My New Guinea Diary

My New Guinea Diary

Staff Sergeant Pilot Ernest C. Ford

White Stag Press
a division of
Publishers Design Group, Inc.

ISBN 13: 978-0979258398

Library of Congress Control Number: 2010928453

Cover Design: Chuck Donald

White Stag Press

a division of

Publishers Design Group, Inc.

Roseville, California

www.publishersdesign.com

1.800.587.6666

Printed in USA

Dedication

THIS BOOK IS DEDICATED to the families and loved ones of the brave men of the U. S. 6th Troop Carrier Squadron who airlifted military personnel and supplies into the battlefields of New Guinea and to the American and Australian ground forces who so valiantly fought to turn back the Japanese advance in 1942, and to drive the Japanese forces from the Island in 1943. The dedication of the 6th Troop Carrier Squadron, the most highly decorated squadron in World War II, was crucial to the success of Allied efforts to stem the tide of Japanese aggression and to begin the march through the Pacific to Japan.

To my wife, my four children, their families, and to generations to come, I leave this story of America's wartime efforts in a far off corner of the world to protect the freedoms and liberty against those who sought to take them away.

God and soldier we adore,

In time of danger and not before.

The danger passed and the wrong is righted,

God is forgotten and the soldier is slighted.

—ALEXANDER THE GREAT, 323 B.C.

Contents

List of Maps

List of Charts, Tables, and Documents

Foreword

I MET MY DAD ON JULY 5TH, 1952—the day I became Ernie Ford's little baby girl. At the time, my Dad was a United States Air Force Captain. I had two older brothers, Steven and Terry. My younger sister Nancy was born in 1961. Although I was made in Japan (where my Dad was stationed), I was born in Minneapolis. Soon after my arrival my Dad was transferred to St. Louis.

As the years unfolded, it became apparent to me that my Dad was 'just' a little different than other dads I had met. I remembered hearing Dad's war stories, and assumed other dads shared their experiences, too. Yet, it seemed my Dad's stories were told only on 'special occasions,' you know when others brought up the subject. Once they opened the door…my Dad would give them precise facts, dates and every detail in between. No kidding, he would even provide the weather report for the day…always lots of details!

I remember my Dad daily leaving for work in his crisp khaki Air Force uniform. I wondered, "where did he go and what did he do?" Yes, I heard he was a pilot and flew airplanes, but to a four-year-old little girl that was a hard idea to wrap my head around. I came to realize that my Dad (though he never said this) was a bonafied hero. This pocket-size man was a 'hero' to his hometown, Manzanola, Colorado, to those who knew him, and to his family.

As you read Ernie's adventures in New Guinea, it is helpful to understand the facts behind his story. When he was five, Ernie saw his first airplane. After that, he wanted to see what was out there. What wonders lie beyond the plains of eastern Colorado and the white-capped Rocky Mountains?

In 1939, at age seventeen and having just finished high school, my Dad left home unannounced. His parents had no idea where he went and could think of no reason for him to suddenly be missing. Dad left no note. His parents did not hear from him for months.

Dad hitch-hiked and worked his way to California, picking string beans in Utah and cherries in San Jose. With little money in his pocket, he headed to the San Francisco shipping piers. Ernie knew he wanted to be a part of a bigger picture and worked to fulfill his dream.

Ernie had often been asked, "Are you going to college after high school?" College was out of the question—his parents simply could not afford it.

While working during high school as a filling station attendant, Dad was approached on more than one occasion by the Standard Oil Regional Superintendent who told him his company had a program that paid hard-working kids to go to college. To qualify Dad first needed to prove himself worthy by working in the oil fields in Venezuela. So Dad figured if he could find his way to California, maybe he could hire on as a steamship crewmember for a 'one way' trip to South America. The shipping company was on to this scheme. They laughed at his plan and sent Ernie on his way.

Dad didn't know anyone in San Francisco and he was running out of money. Determined to find work, he headed to the Army recruiting office. The Army recruiter suggested that if Dad did well, he could become a pilot! For a kid without college education, those words were all he needed to hear.

Without permission from his parents (who still did not know where he was), Ernie enlisted in the Army on November 7, 1939. That afternoon he shipped out to Fort McDowell on Angel Island. He quickly proved he was a hard worker who would do what he was told. On Friday, September 13, 1940 he got what he wanted, his transfer to the Army Air Corps. Dad's life was to change forever, "beyond the blue yonder."

As you read *My New Guinea Diary*, especially his memories of December 24, 1942, and the Battle of Wau in February 1943, you will realize that Ernie was blessed with two co-pilots—the co-pilot assigned to him, and then, more importantly, Ernie had "God as his co-pilot."

In Jeremiah 29:11, the Lord declares, "For I know the plans I have for you, plans to prosper you and not to harm you, plans to give you hope and a future." God certainly protected my Dad and continued to.

Dad, "Thank You" for sharing your *My New Guinea Diary*. And "Thank You" for your Patriotic Spirit in protecting and defending our Constitution. You have demonstrated courage, strength-of-character, and a determination to follow your dreams even when success was in doubt.

You may know Ernie Ford as a friend, neighbor, pilot, veteran, New York Life field underwriter, church usher, computer student, or relative; however, I proudly know him as my Daddy, my Hero. I love you, Daddy. Thanks for the memories!

—Kathy (Ford) Shea
October 2009

Preface

LITTLE HAS BEEN PUT ON THE PRINTED PAGE about the airmanship, courage, and hardships the 6th Troop Carrier Squadron endured in New Guinea in 1942 and the early months of 1943. ALEXANDER THE GREAT in 323 B.C. may have had such a Squadron in mind when he penned:

"God and soldier we adore,
In time of danger and not before.
The danger passed and the wrong is righted,
God is forgotten and the soldier is slighted."

It is high time that the record of the 6th Troop Carrier Squadron, for their first year of combat in WWII, become a matter of Public Record. In our Squadron during this time in New Guinea there were "NO WRITERS, ONLY FLYERS." We did not have the luxury of having a PRO or the PRESS following us around recording and reporting each accomplishment or decoration awarded. The mission of the 6th Troop Carrier Squadron was to: stay alive, evade capture, support the Allied ground forces who were desperately trying to defend Port Moresby, and drive the enemy out of New Guinea. General MacArthur had already decreed that if Port Moresby fell the new battle line would be moved 1,000 miles south to the middle of Australia!!

Many of the military units with the most press did less flying and received far fewer decorations. This is not sour grapes, just check the records. I recall the admonition of Lieutenant Curtis King, 374th TCG, "Wars are fought not only on the battle fields, but also on paper."

The 6th Transport Squadron was activated at Middletown Air Depot, Olmsted Field, Middletown, Pennsylvania on 14 October 1939. It was the second Air Transport Squadron to be formed in the United States Army Air Corps. I, Staff Sergeant Pilot Ernest C. Ford, 19012812, Army Air Corps, was assigned to the 6th Air Transport Squadron on 27 July 1942, at Camp Williams, Wisconsin. It has since been re-designated as the 6th Troop Carrier Squadron. We were the first C-47s to fly from the United States to Hawaii and on to the Southwest Pacific. Departing Hamilton Field, San Rafael, California on 2 October 1942, the 6th was also the first Troop Carrier Squadron to be permanently stationed in New Guinea. The 21st and the 22nd Squadrons were activated in Australia in the spring of 1942, and were stationed in Australia. They would fly up to Jackson Airdrome, Port Moresby, Papua, New Guinea, refuel and go on a mission. They would return to Jackson, refuel and fly back to Australia twenty some hours after departure. There was too much enemy air and ground action to make it safe to RON in the war zone.

The 6th Troop Carrier Squadron arrived at Jackson Airdrome, Port Moresby, Papua, New Guinea on 13 October 1942. Later, the 33rd arrived on 10 December 1942, the 22nd arrived on 14 February 1943, and the 21st arrived on 18 February 1943. The 5th Air Force was activated on 4 September 1942, the 374th Troop Carrier Group on 12 November 1942, and the 54th Troop Carrier Wing on 20 May 1943.

I am writing my New Guinea experience in 1997-2009 as if it had been a daily diary written back in 1942 and 1943. The basic story is true to the best of my memory and after much research, reading Official Military records, viewing the Army Air Corps' micro film on the 6th Troop Carrier Squadron, and corresponding through many letters, e-mails and telephone calls to Squadron members who were there at the time. A diary is a written record of the writer's own experience, observations, thoughts and action at the time. Since it is about one's own life, it is written mostly in first person. If it is accurately recorded, it is a fact and is not boasting or lying. This is my diary of New Guinea. As Mark Twain once wrote, "This will be a long letter because I don't have the time to write a short one."

The purpose of this "Diary" is to provide a record of what my life was like as a C-47 Troop Carrier combat pilot in New Guinea in the early days of World War II. There are those who think only Fighter and Bomber Crews fly combat. That's far from the truth. How wrong they are! General Kenney, the Commanding General of the 5th Air Force, in a December 1942, press release stated, "I classify the transport crews as combat crews and they receive decorations on the same basis as the fighters and bombers. In this time period, P-39 Fighter Pilots lived longer than Troop Carrier Pilots in New Guinea." The lack of longevity was due to the air superiority of the enemy. In the early days, our transports had little or no fighter escort while flying over some of the most challenging terrain on earth with no maps, charts, radio aids, roads, or trains and some of the worst, unpredictable weather on the globe. Landing strips were hacked out of the jungle or up the side of a mountain all by native hands using only machetes and with NO mechanical machinery. There was only one way to transport and support a victorious Army in this Theater of Operations in this environment, and that was by air. That was our mission, and that is what we did.

For our year in combat, President Roosevelt authorized three Presidential Citations, two Battle Stars, 245 Distinguished Flying Crosses and 163 Air Medals to the Flight Crews of the 6th Troop Carrier Squadron for the periods between 13 October 1942, and 2 October 1943. At the time, the 6th Troop Carrier Squadron was the most highly decorated Squadron, of its size in the US Army Air Corps.

Read on and see quotes from Generals Marshall, Eisenhower, MacArthur, and Kenney. At least a few of the "Wheels" must have thought the "Bully Beef Express," as our Squadron was affectionately known, flew combat. There is another way to think about it. Would the President of the United States authorize the awarding of four hundred-eight combat flying decorations to a NON-COMBAT military unit? The 6th Troop Carrier Squadron had a crew loss of 38.5% in their first 354 days in combat.

About the Author

ERNEST "ERNIE" C. FORD WAS BORN IN 1921, in a rural, dusty part of eastern New Mexico, where his father worked as a cowboy and handyman. The family soon relocated to southwestern Kansas where they struggled through the Dust Bowl before moving to southeastern Colorado in 1935.

Upon graduating from Manzanola High School, Ernie ran away from home and headed west. Within months, he joined the Army to pursue his pilot's wings. During his life, he traveled to more than 90 countries, to all 50 states, and to most U.S. territories.

During World War II, his family learned of his achievements through telegrams and letters from the War Department, and through newspaper accounts—they were amazed. The War Department brought him back to the States to headline in U.S. Bond Tours—he had flown a record 364 combat missions in New Guinea before reaching age 22.

While on Bond Tour in Minneapolis, he met Esther Marie Trautner, a preacher's daughter from the Dakotas. They were married in Indianapolis on Memorial Day in 1944. Ernie and Etta were blessed with four children and seven grandchildren. Ernie continued to move and travel as an Air Force pilot until his retirement in 1963. He then relocated his family to Sacramento, California, and began a second career as a New York Life Insurance Agent. Throughout, Ernie and Etta remained active in church life.

In January of 1946, Ernie was given a two-year State Department assignment to fly to Bogota, Columbia. Thirteen pilots were to train Columbian pilots to fly C-47 planes. Ernie's assignment was to fly State Department dignitaries to all the capitals throughout Central and South America. This is what some call "showing the flag". They went to each embassy en route.

When he returned to Columbia, flying over the Andes mountain range, he encountered solid cloud coverage with plenty of turbulence. At 21,770 feet, with no oxygen, and both of his hands frozen to the wheel, Ernie was gasping for air. Flashes of lightening from the nearby thunder storm added to the seriousness of the situation. The Crew Chief along with two others frantically tried to release his hands from the controls. This was a typical case of high altitude bends. Another pilot who was a passenger was able to take over and land safely at their destination.

From then on, Ernie restricted his flights to below 15,000 feet. Flying in Columbia without oxygen at high altitude was in violation of Army Air Corps regulations. As a result of a heart condition, Ernie was returned to the States in May of 1946.

In June 1950, Ernie was flying from Japan to Korea the night the Korean War broke out. Before replacement pilots arrived from the states, Ernie flew 21 combat missions within the first two months of the war, for which he received the Air Medal.

In July of 1958, Ernie was ordered to undergo tests at Brooks Army Hospital in San Antonio, Texas, for a heart evaluation. The EKG discovered that Ernie was a Wolf-Parkinson-White (WPW) patient which required further evaluation. The WPW syndrome indicates a very rapid heartbeat caused by an extra electrical impulse affecting the heart rhythm. Ernie was born with an extra valve in his heart chamber which caused the electrical impulses.

After a week of evaluations at Brooks Army Hospital, Ernie was approved for flying with a waiver. He was allowed to continue to fly because he was a command pilot with so many hours of flying experience. Even though he remained on flying status he was restricted from flying jets.

In April of 1988, Dr. Larry Wolf did an Electro-physical Study of Ernie. Dr. Wolf then cauterized the electrical charge in Ernie's heart, which proved to be a successful procedure.

A few years ago Ernie was asked, "To what do you attribute your long life?" He simply replied, "I never was shot down!" He then added, "God has been my co-pilot!" Ernie always gave God the Glory.

He passed away on March 4, 2010, at age 88.

Acknowledgements

As my life began to wind down, I wanted to write down my day-to-day experiences during the War—World War II—so that they would not be lost to my children and grandchildren. I hope that this is a story worth telling. When I finally sat down to convert my wartime diary into book form, I quickly discovered the challenges imposed both by the number of years that have passed since the events of the diary and by my limited computer skills.

There have been many contributors to the book, too many to mention them all. But my heart compels me to convey my gratitude to my family who encouraged and inspired my efforts. My wife, Esther "Etta" Marie Trautner Ford, who has been "Number 1" in my life for more than 65 years, promoted this project, even when I wanted to keep it small. My daughter Kathy "Ford" Shea consistently encouraged my efforts, my son Steve helped me with my research, and my son Terry helped with editing the initial draft and compiling the final version. Additionally, I appreciated the encouragement and support of my sister-in-laws, Ruth Paynter, Elizabeth "Jane" Hanson, and Lois "Kay" Litin, and my youngest brother, Marvin "Buddy" Ford.

Although there have been many inspirations for my book, in addition to my wife and family, I believe it important that I single out a few individuals whose impact on my life is, only in part, described in the events of *My New Guinea Diary*. I begin with General Jimmy Doolittle, who's Tokyo Raid in 1942, gave hope to our nation in our darkest hour, and who was a special inspiration to my life over the years even before I personally met him. Mary Tornich Janislawski, who taught me—along with a generation of pilots—how to navigate; no other man or woman could have done it better. Amerigo Grassi, my crew chief, who kept our plane in top flying shape and whose "street smarts" and steady demeanor while we were air borne was always appreciated, and George C. Gregg, our radio operator and assistant crew chief, who always remained vigilant.

I acknowledge Ruth and Dick Moorhouse for editing the final text and their neighbor, Zeliko Miksic, a computer whiz, who assisted them more than once to revive their computer. After I finished the initial draft, Ruth felt that *My New Guinea Diary* presented a story that needed to be told and pushed me to continue to move the project forward. I extend a special thanks to Shirley Berger, who spent countless hours trouble-shooting our many computer software glitches during my writing of the draft copy, and to Brian Eberly, who worked to keep my PC humming.

I wish to acknowledge Congressman Daniel Lungren, his staff, and Carol Kohler for their support and encouragement and to Susan Maxwell Skinner, who converted my pictures to digital format, and whose sunny disposition inspired me to keep moving forward.

I also want to thank George Moses, Director of Retiree Affairs, for all of the help he gave to me.

Finally, I thank Robert Brekke, my publisher, and his wife, Terie, for their insights and patience in guiding me through the mechanics of preparing *My New Guinea Diary* for publication.

Author's Note

I TOOK MORE THAN 600 PHOTOGRAPHS during my year in New Guinea. Since the photos were taken in a war zone at the time of war, all had to be censored, stamped, and released by military examiners in Townsville and Brisbane, Australia, and at Hickham Field, Honolulu, Hawaii. When the photos were reviewed in Townsville and Brisbane, nearly all were cleared and returned to me. However, military "censors" at Hickham were not nearly as kind. By the time my photos were reviewed by the Hickham examiners' censorship, more than half, including most of the best ones, were confiscated.

While I do not know this to be true, some photos may have been deemed to be too sensitive. But I believe most of the best photos were kept by the Hickham examiners for their own use after the war so they could make claims about their own wartime exploits!

In spite of my strong protestations at Hickham and my numerous written requests thereafter, more than 300 of my photos were never returned.

The only film we could obtain was military gunship film. This film was of low-grade quality, but was sufficient for use by mounted aircraft cameras to photograph the machine gun results—that is, to confirm their kills.

After more than 60 years, the photos have faded and their clarity has further deteriorated. I hope their quality remains sufficient to help illustrate this important story of what the men of the 6th Troop Carrier Squadron experienced in 1942 and 1943 in New Guinea.

—Ernest C. Ford
November 2009

Acronyms

AO	Air Officer
CBI	China, Burma, India
DFC	Distinguished Flying Cross
DZ	Drop Zone
IP	Initial Point
NAS	Naval Air Station
NCOIC	Non Commissioned Officer in Charge
OD	Officer of the Day
PSP	Pierced Steel Planking (69 lb, 30"x9' per strip)
RON	Remain Over Night
SOP	Standard Operating Procedure
TCG	Troop Carrier Group
TCS	Troop Carrier Squadron
TCW	Troop Carrier Wing
ZI	Zone of Interior (48 states)

Chronological List of Events

17 Mar 1942	Gen Douglas A. MacArthur arrived in Brisbane
4 Aug 1942	Allied Air Forces activated under Major General George C. Kenney
7 Aug 1942	5th AF activated with M/G George C. Kenney, Commander
22 Sep 1942	6th TCS to Douglas Aircraft Factory, Mobile, AL signed for and picked up C-47s
26 Sep 1942	McClellan Field Sacramento, CA to modify air/ft
29 Sep 1942	Hamilton Field, San Rafael, CA Aerial Port of Debarkation
2 Oct 1942	6th TCS Air Echelon departed for overseas
2 Oct 1942	Hickham Field, Oahu, Territory of Hawaii, 14:20 hrs flying time
4 Oct 1942	Christmas Island, 8:25 hrs flying time
5 Oct 1942	Crossed Equator 2257 Z (Zebra Time from Greenwich, England)
5 Oct 1942	Canton Island, 6:10 hrs flying time
6 Oct 1942	Departed from Canton in route to the Fiji Islands
7 Oct 1942	Crossed International Date Line 2332 Z
7 Oct 1942	Nadi, Viti Levu, Fiji, 7:40 hrs flying time
8 Oct 1942	Noumea, New Caledonia, 5:40 hrs flying time
9 Oct 1942	Amberly Airdrome, Ipswich, Australia 5:30 hrs flying time
13 Oct 1942	6th TCS arrived Jackson Airdrome, Port Moresby, Papua, New Guinea, 11:50 hrs flying time
19 Oct 1942	6th TCS moved to Ward's Airdrome, Port Moresby, Papua, New Guinea APO 929 00:05 hrs flying time
26 Oct 1942	6th TCS Ground Echelon departed USA, 11 Officers, 155 GIs
2 Nov 1942	Kokoda recaptured
5 Nov 1942	*Guinea Gold* newspaper first published
8 Nov 1942	Dododura opened
12 Nov 1942	374th TCS activated, Col Paul H. Prentiss, Cmd'
17-30 Nov 1942	19th Bomb returned to ZI
1-13 Dec 1942	6th TCS Ground Echelon arrived
9 Dec 1942	Buna Mission captured
14 Dec 1942	6th TCS opened mess

Continued on next page

23 Jan 1943 Gona-Buna Area captured
23 Jan 1943 Papua and Australia declared saved
 6 Feb 1943 Wau saved
10 Feb 1943 90th Bomb (B-24s) transferred to Wards
22 May 1943 54th TCW activated, Col Paul H. Prentiss,
22 May 1943 Maj John H. Lackey, Jr. transferred to 54th TCW
16 Sep 1943 Lae captured
 2 Oct 1943 6th TCS reassigned to Garbutt Airdrome, Townsville,
Australia, APO 922

6th Transport Squadron

14 Oct 1939 Activated at Middletown Air Depot, Olmsted, PA
14 Oct 1939 1st Commander, Major John R. Dann
 4 Nov 1939 2nd Commander, Major George J. Cressey
28 Mar 1940 3rd Commander, Captain John J. Keough
10 Jun 1940 4th Commander, 1st Lieut. Hawish McClelland
17 Feb 1942 5th Commander, 1st Lieut. John H. Lackey, Jr.
23 May 1942 Squadron transferred to Camp Williams, WI
 2 Jul 1942 Re-designated as 6th Troop Carrier Squadron (TCS)
 6 Aug 1942 Transferred to Selfridge Field, MI
12 Sep 1942 Transferred to Pope Field, Ft. Bragg, NC
16 Sep 1942 Transferred to Dodd Field, San Antonio, TX

Air Echelon

23 Sep 1942 Transferred to McClellan Field, Sacramento, CA
29 Sep 1942 Transferred to Hamilton Field, San Rafael, CA
2-9 Oct 1942 Departed for overseas via: Hawaii, Christmas Island, Canton Island,
Fiji, and New Caledonia, arriving in Brisbane, Australia
13 Oct 1942 Arrived Jackson Airdrome, Port Moresby, Papua, New Guinea
19 Oct 1942 New duty station Wards Airdrome, Port Moresby

Continued on next page

Ground Echelon

1-13 Dec 1942 6th TCS Ground troops begin arriving in New Guinea

13 Dec 1942 Squadron reunited

Squadron's New Duty Station

2 Oct 1943 Reassigned to Garbutt Airdrome, Townsville, Australia

Homeward Bound for Christmas 1943

Five passengers returned to the U.S. on Mrs. Eleanor Roosevelt's LB-30. We were restricted to the lower deck of the aircraft and not authorized to go topside where the First Lady and her entourage were. We were further instructed not to speak to her, if she should come into our compartment, unless she asked a direct question. Mrs. Roosevelt never came and we never spoke!! We only saw her through the port holes as she entered and departed the aircraft.

Another Set Of Orders

IT WAS TUESDAY, OCTOBER 13, 1942, 0515 hours in a little grass cow pasture named Amberly Airdrome at Ipswich northwest of Brisbane, Queensland, Australia. Standing in front of his aircraft, our Commander Captain John H. Lackey Jr., was briefing the thirteen First Pilots on the day's flight. All aircraft had been thoroughly checked and rechecked by each member of the crew. All fuel tanks were full and the crews were ready to go. The Commander told us that we had a long day of flying ahead and the weather should be good. At noon we would make one stop just long enough to eat, refuel and pick up a full load of troops and their gear. We would be flying in loose formation. Each pilot went back to his plane and we were in the air and on our way by 0557.

Four hours and thirty-five minutes later we let down and landed at an airdrome on the northeast coast of Australia near a small town. After landing we were told that it was Garbutt Airdrome, Townsville, Queensland, Australia. Captain Lackey told us to go eat, come back and take on a full load of gas. We would be flying over water with NO parachutes, NO life rafts and NO Mae Wests. The crew's parachutes and Mae Wests were not to be used, worn, or seen by the passengers. They were to be stored in the forward baggage compartment because there was no survival equipment for the passengers. In our aircraft we would have 29 mechanics and all their personal gear including their heavy tool boxes.

We had the same briefing at Garbutt as at Amberly except this time we knew that it would be an over water flight. We did not know where we were going or how long the flight would be. We still had no maps and had only seen two segments of the route since leaving the States on 2 October. I tried to remember from school what was north and off the northeast coast of Australia. In my mind's eye all I could see were a lot of islands scattered throughout the Southwest Pacific.

Once again our aircraft had an overload. Like the flight from Hamilton Field, San Francisco, California to Hickham Field, Honolulu, Hawaii, the plane had a load far more than she was designed for. The cabin aisle was stacked high with tool boxes and B-4 bags. Airborne at 1337 hours we climbed out on a heading of 008° and leveled off at 9,000 feet. The crew chief went back to see how everything was doing. When he returned to the cockpit he said that all the passengers were mechanics. They did not know where they were going and asked him where we were taking them. The secrecy on this whole mission was going too far! What about the need to know? What if the lead plane went down? If we got separated in weather and since we had to maintain radio silence we would be up that well-known creek without a paddle. I guess since this was war, we were expendable.

At about 1700 we began to see a long, low dark cloud on the horizon. The closer we got the longer and darker it became until we could see it was the coastline of a land mass. The land stretched as far as we could see in both directions from the southeast to the northwest. As we approached we descended to 1,000 feet. There on a coral reef a short distance off shore was an old grounded rusted wrecked ship. When over the ship we slowed to 120 mph, dropped our gear, turned left picking up a heading of 317 and flew parallel to the beach in trail formation. After seventeen minutes we came to a large seaport with no ships and a few native grass topped huts. We let down to 500 feet, made a right bank and flew seven miles inland. Beyond a small line of hills was a landing strip.

The runway surface was different from anything I had ever seen. It was made of steel strips all connected with evenly spaced holes the length and width of the landing field. Later we found out it was called "PSP", Pierced Steel Planking. Each interlocking strip was honey-combed. The strips were eight feet long, 30 inches wide and weighted 69 pounds. To make this airdrome, the jungle was cleared, rolled to a smooth flat surface, and a thick coating of ground coral was added. This surface of coral was then watered down and re-rolled. Next the PSP was laid and connected the length and width of the new runway. Following this, fine ground powered coral was spread over the steel surface, watered down and re-rolled.

After landing I asked the Alert Driver, "Where are we?" He replied, "Jackson." I said, "Where is that?" He said, "Port Moresby." Again I asked, "Where is that?" He replied, "New Guinea." I asked again, "Where is that?" As he got back in the old Staff and Command car he said: "Ask your pilot." I told him that I was the pilot. He looked me over, then at my stripes and Pilot's Wings, just shook his head and drove away.

We had flown over a third of the way around the world with only the Squadron Commander knowing where we were going. The only maps and radio frequencies in this thirteen ship formation were with the Commander. At each briefing after Hickham Field, Hawaii 'til we reached Australia, the first pilots and navigators were briefed for the next leg of the flight on one occasion we were permitted to look only at that segment of the Commander's map which he kept. From Amberly on it was basically follow the leader and no looking at the map. Since we departed the United States on 2 October 1942 we had made eight stops, flown 9,776 nautical miles in 59:35 hours flying time at an average ground speed of 164 mph, arriving in New Guinea on Tuesday, 13 October 1942. There were no security leaks in this Squadron!! Putting this all together meant that we were now at Jackson Airdrome, Port Moresby, Papua, New Guinea within five miles of the enemy lines. There were snipers in the traffic pattern and a few pieces of artillery within a quarter of a mile in the hills. I just realized that it was twenty-five months ago to the day that I joined the United States Army Air Corps. Here I am, overseas as a pilot in a combat zone and only twenty years old.

Now let us go back to when and where we first picked up our aircraft at the factory. Before we made this fast dash across the Pacific to what was to be our jungle home base for the next year.

The record of my tour in New Guinea should start at Douglas Aircraft Factory, Brookley Airport, Mobile, Alabama on 22 September 1942. Thirteen flight crews of four soldiers each were flown to Brookley in one old C-48B and a C-53 aircraft. The C-48B was an airline night sleeper that carried twenty-one passengers, of which four could sleep in the Pullman with upper pull-down beds. Upon mobilization the Army left the sleeping berths in place and removed the airline cushion seats replacing them with twenty-six military wall-type troop seats. The C-53 was a twin-prop airline freight carrier that now had twenty-eight military wall type metal troop seats. We were flown from Dodd Field Fort Sam Houston, San Antonio, Texas to Brookley Airport, Mobile, Alabama with orders to pick up thirteen new aircraft from Douglas Aircraft Factory for the United States Army Air Corps.

The next morning at 0800 hours we attended a briefing on the second floor of the Administration Building. After the meeting crew assignments were made. I was assigned as one of the Squadron's thirteen First Pilots. My co-pilot was Staff Sergeant Pilot George W. Beaver age 20. He was three months older than me. Technical Sergeant Amerigo (Reggie) Grassi, (29 July 1918 - 18 July 1987) was our crew chief. He was the oldest and ranking enlisted crew member. Buck Sergeant John C. Griggs, (19 October 1919 - 10 December 1996) was the radio operator. I was the youngest First Pilot in the Squadron. We were an all "dogface" crew. Before World War II enlisted men in the Army were called "dogfaces." Only later during the War were Enlisted Men called GIs.

After a few minutes of introductions our Squadron Commander Captain John H. Lackey Jr., the Commanding Officer of the 6th Transport Squadron, told us that all First Pilots were to go with him to see about test flying and signing for the Army's new aircraft. All other crew members were to wait in front of the Admin Building until we returned. If we were not back by 1130, they were to go to the factory cafeteria, eat and return by 1300 and wait in front of this building. In those days the Aircraft Commander, or Captain of the ship, was called First Pilot and the First Officer was known as the Co-Pilot. All thirteen First Pilots went to the Douglas Hanger and found a small sign that read "War Department Pilots report here" with an arrow pointing to a door. It was a small room with a counter across the middle, two desks and on the other side were three civilians, two men and a woman. Captain Lackey told us to wait outside.

I knew all thirteen First Pilots: one Captain, two First Lieutenants, eight Second Lieutenants and one other Staff-Sergeant Pilot. Of the twenty-six pilots in the Squadron only three had more flying hours than I had. This was a Squadron of real rookie pilots or just plain "yardbirds."

Later we learned that Captain Lackey entered the Army in August 1939 after completing four years of R.O.T.C. at Virginia Polytechnic Institute. He received a B.S. degree in Engineering. After graduating from the Army Air Corps Flying School he served as a ferry pilot flying aircraft to Newfoundland and to Trinidad. He was now a Senior Pilot. In time we would find out that he was a wonderful superior leader, a doer, not a driver, "a puller not a pusher," truly an Officer and Gentleman of the highest class. Before his career ended, he became a General. He was most deserving.

The two First Lieutenants had been out of flying schools two plus years and had less than three hundred hours more flying time than I had. I was next in total flying hours. All the other Squadron-Pilots had just graduated from one of the several Army Flying Schools. I had just completed United Airlines Captains School at General Billy Mitchell Field at Cudahy, Milwaukee, Wisconsin. I received my pilot wings on 20 May 1942 fifteen years to the day after Lindbergh took off for Paris and twelve years to the day after Amelia Earhart made her solo flight to Ireland. I received my pilot wings in Class 42-E, Luke Field, Phoenix, Arizona in P-40s. This was the first class of Staff Sergeant Pilots in the West Coast Training Command. We were also in the first class which had Chinese Lend Lease student pilots through the Lend Lease Program. One of the Chinese student pilots was a Captain. He had six confirmed Japanese kills to his credit. At Luke one of our Ground School Aircraft Maintenance Instructors was Captain Berry M. Goldwater. In later years he ran for President of the United States.

After considerable waiting Captain Lackey came out. He told us to be sure to remember the two numbers that he assigned to each of us. He then called out our names and gave each of us two numbers. My numbers were "2" and "39." He explained that in my case the "2" was my position in the Squadron formation of four elements and three aircraft per element plus a tail-end Charlie. Being the second plane my position in formation would be flying on the Squadron Commander's right wing. When flying in squadron formation we would be the second aircraft to take-off and the second to land. The "39" was the field number of our aircraft. Number "2" meant that since Captain Lackey was number "1", I would be taking the second aircraft off the assembly line. Staff Sergeant Pilot Weedin, number 3," would be the third aircraft etc. for the other ten pilots.

The big olive-drab Army camouflaged C-47A, serial number 41-18539, had a large white field number "39" painted just behind the pilot's and co-pilot's side windows. By the time Douglas had towed all thirteen planes to the Army parking area, tied them down and put the control locks on, it was after 1700. Captain Lackey said it was time to go back to the Admin Building to pick up the rest of the crews, go eat and be off duty until 0700 the next morning. At that time we were to be at our assigned aircraft. In the planes we would find Tech Orders and the flight test forms. Tomorrow would be a very busy day. It was important that we give each aircraft a very thorough inspection, test flight, and have all safety-of-flight "gigs" corrected. The test flight consisted of, filing a flight plan for the local test flight: checking the Ops map for the location of the test area, how to get there and the radio frequencies, climbing to 5,000 feet, doing climbing single engine turns and climbs with wheels and flaps up and down. The radio operators were to go through their check list. Captain Lackey instructed, "When you have completed the printed check list and both the pilot and the crew chief are satisfied land and write up the report. Every pilot must not forget the aircraft is assigned to the crew chief and ONLY loaned to the pilot for one flight at a time. If you and your crew chief do not agree both of you come to me. If you agree take your completed forms to Douglas and sign for the aircraft. Remember that some crew will be flying this aircraft in some part of the world. Be sure it will be safe to fly anywhere in the world for it might be you. If we finish tomorrow we will leave on the 24th. Remember you and your crew are to be here in the morning no later that 0700 with parachutes. Now let's pick up the rest of the crew and go to chow." It wasn't until then that I realized how hungry I was. By the time we started eating it had been over twelve hours since breakfast with no lunch. With all the excitement of being on the flight line and being assigned my first crew and aircraft I had forgotten all about food.

The next morning at 0630 when the co-pilot and I arrived on the flight line the crew chief and radioman were just shutting down the engines. When they got out they were all smiles. The crew chief said it looked good to him. I asked if either of them had ever picked up an aircraft from the factory before. Neither one had. However, Grassi had picked up several aircraft from Middletown Air Depot during the three years he was stationed with the 6th at Middletown. He had been told the procedure was the same.

I told the crew since we had never flown together I'd like to have a few words. I told them: "I like to think of a flight crew as a football team. The First Pilot is the Team Captain and we each have our positions and skills that make the flight run smoothly and safely. Try to fly without a mechanic and you won't get far that is if you ever get the engines started. When you need to call for directions, file a position report, or have an emergency the radioman will make the call. The two pilots have their skills also. Until the crew chief and the radioman tell me that the aircraft is ready to go they are the boss. Once they `hand over the aircraft' we begin to play football. Off the flight line Sergeant Grassi is the ranking enlisted man. Any time any of you have any suggestions speak-up. I may not follow your suggestions, but I sure want to hear from you. Sergeant Grassi, you have been around longer than any of us so you keep us on the right path. Any questions?" There were no questions.

"Now it is time for the pre-flight briefing. As you know we are required to wear parachutes on all test hops and on combat flights. On other flights it will be up to you. I will not be wearing mine except when required or in emergencies. After we fit them either store them or hang them up in the same place each time so everyone will know where to find his own chute. In flight we must use the buddy system and everyone will look after and help one another. In case of a bail-out we more likely will have a chance to talk it over before we have to jump. In any event John you transmit your required messages. George if you have radio contact give out the info on your frequency. Grassi put on your chute and then open the rear door. By this time you other two should have your parachutes on and ready to go. Double check one another. Grassi you can get my parachute and stand by in the tail of the aircraft and help me harness up. If possible we should all try to jump in one string, one after the other so we will land in the same area. I should be the last one out. Anyone that does not jump out ahead of me just assumed command. George, you and I must go over the Dash One (PILOT'S HAND BOOK) until we know it by heart and hope we never need it. Grassi you know more about this bird than any of us. In case of an emergency you speak up and have the Dash One handy. Any questions?" There were none.

"John, will you double check all the radios now and during the flight test?

When in Operations get all frequencies and charts we'll need between here and Dodd Field. If you should find out where we are going from there pick them up also. After the flight test we will all have to stay close to our plane for further orders from Captain Lackey."

"Grassi, will you follow the co-pilot and me as we do our outside walk around inspection? I'll call out the items as we go." In those days there were no published walk-around or cockpit check lists for the pilots. It was in the Dash One and in the Tech Orders but not a hand copy for the pilots. It was all left to the pilot's good judgment and memory. "If either of you see any thing that I miss, point it out because your necks are up there also. As I approach an airplane I want to either get in the air or go back to Ops for another aircraft as soon as possible. This morning, on the way to No 39, I could see that the aircraft has two wings, engines, props, wheels, a fuselage and tail section. All appeared in order. The reason for this cursory glance is that if anything is missing or damaged there is a minimum loss of time. I made this 'look' as we approached No. 39, while you two were still in the cockpit."

"Now let's go inside making the same 'look see' when we get in the cockpit. That is where the real inspection starts." As we went up the steps Grassi spoke up and said: "You're in for one big surprise. I'll wait to see how long it will take you to see what I'm talking about." As we walked up the aisle everything appeared to be in order. When I opened the cockpit door the first thing I saw was a large hole in the instrument panel where the autopilot should be. I said: "We will have to see what the Form 1 has to say about that," pointing to the hole. "We will now start the formal inspection by examining the Form 1 in detail." There were only two write-ups that I took note of. The autopilot was on back order, and there was a note to keep the Sperry Artificial Horizon caged at all times while the engines were running. I was in hopes that Sperry would have worked out the bugs by now. We had found out that when flying with the commercial airline aircraft it was a great instrument for blind flying. In rough weather flying: needle, ball, air speed, altimeter, clock, rate of climb and compass gets extremely fatiguing in a very short time. After reading the Form 1 in detail I went through the complete aircraft inspection item by item. I pulled out a dime, crawled up on the wing and opened the Zus Fasteners that locked the inspection covers for all four wing gas tanks and the two engine oil tanks. This is to visually check and be positive that all gas and oil tanks were full. As we went around the aircraft I gave the tolerances, pressures, measurements and specifications of all controls, wheels and surfaces. Normally this is an 8-10 minute inspection, but in this case it took 30 minutes. I went into great detail for two reasons: one, to let my crew know what I knew about the aircraft, and second, to check out our aircraft before we flew and signed for the Army. When the inspection was completed I asked if there were any questions or comments. The co-pilot smiled and shook his head. The crew chief said, "If you can fly as well as you know your airplane we have one outstanding pilot."

I had been fortunate. Mr. Bernard, Chief Test Pilot for United Airlines, had taken me under his wing the first day we started flying at Milwaukee. My total flying hours at General Billy Mitchell Field had only been 78:35 hours and maybe three times that many class room hours with Mr. Bernard. He had said to me that he "wanted to train a Pursuit Pilot how to fly a real airplane." Surely this was very few flying hours especially for a "rookie" just out of Flight School, but this was war time and the training was intense. When I wasn't flying, I was studying or working with the mock-ups. Mr. Bernard was one outstanding, interesting Instructor Pilot. I was motivated.

After the inspection I told the other three we should go to Operations and have coffee. "One of you get us a table. I'll meet you after I pick up a clearance so we can fill it out for the test hop."

When the four of us arrived at the coffee shop all the other crews were already there. I got some kidding for being so slow. As we had coffee I filled out the clearance and had each crew member print their full name, rank and serial number on the clearance and also on a blank sheet of paper which I kept for future use. I asked George to pick up a map of the local test flight area to study the taxi ways, runways, take-off and landing pattern and get the tower and range frequencies. I would meet them here as soon as I could go to the Weather Bureau and file the clearance.

After the weather briefing I turned in the completed clearance to the Army Operations clearing authority who was a First Lieutenant. He looked at me and demanded to see my identification. Of course at this time Sergeant Pilots had none. I told him that I was one of the two Enlisted Pilots who were here to pick up aircraft from Douglas. I told him that I wanted to see the Operations Officer since I was sure that the base had been notified that I was one of the Pilots who would be picking up a C-47. He said that he was the Operations Officer and for me to stand where I was and to be quiet. He then told his NCOIC to call security. He again ordered me to stay where I was. George came up at this time and saw what was happening and he rushed for our Commander.

Captain Lackey came to my rescue. Basically, he told the Lieutenant what I had said. The Operations Officer said that he would check with the Base Commander first. Captain Lackey said that he would sign for all thirteen aircraft and that "After we land I will file a complaint against you Lieutenant. This base has been notified by Washington and all interested parties have been advised that this Squadron was to receive preferential treatment as we are on a secret rush mission. Further, that there would be two Sergeant Pilots by name in the group as First Pilots, and they were to receive the same treatment as any other pilot. This does not mean refusing to clear them or treating them as a thief. When I land you have an appointment for you and me with the Base Commander. Also have transportation standing by. Do you understand, Lieutenant?" The red faced Lieutenant said, "Yes, Sir." Captain Lackey then turned to all of us pilots and said, "I'll sign your clearances." As Commander on this mission he had command clearing authority. He signed all clearances and handed them to the Operations NCOIC and said one word "File". This was just one of many run-ins while I was a Sergeant Pilot. Most of us received the same treatment. However a few Enlisted Pilots did have extremely harsh and unjust treatment. I was more fortunate.

The reason we were Sergeant Pilots instead of Officers was due to the Army Regulations under which we applied for flight training. When my flying class 42-E applied for flight training in August of 1941 it was during peacetime. At that time all pilots graduating in the Army Air Corps except West Point graduates were commissioned Second Lieutenant Reserves. They would stay on active duty for three years and then revert to an inactive civilian status and would go off active duty and off flying status. It is not like the Military Reserve Officer Pilot program today. The regulation covering Enlisted Pilots was different. In my opinion it was a much better deal if you really wanted to fly. The only difference in our qualifications, I repeat "the only two differences", was that the pilot graduating as an Officer had to have completed two years of college and upon graduation must be twenty-one (21).

The Sergeant Pilots had to be nineteen (19) and be a High School graduate. However, we were required to take and pass a two-year college level test with heavy emphasis on math and science. NO "under water basket weaving courses" were allowed as in some Cadet college degree programs.

My class reported for flight training on 7 November 1941 with our first student flight training on 10 November. On 26 November I soloed in a PT-21 with 8 hours and 7 minutes of total flying time. At this time in aviation history pilots were in an elite flying fraternity. All Aviation Students that were in the Army Air Corps Flying Program prior to 7 December 1941 attended the same ground and flight training schools at the same time and in the same mixed classes together with in-grade Officers and Aviation Cadets. In-grade Officers, Aviation Cadets and Aviation Students attended all the same ground school classes. Each Flight Instructor had four student pilots with a mix of all three. More was expected from Aviation Students than from Aviation Cadets. The reason we were told was that we had been in the Army, we'd had the Manual of Arms, were rifle and pistol qualified, received poison gas training, had a security clearance background, and we knew the routine. The one thing that all individuals going through flying school in those days will agree on is that they did not get enough sleep. We all felt we had too many hours in ground school, PT (physical torture), flying, and studying. After we completed Primary, a Pre-Flight Ground School was added to the program in order to give more classroom training and thus reduce the wash-out rate.

Prior to our first training flight at Primary, Basic and Advanced Flying Schools, the following was read. Each of us had to sign that we understood and would comply, and then we received a copy.

HEADQUARTERS XS/ac
WEST COAST AIR CORPS TRAINING CENTER
Office of the Commanding General

Moffett Field, California,
June 2, 1941.
GENERAL ORDERS): NUMBER 2.)

Breach of Flying Regulations

1.All Post and Detachment Commanders will be held responsible that a copy of this letter is read and thoroughly understood by every pilot and student pilot of his command at frequent intervals. 2.Breach of Flying Regulations, which creates additional hazards to the flying of Army aircraft, is in effect a treasonable and traitorous act. When for pure thrill a pilot hazards aircraft vitally needed by the United States in its present expansion program, hazards his own life and any additional crew aboard, he is in effect "giving aid and comfort to an enemy." No saboteur or hostile pursuit or anti-aircraft fire can so effectively destroy a vitally needed airplane and crew as the thoughtless young pilot who is charged with the responsibility of operating the airplane. The most drastic punitive measures will be taken against any proven case as described above in which the pilot responsible there for survives.

(Signed) HENRY W. HARMS,
Brigadier General, Air Corps., Commanding

DISTRIBUTION "A"
A TRUE COPY
(Signed) DEWEY BARTLO, Captain, Air Corps., Adjutant

I was at King City, CA, in a Civilian Primary Flying School when World War II broke out at 07:53 hours, 7 December 1941. It was a Sunday morning and most of us were sleeping. All Aviation Cadets and Aviation Students were billeted in long single story, Spanish style haciendas. Each building was subdivided into several units. A unit had two bedrooms with a joining bath and each bedroom had two beds and housed four students in each unit. On this morning one of the students in the other room came in and announced that he just heard over the radio that the Japs were bombing Pearl Harbor. Our first question was "Where is Pearl Harbor?" We turned the radio on and we heard direct broadcasting from Hawaii. For the first twenty or so minutes we could hear the on site eye witnessing of this historical event. Then the Army interrupted the program and played martial music. The four of us went to the mess hall. Few there had heard about it. There was some talk. Then most of us dressed in civilian clothes and went to King City, walked around and then went to a movie. During the show a notice came on the screen, "All 9th Core Area men report out front." Many soldiers walked out. In a few minutes another notice came on the screen, "All Aviation Cadets report out front." Shortly after the Cadets left the theater lights came on and a policeman walked down both isles looking for young men. When they came to our row they asked if we were soldiers. No one moved. Then they asked if we were Aviation Cadets and still we remained seated. We were then asked if we were in the military, we replayed, "Yes." "What are you?" "We are Aviation Students." Get out in front, NOW." The amusing thing about the announcement was the spelling of "core." In the military the word is CORPS. 6X6 trucks drove us back to the base and once again we found out in short order that we were back in the Army as soldiers first and as Aviation Students second.

There were only three permanent active duty Army men assigned to the base. This did not include the Regular Army Aviation Students as all other base personnel were civilians. One of the civilians, Mary Tarnish, was our Navigation Ground School Instructor. She was the only lady instructor we had while going through Flight School. In later years she became world famous. I'll speak of her in a later chapter. The personnel included the base civilian guards who did not have the Army Manual of Arms or a background security clearance. So starting the night of 7 December 1941, and continuing until 19 January 1942, when we left for Basic Flying School at Moffett Field, a Regular Army base, Sergeant Pilots had to pull four hours of guard duty four times a week. Of course, we were required to attend and pass every ground school, PT, and all flying classes. If you missed one class without a prior written excuse from the Commandant of the School, you were washed out and sent to the 9th Corps Area for immediate overseas assignment in the Infantry. Being on the West Coast with P-38s with live ammo flying overhead every few minutes at full throttle, with all kinds of reported submarine activity a few miles off the coast with live ammo, with the Officer Of The Day and Sergeant Of The Guard checking every few minutes, and with the Corporal Of The Guard trying to make a name for himself, it's a wonder that a single one of us made it to Moffett Field to Basic Flying School.

In our Primary Flying Class at Mesa Del Rey Flying Field in King City, California, 115 Aviation Students started and 79 completed the training. Later, at Basic Flying School we lost another seven and at Advanced Flying school another six. Of the 371 West Coast Aviation Students that applied for 42-E pilot training only 66 of us received our silver pilot wings. Thirty-one graduated from twin-engine AT-9s at Mather Field, and thirty-five of us graduated in single engine at Luke Field in P-40s. Most of the 36 who were washed out were due to lack of sleep.

At King City we flew open-air cockpit Ryan PT-21 and PT-22 trainers called the "RECRUIT." This was only a few steps beyond the primitive flying of "Old." We flew strictly by the seat of our pants. The same aircraft company that manufactured the PT-21 and 22's design, manufactured Colonel Lindbergh's "Spirit of Saint Louis." Our trainer was a tandem two-seater open air cockpit. We wore khaki cloth helmets, a long white flowing silk parachute scarf, goggles and a T-6 seat-pack parachute. When flying if you got caught in rain each rain drop that hit your exposed face stung like mad. My instructor, Mr. Jack Matlock, flew in the rear cockpit and the student pilot flew in the front seat. The aircraft was not equipped with either a radio or intercom. The instructor sat in the back seat and yelled into a rubber tube that was fastened to the student's helmet. There was no way for the student to talk back. Maybe that was a blessing for the instructors. If the student was not carrying out his instructions or was just goofing off some of the instructors would hold the rubber mouth tube out in the slipstream. The student's helmet would fill up with air and the student's ears would ring and he could not hear for a couple of hours. I'm lucky I missed this "attention-getter." We were to keep the chin strap of our helmet buckled up at all times. One of the students did not like this idea. After warning the student pilot a time or two the instructor held the "tube" out the side of the cockpit in the slipstream and the student's helmet blew off and was lost. The student had to pay for the lost helmet and walk five "demerits."

We were told of an upper classman who, when flying, did not like to keep his lap belt locked. After several warnings the instructor did a half roll and the Cadet fell out. He parachuted down safely and walked back to the base caring his chute. Upon arrival he was washed out and sent to the infantry.

In Primary Flying school, after your first duel instructional flight, a white four inch long tape was stuck on your flight suit. It was located just above your right knee and stayed there until you soloed. In my case on 24 November 1941, the tape was removed when I soloed.

The Ryan was mostly a "Stick and Rudder" tail dragger aircraft. For controls the aircraft had a "Joy Stick", rudder, flaps, and throttle. There was no airspeed indicator. The pilot learned to listen to the sound of the air from the vibrating "wing wires." That way he could judge if the aircraft was flying at a safe speed, near stalling speed, or flying too fast. We were told that the cruising speed was 100 mph with a maximum speed of 125 mph. Our little aircraft had a wooden fixed pitch prop. It was a "trail wheeler" with three extended fixed wheels welded in the down position. To taxi, you had to make "S" turns in order to clear the area in front of the aircraft and allow you to see where you were going. The aircraft had no radios. All ground and air control were one-way communications from the tower by light signals. The instruments were: a magnetic compass, altimeter, needle and ball, clock, oil pressure and RPM. To start the aircraft, a ground mechanic had to hand crank the engine. This was tricky. The mechanic had to watch for the turning propeller and the kick back of the crank. It was like cranking the old "Model T Ford." You could easily get a broken wrist, arm, or, worse yet, get hit by the prop and killed.

While at King City I received one five-demerit tour for attempting to fly formation which was a no-no. Another Aviation Student, Johnny Crouch, and I had to march in "flight formation" five times around the outer perimeter of the airport. Our simulated "traffic pattern" was just like flying an airplane around the outside perimeter of the airport which was a normal box pattern. We were required to wear our T-6, seat pack parachute, banging into the back of our legs with each step we took, with arms fully extended, straight out, shoulders back, eyes moving in all quadrants with each step. When "flying" around the field when we had to change directions, we had to bank our arms. All gigs were walked off on weekends. The only other gig I received in Flying School was in Advanced Flying School for practicing Judo. The Army's policy was that it was OK to be shot at and killed by the enemy in combat,

BUT they could not take any chance of you being injured in the ring practicing martial arts while in flying school. This was an unauthorized activity and too dangerous for pilots. This time I received five demerits and had to march on the Cadet Parade Field for five hours.

After the war started the Student Officers and Cadets proceeded on with their same peacetime schedule with no guard duty and continued to have off-base weekend privileges. They were not trained in the Army's way to shoot a gun, nor did they have a security clearance. Under The Staff Sergeant Pilot's Plan when we graduated we would be promoted to Staff-Sergeant Pilot Regular Army. And every three years when we re-enlisted, unless there was something derogatory in our file in the War Department in Washington, we were to be automatically promoted one grade. At the end of twelve years we would be Senior Warrant Officer, Regular Army. Our only duties were to fly. We could only be promoted or demoted by Washington.

This rubbed many Officers the wrong way. It is true after this "Elite Group" received our wings some of our GI Pilots did walk around with a chip on their shoulder daring anyone to knock it off. Later on when we were at Selfridge after our aborted attempt to fly to England, 67 of us Sergeant Pilots slept in one, two-story, wooden, GI 38-man barracks. The Squadron Commander told us to move into two barracks. The Flight Surgeon said it was unhealthy all to no avail. Our excuse was so we could talk about flying and girls. So the Base Commander came in person with his Executive Officer and tried his hand. The Colonel began his tirade by speaking to the ranking Sergeant in our group. After a few choice words the Sergeant told the Colonel that if there was a complaint about our flying he wanted to hear about it and it would be corrected on the spot. If that was not the problem he asked the Colonel if either he or his Executive Officer had ever read AR 615-150 dated 1 August 1941, stating the regulation setting forth the sole duties of a Staff-Sergeant Pilot. Both indicated that they had not. The Sergeant then said that the Colonel must be aware that we are a pretty unique group and a special breed of pilots. The Colonel was deflated and that was the end of it. After they had left the Sergeant warned us that we had to be on our toes at all times, because if this Colonel could, he'd see to it that we were all grounded on some trumped up charge and off to the Infantry overseas we'd go. There never was in the history of the U S Army Air Corps such a small group that

Who Were the Staff Sergeant Pilots?

Advanced School	A	B	C	D	E	F	G	H	I	J	TOTAL
Columbus, MS							27	45	10		82
Craig FLD, AL								4			4
Napier FLD, AL							17	24			41
Ellington FLD, TX			39	55	59	56	89	98	112	108	616
Kelly FLD, TX	4		54	56	59	39	56	66	?	107	441
Lubbock, TX							54	65	102		221
Luke FLD, AZ				35	24		87	107	3	45	301
Mather FLD, CA					31	40					71
Moody FLD, GA							13	41	68	36	158
Roswell FLD, NM							31	1			32
Spence FLD, GA							26	56	71		153
Stockton, CA								150	2		152
Turner FLD, GA							14	1	17	37	69
Victorville, CA							11				11
Williams FLD, CA							28	43	1	48	120
TOTALS	4		93	111	184	159	436	540	562	383	2,472

"Old Timers"	154
Trained by RCAF	67
Total enlisted pilots who served with the Army Air Corps 1912 - 1943	2,693

Between 1939 and 1945, 193,440 Army Corps Pilots completed training and received their Silver Pilot Wings. This number includes 2,472 Enlisted Pilots, which accounted for only 1.278% of the total number of Pilots awarded this coveted rating.

AVIATION STUDENTS (Staff Sergeant Pilots) West Coast 42-E

Status	Started	Dropped-Out	% Succeeded
APPLIED	371	———–	100%
ACCEPTED	115	256	31%
KING CITY	115	36	21.29%
MOFFETT	79	7	19.4%
LUKE	38	3	9.43%
MATHER	34	3	8.36%
GRADUATED	66	305	17.79%

was so dedicated to flying and flying only. And our record proves it. In the history of the United States Army and Army Air Corps there were 154 Enlisted Pilots between 1912-1933, 2472 Staff-Sergeant Pilots in 1941-1943 and an additional 67 at that time who were trained by RCAF and transferred to the US Army Air Corps after the United States entered the WWII, thus making a total of 2,693 Enlisted Pilots that flew for the Army Air Corps.

In the summer of 1980, 42-E the first class of Enlisted Pilots in the West Coast Sergeant Pilots Program had our first class reunion 38 years after we received our wings. Merle Strauch was the Master of Ceremonies. Here is part of his opening address that best describes The Sergeant Pilot:

"It has been a long, long trip since you took that first flight in your Ryan, PT-22, on November 10th 1941.... When we assembled that memorable day to start flight training we were, you have to admit, a motley bunch, all enlisted men, displaying rank from private to the first three grades. Green was hardly the word. Uncomfortable was more like it. We were, after all, the first class to try the experiment of becoming flying sergeants in the West Coast Training Command, surrounded by officers and cadets that would graduate as officer pilots. No one, it seemed, wanted to associate with us...because we didn't belong. Not to the officers..., we were not Aviation Cadets and we did not fit in the normal enlisted category. We were a bastardly group."

"This was reinforced when the Mess Officer called us from the Flying Cadets mess to be sure we ate with the enlisted - food that was much different. We were, for the first time, realizing discrimination...a word that was hardly ever used in those days. The worst came after we were first pilots on multi-engine airplanes when, often, we had an officer as a co-pilot. We would land at an airfield and out would come a staff car and a 6 X 6 truck. The co-pilot would get into the staff car and the rest, including the pilot, would have to climb into the rear of the 6 X 6 if they wanted transportation."

"But that was acceptable to us because we were enlisted men and we knew the Army Regulations. We also knew we were damn good pilots and in the end, flew everything the Air Force had to offer...along with becoming officers of distinction. One of our group tonight ended up with six DFC's and a host of other medals for flying 385 combat missions; he holds the Air Force's record for having flown the most combat missions. Ernie Ford, take a bow! Another one of our classmates is happy that General Doolittle is here tonight. He flew General Doolittle out of Tokyo after the official signing of the documents signaling the end of the war in Japan. Floyd Barnes, please stand and take a bow! Otherwise, we were like flying cadets everywhere, a group of ambitious and daring young men. I know you have thought about this. Every man here, by virtue of the fact he was an Army Pilot at the very start of WW II - and is alive today, is a legend! Do you realize if you would get down on paper every hair raising event that happened in your flying life time from the scariest missions you have flown it would make a damn good book?"

"I am fiercely proud to be a part of this group and I am sure I speak for everyone of you when I say flight training, the discipline, and the eventual winning of those cherished silver pilots wings, did more to get our lives pointed in the right direction than any other force."

"Please, rise and let's sing God Bless America!"

That was the end of Merle's opening remarks.

When we were invited to the reunion we were instructed to give a two to three minute speech on what had transpired in our lives since receiving our wings on 20 May 1942. Before giving my speech I read the following:

"Ladies, General Holstron, Mr. Mason and Ex-Sergeant Pilots. As far as I am concerned, the highest tribute that can be bestowed on us Ex-Sergeant Pilots is the honor that we have been paid this night by having MR AVIATION come to us in person. What can be said of this man of letters that Kings, Queens, Presidents, the man on the street or pilots have not already been said? Sir, you were my idol long before the Tokyo Raid. My Grandfather used to say, 'Jimmy Doolittle can fly in the clouds and not even the birds can do that!!' Thank you Sir for coming."

Now a little United States Military "Aeronautical History" background...

In the 1790s, Ben Franklin first proposed using balloons not only to spy, but to put an early version of the commandos behind enemy lines. The French used balloons for reconnaissance during their revolution. The American Union Army used them in the Civil War and the Spanish American War. Eventually the Army became interested in dirigibles. Not only could they fly, weather permitting, but they could to a degree go when and where the pilot wished to go.

The "Air Age" was ushered in with the first successful heavier-than-air flight in an airplane. It took place at 1030 hours, Thursday, 17 Dec. 1903, at Kill Devil Hill, Kitty Hawk, North Carolina. The morning was cold with an on shore wind of 27 mph. Orville Wright (19 August 1871 - 30 January 1948) was the pilot and his brother Wilbur (16 April 1867 - 30 May 1912) ran alongside the right wing-tip. The biplane with a four-cylinder, twelve-horsepower engine with two wooden propellers and on skids flew for 120 feet in twelve seconds. This was the start of Aviation. It was a true "wood and cloth crate." The flight changed the entire world. Prior to this, the average man could travel 20 miles a day. Today he can travel over 1,500 miles in one hour. Astronauts circle 370 miles above the earth every 90 minutes!!

On 1 August 1907, the Army began an Aeronautical Division and placed it under the Chief Signal Officer. The Division was set up to take charge of "matters pertaining to military ballooning, air machines and all kindred subjects." The Officers who had flown in a number of balloon competitions—Capt. Charles Chandler and Lt. Frank Lahm—were put in charge. In the summer of 1908, the Army held trials at Fort Myer, VA, for what was to become its first dirigible competition with the aircraft. Then Wright Brothers finally convinced the Army to consider buying a powered aircraft. It would make an even better observation platform than a lighter-than-air aircraft. The Army bought both kinds of machines and continued to use balloons for many years. The airplane gradually gained the edge.

By 18 July 1914, military flying had graduated from an aeronautical division to become the "Aviation Section" with twelve Officers, 54 enlisted men and six airplanes.

On 15 May 1918, the Army took aviation away from the Signal Corps and set it up in two separate departments: the "Division of Military Aeronautics" for training and operations and the "Bureau of Aircraft Production."

On 2 July 1926, Congress created the Army Air Corps. The air arm wasn't a separate service, but it now was on a par with the Army's other Corps. Fifteen years later the Army Air Force was formed on 20 June 1941. Then on 18 September 1947, the United States Air Force became a separate branch of the armed forces and came into being. It is interesting to note that my youngest child NANCY JANE was born twenty years to the day after the Air Wing of the US Army became the Army Air Force.

A footnote to aviation history: the Wright Brothers called their Kitty Hawk flying machine the "Bird of Prey." It became the most famous airplane in aviation history. Yet today few have ever heard of it by name.

The following two paragraphs are from pages 10 and 11, in the book *THE AMERICAN WAR WITH JAPAN, EAGLE AGAINST THE SUN*, by Ronald H. Spector, The Free Press, A Division of Macmillan, Inc., 866 Third Avenue, New York, N.Y. 10022.

"On Armistice Day after WWI the (Army) Air Service had 20,000 officers, one year later it had been reduced to 200. It was a tight-knit, hard-drinking, hard-bitten, long-service army: an army of inspections and close-order drill, and long evenings over drinks at the officers' club."

"Of regular enlisted men in the army prior to Pearl Harbor, high school graduates were rare; outright illiterates were common. Over 75 percent had failed to complete high school and 41 percent had never been in high school at all. Most of the non-commissioned officers had seen twenty or more years of service."

Now back to Brookley...

The test flight was uneventfull. We wrung the bird out and it passed with flying colors. We landed first after Captain Lackey. He asked if we had any write-ups. I told him only the two that were on the Form 1. He said go sign for your plane, then go eat and be back by 1400. Tell all the other Pilots to do the same. We will have no more aircraft maintenance here unless they are safety flight items that have to be corrected. He then told me that Weedin's aircraft and mine were the only two aircraft that did not have auto pilots or artificial horizons that would work. They were on back order.

He then left for Operations. The Operations Officer was standing at attention with the right rear staff car door open. He gave a snappy salute and Captain Lackey got in and they drove off. After about 45 minutes they returned. By that time all pilots were at Douglas. They would not let Weedin or me sign for our aircraft as we were not officers. They could not believe that we were pilots or that we had test flown two Douglas aircraft. When Captain Lackey arrived he told the senior civilian in charge that we were pilots and that we would sign for our aircraft. The man behind the counter said that he could not do that. Captain Lackey picked up the phone, gave a number to the operator, then identified himself, told the party on the other end to get it straightened out within ten minutes or he would call General Marshall. Then he handed the phone to the civilian. The civilian said over the phone, "I do not take orders from the Army" and he hung up.

Captain Lackey began to look through his papers for a phone number. As he was placing his call, another phone in the office rang. Before Captain Lackey got his call through the civilian hung up the phone. He turned to Weedin and me and said, "you may sign." Weedin started to sound off. Captain Lackey said, "Forget it, he's only following orders. Sign, then let's all go eat. I'll get a formation clearance then meet me at my aircraft for a briefing."

From Brookley we flew loose formation back to Dodd Field in Texas. The last few miles we pulled into tight formation of four elements of three each with a tail-end-Charlie. Landing at Dodd we were told to refuel, have full tanks, get chow, and a good nights sleep. Tell no one where we had been or that we would be leaving at 0600 in the morning. Don't forget, "Loose lips, sink ships; whether it is on the water or in the air!!" We were to take everything we owned and had signed for. Have a good night's sleep, a good breakfast and to be at your aircraft no later than 0520 ready to fly. The crew chiefs and radiomen will do their pre-flight and engine run-up while the pilots will be at my plane being briefed. We were all restricted to the base until we would leave in the morning.

The next morning we found out that we were going to be landing at Kirtland Field, Albuquerque, New Mexico. The airport is on a flat plateau, 5,250 feet elevation, on the west side of a mountain. Off the west end of the runway there is a steep three hundred feet drop off to the Rio Grande River below with the city mostly on the west side of the river. We had to be careful on landing at this altitude coming in over the fence no slower than 95 mph and no faster than 100 mph. We were reminded not to forget that when your indicating 10,000 feet you're less than 5,000 feet above the ground. There are mountains 10-12,000 feet high in the immediate area. The weather was forecasted to be good, but if it turned sour we would turn back, find a field and wait until it cleared. We were to fly loose formation. I was lucky for I had landed at Hill Field, Utah once and Lowry Field, Colorado twice. Both are higher than Kirtland.

After refueling and eating at Kirtland, we were cleared to McClellan Field, Sacramento, California. About 1500 hours still in trail formation in clear weather we saw a beautiful mountain valley below the tops of two very high waterfalls. Later, we learned that this was Yosemite National Park.

Upon landing at McClellan Field the control tower instructed us to taxi to the south end of the ramp to the farthest hanger, staying in line close together on the west side of the ramp. We were to cut engines, take all gear, personal and GI, and put it on the ramp near the rear door of our aircraft and stay there until picked up and brought to Operations. Then at all times stay with your gear by the hanger door until told otherwise. Being the second plane to land it wasn't long before security people arrived. They gave each of us a green identification tag that we were to wear at all times while on the base and a base map with the green area marked indicating where we were cleared to enter. This tag had to be visible at all time when on base. There were very few places that we were cleared to enter. The base was divided into color-coded areas. The security people told us that when all crews have the same information we would be picked up for a very short briefing. In the meantime, we were to stay with our aircraft. Each crew was to stay together as a crew for the briefing.

In about 30 minutes security completed their rounds to all the crews and three newly painted Army buses arrived. You could still see the school district printing on the side of the buses which the Army paint had not completely covered. The drivers drove us to Operations. They told us to follow the waiting sergeant and that the buses would wait with our gear. We went through a green door and entered a briefing room.

When all crews were there Captain Lackey told us that we would be at

McClellan Field for two or three days to have our aircraft modified. He told us that we were not to talk among ourselves or with any one else about where we have been or may be going, what type aircraft we're flying, what the Depot is doing to our planes or any thing to do with the Army or the war. We were told not to forget there are a lot of security people around both in and out of uniform on and off the base. They will be asking questions just to get you to talk. If you do, you will not be going with us. Twenty years at Fort Leavenworth is a big price to pay just for sounding off. We have open-post tonight and tomorrow night. Every day while we were here, all crew members were to report to this room at 0800 hours in flying uniforms. You'll be excused as early as engineering releases us. Do not plan anything before 1600 and you may not make it then. When we meet here in the morning I'll give you the latest and then we'll be escorted to our planes. Do not get in the way of the work crews. They are highly skilled civilians. We are on a high priority mission. They cannot stand around talking with us. If you have any questions bring them back to this room and I'll try to get the answer. If it is when and where we're going, do not ask. Do not forget security on and off base and think of every girl as having VD, being a spy or worse yet, a traitor.

"Now I'll introduce you to the newest member of your crew, your navigator. Each pilot, as soon as I call out your plane number step forward, introduce yourself, shake hands, then the two of you go and you introduce your navigator to the rest of your crew." Then the green door opened and in came thirteen "old" Second Lieutenants. I doubt if any member of the 6th's ground crew was as old. Our navigator was Second Lieutenant Andrew H. Sambor, Jr. After a few minutes we were sent to our bus. When we arrived at our bus the last of our airplanes were being towed into the hangers.

This was my second flight to McClellan. The first time had been in the spring of 1941. I flew as an Observer for Second Lieutenant Frank N. Graves in an O-46 from Gray Field, Fort Lewis, Tacoma, Washington, where we were stationed. As a Private First Class, Third Class Specialist, I was assigned to Headquarters and knew all the base pilots. On occasion one would ask if I would like to go for a flight and be his observer. All this entailed was to keep a sharp look out at all times in all quadrants for: airplanes, balloons, birds, clouds and mountains while the pilot was practicing flying instruments under the hood. I remember once flying as an Observer for First Lieutenant

Felix M. Hardison who was later grounded and transferred to the 4th Infantry in Alaska for doing loops around the Narrows Bridge. My immediate Supervisor Officer was Major Hannie B. McCarmick a Balloon Command Pilot. He would always say, "If your work load will permit, have a good safe flight and do exactly what and when the pilot tells you." The base was assigned: Beechcraft F-2s, Martin B-10s, Douglas B-18s and C-46s, North American O-38s, and O-47s, and a Squadron of Barrage Balloons.

Major McCarmick once took me for a balloon flight. The balloon was tethered on the ramp. The basket was resting on its side on the ramp. To get aboard in the basket the Balloon man a Sergeant up righted the basket. He placed a three-legged step ladder with one leg in the basket and the other two legs straddled over the side of the basket standing on the ramp. We took three steps up and three steps down the other side of the ladder and we were in the basket. The Pilot, Major McCarmick, told the Sergeant that he was ready. The Balloon man removed the ladder, released the tension on the cable and we were lifted up. We were now in the air four feet off the ramp and there we stayed for one hour. We stood in the basket and he told me about flying balloons in France and Germany during World War I. When his flight time was over the Balloon man started the gasoline engine and reeled us down. Another six steps on the ladder, one hour flight time in a barrage-balloon and my balloon flight experience was over.

One of the Base Squadrons, the 2nd Photo, mapped Alaska in F-2s and B-18s prior to World War II. What stories they told about the weather! Master Sergeant Raymond W. Stockwell, was undoubtedly one of the best pilots, if not the best, in the Aviation Service or Air Corps at that time. He received his wings in October 1932. He was afraid of no man. Until you became his friend you quaked in your boots when he growled. This included West Point full Colonels. More Generals knew him personally than any other Pilot in the Air Corps including Officers and enlisted men. Most of equal or higher rank called him "Uncle Chew" because he always had a mouthful of chewing tobacco. Each pilot was assigned to a specific airplane. His was always well marked inside and down the left outside of the aircraft from the pilot's side window to the end of the rudder. One of his more outstanding accomplishments was when National Geographic Magazine published his pictures and gave him full credit for mapping what one day became the Alcan Highway. I am proud to say that Master Sergeant Raymond W. Stockwell knew me by name and so called me. I have a photo of me standing guard duty on the B-18 he flew in Alaska.

That night George asked, "What are we going to name our airplane?" I had never thought about it. The four in my crew were billeted side by side. So after a few suggestions I said, "think it over and we will decide tomorrow."

The next morning Sgt Grassi met me with fire in his eyes. It seems that the Navigator had Grassi out until after 2300 hours looking at the stars and trying to locate them on a chart. Grassi told me to call him off and that we should get another "Stargazer" as this guy doesn't have any confidence. The navigator told Grassi that he had never flown anything like this before.

When our briefing started Captain Lackey told us our aircraft were being winterized. At 1000 hours there would be a movie in this room on winter flying in cold weather. Those that wanted to could go to see their aircraft at this time. "The escort will be here shortly, but be back here before 1000 hours. Only go to and from your airplane and only with your escort. If you're picked up in an unauthorized area you can go to the guardhouse. Don't forget this is wartime." All crews went to see their birds. What a busy place with eight men working on each airplane. On my bird they were nearly finished with all deicing boots and were working on the prop deicer slinger rings and were installing the inside alcohol tanks.

Just then a forklift drove up with a flat stack of big black empty rubber sacks. Grassi said, "We're going on a long over water flight. Those are inflatable cabin gas tanks. Next came a load of lumber for the frame to hold the tanks. Our escort then took us back to see the movie. After lunch we were excused until 0800 next morning. On the way to the bus I told Lieutenant Sambor to please take it easy on the crew chief as he did not need any more cross training into navigation. That was the end of that.

That evening several of us Sergeant Pilots went to the Capital Hotel in downtown Sacramento across from the State Capitol. When we arrived most of the squadron's Second Lieutenants were on the second floor balcony overlooking the main dance floor directly below. Of course, being an enlisted pilot we could not join the other Squadron Pilots, so we stood around the main floor in the crowd and watched and listened to their loud singing. Some of the Lieutenants were already pretty high (drunk) when we arrived. At the table below the Lieutenants were the girls. One of the Lieutenants had been talking (shouting) with them before we arrived. This young "Birdman" called down and said, "If I can have a date I'll fly down and get you." One of the young ladies told him that if he could fly to come on down. He stood up in his chair and then on the banister. With arms straight out he took off singing the Army Air Corps song! Somewhere about "The wild blue yonder" he crash-landed on their table. The only good thing about it was that all the young women got out of the way and none of them were hurt. Our fly boy was hauled away in an Army "Meat-Can" with what turned out to be only a broken leg, a lot of bruises, cuts and scratches from the broken glasses. That was the last we ever saw of him. Two days later we had a replacement. That broke up the party and everyone returned to base and all of the drunks sobered up really fast.

At the briefing next morning the Commander told us that last night one of our young pilots stupidly got hurt and was no longer with us. He had taken some mighty drastic action to keep from going overseas. That was the first time we had heard the word "Overseas" since our aborted attempt for Europe prior to going to Selfridge Field.

While waiting for our aircraft to be winterized we attended a sea survival class and a movie on ditching and life in a raft at sea. Being a poor swimmer and afraid of water, I knew this was not my cup of tea. We were each fitted and issued an all-weather survival suit and an oxygen mask. There was a short movie on the proper fitting and use of the gas mask. All present had seen the movie before and had been through the actual "Tear and Mustard Gas" course and for most of us GIs, several times. The instructor and Grassi had at one time been in the same squadron and were good friends. After the two hour lecture, demonstration and movie, the instructor asked Grassi to stay for awhile so they could talk about old buddies. Later when all the survival equipment arrived at our plane we had double portions and more different items than any of the other airplanes. Months later we were still eating our C-rations thanks to Grassi's "Friend." Grassi told me to look over our aircraft with a fine tooth comb for his friend had told him that this was the same hanger crew that had fouled up General Doolittle's B-25s. I passed the word on to the Commander.

When maintenance released our plane, the crew chief was to fully refuel the wing tanks and put 50 gallons in each of the eight cabin tanks. No more or no less. He was to double check for leaks before starting the engines. We were reminded not to smoke on or near the aircraft as long as there are cabin fuel tanks aboard. Remember empty gas tanks are more dangerous than full tanks. Aircraft Number "39" was released during the noon hour. I had already completed the clearance except for Weather and Ops signature. George and I had studied the local test area map and had the tower and range frequencies. Returning from lunch we had our clearance in short order and walked to our plane parked on the ramp across from Ops. Grassi and Greggs were waiting for us. The co-pilot and I did our pre-flight. Alert stood fire guard and we were on our way. The basic test flight was the same as at Brookley. We ran five minutes on each of the eight inside cabin tanks and the Navigator swung the compass. Upon landing, Alert parked us in the same spot across form Ops. I signed the Form 1 and the test flight release forms. When I turned in the test flight forms, maintenance released the airplane to the Squadron. No 39 was now released and ready to go somewhere overseas, but when and where?

Upon landing, several of the other aircraft required further maintenance before they were released. It was not until the next afternoon that all Squadron aircraft write-ups were cleared.

That night most of the enlisted men, Sergeant Pilots, crew chiefs and radiomen got together. Shortly, we were talking about weather flying and survival. None of us had ever flown in real cold weather. The perils of flying and surviving in such an environment would be a new experience for all of us. A few of us had heard pilots and crew members talk about flying in Alaska. They all told of the same difficulties and hazards of flying: strong head winds, low ceilings and visibility, ice-fog, snow everywhere, iced-up wings, fuselage, tail section, control surfaces, props, carburetors, air intakes, windshields, pitot tubes, radio antennas, with little or no radio transmission or reception, engine oil congealing, tires that freeze to the ramp. But worst of all was the erratic magnetic compass that only points north. It looked to me that we had plenty to learn and very little time to learn how to fly and survive in such extremes. But I knew that if the old-timers like Stockwell could fly a B-18 and F-2 for so many hours and live to tell about it, we could too.

At the briefing next morning I asked the Commander if he could get us some books on Arctic Survival for the protection of the crews and the airplanes. He said that he would see what he could find. We were told that when this meeting was over we were to go to our quarters and pick up all our gear. We were to put it in our planes and to stand by either our planes or around Operations. As the airplanes were released they were to be parked across from Operations. At 1130 we were to go by bus to eat and then come back to our aircraft and wait. We were scheduled to depart as soon as the last plane was ready.

As we walked across the ramp we were in for a surprise for we could plainly see "Irene" had been painted on both sides of the nose of our bird. Grassi spoke up and said that was his wife's name. No one objected. Irene was the best airplane any crew could ever wish for.

After a long hurry-up-and-wait, the Commander called all Pilots to his plane and told us that we were now leaving for Hamilton Field, San Rafael, California. It would take about 35 minutes and we would be flying in formation. So off we flew. We all knew that the next flight after that would be a long over water flight. Why not fly inland up to McChord and then on up the coast to Alaska?

When we landed at Hamilton we were parked on a closed taxiway. Before we were out of the aircraft there were posted armed guards at each of our thirteen aircraft with two mobile roving guards, one driving in front of the planes and the other guard driving in the rear of the aircraft in the other direction. Our guard told us to take everything with us that we would need for this was a secured area. The only way we could get back to our plane was to be escorted by the Operations Officer, the Sergeant of the Guard, or the Officer of the Day.

6X6s trucks came and drove us to Operations. A Major came out and welcomed us to Hamilton Field. He said, "As soon as your Commander clears Operations and reports to the Base Commander, the trucks will drive you to your quarters. The Officers will go to the BOQs and the enlisted men will be dropped off at their barracks. When you check in, and this goes for both Officers and enlisted men, you will be given instructions on the black-out rules. This is one rule that will not be violated." Then he made a big hit with thirteen of us. He said, "I understand some of you pilots are sergeants. You have some big shoes to fill. All the former Enlisted Pilots now in the Army Air Corps are either full Colonels or Generals and they are all outstanding pilots. I wish you the very best." Thirteen of us gave the Major a hearty applause. This was the first time as a group we had ever received any recognition.

When Captain Lackey returned he told us that we were all restricted to the base until notified differently. "Do not try to sneak off base. When you get to your quarters you will be given two very important bits of information. One, study the base map and know where you may go and what is off limits. Second, do not goof up on the other one and that is the blackout regulations. If you let any light out a door or window, light a match, smoke outside, turn any lights on outside, you will be Court Martialed, that is, if someone does not shoot you first. All guards have live ammunition and have orders to use it. Repeat, no lights that can be seen outside after it starts to get dark until after sun up. The trucks will pick us up at 0745 in the morning. Leave all your gear in your quarters. No letters or telephone calls to anyone, period."

All GIs were billeted by crews. Again we were well briefed on the blackout rules: how to get in and out the double doors that were hung with heavy blackout curtains which are the same as those that are used to get in and out a photo lab darkroom. We were briefed on the base restricted areas and how to find the mess hall. Before dark the four of us had returned to the barracks and did not leave until early chow next morning.

Next morning at Operations Captain Lackey told us that we were going to Fort Mason in San Francisco near Crissey Field on the other end of the Golden Gate Bridge. We would be picking up our winter clothing and survival equipment. We were now to go out front, load in the 6x6s by crews, and to stay with your pilot. Off we went to the Army to get our gear. They were waiting for us with everything that was on the Order Request. All the gear fit: complete winterized fleece-lined flying suits, pants, a one piece long coat with fur hood, snow glasses, whistle, wrist compass, knife, survival mirror with an attached cord to hang around your neck, a woolen sock cap, two pair of nylon gloves inserts, gloves with an attached cord running through the coat sleeves, one pair of winter leather fleece-lined high topped buckle boots, four pairs of heavy woolen winter electric heated socks with a box of twelve batteries (to be used only when not hooked up to the aircraft DC power), two pairs of winter long-johns, a steel helmet, liner, and trench axe. The navigators and the pilots were issued an automatic .45 caliber pistol for a side arm, four ammunition clips, 100 rounds of ammunition, webbed cartridge belt, leather holster, ammo pouches, medical kit, water canteen with canvas holder and our own personal Gas Mask. The other crew members were issued the same except for the weapons. They were each issued a carbine and 1,000 rounds of ammunition. All crew members were issued a large heavy duty B-3 bag with lock.

When it came time to sign for all the gear for each crew the pilot was asked to sign. But the Army would not let Weedin or me sign. Since they had been so nice and were waiting for us with all the equipment and correct sizes, I asked Lieutenant Sambor if he would sign for our crew. He said yes, if he could get a copy of what he was signing for. After signing we went to the mess hall.

After chow we headed back to Hamilton in the back of the 6x6s. Most of the 66 Officers and enlisted men, thirteen crews of five each and Staff Sergeant Goldstein, our Administration NCO, had never been in San Francisco before. They were only getting a glimpse of the city through the dusty, flapping rear tarpaulin flap on the bumpy tail end of an Army truck. I had spent some time there before the war, a week at the World's Fair, three weeks at Fort McDowell when I enlisted in the Army Air Corps and two days on the way to Flying School.

After storing all our gear in a secure room at Hamilton Operations, the Commander gave us open post until 0200 the next morning. He told us that there was an off base GI bus schedule on the wall in Operations. Then he said: "have a good and safe time, go in groups and use your heads. If you miss the last bus at 2400 it will cost two weeks' pay to get back to base. Remember the black-out and security. Think of every girl downtown as a spy with VD."

At 1700, four 38-passenger GI buses departed for 5th and Market Street in downtown San Francisco. Two of the busses were to return at 2200 and the other two at 2400 hours. Most of our flight crews were aboard and ready to see the city. All vehicles drove with black-out lights and the city was in a brown-out condition, no bright or flashing lights anywhere. As we were getting off the bus I overheard some of the officers talking about the Top Of The Mark. I then knew that was one place I would not be seeing. Eddie Silsby and I stuck together for the evening. We walked two blocks to Powell Street, caught a trolley to Union Square only because we had heard about it. Then we went on to Chinatown. Eddie had been there before, but it was the first time for me. I thought it very interesting and some of the snacks were most unusual. From there we went by trolley to Fisherman's Wharf. A trolley ride in San Francisco is always fun and more so at night in a black-out condition, straight up, then straight down to San Francisco Bay which is almost to the water's edge. We had to walk the last couple of blocks. Half the Army and Navy were there along with a good number of MPs and Shore Patrol. Most either had a girl or were trying to get one. Of course, all of us were just on our own. It seemed that all the military (in wartime all military personnel must be in uniform) were having a good time and all were on good behavior. I did not realize there were so many different kinds of fish and all tasted so good, but what would you expect from a "drylander?" When we had our fill it was time to head back for the 2200 bus. We made our way back to our barracks in the dark.

At next morning's briefing we were told to pre-flight our aircraft: run up the engines, check radios, then fill all tanks to the top, gas, oil, alcohol, hydraulic fluid, oxygen bottles and drinking water. We were to check the tires, then make sure everything inside was tied down and in its proper place. This was especially true for the two life rafts, Gibson Girls (emergency radio), Very Pistol (Flare Gun), emergency food, water and survival kit, the two aluminum oars, two hard rubber 2" X 10" X 10" pads, and a tarpaulin. The tarpaulin was to cover the raft to keep the rain, cold weather and or sun out. One of the pads was to be placed in the middle of the bottom of the rubber raft. Lace it down in the marked area as indicated. Unscrew the oar paddle from the aluminum handle. Place the handle in the designated notch on the pad in the bottom of the boat. Put the second pad on the other end of the oar handle. Lace this pad to the designated marked area of the tarpaulin. Then raise and secure the edges of the canvas. In the kit were: sea-marker dye, fish hooks, a 300-foot nylon line, hunting knife, medical first-aid kit, a plastic water bag, waterproof matches, whistle, shark repellent, water purifier, sunburn preventive, signal mirror, and a plastic-coated manual of survival instructions on land and sea in all climates and regions of the world with maps and compass. We attached the two life rafts with a good strong lanyard tied to a floor "D" ring just inside the main cabin door. We would be wearing our Mae West at all times while over the water. "The Navigator will let you know when we reach cold water. Then take-off your Mae West, put on your survival suit and then once again put on your Mae West. If you inflate the Mae West while in the plane you will be too big to get out the cockpit or passenger door. If you have your parachute on and pull the Mae West cords you'll die from a crushed chest. So remember to stay alert and help your buddy. It would be nice to think that all of us will return to San Francisco. However the odds are 25-50 percent of us right here now will not make it. Be on the ball at all times so you will beat the odds. Pilots, remember you are the lawful guardians of your crew, passengers, cargo, and aircraft. You are commander of your ship, so take care.

"There will be another meeting in this room at 1600 this afternoon. The Squadron is restricted to the base until we depart. From here go pick up your survival gear and meet the trucks out front to take you to your airplane. Stay with your aircraft and do not leave that area. Refueling should be there in about 30-45 minutes after you arrive. This will give you time to pre-flight. Do not rush! Remember there are no gas trucks over the ocean so fill it up and fill all tanks all the way. The trucks will return at 1130 and take you to eat. After chow, if any crew needs to go back to the plane tell the truck driver when he lets you off at the mess hall so you will have transportation. After the noon meal those that do not go back to their airplane are off till 1600. You might want to go to the PX for there is no telling when you will be able to visit one this well supplied. An afternoon rest might be in order. See you at 1600. After taking their gear to their aircraft the navigators should check their charts, study their navigation books, and talk to the weather people."

Prior to 1600 hours all were present and anxiously waiting for the big news. Captain Lackey asked for any crew chief to sound off if his airplane needed any maintenance: "Are all twelve gas tanks full, oil and extra hydraulic fluid, alcohol and oxygen? Do you have the two twenty gallon drums of fresh drinking water full? Would you feel safe in flying this aircraft for 20 hours non-stop over the ocean?" There were no comments. "OK. You know that this aircraft was designed for a maximum payload of 5,000 pounds. We will be taking off with over 10,000 pounds, more than 200% over the recommended weight. Your aircraft will not maintain level flight with take-off power on a single engine at sea level. So you do not have a single engine security until you've flown at least ten hours or you will be in the water. It is as simple as that. This is war and we have no other choice but to go. If all the planes are ready, go to your quarters and pack everything except your shaving kit. Then go eat and return to your quarters and go to sleep. Wake up time is at 0100 hours. Yes, I said 0100! Be ready in flight suits at 0115 for a base sergeant to walk you to the mess hall. Remember, it will be night, dark, blackout rules, security, and we will be on a tight schedule. Other people will be sleeping, use only flash lights to the minimum in the sleeping quarters. In the latrines the lights will be on. No talking in the barracks and not until you are inside the mess hall."

"All co-pilots stay at the mess hall and pick up and sign for ten sack lunches, that's two lunches for each of the five crew members. My co-pilot will pick up two extra lunches. They are for our Sergeant Major. They know that Sergeant Pilots will be signing for a total of 112 sack lunches. The two Lieutenant co-pilots will sign for twenty at the Officer's Mess. The truck drivers will be at the mess hall waiting to take you to your barracks for a 15-minute stop and then will take you on to your airplane. When you arrive at your plane if the engines are not running put your gear and the lunches on board. Put two sacks lunches in the seat of each crew position. Co-Pilots stay in the plane until the run up is over. Stay in the back so the crew chief can do his run up. When the run ups are completed the trucks will bring you to Operations. Do not forget the blackout rules. There are security and armed guards that have live ammunition and they may be trigger happy. Be in this room no later than 0235. Remember NO LETTERS OR TELEPHONE CALLS. See you here in the morning. At Christmas you will find out why we did not go to England and the reasons for all the rush and secrecy of this flight."

A group of us went to the PX. The only thing I bought were two rolls of 35mm black and white film. They had an ASA rating of "25" that was the fastest on the market in those days.

Later at the mess hall, I learned that Grassi was the only crew chief that went back to his aircraft. There he once again topped off all twelve fuel tanks. By squeezing and shaking he thought that maybe we now had another half hour of flight time. This is only one of the many reasons why when Grassi came aboard I knew that the airplane was safe and ready to fly. He knew how and he always made sure the bird was ready to fly before he would say, "OK, she's ready," or he would give a thumbs up.

Back in the barracks, I packed my B-4 bag, everything except my flight clothes, 45, shaving kit, and flash light. Then I took a shower. From then until lights out most conversations were about Alaska and Arctic flying. Even after the lights were out, most of us had a hard time going to sleep. Several times I'd pull the blanket over my head turn on the flash light and check my watch. At 0030 I was wide awake, got up, dressed and was ready along with all the enlisted crews by the time the CQ came to wake us. Without a word all thirty-nine enlisted crew members and our Administration NCO followed the CQ to the mess hall. After breakfast, a staff and command car took Weedin and me to the barracks where we picked up our gear and then went to our planes. After we had stored our gear the driver drove us to Operations.

Prior to 0233 hours, 2 October 1942, all sixty-five crew members and Sergeant Goldstein were standing in the hall outside the briefing room. The door was closed with a posted armed guard. That was a big joke for all sixty-six of us were also armed! At exactly 0235 the door opened and out came the Operations Officer and the same Major that had met and spoken to us on our arrival at Hamilton. He told us to come in by crews, for us to stand in the back behind the roped off area and for the guard to close the door and not to let anyone in or out after we all had come in and he had closed the door. The Major then asked Captain Lackey to verify that he personally could iden-tify all sixty-six of his men. Captain Lackey told his four crew members and Staff Sergeant Goldstein to take seats as a crew in the front leaving a seat for him. Next he called "Ford," and my crew of five moved forward and were seated. Then Weedin's crew, and so on until all thirteen crews were seated and no one was left standing.

The Weather Officer was first to speak. He gave us the weather from San Francisco up the coast to Anchorage and on to Fairbanks with the upper winds.

Then the Intelligence Officer told us that the Operations Officer would have each pilot sign for a classified weather report, radio frequencies and landing approach instructions for our next airport, all in a sealed envelope. Each pilot was to put the sealed envelope in his upper left zipper pocket of his flight suit after signing for it. "Do not remove it until one hour after take-off. After take-off and passing over the Golden Gate Bridge pick up a heading of 270° and climb to 6,000 feet. The pilot is to open the envelope one hour after take-off. Take the sealed envelope from your pocket, break the seal, read and follow the enclosed SECRET ORDERS." Each pilot must return the envelope with all enclosed orders and documents to his Commanding Officer upon landing at the first airport.

The Operations Officer told us to start our engines when the Squadron Commander started his. Remember: "Total radio silence, no more use of the radios on this mission until advised to do so, no landing lights, cabin or flash lights. The guards have orders to shoot out any lights that are not out on command. With engines running you can not hear so do not turn on any light. Be careful and follow your orders to the letter. If any engine will not start or there are other problems that will prevent your departing on time and in assigned sequence with your Squadron, stay where you are. A ground maintenance crew will come aboard your aircraft and check it out. If there is a valid maintenance problem your aircraft will be repaired at a later date and you will be rescheduled later. If it is not a valid problem, a Court Martial will follow. This is war. Captain Lackey will now conclude the briefing. When the briefing is over, all first pilots come forward and sign for your classified material."

Captain Lackey stood, "We have trained to fight, now fight like we have been trained; if you do not know it by now, it is too late. Remember no lights or radios, and no smoking. Our aircraft are the only ones that will be running at this hour, so when you hear or see an engine running, start your engine running. Set both altimeters at 29.92" Hg and do not reset until you hear the landing instructions. Taxi and take-off in your assigned order. Stagger sides of the runway for take-off. I'll be at the very end on the far left side of runway 14. Ford will be on my far right and Weedin will follow in my position and etc. Odd position numbers on the left side of the runway and even numbers on the right side. Release your brakes for take-off at 30 second intervals. After take-off, climb straight ahead for three minutes, then a left 690 rolling out the second time around on a heading of 170° and head for the Golden Gate Bridge. Be on the look out for the bridge towers, for they will be about your flight level depending on your rate of climb. When crossing the bridge pick up a heading of 270° and climb to 6,000 feet."

"One hour after take-off open your sealed secret envelope and follow the instructions. We will be in a very loose formation. You may not see any of the other aircraft after take-off until we land. If we get in weather, the sealed orders will tell you when, where and what to do. Our next meeting will be in Operations after we land. Pilots, bring your envelope with all documents and turn them in to me for your signed receipt. Now, go to your aircraft, be careful and remember be quiet, use no radios and keep 'em flying."

Each first pilot went forward, signed for his sealed envelope and zipped it up in his flight suit. The three briefing officers wished each of us a safe flight and a safe and speedy return. Then they shook hands with each pilot. The door opened and we were on our way. This was the second time in three months that we had started for overseas. The other time we were headed for England. I hoped that this time we'd make it.

As we stood to leave someone began to sing and then we all joined in.

"We live in fame and go down in flames, but nothing can stop the
Army Air Corps and off to war we go!!"

Each crew was dropped off at its assigned aircraft. Our guard said no one had been in the plane since the crew chief had filled the tanks yesterday. I thanked him for watching our bird and told him that if he got overseas and should run into No 39 to come and see us and I would give him a ride. Since all of our crew had arrived at the same time, the co-pilot and I made an outside walk around in the dark in record time. Grassi drained and safied the fuel sumps (drained the water condensation out of the gas tanks). Beaver and I pulled No.1 prop through while Grassi and Gregg pulled No. 2. The crew chief stayed outside and stood fire guard. Being parked next to the lead ship we were able to start our engines as soon as their prop started turning. Both engines caught on the first try. Lieutenant Sambor helped the crew chief climb aboard. There were no outside lights as far as I could see anywhere on the base and very few visible from off base. All outside doors and windows had either blackout curtains or roladins. With thirteen aircraft in a close area and all engines running the only light was from their exhaust stacks. There were no landing lights or cabin lights on. There were no wing walkers. We only had the one Alert Truck to lead the Commander to take-off position. Those were the days before there were red rotating anti-collision beacon lights or formation lights. The cockpit lights were so low that only the crew chief could read the instrument panel and then only when he was on his knees looking over the pedestal. The co-pilot and I both set our altimeters at 29.92.

Very slowly we followed the Flight Commander to the run-up area adjacent to the end of the SE runway. When taxiing it was easy to tell that we had a load. It required more power to move and more braking distance to stop. We were just lumbering dangerously close to other parked aircraft with no lights or wing walkers even though we were just creeping. As we swung around for run-up and magneto check, George thought he could count the exhaust of all thirteen birds. What a black night to be feeling your way around in a very crowded area with thirteen aircraft all over-loaded with supposedly 1,620 gallons of 91 octane aviation fuel. This was in the days before 96 or 100 octane was available. If any two of us had collided, all thirteen aircraft and sixty-six Army men would have gone up in one loud bang. There were sixty-five crew members in addition to the Squadron Personnel Sergeant Major who was aboard Captain Lackey's aircraft.

Shortly the lead aircraft started taxiing into position. We followed stopping at the very end on the far right side of runway 14. We advanced the mixtures to emergency rich, props full forward, dropped a quarter flap, cowl flaps trail, tail wheel locked, tightened the friction lock for the throttles and stood by to add power. Above our engines I could hear the build up roar, as power was being added to the Captain's engines. Looking out my side window I could see his right engine exhaust had changed from a short fiery exhaust to a steady solid long stream of vivid white flame. I told George to stand by with his left hand on the wobble pump and his right hand behind the throttles so they would not creep back and lose power on take-off. Once again I checked the controls for full travel and then called out that we were about ready to roll.

The Squadron Leader was moving on his take-off roll. With brakes locked I slowly eased the throttles forward until reaching 40" Hg. The attitude of the nose did not change. When our 30-second interval was up I released the brakes, applying full emergency war time power, 2800 rpm and 52" Hg. We only began to creep forward and the tail was still on the runway. For the take-off Grassi was on his knees between the pilot and co-pilot looking over the pedestal calling out the power settings and air speed. The co-pilot was keeping an eye on the cylinder-head, oil temperatures and oil pressure with his left hand on the wobble pump and right hand behind the throttles. It seemed like an eternity before the tail-wheel broke ground and we started moving up and got on the step. The bird was straining and groaning for all she was worth to break ground. Grassi said that the Commander had just got airborne. We were far enough to the right and so heavily loaded that there was very little prop wash. At 80 mph the plane was solid on the runway and felt like it had no intention of ever getting airborne. At 90 mph with back pressure on the wheel and the end of the runway racing towards us I pulled it in the air at 0401 hours on 2 October 1942.

A history footnote regarding this same date on 2 October 1942, at Mojave Desert, California, Army Air Corps Major Bill Craigie was the first American Military pilot to fly America's first jet powered aircraft, the P-59A.

As I called for wheels up, George and Grassi both called out: "We just cleared the sea wall." We climbed straight ahead at 200 feet per minute using emergency rich and slowly increased airspeed to 120 mph. At 400 feet we milked the flaps up and then started a single needle width bank to the left the second time around rolling out on a heading of 170°. At the end of the 690° left turn with normal take-off power we were just indicating a 200 foot a minute climb and had lost 200 feet in the bank. We had a cylinder head temp of 290° C. This was 30°C above maximum temperature for take-off. It was too hot, but there was nothing I could do, because at that time we were using 91 octane fuel. I could only hope that when we straightened out and had more lift it would start climbing before the engine detonation put us in the bay. The oil temperature was 15°C above the allowable. Both engines should freeze up and conk out, but we were still climbing.

Looking out the right side window, the co-pilot said that he could still see lights from the exhausts of some of the planes still on the ground, but nothing from the one aircraft ahead of us. Hopefully, she was still airborne somewhere in front of us. It was still dark in the early morning and we could see a few stars and patches of fog. The wake of a ship in the bay gave off a V-shaped phosphorescent shimmering glow in the water, like neon lights in the morning darkness. By dead reckoning we should be at the bridge. Since the start of the war all obstruction and outside navigation lights had been turned off. Climbing in the pitch dark with scattered fog and at an indicated altitude of 710 feet—where was the bridge?

After take-off the navigator came forward and was standing behind the crew chief. He asked if that was one of the bridge towers. I said that I could not see anything and was going to make another 360. At that instant a tower came into view dead ahead. If I'd tried to make another 360 I'm sure the centrifugal force would have pushed us into whichever tower was in front of us. I pulled back on the yoke, added full rpm and throttle, dropped a quarter flap, in a steep straight ahead climb at 90 mph and then went to emergency rich. We got the elevator effect and God only knows how, or which tower, we missed. At 900 feet I lowered the nose, picked up airspeed to 120 mph, reduced to normal climb power, turned right to a heading 270° and continued climbing. Years later I found out that the bridge towers were 746 feet high. We should have been briefed on the height of the bridge towers and instructed that after take-off to make a third left 360° turn before heading for the bridge.

George was looking out and down from the co-pilot's side window when he thought that we were passing a dirigible flying parallel to our flight and just below us. I told him that it more likely was a Navy submarine patrol balloon. When I was in Basic Flying School at Moffett Field just south of here the Navy would send a balloon up ever morning, weather permitting before daylight, to patrol the entrance to San Francisco Bay. They would stay on station until after dark if the weather held out. At 6,000 feet we leveled off and switched to the rear cabin tanks taking note of the time. I kept my own record of time, heading, altitude, indicated airspeed, free air temperature, fuel consumption, time changing tanks, and power settings. We had no available information on long distance cruise control so each pilot was on his own. Below 10,000 feet I used 1800 rpm and 27" Hg. Above 10,000 feet I pulled the rpm all the way back and the throttles all the way forward. With the bird trimmed up it indicated 140 mph. We kept a sharp eye on the oil and cylinder head temperatures and the oil pressure. By this time they had come down to safe limits.

When our one hour was up, there was no head room in the cockpit for the radio operator so he went back to his station. I broke the red waxed seal on the envelope and took out all documents. The envelope and each enclosed sheet was stamped "SECRET" in big red letters at the top and bottom of each sheet. There was a flight order, weather chart, approach, let down instructions and radio frequencies to guard. When Lieutenant Sambor got a glance at the orders he said, "Pick up a heading of 210° and climb to 12,000 feet. We're heading for Hawaii!! I'll be back shortly with a corrected heading, ETA and to take a Sun Line." We were climbing through 10,000 feet when he returned and gave me a new heading of 243° and an ETA of 1620 Hawaii time. Don't forget Hawaiian time is two hours earlier than the West Coast.

As I review this in August 2004, it is interesting to note that when we departed from Hamilton Field my Form 5 military flight log indicated that I ONLY had a total of 451:40 hours of pilot flying time. Only three of the pilots in our squadron had more flying time than I had. What a bunch of rookies pilots!! At that time the airlines required a minimum of 4,000 flying hours in the DC-3/C-47 before they would even consider checking a pilot out as a Captain. But this was war and we were expendable!!

6TH TROOP CARRIER SQUADRON

Squadron aircraft flight formation positions from Hamilton Field, San Rafael, California to Jackson Airdrome, Port Moresby, Papua, New Guinea between 2 October and 13 October 1942.

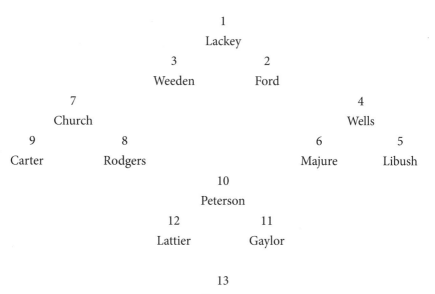

Aircraft formation, Serial Number, Field Number,
Aircraft Name, and Crew Assignment:

Position 1, C47A, 41-, 51, LINDA ANN
P Capt. Lackey, John H., Jr.
CP S/Sgt P McFarland, Orland W.
N
CC T/Sgt Janavich, Vincent J.
RO Cpl NcMann, Lyle G.
X S/Sgt Sidney B. Goldstein

Position 2, C47A, 41-18539, 39, IRENE
P S/Sgt P Ford, Ernest C.
CP S/Sgt P Beaver, George W.
N 2nd Lt.. Sambor, Andrew H. Jr.
CC T/Sgt Grassie, Amerigo
RO Sgt. Gregg, John C.

Position 3, C47A, 41-, 61, FLAMINGO
P S/Sgt P Weeden, Wibbur H.
CP S/Sgt P Silsby, Edward M..
N
CC T/Sgt Kopko, Casimir J.
RO T/Sgt. Palmer, Gerald L.

Position 4, C47A, 41-, 63, HELLS BELLS
P 1st Lt. Wells, William D.
CP S/Sgt P Webb, Glenn E.
N
CC M/Sgt Kullich, Michael
RO T/Sgt. Proctor, William E.

Position 5, C47A, 41-, 59, MISS AMERICA
P 2nd Lt. LIBUSE, Frank C.
CP 2nd Lt. Malmstone, Blesch
N
CC T/Sgt Iles, Ward C.
RO S/Sgt. Parker, John W.

Position 6, C47A, 41-18585, MAXINE
P 2nd Lt. Majure, Harold B.
CP 2nd Lt. Burleigh, Albert H.
N
CC T/Sgt Stephens, Clifford D.
RO T/Sgt. Branner, Delmar C.

Position 7, C47A, 41-, 62, SWAMP RAT
P 1st Lt. Church, Frank C.
CP S/Sgt P Dial, Irwin W.
N
CC T/Sgt Shireman, Paul
RO S/Sgt. Noggle, Willis

Position 8, C47A, 41-, PEGGY-POLLY
P 2nd Lt. Rodgers, Jeffus M.
CP S/Sgt P Fairey, John P.
N
CC S/Sgt Large, Shadrack J.
RO Cpl. Klar, Wesley W.

Position 9, C47A, 41-, CAJUN RAT
P 2nd Lt. Carter, Wilson C.
CP S/Sgt P Bronson, Hurbert S.
N
CC M/Sgt Mackey, Donald A.
RO Sgt Millis, Curtis T.

Position 10, C47A, 41-, 54, DUMBO
P 1st Lt. Peterson, William A.
CP S/Sgt P Meeks, John R.
N
CC T/Sgt Stofocik, John M., Jr.
RO S/Sgt. Neal, Jasper F.

Position 11, C47A, 41-, 58, MISS OHIO
P 2nd Lt. Gaylor, Don G.
CP S/Sgt P McWilliams, Joseph W.
N
CC Sgt Proffitt, Authur
RO Cpl. Bunke, Harvey C..

Position 12, C47A, 41-, 57, NORMA-YARDBIRD
P 2nd Lt. Lattier, Earl B.
CP S/Sgt P Vaughter, David C.
N
CC T/Sgt Paul, Joseph E.
RO Sgt. Believe, Authur

Position 13, C47A, 41-, 56, DEAR MOM
P 2nd Lt. Simpson, Jerome L.
CP S/Sgt P Thompson, Thomas G.
N
CC S/Sgt Korhals, Albert H.
RO T/Sgt Shandor, Frank D.

Key

P	=	Pilot
CP	=	Co-Pilot
N	=	Navigator
CC	=	Crew Chief
RO	=	Radio Operator

NOTE: I was unable to fill in all the blanks. You would think that each crew member would remember the number of the aircraft, field number, and the other crew members on their flight.

2

A Tour Of the South Sea Islands

I HANDED THE NAVIGATOR ALL THE WEATHER INFORMATION and asked him to give the radio operator the radio frequencies that he was to guard. I also instructed the crew to return all documents to me before landing. We climbed to 12,300 feet, then gradually eased down and leveled off at 12,000 feet. The reason was to pick up a faster cruise airspeed. At flight level it was CAVU (Ceiling and Visibility Unlimited). I turned the controls over to the C0-Pilot and got out of the pilot's seat so the navigator could take a sun line. At that time C-47s were not equipped with a celestial dome. It was more commonly known as the navigator's bubble or dome. The navigator had a make-shift position in the tail of the aircraft. It was an attached folding table, steel folding chair, no light, a drift meter, and no intercom. Of course, neither the navigator nor the crew chief had seat belts. The crew chief did not even have a seat. On take-off he would be on his knees behind the control pedestal. For the remainder of all flights he would have to stand or walk around. In rough weather he would stand holding on to anything available. The navigator's chair was not bolted down and he could move it anywhere he wished. On take-off, landing, and in rough weather he would fold the chair up and tie it to a floor "D" ring. Then he came forward and hung onto the crew's luggage rack behind the standing crew chief.

Every 30 minutes of flying for the rest of the flight while the navigator was with us he would take a sun line. Then in a few minutes he would give me a new position report, ETA, ground speed, time since departure and last position fix, gas consumption, hours of fuel remaining, and time to the point of no return. He would then take another sun line, check the four wing tanks fuel quantity gages, dip stick the eight cabin tanks, and compute another position report. This was one busy navigator. Several times during the flight he made a remark to the effect that he had never made a flight like this. On a clear night the navigator could get lines of position on two or more stars. At the intersections of these fixes would be our exact geographical location at that time. But during day time with only the sun as a guide he was able to make only one line of the fix. By dead reckoning the navigator could only assume a position on that line.

At cruising level we were above all scattered clouds in the clear sunshine. In the pilot's seat with the sun beating down on me, it was hot. George and I took turns hand flying. It was interesting to watch the cloud formations below change as we flew from one weather system to another. Sometimes we could see white caps on the ocean below. Looking out the pilot's side window on occasion you could see a drop of engine oil on the cowling. It would spread out to make it appear like there was one big oil leak.

After we had been airborne for about four hours one of our pilots came on the air in a frantic call to our Commander stating that he was running out of fuel. We had strict orders that under no circumstances were we to use the radio. After several calls, with each sounding more excited, finally Captain Lackey came on the air and said, "Silence, if you cannot make it return to where you departed from. No more calls". Our crew chief told us that the reason they were running low on fuel was the way they had filled the cabin tanks. It was the way the tanks were installed in the aircraft cabin do to the tail-wheel being lower than the main gear. When the aircraft was on the ground all the tanks were on a slant. If you filled only the front cabin tanks on each side of the aisle there was trapped air in the back tanks, and the tanks would not fill all the way with gas due to the trapped air. Since our Squadron was the first to fly C-47s from the States to the Pacific there was no procedure on how to fill the cabin tanks or what power settings for such a long flight. Our crew chief had taken all eight cabin gas tank caps off, then filled the back tank on both sides of the aisle, put on their cap etc., moving forward until all eight tanks had been filled. He then filled the four wing tanks in the same way with a total of 1,620 gallons of 91 octane fuel. Taking into account our fuel consumption for take-off, climb and cruise, I calculated we should have more than 20 hours of flight time.

After the navigator had made his 1230 hour sun line fix and calculated the course, he informed us that if we were on course the ETA to rendezvous should be at 1450. That would be one hour and thirty minutes before landing time at Hickham.

Irene flew like the lady she was! The two Pratt and Whitney R-1830-92s with Hamilton Standard, three blade metal props never missed a beat. In perfect synchronization the fuel consumption was only 69 gallons an hour and that included take-off and climb. The steady drone of the Pratt and Whitney was the sweetest music you could hear. At that rate we would beat Captain Lackey's prediction of twenty hours by at least another three plus hours.

After departing San Francisco Bay we had not seen a single aircraft. Since we should be in a loose trail formation and our gas consumption was well below schedule, I asked the crew chief if he would have the navigator come to the cockpit. There was no intercom at the navigator's table. I told the three of them that we were using less gas than was expected and that we should be in loose formation before landing. I asked the co-pilot, navigator and crew chief what they thought of increasing the power to 30" Hg so we could catch up. All agreed. At 1328 we saw the first speck on the horizon and 30 minutes later we had caught up. In a few minutes the co-pilot of the lead ship left his seat and their radio operator took the co-pilot's seat and began to flash his light (Aldis Lamp). I held up the palm of my left hand to indicate wait. Our radioman came forward, took my seat and then there was a fast exchange of dots and dashes. Gregg said that they wanted to know our position. Grassi got Lieutenant Sambor and our position was relayed. In return, we got theirs. Both positions agreed as of 1400. I thought this was mighty good after ten hours of over-water day time flying, and both navigators had us at the same spot.

When I got back in my seat I took out the SECRET envelope and studied the orders, the approach and let down instructions. Then I passed them around again for all to study. I assigned different quadrants of the sky for the four of us to watch for the intercept. George was to look from the center nose of the aircraft to the right wing-tip from flight level to the ocean. I would cover the same on the left side. Grassi was on his knees behind the pedestal between the two pilots. He was to cover from flight level and up and from wing-tip to wing-tip. The navigator standing behind the crew chief had a band 10-15 degrees above and below flight level. I reasoned the intercept would be coming in high out of the sun. We took up our watch 15 minutes before intercept time. Within seconds of the navigator's ETA, George picked up two Martin B-26 Marauder's skimming above the white caps. The moment I saw them they split. One made a steep climbing turn to the right. The other one was doing the same going to the left. At this time I could only see the first element of our squadron formation. Of course our view to the rear was almost completely blanked out. One of the 26s came in high above us and on the left wing of the Commander. The other one was above and behind Weedin and me. On both B-26s, the side turret's twin 50s' were simulating raking us with machine gun fire from nose to tail. It was a good time to be friends. The dots and dashes began to fly between the lead Martin and our leader.

Just as we were making our extended base leg one hour out, a flight of four P-40s came roaring in from high and out of the sun. They came so close that we got their prop wash and bounced around some. By this time the second and third elements were in position. We could not see tail-end Charlie. So either that was the plane that had returned because he was running low on gas or he filled in the slot for the aircraft that had returned to Hamilton Field.

The SECRET orders for us were when one hour out to descend to 1,000 feet and pick up a heading of 270° until Honolulu radio was off the left wing tip. Then we were to slow to 120 mph indicated and lower the landing gear. When the compass needle read 225° we were to pick up a heading of 180° and maintain 1,000 feet. Again when the radio compass needle indicated 270° we were to make a left 90° and track inbound still holding at 1,000 feet. While on the extended final we received a radio message, "Altimeter setting is 30.04. When the runway is in sight and a green light has been received from the tower reduce power, drop flaps and make a normal straight-in approach. After landing follow the Alert Vehicle." The fighter escort stayed with us until the last aircraft had landed.

Irene touched down at 1621 hours Hawaiian time 2 October 1942. I was the second C-47 pilot in the history of aviation who ever flew from the States to Hawaii. We landed within 30 seconds after our Commander. It took us 14:20 hours at an average ground speed of 167 mph, or should I say "Water Speed" or is it "Knots." I was greatly disappointed that no young Hawaiian girls in grass skirts met us as we deplaned from our aircraft, placed an orchid lei around our necks, gave us a welcoming kiss and greeted us with a big "A-lo-o-ha!!" In the movies they always meet the Matson Cruse Line as the band softly played the strains of the Islands' music.

A "Follow-Me" weapon carrier parked us. I collected all the classified documents and put them back in the envelope and zipped them into my top left flight suit pocket. I filled out the Form 1 with no write-ups. When we got out of the plane the Alert Driver asked where is the pilot. I, with staff-sergeant stripes on my flight suit, said that I was. He asked again, "Who is your pilot?" I told him that I was. He got back in the weapon carrier and left. We unloaded our B-4 bags taking our guns with us. Grassi locked the plane. At this time in aviation, all cargo aircraft could be locked. In the meantime the Alert Man returned to Operations and reported that two Sergeants had stolen aircraft in the States and were trying to fly off to war. By this time Captain Lackey was at the counter. He told them if they would go check they would find that two other Sergeants had just flown in a Douglas from Hamilton Field also. The same Alert Man came back to pick us up. He said that Operations told him to pick up the five of you and bring you to 0perations. Then looking me straight in the face, he said, "Are you a pilot?" All the crew said "Yes." This time he asked, "How old are you?" I told him that I was twenty years old. He said, "In how many more years?" Lieutenant Sambor spoke up and told us to put all our gear in and for the driver to take us to Operations. When we arrived at Operations the driver told us to unload our gear on the ramp.

When our crew arrived at the NCOIC Operations we were told to take our classified material and guns and go to the third room on the left at the end of the hall. That was our briefing room. All other crews were already there. I turned in my classified material to Captain Lackey and he returned my signed receipt, which I promptly destroyed. Captain Lackey asked how our planes were and were there any write-ups. No one spoke up. "There will be a briefing at 0800 hours in this room tomorrow morning. Eat before you arrive and be in flight suits and leave your B-4 bags at your quarters. Buses are out in front. Officers take the first two and the enlisted men take the last two. The drivers will pick you up at 0745 in the morning where they let you off. We have open post till 2400 hours. This is the military curfew for the Island of Hawaii so be in quarters prior to then. The night light restrictions are 'Brown Out.' That basically means no bright lights and a special dim light for vehicles. Again, think of everyone as a spy, especially those in uniform, and that all the girls have VD. From this room walk down the hall and turn to the right past the dispatch office to the end room on the left and check in your guns. Be positive that you check and re-check the gun number before you leave the counter. Do not pick up your gun until told to do so. Do not lose your receipt. Then go to the buses and have a good safe time. Remember you must carry your gas mask and helmet with you at all times. See you in the morning." Checking in my gun was faster than I'd expected. The bus driver drove us down the flight line. It had been almost ten months to the week since the Pearl Harbor attack and you could still see plenty of damage. The two end hangers were all fenced off and abandoned. Weeds were growing between every crack in the cement and all around the edges of the hangers. The walls that were still standing looked as if they had been used for target practice. All windows and doors had been either shot or blown out with the roof's twisted steel girders sagging to the hanger floor from the bomb damage.

The climate and natural surroundings were even more beautiful than in the movies. It was warm with a nice ocean breeze. This is truly an Island Paradise. I'd better start looking for Dorothy Lamour and Betty Grable for they must be behind one of these palm trees in their skimpy sarongs.

After showering and putting on a fresh class A uniform I was ready for Honolulu. In our haste to get going we had failed to get off-base passes. All Enlisted Pilots walked across the parade ground to Operations and orally identified ourselves and asked for off base passes. The Airdrome Officer had just come on duty. His first question was, "Why are you Sergeants wearing pilot wings?" We told him that we were pilots and that today we had flown in the twelve C-47s that are parked out on the ramp. He asked who was our Flight Officer. We told him. He then tried to locate Captain Lackey by phone with no luck. One of our group suggested that he get out Operation's copy of the formation clearance that Captain Lackey turned in upon landing. After looking over the clearance he was convinced that there were Sergeant Pilots, but he asked, "Was that us and why don't you have passes?" Would he get us passes if we could prove who we were? He said, "Yes". The plan was for all of us to go out in front and come in one at a time on his call. The Captain with clearance in hand would call in one of us at a time and ask our name, serial number, aircraft serial number, field number, name of other crew members, flight positions, etc. After he interrogated two Sergeants he said that is enough. He called the base Provost Marshal Office and told them to issue each of us an all-night off-base pass. We thanked him and got our passes. All this had lost us nearly two hours.

We caught a bus to the main gate. While waiting for the city bus one of the MPs at the gate raised a fuss about our wings. We told him to call Operations. The bus came and we went to downtown Honolulu. We walked around for a while, saw some Army personnel, but the whole Navy must have been in port. Everywhere you looked some girl was trying to get your attention. None of our group took the bait. Walking around we came across a photographer who would take your picture with a Hawaiian girl in a grass skirt in front of a grass shack for 25 cents. We waited in a long line and had our pictures taken. By then it was time to head back to the base.

Next morning the Base Briefing Officer filled us in on some history of the Pearl Harbor bombing. Admiral Isoroku Yamamoto was the Tack Force Commander of the six aircraft carriers and supporting fleet. The fleet sailed undetected to a point 235 miles north of Oahu, Hawaii where their aircraft were launched on Japanese code name "OPERATION Z." After becoming airborne Air Commander Mitsuo Fuchida, the Flight Leader led the air attack. He tuned into the Honolulu radio station KBMB and tracked the needle all the way to the target. He lead the "Eagles of the Sea" in the first wave of 183 bombers and torpedo dive bombers striking at 0753 hours Sunday, 7 December 1941. The second wave attacked at 0855 hour with 167 aircraft. A total of 2,403 Americans were killed, 1,178 wounded and 64 Japanese crew members died. We lost 169 aircraft, 3 battle ships destroyed and 18 ships damaged. Earlier at 0640 hours the minesweeper USN Ward sank a Japanese midget 2-man submarine while patrolling the entrance to Pearl Harbor. These were the first shots of World War II by the Americans. The submarine Captain, Ensign Kazuo Sakamaki was captured alive uninjured by US Marine

2nd Lieutenant Stephen Weiner and thus became the first POW in our war with Japan.

We were told that for sometime before the war all the P-40s at Wheeler Field were lined up wing-tip to wing-tip on a closed runway parallel to and across from the ramp and insight of Operations so as to be safe from sabotage. On Sunday morning just before the Pearl Harbor attack one of the regular Japanese civilian on a base milk truck was driving the perimeter road adjacent to the ramp. The truck speeded up, drove across the grass area, over a taxiway, then over another grassy way and onto the closed runway where the Curtis Fighters were parked. He then drove the milk truck down the row of parked Fighters either damaging or destroying the rudders and/or elevators of most of the parked aircraft. In 1926, Billy Mitchell warned that "Japanese planes would seize Alaska, Hawaii and the Philippines." For this and other out spoken statements about the advantages of the aircraft he was Court-martialed.

Captain Lackey told us that the aircraft that had returned to Hamilton was running low on gas. Before we departed Hickham, the "thirteenth aircraft" caught up with us. Grassi was correct as to what went wrong. Captain Lackey then told us following the briefing to go to our planes, do a very thorough pre-flight, fill the wing tanks and the front two cabin tanks. We were to be in this room tomorrow morning at 0530 hours ready to leave. Don't forget in the morning to pick up your gun before you get here. "When you are through at the plane you're off until curfew at 2400 hours to-night. Do you have any questions? "Yes, may the enlisted pilots get off base passes?" "Pick them up at dispatch after returning from your aircraft. Tomorrow we will be flying out so get a good night's sleep. Remember security, curfew, and VD."

As we were leaving the briefing Second Lieutenant Harold B. Majure, one of the first pilots, stopped to talk with me. He said that he has a brother who was a Lieutenant Junior Grade in the Navy. He was in the submarine fleet and his "boat" was tied up at Ford Island here at Pearl Harbor. Tonight his brother was on inner harbor patrol which meant that at certain times he and a group of sailors would depart from Ford Island in a small motor launch. They will tour and inspect the inner harbor all around the inner mouth of Pearl Harbor to make sure the inner submarine net is still in place. There are two sub nets, an inter and an outer net. When the nets are up this prevents enemy submarines from entering or leaving the harbor. This was interesting. But, why was he telling me? Then he asked if I would like to go on night patrol with them tonight at 1900 hours. I replied, "Yes sir, this sounds great, when, where, and what uniform?" I also told him that Enlisted Pilots still did not have any identification cards. He said that was OK because I would be with him. This was a great surprise to me, but I was glad to be asked. We then departed and I went to my airplane.

We checked Irene from stem to stern and she looked like new. The crew chief and radio operator did the run-up while the co-pilot and I rearranged the gear in the cabin. The navigator cleaned his area in about two seconds. Then he looked over and checked the two life rafts and gear and the Very Gun that would shoot a bright orange flare. The fuel truck arrived. George and I filled the wing tanks, and the crew chief put 300 gallons in the cabin tanks. I had Grassi add an extra 100 gallons, just in case. The oil truck was next. That only left checking the drinking water. Here came a converted civilian milk truck that filled us up with drinking water. We required no oxygen, hydraulic or alcohol. At 1100 hours the five of us were back in Operations and George and I picked up our passes.

Our Enlisted Crew decided to go to the city on our own. I told them that I had to be back in Operations by 1800. George said, "Oh, that's what you and Lt. Majure were talking about". I said, "yes" and said no more about it. We went, cleaned up, changed to class A uniforms and met at the main gate at 1200 hours. On the way to Honolulu the driver pointed out Aloha Tower and let us off one block from Waikiki Beach near Fort Derussy. We stopped at a hamburger stand for lunch. Again it was mostly sailors and they were all on good behavior. We walked in the sand the full length of the beach all the way to the Royal Hawaiian Hotel. The grounds were manicured. I'd expected a much longer beach. Diamond Head stood out so clear just a short distance to the east. As we arrived at the hotel there was an afternoon shower and everything outside was washed so clean by the rain. I do not think the hotel management appreciated non-resident GIs in their hotel. When the rain stopped we were glad to leave.

Palm trees were everywhere along with exotic flowers and plants that I had never heard of or seen. By now the sky was a beautiful blue with a light on-shore breeze. We walked west to where we had started. I saw some white dirty looking coral in the sand. It was the first coral that I had ever seen. In the sand I picked up a green glass coke bottle. Engraved in the bottom of the bottle was Honolulu T.H. I still have the bottle. We went back to the same hamburger stand and had a coke. A bus drove up with a Hickham sign so I left the crew and returned to the base arriving at 1600. I walked to the mess hall and had a good meal and all the fruit I could eat.

After supper I walked to Operations and waited out front for Lt. Majure. At about 1730 a weapon carrier drove up with the Lieutenant in the back seat. I saluted and got in the right front seat and away we went. The driver drove us to the west side of the base behind the hanger line to the Air Rescue boat dock. There we got out and took a few steps to the waiting "Crash Boat" which took us to the submarine dock on Ford Island. The Navy challenged us before we could disembark. The Lieutenant identified himself and explained our business. They let us come on the dock. The guard pointed out and told us that among all the wreckage at Pearl Harbor the battleships USS Arizona was over there. He pointed to the USS Utah on the other side of the Island. Shortly a head appeared out of the docked sub's conning tower. The big smiles on the two Lieutenants' faces told me who he was. When I was introduced he returned my salute and we shook hands. He then looked very closely at my wings and then his brother's wings. We then walked a few steps to the end of the pier where there was a shore patrol guard watch station. It was a very small one room. It was glassed in on all four sides with a phone, several light switches, a blow horn and another guard. The Navy Lieutenant introduced his brother and then me and said that we were going with him on the 1900 hour inner sub net inspection and when we returned we would be going aboard his submarine. He also told the guard that at 2130 hours the Army Air Rescue boat would come back to pick up the two solders.

Shortly, a US Navy launch pulled along the dock with three sailors aboard. There was a coxswain (the pilot), a signal man, and the rear machine gunner. We saluted the flag in the rear and climbed aboard. The gunner handed each of us a life vest and we were on our way at 1900 hours sharp. The Navy Officer, now the boat's skipper (pardon, I mean Captain) stood behind and to the starboard of the pilot and was giving him orders. We two Army airmen took a seat in the back. The Lieutenant was on the starboard and I was on the port side of the vessel. The launch went up the west side of the channel. As we approached where the submarine net was stretched across the inner opening to the harbor we were challenged by a series of on shore flashing lights. The boat immediately reduced speed to a slow walk. The exchange of blinks (flashing lights) was far too fast for me to read. Our signal man flashed back. The shore lights blinked again and we picked up speed and continued on to where they said the net was submerged. In the dark I could not see what the Captain was doing leaning over the starboard side of the boat as we slowly moved from the west to the east side of the inter mouth of the harbor. We picked up speed and then went down the east side of the water way and back to the dock. We were told that to either open or close the net two tug boats were required to draw aside the submarine net that guarded the opening to the harbor entrance. The Navy Officer checked in with the guard on duty at the guard house. This was a forty-five minute boat ride. Then we went to his vessel which was a real submarine!!

As we stepped aboard the sub we saluted the flag at the aft of the boat or pig boat. That is what they call a submarine. This was the first time I had ever seen a submarine let alone boarded one. We then followed the Navy Officer down the ladder through the conning tower's hatch to the control room. I had no idea they were so small and had so many instruments, valves and handles. The Captain's quarters were very small but the crew's bunks were unbelievably cramped. They even had to take turns sleeping in the same bunks. All I could say is, "No, thanks, but thank God we do have them." No wonder the submariners are called the Elite Corps of the Navy. We talked to several of the men and they said that they would not trade positions with us, not flying up there in the air so everyone could see you and being shot at. I guess it's all what you get started in. It was now time to go. We said our good byes and departed. In looking back this was the last time that the Army Lieutenant would ever see any member of his family. He and his crew were shot down and all killed just one month and a few days later.

On the way back to Operations I expressed my thanks for a most interesting experience. Then I asked why I was so fortunate to be asked. He told me that he remembered several remarks I had made in Milwaukee after the 4th of July overnight ferry-boat ride on Lake Michigan for all the pilots going through United Airline Captains School. Again at Hamilton, I'd said that during the World's Fair I rode the ferry between San Francisco and Treasure

Island several times and how I liked it. Another time I said something about being a drylander or landlubber. Again I thanked him. I did not know if I should tell anyone or not as Officers and enlisted men do not socialize. So I decided that if anyone should ask, I would tell them that we went to the Army rescue boat dock. From there I could see the submarines which we had just visited.

On my thirty-seventh trip through Honolulu in 1969 something very amusing happened at the airport. My family had been on a Christmas Holiday and was in the airport waiting to return to San Francisco aboard a DC-9 when a roving TV reporter started to interview our daughter Kathy. He wanted to know how she liked her vacation and how long we had been there and was this Kathy's first visit to the Islands. Looking straight into the camera and with her big eyes and smile she replied, "For a week I had a great time and a lot of fun and no this is not my first time to Honolulu... The other time I was here my view was slightly restricted because my Mother was seven months pregnant with me." The terminal roared with laughter. While Kathy was talking to the reporter our family was standing beside her. When she said, "I have been here before." We could not imagine what she was going to say for this was the only time she had been to Honolulu. What she did say was technically true. In April 1952, my wife Etta was seven months pregnant with Kathy. Pregnant Etta and the boys, Steve and Terry, were on a thirty-five hour flight from Tokyo to Travis Air Force Base, California.

Next morning at 0530 I had my B-4 bag in the plane and was standing in line to pick up my gun. From there I went to the briefing room. The briefing was pretty much the normal format. There were only two items of importance. We would have four P-40 Fighter Pilots as passengers and we were going to Christmas Island. Where was Christmas Island? No one had ever heard of it. It turned out to be 1160 nautical miles, 175° south of Hickham. Our passengers would meet us at our aircraft. The four passengers were First Lieutenants C.E. KLEEN, Fred A.HARRIS, J.A.GRIMAN and W.F. HARRING. (After WWII I found out that Captain Frederick A. Harris became an Ace by shooting down eight confirmed "kills." I could find no information on the other three pilots.) Our orders were: "Today, keep in sight until the last hour of flight and then close formation. Same safety precautions as before and no, repeat, no radio transmissions. Pilots brief your passengers, emphasize no smoking and how to egress the plane for both bailing out and ditching. They have their own Mae West's and parachutes. Same taxi and take-off instructions as at Hamilton, but this time the aircraft are roughly 4,000 pounds lighter and its' day time with no obstructions. Your bird will still not fly on one engine for at least two hours after take-off. Have a good safe flight and no more running out of gas! We cannot have any more screw-ups. On the way out your navigator will pick up his canned flight plan" which I still have. This was the only leg of the flight that we received a pre-planned flight plan for this entire mission.

When the crew arrived at our aircraft the four Fighter Pilots, all First Lieutenants, were waiting by the cargo door with their flight gear and B-4 bags. I introduced the crew, told them that while the pilots did our walk-a-round the crew chief would get them set, and that they should put on their Mae West's and parachutes. After the outside inspection I came aboard and briefed them. I told them it should take 8:34 hours. After we level off they were welcome to come forward, not more than two at a time, as often, and stay as long, as they wished. "Sorry that we do not have better facilities, but as Eleanor says: "This is war." Remember bail out only as a last resort. The entire flight will be over water and we cannot use the radio. Once you go out the door you'll all be on your own with just you and your dinghy. Those are not very good odds. If we have to ditch the odds are only a slightly bit better. Keep the walkway to the cockpit clear at all times because the navigator has to use it at least four times an hour. No smoking on or near the aircraft at any time. This is a bomb just waiting to be ignited. Don't light it! We have 1,104 gallons of gas aboard. "How far are you going after Christmas?" They did not know where they were going. They only knew that they were to go with us until told otherwise. It did not take long to see that there are no security leaks on this plane, since no one including the crew knows where we were going!

We fired up, taxied out in formation and did our run-up. All thirteen of us were ready to go when we got the green light. What a difference on take-off with a lighter load and a longer runway and in daylight! Wheels were up at 0702 hours 4 October 1942. We could climb with normal climb power at 300 feet a minute at 120 mph with no trouble. How much safer! When abreast with Diamond Head we made a right turn and picked up a heading of 178°.

From 2 to 8,000 feet we climbed through broken to scattered clouds and then came out on top. The navigator tapped me on the shoulder and said that if I'd keep an eye out on my left between 0810 and 0815 I would be able to see two snow covered mountain peaks both over 13,000 feet and 26 miles apart on the Island of Hawaii. Shortly off to the left they were glistening in the morning sun. I told him to point them out to the crew and passengers. He said that when I leveled off at 10,000 feet he would like to take a sun line. After leveling off George took over and the navigator got in my seat.

I went to the back to talk to the passengers. This was the first time any of them had ever been in any type of aircraft other than single engine planes, both in flying school and pursuit. They were now flying P-39s and P-40s. They couldn't get over our slow rate of climb. They were very hesitant in taking off their parachutes. I told them that all the crew had their Mae West's on, but the crews' chutes were hanging there by the door and that we had not moved them since McClellan. Then I told them that I was in 42-E at Luke in P-40s. This came as a real surprise and they wanted to know how come I was assigned to transport. When I graduated, three classes of Enlisted Pilots were assigned to a new expanding branch of the Air Corps. Most of us put up a real squawk, but of course it did no good. I now had been flying transport a little over four months and it wasn't so bad. "Come up front as often as you wish, one or two at a time. You will have to stay clear of the walk way so the navigator can go back and forth between his position and the cockpit. The crew chief's position is between the pilot and co-pilot, but there is still head room."

As in the first leg the navigator was one busy man. Later in the morning as I was going to the latrine (a relief tube in the rear of the aircraft). I over heard the navigator telling the passengers that, "This is my first flight like this but it is working out OK."

After lunch I was back having the navigator check me out on the drift meter when the bail out bell rang. On the first sound of the bell the four pursuit pilots were on their feet reaching for their parachutes. I shouted, "Get ready, do not jump, do not open that door, I'll let you know". Few pilots ever got from the back of the aircraft to the cockpit door so fast. When I opened the door, George was looking back down the aisle with a big grin from ear to ear. If I'd had my 45 on I might have shot him at that moment. Beaver said,

"I just wanted to see what you'd do and how long it would take you to get up front." I turned, went back and told them it was a false alarm as the co-pilot was just playing around. "Don't let me throw him out, but I'm plenty unhappy over his stupidity." In the seconds it took me to get from the back to the cabin door, look in and turn around, the four pilots had their chutes on over their Mae West's and were helping the navigator with his. Only twice in my twenty-three years of flying as a Pilot in the military did I ever really get mad with a crew member. This was the first time. I walked forward to my seat. I said "Your stupid shenanigan nearly bailed out four pilots and a navigator. They were ready to go before the bell stopped ringing and that would have been nothing but murder. In the olden days a ship's Captain could have made you walk the plank. If ever, while flying with me, you do any horsing around when on or near an airplane, on the ground or in the air, I'll bring General Court Martial charges against you. Subject closed, do not bring it up again and do not answer." For the rest of the day's flight the atmosphere up front was very cool.

The navigator made his usual fixes and gave us the report. I told him to give it to the passengers also. All of the pursuit pilots had been up two or more times to look and talk. They remarked at the number of instruments we had. I explained everything was in groups and once it was explained and you studied it for a while it was not as difficult as it appears. The hardest thing for me was to learn how to taxi this bird. "You know in P-40s to taxi its throttle and rudder making "S" turns. But in this airplane, to taxi it requires mostly manipulation of the throttles.

After a while Grassi came from the back and told me to make a smooth landing for they are betting for and against you in the back. At 1430 hours we received a few blinks from the lead ship. I sent for Gregg and his biscuit gun. They wanted us to pull into tight formation. I guess the purpose was so we could show the pursuit pilots that we too could ALSO fly good formation. It wasn't long before two of the pilots were standing right behind Grassi and were very nervous. We flew that way until we came over the runway and pulled up on the downwind. We kept the downwind and base legs in close but not as tight as the P-40s. Luck was with me. I made a good smooth landing at 1527, 4 October, on the right side of the runway, 25 seconds after the leader touched down. This leg was 8:34 hours with a ground speed of 135 mph.

They parked us on a coral parking area in front of Operation's grass shack. I filled out the Form 1, picked up my B-4 bag and got out. The other eight were waiting for me outside in the shade under the wing. The alert crew driver had told them that we had to pack our own bags to Operations and that a GI truck would take us to our huts. As we were walking in, one of the Lieutenants said, "A very good flight, excellent formation and landing. Why are you only a Sergeant?" Then I explained what the difference was and that I had the best deal since I loved flying so much.

Captain Lackey closed our flight plan and told us to be here by 0500 in the morning. He told the crew chiefs to go back to their airplane and fill up the same as when we left Hickham. Each crew member and passenger was to pick up his own sack lunch and all the fresh fruit we wanted the next morning as we leave the mess hall. He then told us that there were no off-base towns or places to go, only a small base with plenty of palm trees, coral and sandy beaches. "After dark either stay in your hut or in a lighted area. Do not go wandering off in the dark because a patrol might mistake you for a Japanese landing party. They might shoot and ask questions later." While waiting, I noticed a B-17 parked down the ramp with No. 2 engine missing.

Three beat-up old 6x6s trucks came for us. We were all let off at the same hut about a half mile from our planes. The driver told us that the officers were to pick out a hut on the right side of the road and for the GIs to wait in line in front of this hut and he'd be back to check out our bedding. He pointed to a larger grass shack and told us that it was the mess hall. Officers this end, GIs the other end. Transportation will leave here at 0445 in the morning. Chow is served from 0345 on. Two 6x6s returned to pick up the rest of the crews. Each GI was issued four items: a towel, bar of soap, one pillow and a mattress cover. Eight GIs went to a grass hut equipped with eight GI cots and mosquito nets. A latrine was a dozen palm trees down the road away from the mess hall. The shower consisted of several 55-gallon gasoline barrels on an eight-foot-high platform. All barrels were connected into one common manifold which had several faucets with an attached shower head on each. The barrels were filled each morning with sea water and heated by the sun. Several signs read, "Hot water, be careful." We did not need the soap for it would not lather in sea water.

After chow most of us went for a walk on the white sandy beach. While there, we met the Base Historian, a GI who filled us in on the Island's history. Captain James Cook, an English sea captain, discovered Christmas Island on Christmas Eve, 1777. This was a good sized island and totally flat. The highest land point was 12 feet above sea level. It is the largest coral atoll (140 square miles) in the world. It lies 119 miles north of the equator and has 94 miles of coast line. The average rain fall is 30 inches a year. The temperature is about the same every day in the mid 80s with a breezy 72° at night. There were plenty of coconuts and fish, but there were no natives on the Island. They had been evacuated for the duration.

The next morning at 0410, just as I was setting down my mess kit, a Tech Sergeant across the table stuck out his hand and said, "Ernie Ford. What a surprise!" It was Gaylord King from my own little hometown of Manzanola, Colorado. Four years before my parents had bought his parent's home. Gaylord was the crew chief of the B-17 that was waiting for an engine. After a few minutes of hometown talk I had to leave. We never met again during the war.

At 0500 we had our morning briefing and found out that we were going to Canton (Kanton) Island and that our passengers were going with us. Someone asked about our final destination. The answer: "When we get there you will know. Do not ask again." The crew chief and radioman had already pre-flighted by the time the rest of us arrived. After the pilot's walk around, I asked the five Lieutenants if any of them had any questions. Hearing none, I told them that I do not believe that we will have any more false alarms. A compass heading of 253°, 855 nm, 6:10 our flying time at a ground speed was 139 knots with an ETA of 12:10 local time. By leaving early the weather was forecasted to be better. If we left at 0800 we would be in thunder storms. "Remember, after we are airborne you may come up front any time and as often as you wish. Just make room for the navigator and crew chief." We had wheels up at 0600. We climbed out on course to 10,300 feet, eased down to 10,000 feet and leveled off at 0635. The navigator was waiting to take a sun line. When he came forward for his fourth fix he said that at 0857 local time 5 October 1942, we should cross the Equator. That would be 1857 Zulu time 5 October 1942. It is traditional when crossing the Equator to celebrate with Davy Jones by having a drink. I told the navigator to spread the word. As Captain of the ship that was all the celebrating I could provide as the "Bar" was left back in the ZI.

Touch down was at 1210 local time 5 October. The field was only for a refueling stop and was just a way to skirt around to the south and east of the area where the Japs had air superiority. The control tower was manned by a Sergeant seated on the tail gate of a 6x6 with a biscuit (light) gun. When a plane was due, a flag to serve as a wind sock was raised from the back side of the truck cab. The refueling was from 55-gallon barrels on the back of a GI Army truck and were all pumped by hand. Canton Island is nothing but a coral atoll with a lagoon in the middle. Up until last night the base had one palm tree but a Japanese submarine had surfaced close in off shore just after dark and shot the top out of the tree. It now looked like a short telephone pole stuck in the coral. The only island defense was one P-40. After the shelling started the pursuit got airborne but the sub got away. Upon landing we were told that we could expect shelling tonight and to park our aircraft some distance apart. In that way if one airplane got hit and exploded the other planes would not all go up at once. By spreading out, it would take at least one direct hit for each aircraft. There was no other protection for the air-craft and no place for the troops to hide.

We had the routine debriefing and were told to fuel up now and be here ready to go at 0800. We were urged not to forget to pick up two lunch sacks and fruit, but no more than you will eat. "Remember every single bite of food except fish comes from some place else and that includes drinking water. So be sparing with everything. The pastime for all field personnel is to fish for the evening and morning meals. If you hear three quick gun shots in short order hit the deck because the enemy is here. In the event of a shelling, spread out and lie as close to the coral as you can. Do not get up and start running. If there should be an invasion, let the base personnel take care of it unless they ask for help. Then be positive it is an American that is asking for help. Don't forget some of the Japs can speak perfect English with no accent. Keep your guns holstered and your powder dry. Sleep well!" A truck came and we put our B-4 bags on and we all walked to find a vacant tent. There was very little room on this island except for the runway. Unless the P-40 took off there were no scheduled take-offs or landings until we depart tomorrow morning.

While walking to our tents, our four passengers asked what I thought about the four of them volunteering to fly night patrol in the Kitty Hawk. I told them it sounded great to me. "Let's catch up with Captain Lackey and ask him." When they told him he also thought it was a good idea especially since we had a quarter moon and it might afford some protection for our planes. After Captain Lackey and the four pursuit pilots had found a cot, the five of them walked back to Operations and made the suggestion. The Base Commander and Operations Officer, a First Lieutenant, all one and the same, thought it a good idea. Then he explained why we could not do it. All parts and fuel come from Hickham and the P-40 was over due for an inspection. At this time they could only fly in case of an actual attack. Their only pilot was in the lagoon fishing. "When he returns, I'll tell him that we have four P-40 pilots staying over night with us. I'm sure that he'll be looking you up. I thank you and hope we don't require your services."

It was hot in the tents, hotter outside and no shade on the island, not one single tree, not even a leaf. All tents had the ends of their flaps and sides stretched out tight parallel to the ground on steel poles with three guy wires to support each pole in the wind. As you walked by an empty tent you could look straight through. The only thing inside the tents were empty cots with mosquito nets. While the sun was up most, of us stayed in the shade of a tent so we would not get roasted alive. The only people on the island were 32 American Army troops. They were as sun burned or black as I'd ever seen a white person. After sunset we walked on the beach. All of us were armed and ready for war, but no one showed to do battle. In retrospect, how fortunate there was no battle, because most of our troops would have shot one another. There were some of us GIs that had infantry training. The enemy did not visit us during our stay on Canton Island on the night of 5 October 1942.

By 0700 the next morning everything was on board, pre-flights and engine run-ups completed with all thirteen crews and aircraft ready to go. We were just waiting for the briefing. Most of the field personnel were standing around listening. Several times some of them had said that they would trade us places or go in our place. One corporal even asked Grassi if he could hide aboard and go with us. The Base Commander in private told our Commander that war had to be better than this. We found out that the next stop would be Nadi (Nandi) Airport on the main Island of Fiji. There was the same procedure as before: set the altimeters at 29.92" Hg, heading 212°, 1178 nm, flight level 10,000 feet with 7:40 hours flying time.

We made a normal take-off at 0800 local time on the 6 October, and climbed out on course. The navigator told us, pointing out at about 5 O'clock, that out there about 350 miles is Howland Island. That is where Aviatrix Amelia Earhart and her Navigator Fred J. Noonan, were headed for on 2 July 1937, when they disappeared and were never found. They had departed from Lae, New Guinea. Most of the islands in a 1,000 mile radius of Howland Island were searched with no luck. Since then several books and hundreds of articles have been written and a few movies have been made about what happened and where they may have gone down. Here it was a little over five years later and not a trace, so "Davy Jones Locker" must have them.

This turned out to be a most unusual and memorable flight. We took-off at 0800 hours and landed 7:40 hours later and it was tomorrow, 7 October 1942!! This leg of our flight plan took us across the International Date Line and we gained one day. There would be no celebration for this Neptune crossing. Forty-two years later on 20 September 1984, a picture was taken of me standing straddling Longitude Zero, the Prime Meridian of the World at Greenwich, London, England. This is where Zulu, Greenwich meantime starts.

At times the clouds below reminded me of a white bed sheet so smooth stretching as far as the eye could see. As we approached our destination other islands came into view. I asked the navigator if he had any idea of where we were going. He replied, "There are many battle fronts north and west of us and the farther we go there are more, but if I was betting it would be Australia. But as you know that is only a guess on my part." He said, "You realize that all the navigators receive their charts for that leg of the flight after the morning briefing and our Almanacs cover the entire world so we have no better clue than you."

We made a PORT OF CALL at Nadi Airport, on Viti Levu, Fiji's largest island, at 1440 hours 7 October. The Island is located 18° south of the Equator and the airport is 177° east. This is one of the larger Islands in this part of the Pacific. Our debriefing was delayed while Captain Lackey talked to the weather people. It seemed that tomorrow there would be a lot of weather across our path. We would be flying to the French Island of New Caledonia taking off at 0600 hours weather permitting. This was to be our shortest leg so far, but due to the weather we may be doing a lot of zig-zaging and flying around before we land. We put the same amount of gas on board as we loaded for this leg of the flight. Fiji was a British Colony so were told to mind your manners. We were their invited guests, so don't be like Captain Bligh's crew. Their customs may be foreign to us. The same story about VD and spies were heard here also. We were to stay away from both. We were billeted in modernized grass shacks with eight to a hut. The natives never had it so good.

Most of us caught an off-base bus to the nearest town, Nadi. It was like walking straight into the last century. There appeared to be three races of people: the native Fijians, Indians from India, and Americans. All spoke English. We saw no English but we were told that they were all in Suva, the Capital on the other end of the Island. There were a few shops, beaches, palm trees, the ocean, and that was it. Some of us went back to the airport and rested under the shade of the coconut trees next to the beach. All flight members had sun glasses and I was glad! The sun was so bright that the sand and water nearly blinded you. Over ten minutes at a time was too long to stay in the hot scorching sand and blinding sun without being in the shade.

I had no way of knowing that twenty-seven years later my wife, Etta, whom I had not as yet met, and I would have our youngest son Terry living here as a US Peace Corps Volunteer Teacher in a private high school on an outer island in Fiji. Two years later when he returned to the States he told us about many of their customs. One that stands out is that shortly after he arrived his class told him that their great-grandfathers did something his great-grandfather did not do. They were all cannibals or head hunters. That means that when I was there some of their grandfathers may have been still eating their neighbors.

This was a lovely island but we had to move on. So the next morning all were ready to go on to another island in the South Pacific. This was the first time that we got to look at a map since we left Hamilton. The map showed only this segment of the flight. The weather en route was forecasted to be lousy, but we should be able to make it. Three thousand feet would clear anything from here to our destination with a good safety margin. Before entering any clouds we were to go into the Weather Penetration Formation. We were briefed that as we approached our destination if we did not have good visibility to descend and come in over the water. There is a 5,400 feet mountain to the north and east of the airdrome and another one at the other end of the island to the northwest.

We were in the air at 0600 on 8 October 1942, for a 640 nm flight to the southwest on a heading of 225°. Between take-off and landing a front and a squall line were forecasted. It should be clear at both ends but enroute was something different. We climbed to 6,000 feet and leveled off in the clouds. At that time we were in a very loose formation. Just before entering the weather we went into weather penetration formation. The lead aircraft maintained the same heading, indicated airspeed and altitude. His two wingmen made a 45 degree turn from the leader for two minutes and then came back on course. The right wingman climbed 500 feet and the left wingman descended 500 feet. The right element leader at the same time climbed 1,000 feet. His two wingmen made a 45 degree turn from him for two minutes then back on course. His right wingman descended 500 feet and the left wingman climbed 500 feet. The left element at the same time made the same maneuver but descended 1000 feet. The tail-end Charlie element did a 360° single needle to the right when back on course. The two wingmen made a 45 degree turn from their leader. The right wingman descended 500 feet and the left wingman climbed 500 feet. All aircraft kept the same indicated air speed. This way all aircraft were spread out and are less likely to collide. As soon as we entered the clouds we started to pick up light turbulence. I told Grassi to have everyone to get hold of something and hang on tight. The two pilots and radio operator were the only ones that had seats and seat belts. All cabin seats were folded up against the side walls to make room for the eight inside fuel tanks.

The navigator was standing behind me sharing the aisle with the crew chief with his stop watch and a writing pad in hand. He said it would be dead-reckoning until he could take a fix. I told him to hang on and try to keep us near our track. If anything, stay to the north of course so when we broke out we could make a landfall to the left. That way we would know which way to turn so we would be able to locate New Caledonia. I lowered my seat as far down as it would go, pulled my lap belt up good and tight, turned all cockpit lights up bright, took off my head-set and put on my sun glasses. This was the most violent weather I had ever flown in. The up-and-down-drafts seemed to be going both ways at once. It was raining so hard at times you could not see the wing tips. I was flying on needle, ball, airspeed, altimeter, rate of climb, compass, and clock. We earned our flight pay on this one leg. As a Staff-Sergeant Pilot on flight pay I received $135.00 a month. We were on a roller coaster ride, up 1,000 feet, down 2,000 feet, then the other way around with sudden violent changes of attitude. Holding the wings as level as I could and reasonably close to the heading and porposing like riding a wild bronco we roller coasted on. One minute the gear was down to try to stabilize and slow down our rate of climb, and the next the gear was up with take-off power to get us out of a dive. We were tossed about like a rowboat in a typhoon!! While going through these gyrations we had a gremlin visitor, Saint Elmo's Fire! Wingtips glowed an eerie circular blue light. The whirling propellers had blue circles of fire and balls of fire rolled down the aisle. We were flying through "Electric City." The static was so deafening that we were unable to wear our headsets. The flashes of lighting were blinding even with my seat all the way down wearing sun glasses and concentrating on the instrument panel. This was the only thunderstorm I ever flew in that I saw the lighting and heard the thunder at the same time. The rain, turbulence, and lightening were unrelenting. The cockpit was like a sieve. Water was oozing out of the tops of the two pilot's GI boots. The rest of the plane was dry, just shook up. After one hour and thirty minutes of these wild maneuvers the storm calmed, but we were still in clouds with heavy sheets of rain. We could not see the ocean below or the sky above.

Then we hit another storm cell, but nothing like the first one. I asked the navigator if he had any idea of where we were. He said that with a no wind factor we should be close to course. However, we must be far to the right of track. We should be in the clear within the next 30-40 minutes at the most. He said he'd never been in any worse weather, especially with only half a panel of working instruments. Looking up, I saw one of our Pursuit Pilots hanging on to the luggage rack. I asked him how would he like to take over and fly for a while. He shook his head and said, "NO, thank you!!" The co-pilot asked him if he'd like to be in his P-40 flying in this weather. He replied, "I'd never make it, if I could not get above it," and that was all he said. The navigator said, "Remember, Davy Jones takes no prisoners." Three hours and twenty-eight minutes after take-off the storm abated and we broke out in the clear. We could not see a cloud in front of us. The sea and sky were crystal clear. No one but a flyer will ever know what it is like to fly out of a violent storm and see the beauty of clear skies above, ahead, and a clear ocean below.

I was glad to let George fly while the navigator took a fix. In a few minutes he was back and said that according to the fix and driftmeter reading we were at least a hundred thirty miles to the north of course. Pick up a heading of 200° and hold it until we see land. There were two sets of islands running roughly parallel to our intended flight path. The smaller set of islands were about two hundred miles from our landing area and the other set were roughly ninety miles out. He thought that when we got back on course we should be closer to the 90-mile islands and would very likely never see the first chain. "Keep your eyes open." It wasn't long before a small sand bar came in sight. This was the closer chain of islands. From 6,000 feet up we began to see several very small islands. We made a 25° correction to the right and according to the navigator were back on track 90 miles out. From there on it was clear sailing all the way to New Caledonia. For this leg of 640 nm we made an over-all average ground speed of 94 knots. The upper air wind while in the weather had averaged out at 110 knots from a heading of 185°.

Once again on 8 October, we were second to land on a red clay runway before Captain Lackey turned off the runway. It was one hour and twenty-two minutes later before the last plane landed. We all had the same story. It was a wild, rough, harrowing ordeal. What an indoctrination to flying in the South Pacific! Before landing I'd learned to trust the beat of the engines as I trusted the beat of my heart without ever giving it a second thought. The basic seven flight instruments will get you there if your strength will only hold out. This type of instrument flying drains everything out of you and you're completely exhausted. ONLY with the help of supernatural power can you make it.

As the crews landed they refueled the same as before this leg. We waited around Operations until the last plane had landed. It was a long wait. None of the pursuit pilots had ever been in any weather to speak of and the Saint Elmo's fire gave them a real scare. With the partly empty fuel tanks in the cabin they were sure that the plane would explode any minute.

We were told that we had open post and to be back no later than 0700 in the morning. The weather was forecasted to be CFR (Contact Flight Rules) all the way. This time we were on a French Island so we had to watch our conduct. Guadalcanal isn't too far north of here with troops going and coming. Some troops had short tempers and big ears. We were advised to stay in groups with our mouths shut and no talking about military information.

All GIs were billeted in Quonset huts. In the tropics after an all night rain and with the afternoon sun beating down on the tin roof the temperature and humidity were all but unbearable. One of the crew asked if we were going to town. Across the aisle and a few cots down was a small soldier cleaning his rifle. I replied that I would ask that Limey how to get to town and where to go. This young fellow nearly came unglued, jumped to his feet, all 5' 4" and shouted: "I'm no Limey! I'm from New Zealand, a Royal—something or other." Each of us was armed, but his rifle was dismantled. I think that is all that saved an ugly incident. Another chap without a chip on his shoulder gave us directions and we found our way to Noumea, the island's Capital. There were troops from many different countries speaking different languages and they were mostly in the pubs. We walked the streets in the downtown section and went to one dirty, run down overcrowded water front park. Someone suggested that we go to a French Restaurant. This type of food does not please my palate. Everywhere you looked the ground was red with a very high content of iron. You could still pick out the aircraft that had landed at Noumea six weeks later even after flying in heavy rain storms almost every day. It was good to get back to the airdrome. This was not a clean place.

By 0730 next morning all aircraft were ready to go and the flight crews were having coffee or hot tea. One of the fellows had a French newspaper with a map of the Solomon Islands and New Caledonia on the front page. Of course, none of us could read French.

When Captain Lackey arrived for our briefing, someone asked if we were going to Guadalcanal. He replied that we were going to Amberly Airdrome, at Ipswich, a short distance from Brisbane which is on the east central coast of Australia. There was a loud shout of "good, good, great." The briefing was the usual: 29.92, track 228°, flight level 10,000 feet, 5:30 hours enroute. The weather was forecasted to be good with some lower scattered clouds. "We should double our ground speed of yesterday, that is, for some of us. For you that got in later your speed will be even better. Fly a loose formation until we reach the coast then close in and make it a good tight formation. Do not use your transmitters. We should be at Amberly for at least three days. While in flight pack up everything, your own gear and everything you signed for, B-3, B-4, Mae Wests, survival suits, parachutes, and life rafts. Take out everything inside the aircraft that we signed for at Brookley Airport and Fort

Mason except the fuel tanks. They were installed after we signed for the planes. Yes, we will keep our aircraft but there will be some maintenance work on all our airplanes while we are there. We want our gear out of their way and we do not want to lose anything."

"Nothing has been said about our Navigators, and since they will be leaving us at Amberly, I'd like to tell you something about their background. They are all Army Air Corps Reserve Navigators that have been called back to active duty. All thirteen have been flying on overseas flights with the airlines. Now you know why they worked their tails off in getting so much information so often and having such exacting ETAs. Gentlemen, we have had the best navigators in the world, and they are right here on the ramp in-front of my aircraft right now! We wish to thank each of you." There was a standing applause.

"One more thing, all our passengers will be leaving us at Amberly. Have a safe flight. See you in Australia as it is now time to bid adieu to this island hopping and to get on with our mission."

Now we knew our next stop would be to the continent down under. It reminded me of the first flight from Oakland, California to Ballina, near Brisbane, Australia. I had read that this flight was made in three legs: Wheeler Field, Hawaii, Suva, Fiji and Brisbane, Australia, departing the States on 31 May 1928, and completing the historic flight 9 June 1928. This 7,332 statute mile flight required 83 hours and 15 minutes flying time at an overall average ground speed of 88.07 mph. Australian Squadron-Leader Charles E. Kingsford-Smith and Flight Lieutenant Charles T.P. Ulm were the two pilots. The other two crew members were Marine Navigator Harry W. Lyon and James W. Warner radio operator. Both were Americans. As you see our flight was a real improvement.

After we were airborne, I went back and told the navigator what a terrific job he did for us and that I would like to fly with him anytime. This turned out to be his second flight to Australia and he had made two flights to Manila. I then wished the fighter pilots good luck and happy hunting.

The flight to the coast of Australia went as planned. We were very eager to get there. Even before we crossed the coast we were in good formation and then we pulled into a tight formation. We couldn't see the other elements, but Weedin and I had our wings tucked in half way to the fuselage of the lead aircraft. We had some mighty nervous pilots aboard. I could not take my eyes off Captain Lackey's right wing for both peripheral and depth vision are essential. However, I heard each of their voices as they would come up front to look and talk. They must have thought that fighter pilots were the only ones who could fly close formation. Touchdown was at 1332 local time 9 October 1942.

Just three weeks after making our flight across the Pacific Eddie Rickenbacker on 21 October 1942, made his ill fated ditching. He was lost at sea somewhere between Hickham Field and Palmyra Island and spent 43 days in a raft in the open sea before being rescued.

3

Australia

AMBERLY AIRDROME WAS A LARGE COW PASTURE with rolling grassy hills surrounded by many tall eucalyptus trees. There was no hard surface outside the two hanger floors. There was a line of US Army 6x6 trucks waiting for us to park. The drivers, all American Army GIs, had been well briefed on what to do and where to go. The first trucks picked up all the life rafts. The next one took the navigators and their gear. It took three trucks to handle all the fighter pilots and their gear. That left four trucks to pick up the 53 squadron personnel, 52 crewmen and our Sergeant Major. Each of us had a parachute, Mae West, gun, B-3 and B-4 bags to look after. The driver told us that there would be one stop before we arrived at Headquarters for our briefing. The main post was about two miles from the airdrome. Our truck pulled up in front of a new building surrounded by a high cyclone fenced-in area with a guard at the gate. Another armed guard opened a side door of the building and told us to leave everything here except our gun and B-4 bag. Then we went to the other end of the building and checked in our guns and ammo and got a receipt. The driver then drove us with our B-4 bags to the briefing. He told us to leave our bags in the truck and when the briefing was over to come back and he would take us to our billets. Latrines and coffee were inside on the left and our meeting was at the end of the hall.

The briefing started with an older Australian civilian welcoming us, "All you aviators on behalf of my country and for coming with your aeroplanes to help defend such a large area with so few people." He gave a very nice short speech. He then excused himself and left. An American Army Air Corps Lieutenant Colonel stood up. He told us that we would never know how glad the Australians, General MacArthur and General Kenney were that we had come to their rescue. "The war situation is not good, the Japs have air superiority and we are only hanging on by a thin thread. We are glad you're here." He then told us that General Douglas MacArthur arrived in Australia on 17 March 1942. As the Supreme Commander he had been ordered by President Roosevelt to stop the Japs, turn them around, and win the war in the Pacific. On 4 August 1942, General George C. Kenney was appointed Commander Allied Air Forces Southwest Pacific. The 5th Air Force was officially constituted on 4 September 1942, with General George Churchill Kenney as the Commander. He was born in Nova Scotia on 6 August 1889. General Kenney was only five feet six inches tall.

Captain Lackey then took over. He told us that it looked like our work had been cut out for us. We are to be here for at least three nights. Pilots are to be at their aircraft Monday morning, 12 October at 0500 hours. You are to be in flight suits with gas mask and guns, with B-3 and B-4 bags already in your airplanes and ready to fly. The local Air Corps maintenance crews will be removing from our aircraft the cabin gas, extra oil and alcohol tanks and correcting all the write-ups and due inspections. "While the First Pilots are with me on Monday the 12th the rest of the crews are to inspect the aircraft extra thoroughly. Be positive there are no open lines or valves where the fuel, oil and alcohol lines enter or exit the cabin. We are taking the drinking barrels with us. Check for all cabin seats and lap belts. The driftmeter and the navigator's chair stay with us, the table goes. These are not Depot people so recheck everything including all write-ups they work on and sign-off. When your pilot arrives at the airplane he will have the latest information. He will then make his own pre-flight."

"Pay close attention to the next item for it will get you in a lot of serious trouble real quick if you disobey this regulation. It is mail censorship. The law is simple: you cannot write anything to anyone that will be of any value to the enemy. Such as: what you are doing, where you have been, where you are, where you're going, what squadron you're in, what you're flying, nothing about the weather. Do not ask questions so that they can guess what you wanted to tell them, etc. Each letter is to be censored at least once. All letters will be postage free on "V-mail" forms. V-mail is a special letter form you receive from the Orderly Room. You write your letter in accordance with all the censor regulations. Do not seal it, there can be no enclosures, then drop it off in your own Squadron's out-going mail. One of the assigned Officers of the Squadron has to read every word of the letter. He then seals the letter, and signs and dates the letter on the outside. This is a must. Both of you must be in the same squadron. Then the V-Mail letter is forwarded to the US Army Post Office. Daily, hundreds of letters are opened by the US Army Post Office inspectors at random and re-read. For any and all violations the writer will be charged along with the Squadron Censoring Officer and both will receive the same punishment. When all the censoring is completed, the V-Mail is electrically sent to the Post Office in the U. S. nearest to where the letter is addressed. It is then printed on the same kind of V-Mail and sent to the state-side addressee as regular mail. This does several things. It speeds up the mail by several weeks, and keeps the sender from using invisible ink on chemically treated paper. All original V-Mail letters are kept on file to be used against anyone charged with violating the censor law."

"When this briefing is over, all Sergeant Pilots go to the front office in this building on your left and pick up your off-base pass. Sergeant Goldstein is making out the passes and getting them signed. Trucks will take you to your billets, from there to the mess hall."

"For those wishing to go to Brisbane, the Mess Sergeant will tell you when and where to catch the buses and when they will return. Remember, we are in a foreign country and we are their guests and act accordingly. Their customs may be different from ours, but it is their country. I cannot over-stress the importance of good conduct, VD and spies. You can now be positive that there are `Big Ears' every place, a word from one, another word from another and `Tokyo Rose' will put the whole story together. Have fun and a safe time. Keep your gas mask with you at all times. I'll be in Brisbane at GHQ in meetings for the next two days."

By 1530 we had picked up our passes, dropped off our B-4 bags at our assigned quarters, had dinner, showered, changed into class A uniforms and were on our way to Brisbane in GI buses. This was spring time below the Equator. Brisbane is about as far south of the Equator as Tampa, Florida is north. The terrain is beautiful with rolling green hills with grass and scattered trees everywhere.

From the bus stop we headed for the main downtown Service Club. About two blocks away we were met by a wall of humanity: American service men (GIs) and Australians (Diggers) in uniform coming towards us on the run as if they were being chased. Then we began to smell gun smoke. We tried to stop and talk to several individuals before one Yank told us that an Australian Infantryman who had spent over two years in North Africa before the Japanese entered the war, had returned to his outfit to defend his homeland. While fighting up north he had been wounded and was now on a medical recuperation leave. When he arrived at his home, no one was there. Looking around he saw baby cloths and an American Navyman's uniforms and gear. Going next door, he found out that his wife had a son six months before by the sailor. He also found out that she and her Yank lover were likely to be found at the Service Club. Arriving at the Club, he found them sitting on bar stools drinking. When he walked up she said, "So the bloody bloke returned." The wounded soldier wanted to talk. She told him that he had deserted her, had been gone for over three years and now returned all shot up, so get lost. He said: "is that the way you want it?" She replied, "Yes." He stepped back pulled a hand grenade from his amo-belt, pulled the pin and rolled it under their bar stools. All three were killed and several more were wounded. Military Police rushed to the scene to prevent further bloodshed between the Aussies and Yanks. As the Aussie would say, this could have been one "Jolly good donnybrook." It was a real brouhaha. That's when the club emptied. We did not get to the Service Club until Sunday.

In my opinion, most of the trouble between our troops was the difference in pay and lonely Australian women and lonely Yanks. The fact remained that most of the Aussie men between 14 and 70 were off to war. The Americans were there with plenty of money to spend and the Australian women were lonely. At this time, an Australian Captain on flight status received the same pay as an American private on flight pay.

We were told the Army had transit housing, so we went and signed up for two nights. We were furnished a towel and soap. We bought a tooth brush and tooth paste. Although I was 20, I had not started shaving. (When I first entered the service each recruit was issued a long-bladed razor commonly referred to in the Army as a "cut-throat razor." When the draft started these razors were turned in for safety razors with double-edged blades. The reason was that too many of the troops used the long-blades in fights with our own troops.) We then went out and ordered fish and chips. This was the first time I had ever heard of them. They were very good. We went to a south sea Island movie. In my fifteen months in the Southwest Pacific while on this tour I never saw one native that looked anything like the native girls in the stateside movies.

Next morning we went for a ride to the city park and the zoo in a wood burning taxi. That was quite an experience: smell, smoke, flying burning embers, and with no speed or power. All of the cabs I ever rode in while in Australia must have been early 1930-ish models of some sort. There were many strange animals at the zoo: kangaroos, wallabies, wombats, penguins, ostrich, emu, koala bears, dingos, camels and many more. All of these except the camels were native to Australia.

Late that afternoon we went to a pub. It was interesting to watch the Yanks try to drink the girls under the table. The heat, high alcohol content of the beer, and the size of the bottles would get any Yank down that tried it. We had a hard time understanding the Aussies because they talked so fast. One of the first things we noticed was that most woman over twenty-five years old very likely had false teeth. For each girl there must have been at least ten fellows, so she was dancing every dance. One of our fellows asked one of the girls for a dance. She said, "No, thank you, Yank I'm all knocked up. Go jazz my sister." Now, that took some time to translate into English. We finally determined what she said was, "No, thank you, Yank, I'm tired, go dance with my sister." Every few minutes the band would play Waltzing Matilda. After my second coke, we left, returned to the fish place, then back to our billet.

Next morning was Sunday, 11 October 1942. I could interest only one other fellow in going to church. I still have the picture I took of the Baptist Church we attended in Brisbane. After the service it seemed like everyone wanted to invite us over for dinner. Eddie and I stayed together and joined a woman and her two daughters. They were both just a little older than we were. The older one had lost most of her teeth. Their father was away in the Army the older daughter's husband had been killed in action. The younger daughter had never been married. That evening the two of us went back to the Service Club before catching a bus back to Amberly Airdrome. The club had reopened for business. The bombed out part was roped off. We could still smell the gun powder from the grenade. We talked to one of the Yanks who had been in the club when the "family argument" started. He stated, "To him it was like a knife fight in a phone booth, not room enough to get out of the way and no time to get out before the fireworks started!"

When we arrived back at the Airdrome we were notified not to report for duty until 0500 hours 13 October. The next day was spent on the base, "hanger flying," resting, and eating.

By 0450 hours on the thirteenth we were at the Commander's aircraft ready to go. All planes had been thoroughly checked and rechecked by each member of the crew. All crews were eager to be on our way. The Captain told the First Pilots that we had a long flying day ahead of us. Weather should be good and we would be making one stop at noon. While there, we would eat, refuel, and pick up a load, and then fly on to the next airdrome. We would be flying in loose formation. "Is everyone ready to go?" We all twelve called out, "Yes, Sir." At 0557 we were airborne overland, heading up the northeast coast of Australia.

Four hours and thirty-five minutes later we started letting down and landed at a small airdrome on the coast near a small city. After landing we found out that this was Garbutt Airdrome, Townsville, Queensland, Australia. Between the very end of the runway and the beach was a cemetery. "I do not know if it was for takeoff or landing, but a most unusual location." When we landed, Captain Lackey told us to go eat, come back, take full service and that each plane would have another full, heavy load. The next leg would be over water. There would be no life rafts, only the crew's Mae Wests and parachutes. In our plane we would have 29 Army Air Corps Enlisted Men, all their personal gear along with 29 heavy tool boxes. We were not to wear our Mae Wests. We were to keep them and the chutes out of sight because there were none for the passengers. In an emergency we could not use either, and it was the pilot's responsibility to see that they were not seen or used. Just go down with the ship like all the passengers.

We had the same briefing as at Amberly except that this time we knew that it would be an over water flight. We did not know where we were going or how long the flight would be. We still had no maps and we had only seen one leg of the journey so far. I tried to remember from school what was north of the northeast coast of Australia. All I could see in my mind were a lot of islands scattered through out the South West Pacific.

Once again the plane was overloaded, not as much as it had been from Hamilton to Hickham, but far more than she was designed to fly. We took off at 1337 hours, climbed out on a heading of 008° and leveled off at 9,000 feet. The cabin aisle was stacked high, with very little foot room. Grassi went to the back to see how everyone and everything was doing. When he returned he said that all our passengers were aircraft mechanics. They did not know where they were going and asked him where we were taking them. This secrecy is going too far. What about the need to know? What if the lead plane went down, if we got separated in weather and were not able to use the radio? I guess since this was war, we were expendable.

At about 1700 we began to see a long low dark cloud on the horizon. The closer we got the longer and darker it became. Then we realized it was the coast line of a land mass. As we approached we descended to 1,000 feet when we saw an old rusted shipwreck on a coral reef, a short distance off the beach. When over the ship, we slowed to 120 mph, dropped our gear, turned left and flew parallel to the beach in trail formation. About 50 miles from the ship there was a seaport and a small village mostly made up of native thatched huts. There appeared to be a large harbor without any wharves and no ships or boats of any size. There was one bombed out ship on its' side in the middle of the harbor. Banking to the right seven miles inland we came to a landing strip. The runway surface was different from anything I had ever seen. It was made of steel, all connected with evenly spaced 3-inch holes the length and width of the landing field. Later we found that each plank was 8 feet X 30 inches, weighted 69 pounds and was called "PSP", Pierced Steel Planking. All mats were interlocked together to make one solid runway. On all takeoffs and landings this made a loud rumbling sound. There were no runway lights. The control tower was a small 4 X 4 foot platform on 10 foot poles with a small open thatched roof for shelter from the sun. The only equipment was a biscuit-gun light, a field phone to operations, a hand cranked siren, a pair of binoculars, and a rifle to sound an air raid.

After landing I asked the Alert Driver," where are we?" He replied, "Jackson." I said, "Where is that?" He said, "New Guinea." I said, "and where is that?" He got back into the old beat-up staff and command car and told me to "ask your pilot." I then told him that I was the pilot. He just looked at me, then my stripes, and then he must have spotted my wings. He shook his head and drove away without saying another word. We had just flown over a third of the way around the world with only the Squadron Commander knowing where we were going. I was the first Army Air Corps Staff Sergeant Pilot to fly in and land in New Guinea. The only map in the thirteen aircrafts was with the Commander. At each briefing after Hickham, until we reached Australia, the pilots and navigators were briefed for the next leg of the flight. Only one leg of the flight did the Pilots get a look at that leg of the trip. From Amberly to Garbutt and on to Jackson there were no briefings and no look at a map. We were to just blindly follow the leader.

Since departing the United States on 2 October 1942, we had made eight stops, flown 9,886 statute miles in 58 hours and 35 minutes flying time. Putting this all together meant that we were now at Jackson Airdrome, Port Moresby, Papua, New Guinea within five air miles of the closest enemy ground troops!!

Some sixty years later, my son Steve pointed out that, "I found New Guinea 450 years to the day after Columbus discovered America. When it is 13 October in New Guinea it is still the 12th of October in America."

My wife, Etta, and I flew from the States to Australia, fifty years to the month later in 1992. We flew over in a Qantas 747 in 13:56 hours making only one refueling stop in Hawaii. On this flight there were nine flight stewardess and 341 passengers. We all flew in perfect comfort with hot meals, movies, and above all the weather traveling in smooth air.

Flight Route of 6th TCS from San Francisco

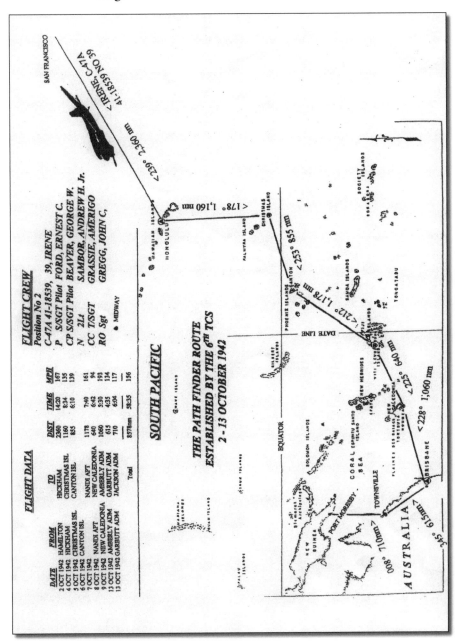

4

Welcome to New Guinea

IN SHORT ORDER, AFTER PARKING OUR AIRCRAFT, all First Pilots met at Captain Lackey's plane. When the briefing started he informed us, "This is our new duty station, our home for now. We are now in a war zone and can expect bombing, strafing, ground and artillery attacks, several times daily. We are truly in harm's way. Each crew member will carry a loaded gun at all times while in the combat zone. Do not draw your gun unless you need it. Officers, this is one time the Sergeants have had a lot more training than we have, so if there should be a ground fire-fight try to be near a Sergeant for advice. Remember the 6th is an old Regular Army Air Corps Squadron with very few short timers and no draftees. As a whole, each enlisted member has had several years of combat infantry training and knows how to protect himself and his squadron. This is serious business. Your life depends on the correct decision made at the right time. This is one time to say, 'Carry on Sergeant' and follow his lead and instructions. In the Army you are paid to do, not to question, so just do your job. When the briefing is over, return to your planes. Open the two big sealed boxes that are still in your aircraft and take out one mosquito head net and a mess kit for each crew member. Then open your B-3 bag. Take out your helmet and liner, insert the mosquito head net between the two and reassemble. Be positive that you have your gas mask with you at all times until you are told differently. Leave all other items in the boxes. Keep the crew's five parachutes out so they can be immediately available, if needed. Keep your head gear, gun and gas mask with you at all times. Carry all these items with you everywhere you go until you leave New Guinea. Never take your 'Dog tags' off, even in the shower, in bed or at anytime. They are just part of you. Have them around your neck at all times. During the war you will hear a lot said about being the first to fly some route. You can now say that the 6th WAS the PATH FINDERS from the States to New Guinea."

"Vehicles should be here shortly to take us to chow. When we get there we each have to wash and sterilize all our eating utensils. Then fall in at the end of the chow line. Do not crowd in front of anyone or you

The author posing in his helmet between air raids in the slit trench in front of his tent in October 1942.

might get a bullet in your back. You may see a General in line behind a private! There are no jails in New Guinea and no one will be sent to Brisbane for trial, so justice will be swift and on the spot. Eat everything on your plate. Do not throw out one bite of food. The Army men we flew up will be our mechanics and work on our aircraft until our ground crew arrives by ship in about four to six weeks. As soon as we eat, an Australian Army Infantry Officer will be here and give us some very important information. Listen to what he says; it is important. Now go back, tell your crew, and wait for the trucks. Stay in one group."

When I returned to Irene our passengers and their gear were being offloaded into trucks. The flight crew was sitting on the PSP under the left wing, swatting mosquitoes. I went over to one of the trucks that had the most men in it, climbed up and told them what Captain Lackey had told us. We would be seeing them around and I thanked them for coming to help us until our ground crew arrived. My crew could hear everything I said. The flight crew opened one of the boxes. We each took out a mess kit, mosquito head gear

Our "not-very-private" outdoor privy The American female nurse caught Cortez Houston with his pants down. She might have been embarrassed, but he got a date with her and a lot of kidding from us, too.

and assembled our webbed belt. I told the crew, "Come on fellows let's go. I'm hungry and cannot wait to try out an actual combat field mess."

Three old, beat-up Australian Army trucks that looked like they had been through the North African Campaign picked us up. The field kitchen was located a mile down a very bumpy, dusty road on the other side of a small hill in a coconut grove. The "Mess Hall" consisted of two tents for storing supplies. One large square of canvas was strung out between the trees about twelve feet above the ground for the cooking area. Two long 16 x 20 foot canvas sheets tied end to end hung above the ground between the trees. This was used as the serving line. Above the whole area was a camouflage net. The "Dining Room" was anywhere you wanted to stand, that was out of the way the line of troops waiting to be served. So far, no one had the time to cut logs to sit on. Except for the mutton and the mosquitoes, the meal was not bad.

Looking around, I spotted a sign that read, "Los Angeles City Limits, City Hall 9,000 miles." An arrow was pointing towards what I figured to be Southern California.

At the end of the serving line was a large metal trash can to scrape anything that was left on your mess kit. A rough, loud mouthed army sergeant stood there looking at each crumb that you put in the can. He had a chant that went like this, "Son, you can't waste any good food here, it costs the Army too much for you to throw out and waste good food, stand there and eat every bite on your mess-kit!" Next there were two large steel barrels. The first one was filled with hot soapy water with a long handled brush to wash your utensils, and the last barrel was filled with very hot, boiling, steaming water. There were several long steel wires with a hook on one end and a wooden handle on the other end. They reminded me of a long-handled hay hook. You were to hook all your mess gear onto the one wire

In November 1942, I moved into this four-man tent at Wards, which served as my home until May 1943. During bombing raids, which occurred almost nightly, I also spent time in the slit trench.

hook, and then sterilize them by submerging them several times in the rolling, boiling hot water. Once you took them out of the scalding hot water they dried very fast in the open air. And still another sign, "If you don't do it, you'll get the GIs and the Doc will know why."

The very first thing we noticed as we got off the aircraft were the mosquitoes. They were everywhere in swarms, and could they bite!! They drew blood most of the time. It was a race to see who could eat the most, the mosquitoes or me. One hand was required to eat, one to swat the insects and at the same time try to hold on to and not drop or knock over your mess-kit. It seemed that for each mosquito you killed one hundred took its' place. This battle continued whenever we were outdoors from just before sundown to just after sun up for the next twelve months, until our squadron was rotated.

Only God and the Medics know why we didn't all died from malaria.

There were other Allied flying originations. Fighter, bomber and transport flew in the area. The 21st and the 22nd Transport Squadrons were formed earlier in 1942 on 3 April. The 21st was at Archer Field, Brisbane and the 22nd at Essendon Aerodrome, Melbourne. Between them, they had twenty-four transports, of which there were nine different types of aircraft: one B-10, a B-18, and a number of B-17Cs, C-39s, C-40s, C-47s, C-53s, C-56s, and two L-4s. This was one monumental supply and maintenance headache. They would fly in from Australia and were staged out of Jackson. Most of the time they flew in, refueled, flew out on a mission, returned to Jackson, gassed up, and flew back to their home base. On occasions they flew up and stayed over night, and then returned. They would RON only if maintenance or weather required it. This put a heavy drain on the flight crews.

Some squadron had to be the "Guinea Pig," so the 6th Transport Squadron with thirteen unarmed C-47 aircraft got the honor of being the first permanently assigned flying Troop Carrier Squadron to be stationed in New Guinea. We were also the first Transport Squadron to fly across the Pacific Ocean from the United States to Australia and then on to New Guinea.

A tall slim Australian Infantry Officer, Captain Norman R. Wilde, arrived at 1830 hours. Over the next year, I ran into him several times at different advanced fields all the way from Jackson to Lae. Captain Lackey met him and after a few minutes all the flight crews moved a short distance from the mess area. The Australian Captain welcomed us to New Guinea and began his briefing. "The Japanese made their first landing on this island on 21 January 1942 at Milne Bay, and on 8 March this year at Lae and Salamaua. That is when the Tokyo War Lords were sent from "The Land of the Gods," the "Sons of Heaven." That is what the Japanese fighting men are known as in Japan and here in New Guinea. You will hear a lot about the Coral Sea Battle. It was over on 8 May 1942. The Japs tried to land troops here at Port Moresby and your navy gave them a beating. They lost several ships and many aircraft. On Tuesday 21 July this year they landed 16,000 troops at Buna. (After WWII it was published that only 700 of this force survived. Thousands had been bypassed and left to "wither on the vine.") They are now trying to take Moresby by land over the Owen Stanley Mountains. That is why you are here to stop them!! The Japanese are a fanatically determined enemy. The fighting qualities of their soldiers, seamen and airman should not be underestimated. They are a real fanatic adversary. These Japanese "Spirit Warriors" have a motto, "Victory or Death." We have to win the war so we Aussie's can live in peace."

"This is a disease-ridden island with malaria, dengue fever, diarrhea and all other known tropical diseases, and a hostile environment. It is a "hole, known as the GREEN HELL." The mosquitoes start swarming in clouds well before sundown and stay until after sunrise. All stagnant pools of water are the primary breeding place for mosquitoes."

"At a forward base like this, the facilities and all maintenance are primitive or lacking. The only spare parts or tools for your aircraft are what you brought with you. Service and maintenance has to be improvised on the spot by your own mechanics, "grease monkeys" as we call them. All work is out in the open, rain or shine, day and night, seven days a week. You can say that you are now in the bonnies, boondocks or "out back", as we blokes call it."

He explained how badly our giant transport aeroplanes were needed and how critical the situation was. "At this time the Allies are losing the war on all fronts in this Theater. If the Japs are not stopped before they take Jackson Air Strip, all of New Guinea and the northern half of Australia will be abandoned. The reason: we do not have the means, the manpower, or the equipment to defend it. This is known as the MacArthur Line. As we speak, all of the immediate hills to the east, north and west are under enemy control and they already have air superiority. All we are holding is this small area between here and the sea and a few hills beyond the first row of hills to the east end of this airdrome. The main enemy force is only five miles up the trail in the hills at Ioribaiwa. However, they have snipers in this area and at times they do take a pot shot at low flying aircraft. The Allies control only three airdromes in all of New Guinea. Two are here at Moresby and one is at the far eastern tip of the Island. Our ships can only load and unload under cover of darkness. They go out to sea and hide during daylight. This keeps them from the enemy bombers and strafers. Look in Moresby Harbor and you will see the sunken wreckage of the 4,630-ton motor vessel `Macdhui` that the Japanese sunk less than a fortnight ago. War is a tough business and if you are not on your guard at all times you will be killed. As the Yanks say CYA. CYA, which means, `Cover Your Ass' and this means at all times on the ground or in the air."

"The enemy are getting reinforcements by the hundreds every week. They all go on foot over the Kokoda Trail. This is all by foot on a series of native trails that start at Buna on the shores of the Solomon Sea on the north side of the Island. This route known as the Kokoda Trail winds its way through one hundred and fifty miles of swamp, jungle, up and through an 8,000 foot gap in the high Owen Stanley Mountains and then down to Moresby on this side. This is all done by foot. The mountain pass is so narrow that pack animals cannot be used. Supplies can only be moved on the backs of men. This break in the mountains is known as the Kokoda Pass. Almost daily we bomb and strafe the Wairopi Foot Bridge where it crosses the swift running Kumusi River at Kokoda. About as fast as we knock it out, they manage to repair it. They use it at night or in bad weather when our Air Forces cannot bomb or strafe. This is a suspension bridge made of wire cable, hemp rope and slabs of newly cut trees for the flooring."

"Since there are no roads or railways and none can be built, you must become the freight cars of the skyways and the `Biscuit Bombers' of this war. Your job is to stop the enemy! If you can carry Allied soldiers, supplies, and evacuate the wounded when and where we need them, in the quantity required, all without air cover, we can stop and turn the Japs around. The only escort you will have is one 'Wirraway' aircraft. You Yanks call it an AT-6. It has two 30 caliber machine guns. The plan is for the T-6 to fly 5,000 feet above your flight leader. When the pilot sees enemy aircraft he will go into a dive for the trees. At the same time your planes are to break formation and fly as close to the trees as you dare. Fly just above treetop level and blend in with the foliage. This is the only protection we can give you. I've been told you like to buzz. Well, as of now, IT IS NOW LEGAL!! I've also been told that you Pilots are a special breed. Now is your chance for us to find out."

"As you can see we have a beautiful tropical moon. Shortly, you will be cussing it. The reason: that's when the enemy bombers come. The strafers usually make their calling when we're eating breakfast and supper. We were lucky tonight but they will make up for it later tonight. Tomorrow morning `Tokyo Rose' will announce your arrival. We may get a few rounds of artillery shelling. Artillery shelling is very accurate and deadly. The only reason we do not get a steady bombardment is that they have to hand carry everything ninety miles through a steaming, humid, snake, crocodile and mosquito infested jungle. Then they have to go up and through the 8,000-foot Kokoda Pass and sixty miles of the same type of jungle down this side of the Pass. They already have four light artillery pieces up there now and if they could move them closer or bring in heavier artillery we would be in for it. The enemy will fire a few rounds and then move to another location so our planes cannot find and destroy them the next day. War is not a good place for nice people. Death is the only certainty in this world. As long as you are in New Guinea, danger is always your comrade-in-arms."

"There are no maps of New Guinea, so I'll trace you a rough outline here in the dirt. It can be said that this is a war of distances. All pilots should take a good look." With a stick, he scratched out a squiggly line in the dirt of the south coast of New Guinea. Then he sketched a couple of hundred miles in both directions from Port Moresby. He made a wiggly line north of and parallel to the south coast. "This is the Owen Stanley Mountain range which runs down the center of the full length of this 1,500 mile long island. New Guinea is the second largest island in the world and has an area of 316,856 square miles. It has a land mass slightly larger than twice the area of your state of California. At the southeast tip of the Island the mountains are down to 4,000 feet. At the far northwest end there are several snow-covered peaks over 16,400 feet. The highest is Mt. Puncak Jaye at 16,503 feet. The highest peak in this area is 13,400 feet. New Guinea was discovered in 1511 by a Portuguese Sea Captain by the name of Francisco Serrano."

Our Australian Advisor placed the stick on the coast line a little way southeast of Port Moresby. "You remember when you flew in from Townsville? You turned left at Hood Point where there was a shipwreck just off shore on a coral reef. This is 50 miles down the coast. Whenever flying into Moresby from over the Coral Sea, join the coast at this ship, descend to 1,000 feet, or below the base of the clouds, slow down to 120 mph, lower your wheels, turn left up the coast to Port Moresby. If it is at night or you are in the rain turn on your landing lights. This was a German cargo ship that was chased by an Australian destroyer in World War I and it ran aground. It is now used for an identification point and for aerial gunnery practice. Within a fortnight we will be in the monsoon season. In New Guinea the rain is from

80-400 inches a year. In the Moresby area it may hit as high as 80 inches a year. Yes, I said in some parts of this Island the rain may be over 33 feet 4 inches. That is deep enough to float one of you aircraft carriers. So get settled in, for it is coming. This is one of the few places in the world that you can be in mud up to your knees and still get dust in your eyes!"

He then sketched on up the south coast to the northwest and then scratched in the Fly River. He proceeded to show and tell how we could walk out of New Guinea. "Remember you must maintain radio silence at all times. Jackson has a control tower, a small 4x4 foot thatched roof shack on 10-foot poles. They have a telephone line to Operations and a light-gun for aircraft and ground vehicle control. A rifle is used to sound an air alert and the all clear. They have no radio. All take-offs, landings, and airdrome ground control are by the standard light signals. If at any time you should return from a mission and the airdrome is under ground-attack, or a red flag is displayed, or there is no tower, fly as low as you dare and as far up the coast to the northwest as you have gas. When you run out of fuel either land or crash land on the beach. Take your gun, all the ammunition you have, your knife, gas mask, first aid kit, mess kit, mirror, both your head net and sleeping mosquitoes nets, all the food and water you can carry with you. Take the aircraft survival kit, the book of instructions, and the fish hooks, which are essential for you to make an escape. Walk up the coast next to the trees. Do not walk down on the beach by the water. Sure it is a lot easier to walk there, but if an enemy strafer sees you, you're dead before you can make it to the trees. That will be the end of the war for you. If you should hear an airplane, hide in the trees until you have identified it. If it is an Allied aircraft use your mirror to signal. If it is an enemy aircraft stay out of sight."

"I would guess it to be at least 450 miles by foot with all the twists and turn of the coast line from the west coast of Moresby to this side of the Fly River. So the farther you fly the less you walk. In the sand next to the trees, with the load you will be carrying, twenty miles a day would be a good gage to go by. When you come to the Fly River follow the native footpath on this side of the river inland for at least a fortnight. This is one very large, swift river. Ocean going vessels have navigated up from the mouth of the river as far as 800 miles inland. If you get slowed down walk faster. When on the footpath you cannot see planes above, and they can not see you due to the

Map of New Guinea

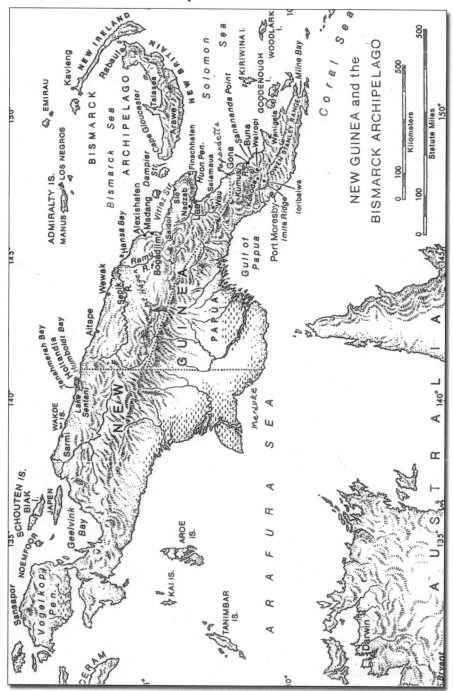

NEW GUINEA and the
BISMARCK ARCHIPELAGO

jungle foliage above the trail. Then make a paddle, find a log, pray, and start paddling for the other side of the river as fast as you can. The river is very wide and the current is very swift. By the time you reach the mouth of the river you should be on the other side. The river is so thick with crocodile that you might be able to walk across on their backs! Once you get to the ocean the sharks are just as thick. Take no chances. They are both killers. Once you get on the other side of the river continue walking northwest next to the trees until you see islands on your left. Take your mirror which should be hung around your neck at all times, with your "dog tags" and your tin can opener, and start flashing to the natives on the island. They have been instructed and will be paid by the Australian Government. If they see any flashes they will paddle over in their dugout canoes and take you to their Island. They are friendly and will ferry you from island to island until you reach the mainland of Australia. This is a total distance of just over a 100 miles over water from New Guinea to Australia. When on the continent start walking down the east coast of Australia until you join up with an Aussie or Yank fighting force. Unless you can fight and swim like Tarzan do not try to swim it!! Within a few strokes in the ocean a shark will have a meal. The same goes for the crocodiles when in the river."

"You must have a contingency plan and an escape plan in your mind for each mission. Nothing is stable. Elements of the war are changing minute by minute, so be ready to change and roll with the battle. No battle plan survives after the first contact with the enemy. Each pilot will have to make the decision on his own. When in camp, do not go walking out of the immediate area and always go with at least one buddy. Do not skip a meal for there is no way of knowing when and where you will have the next one. Hardships are a part of war and we are at war with the Japs and the elements. Both are enemies and killers."

"As you may or may not know, there are still plenty of cannibals in New Guinea.

"Yes, if they catch you they will eat you. Since the end of World War I there have been Missionaries in parts of New Guinea. When they go into a village and are of the opinion that it is reasonably safe, and that the natives are not practicing cannibalism, they will have all the village thatched roofs dyed red. There are many hostile indigenous tribes in the mountains west of

Moresby. The reason for the dyed red roofs is so that when an airplane is flying over a village the pilot will know that it is probably safe to land in an emergency. Of course, after a while the natives may change and go back to eating their neighbors. This is only a rule of thumb to say that you should be safe. If the roofs are not red, be very leery. There are no cannibals within 120 miles of Port Moresby or within 50 miles of the coast, and none from here going north to the other side of the Island. They are all to the northwest of here in the higher mountains. The same goes for the headhunters. The only difference is headhunters cut off your head and put it on a Trophy Pole for religious ceremonies."

"You will see some of the most beautiful scenery and strange exotic animals, birds and plants that you can imagine, with wild orchids everywhere. The dense, dark, all but inaccessible, forest has many trees exceeding two hundred feet in height. There are plenty of snakes and lizards over 10 feet in length. Keep away from the enormous crawling red ants. All waters in and around New Guinea are filled with either man eating sharks or crocodiles. Remember unless you can swim and fight as efficiently as Tarzan, stay clear!"

"Now as to why you are in New Guinea. The war in New Guinea will be won by the side that can get the most soldiers and their supplies and equipment on the battle field first and keep them supplied. Here is the plan. It has worked the few times it has been tried. As our trucks back up to your aircraft, your mechanic is to open the aircraft's cargo door. The Aussie's truck will off-load 5,000 pounds of supplies aboard your aircraft. It may be in boxes, sacks or just loose, or a combination. The cargo will not be individually tied down. Ropes will be strung across the back of the cargo so it will not slide to the rear of the aircraft on take-off. The cargo will not be tied down as is the usual load. The last truck to pull away will leave four or five of our men aboard your aircraft. These are the men that will push the cargo out the cargo door when the pilot gives them the green light and the bail out-bell is ringing. When your mechanic comes aboard for take-off, he will remove the steps and the paratrooper door and store them in the aircraft latrine."

"There are no straight battle lines or trenches as in Europe. So do not forget, NO battle plan survives after contact with the enemy. Keep your eyes open at all times, both in the air and on the ground. The enemy has and controls all the surrounding hills you can see around Jackson. We still control

some of the hills and valleys behind here to the east. At this time we are trying to cut off their supply line. To get where we want you to drop supplies in
the morning is pretty much in a straight line form here. It's on an azimuth of
60°. By air I would judge it to be 20 miles. The drop zone is at 2,200 foot and
it is surrounded by three peaks up to 3,000 feet. There are peaks just to the
north and east of there that are over 10,000 feet. After take-off the pilot
should fly as low as he can up this valley (pointing to the southeast) until on
the other side of those 300-400 foot hills that are on the north, east and south
of this airdrome. The reason is that on occasion enemy snipers infiltrate the
area and take pot shots at our aircraft when in the traffic pattern. When on
the east side of these hills, circle up until you are at 2,600 feet. The terrain
gradually slopes up to about 1,500 feet with peaks up to 3,000 feet. In the 15
miles from the other side of those hills beyond the end of the runway to the
drop zone you may encounter some ground rifle fire. Do not climb any
higher than 3,000 feet for if a Zero is in the area and he spots you, he'll shoot
you down before you can get to the trees. We control all the peaks around the
2,200-foot hilltop that is the drop zone. You should not expect any ground
fire in that area, but always be on the lookout."

"You will find the Drop Zone (DZ) in the middle of the three 3,000 foot
peaks, on an azimuth of 60° and 20 miles from here. It is a small, 2,200 foot
flat-topped hill. There will be two smoking, smoke pots. They will be lined up
in the wind and as far apart as there is a clearing. That will give you a drop
zone of maybe 200 feet wide with a maximum of 500 feet in length. Spiral
down inside and as close to the higher peaks as is safe. Turn on the red light.
Let down to between 300-400 feet above the drop area as far out on a final as
you can with both the wheels and flaps up at 90-100 mph. When lined up
with the two smoke pots with their smoke coming towards you, then descend
to 50 to 75 feet above the ground. This will put you well below the treetops.
Always be sure that you are lined up with the two burning flare pots and keep
them in plain view while descending. At this DZ which is on a hill top all
the trees to the approach to the drop area are below the actual DZ. This is not
usually the case. Just before the first smoke pot goes out of sight under the
nose of your aircraft turn on the green light and the bail-out bell."

"When the Aussie cargo pushers see the red light they will get ready to
push out one circuit of supplies. When the bell and the green light are on,

they will push out the supplies as fast as they can. After you turn the green light and bell off you will keep circling in the same pattern until all supplies are dropped. After the last drop return to Jackson for another load."

"Free dropping of supplies and equipment from an aircraft to units in isolated mountain sites will be at the nearest clearing that can be located to the fighting unit on the ground. In most cases it is on a flat topped kunai grass ridge. Military necessities may require the clearing of trees on mountain sides or in a native village at the bottom of the valley."

"When free-dropping the plane is usually well below the treetops, and with the dead weight of the cargo and such a short fall the wind has very little effect on the falling packages. When dropping by parachutes at 200-300 feet above the DZ wind drift has to be taken into consideration."

"If at any time you see any aircraft, except the one lone T-6, break formation, scatter and fly as low to the treetops as you can. Do not keep flying in a straight line at treetop level. If the enemy pilot should see you it is much easier for him to line up on you then if you do some zigzagging. The top of the trees are leaves with small twigs, so when the prop hits them it will not do much damage to the propellers or the under carriage of the aircraft. Oh, sure, it will leave its' marks and the maintenance men will know that you were in the trees. After you land, clean out all the leaves from the oil coolers and check the props for nicks or damage. Do not hand move a hot prop for it will kick back, cut off an arm, leg, head, or just plain kill you. If you should crash or parachute in the jungle, just head south to the coast and the natives will get you back to Moresby."

"When you have a day off, have one of our infantry men take you a mile or two into the jungle. You cannot imagine how thick the foliage is. It is an almost impenetrable dense, thick tropical jungle that is roofed over by nature. The floor of the forest is covered with ferns and decaying moss, tree roots and fallen trees, if it is not a greenish swamp. In the jungle while on the ground at high noon on a clear day you cannot see the sky or any direct sun light. From below it is perpetual twilight at all times. It may take you a day to cut 50-100 feet off the beaten path. The jungle is so dense that one of the B-26 crews bailed out three miles from the airdrome and it took them a week to hack their way back to base, and they knew where they were and which direction to go. Do not waste your time if you come down in the jungle by calling or using your mirror. If someone else goes down with you, blow your whistle a few times. If you were up there, more likely the enemy are below you. Try not to give your position away. Do not build a fire unless you want to be captured. Wait until you're in a clearing to use the mirror. Be cautious of any voices calling you in perfect English. Don't forget some Japanese can speak fluent English. That is one of their favorite tricks. If you are by yourself, the only time you should use your gun is for food. If you shoot at, hit, or kill one of the enemy, you're dead. In the jungle you can be within twenty feet of an enemy patrol in day time and never see or hear them. Most of the flight crews in New Guinea carry at least four full magazines of ammunition in their webbing, another fully loaded clip in their .45, plus one extra round of live ammunition in the chamber. The extra round is for themselves. Thirty-six (36) rounds are not much fire power in New Guinea. If they see that they are going to be captured either by the Japs, the headhunters, or cannibals, realize neither take prisoners and let them live. The headhunters cut your head off. The Japanese will torture you until they have all the information they think they can get out of you, then kill you. The cannibals, just like in the movies, put you in the pot alive, boil you until you are dead and well cooked and then eat you. This is war, a serious business, and it is for keeps, so treat it that way. At this time in the war neither side takes prisoners and lets them live."

"About the only way to protect yourself when on the ground during a shelling, bombing, or strafing raid, is to be in a slit trench which is a hole in the ground. When you go into an area and you will be there for a few hours or more, find, or dig a slit trench. That was one of the first items to do on the list when setting up this field kitchen. Look all around on either side of this path. See those trenches? They are 4 feet deep, 24 inches wide and 6 feet long. That will provide for two or three men. If there is a need for more, dig another trench or an adjoining one at 90°. Do not dig one long trench, for the strafers will line up on it length wise and kill everyone in one pass. Do not shoot at a strafing aircraft with a side arm or rifle, for he or one of his wingmen will come back and bomb the site and all in the trench will be killed."

"Another thing to watch out for if you should be on the ground in the jungle, there are Japanese Infantry snipers who climb up in the trees and shoot anything that moves on the ground. Unless you can see the sniper do

At times when there was no enemy action, groups of native women gather as a social event
upon the arrival of an aircraft while men and boys (next picture) offloaded supplies.

not waste your time or ammunition with a rifle or side arm, just use a hand
grenade. They booby-trap any and everything from using land mines, trip
wires across the paths, all war souvenirs, and dead bodies. Another trick they
use is to hide behind a coconut tree, pop out, and take a shot at you, then
duck back behind the tree. Their little 6.5 mm rifle will not penetrate a tree
over 8" in diameter. The American M-1 will go through most trees in New
Guinea and kill anything on the other side every time."

"Now for the dress code to follow while in the combat zone. General
MacArthur has an order something to this effect. 'Use the uniform, which
will feed the most ammunition to the enemy and meets with medical requirements.' That is it! What this means is dress any way you wish during the day.
At night cover up to protect yourself against the mosquitoes. No saluting or
spit and polish. This is a war zone. An undisciplined army is like a mob. So
DO NOT forget your training even though there is no spit and polish. You
cannot have a war without people dying. The hospital reports show that
'down here' we have a big war going on. Life in wartime is not like in the
movies. Here you are likely to be killed or at least wounded. Remember, it is
accepted in law, ethics, and religion that if a soldier kills in war in the line of
duty he is not a criminal. That is why we are here! TO KILL THE ENEMY."

"One other thing I should tell you. These natives are truly primitive people. They are in the 'Stone Age' and are at least 5,000 years behind today's

Organizing native men and boys to carry military supplies offloaded from the C47s

civilization. The rugged terrain in New Guinea keeps the natives so isolated that there are over 700 separate languages spoken on this Island. That is over one quarter of the world's languages. Do not take advantage of them or expect much from them. Their customs and culture are much different from ours. Tomorrow you will see more nude women in one hour than you will see in your entire life unless you're a Medic. Many come here to work. They will not steal. All women are bare from the waist up. Most wear a grass skirt. On occasion you will see a native woman breast feeding a piglet. You can buy the women's grass skirts for one cigarette. She wears all she owns, which is two not over three. You will only do it once for it is so filthy and stinky that you will not want to touch it or be around it. Before the age of puberty, which is age nine or ten, all the kids are nude."

"Most of the aboriginal men have large wide noses, broad foreheads with athletic bodies, and woolly black hair. Some dye their hair red. All have wide thick-soled bare feet. Their only dress is a banana leaf rolled up into a long rope and tied around their waist. A second banana-leaf rope is tied to the rope around his waist and then pushed around his side until it is hanging down in the middle of his back. The hanging end of this banana-leaf rope is drawn up between the cheeks of his buttock and up between his legs and tied to the waist band in front. He then places one of his testicles on either side of the rolled banana leaf and his penis vertical behind the leaf rope. In the case of the men, nothing is hidden from view. The reason for the banana-leaf is so that when a man runs his sex organs will not flop around. This is not the loincloth that we see in the movies."

"All men have some tattooing and many have most of their body covered. A few of the women have tattoos. Some of the men have bones or carved wood through their nose, ears or the skin on their chest. A few of the men wear feathers in their hair. Some of the men, but more of the young women, wear bright colored grass woven arm bands. Occasionally you will see one around an ankle. There are no rings or jewelry for they have no metal."

"There is a death sentence against touching or having sex with their women. Don't give it a second thought. From the first minute you get near them they will remind you of a cow in the field. Once you get within a few feet of a native your nose will tell you why. Their odor is something you cannot imagine or stand. They stink!! To my knowledge the only white man that has ever fathered a native child in New Guinea is the Australian movie actor, Errol Flynn. His eight year old daughter is at Hood Point. When the authorities found out they barred him from the island and he has never seen his child. Of course, he could care less." (A few months later I flew down to Hood Point and took pictures of her and she does look a lot different.)

"When you are in a camp area walk on the paths. If you fall in a slit trench you have a good chance of breaking a leg, arm, back, or your neck. The holes are every place. To fall in a straddle trench would even be worse!!"

"There is only one non-Allied radio station in all of New Guinea that you can tune into, and that is Tokyo Rose. She plays the latest American Hit Parade songs and has the cleverest propaganda you can imagine. Do not believe all you hear coming from her radio station. Of course, a lot of it is true, and most is very persuasive. Our G-2 believes one of the several Tokyo Roses is an American." (On October 6, 1949, American-born Iva Toguri D'Aquino was convicted in San Francisco, sentenced to 10 years in prison, and fined $10,000 for being one of several Tokyo Roses.)

"All of you have had 'gas mask drills' several times. If it will ever be needed it will be on this tour of combat. Keep the mask with you at ALL TIMES. Do not go wandering around without it. Wear it like you do your dog tags. If needed, it will save your life. The last item is when your Captain is finished go to the tent down this path to the Medics and pick up your supply of Atabrine Pills and Salt Tablets. Take them daily as the Doc directs for malaria and dengue fever control. If you take them, your skin will turn bronze like mine. If you don't take them you'll either end up in the hospital or the grave. If you live you will be Court Martialed. Before the war we used quinine. Now that the supply is cut off, we now use Atabrine."

We thanked the Aussie Captain and he left so he could be at the drop zone when we arrived in the morning. Think, the Aussie had only twelve hours to walk twenty miles leaving at sea level and going up to 3,000 feet, slipping through the enemy lines, all at night, in the jungle without any sleep or lights. I wondered when he last had any sleep? One of the troops said, "That Captain is so hard he could chew wire and spit out nails! I'm sure glad he is on our side."

Captain Lackey told us that, "From now on we will hold our briefing just before flight time. In that way there is less of a chance of 'Big Ears' hearing. As a rule of thumb, weather permitting, the CQ will wake the flight crews at 0400 hours. In that way we will be airborne and out of the area before the enemy strafers arrive. Have breakfast and all First Pilots be at my plane no later than 0445. Crew chiefs and radio operators pre-flight and do your run-up while your pilot is being briefed. Co-Pilots, do a walk around inspection and keep a close eye on the loading of the aircraft. Crew Chiefs, keep all fuel tanks full at all times, then refuel after the last flight each day. The gas and oil trucks are 6x6's loaded with 55 gallon barrels and are hand pumped. It sounds like we might have to walk out of here so the more gas the shorter the walk. Remember always have your gun, gas mask, mosquitoes nets, all the survival items you carry on your web belt and your steel helmet with you while in New Guinea. When you do not need your entrenching tools in the camp area, keep them in your aircraft. Keep one full barrel of fresh water and at least four unopened cases of C-rations in the plane at all times. Wear your dog tags, signal mirror, and a can opener around your neck at all times. Don't forget to also keep your compass with you at all times. Take good care of your gas mask and pray that you will never need it. As you can see we are now in the business of war!!"

"Do not talk over or use your radios, just listen. There are no radio aids or let down ranges in New Guinea. If you receive any radio instructions from anyone, the tower, or a voice claiming to be me or anyone, just listen and ignore them. Do not answer or follow their instructions. When you return, report it immediately. The two pilots and radioman are to monitor the radios at all times. Most of the time all you will hear is 'Tokyo Rose.' They say she has the latest hit songs along with her propaganda."

"Before you try to fly instruments in New Guinea, allow 5,000 feet above the highest known mountain in the area, 5,000 feet for altimeter error, 5,000 feet for your mother, 5,000 feet for your father, 5,000 feet for your wife or girl friend, since this bird cannot fly that high do not try to fly instruments in New Guinea. Trying to fly instruments in New Guinea is synonymous with suicide and that is not permitted. If the mountains do not kill you the thunder storms will tear the wings off your aircraft!!"

"There are two other Transport Squadrons that fly in and out of Jackson, the 21st and the 22nd. They are stationed in Australia. They fly in, refuel, go on a mission or two, then fly back to home base. They fly whatever type of aircraft that could be picked up in this part of the world when the war started. They are not fully manned, either in manpower or aircraft. Their biggest problem is parts for nine different types of aircraft. Their crews have been trained mostly in bombers or fighters, or whatever was available."

"Once a week clean and oil your guns, do a good job. There are only two times that your gun is to be out of the holster. It is for cleaning or for self defense. No fast draws. You know the rules, follow them."

"From here, go to the Medic's tent. Then return here for the trucks to take us to our planes. When there each of you take out of the boxes an Army cot, one blanket, pillow, mosquito net and your toilet kit. Come back to the sleeping area behind the medical tent. Find a tree and set up your cot and mosquito net below it. Locate several slit trenches and straddle trenches. Do not get them mixed up in the dark!!" Much laughter!! "All of us are to sleep in the same close, compact area. In the morning, take all your equipment back to your plane for we may not sleep here again. After dark, do not go walking around for you could easily get shot. Jackson Airdrome has an Australia outer-perimeter patrol. The American Infantry is the on-base guard. They may shoot and then ask questions. When you hear three rapid shots, grab your pants, shirt, shoes, gun belt, gas mask, helmet and mosquito head net and get in a slit trench. If that takes you thirty seconds, you're too slow. Pilots, leave your guns in the holsters. Dress when in the hole. No lights or smoking. As you can see, we are now out in the boondocks!! There is no room for screw-ups while in the combat zone. Remember, flying in itself is not inherently dangerous, but it is terribly unforgiving for incompetence, carelessness, or neglect." Gentleman, as you can see this will not be a cake walk so be alert at all times on the ground and in the air. In our ignorance we thought we were ready!!

When the briefing was over and we were heading for the Medic's someone said, "It looks like if the red flag is hanging from the tower, or there is no tower, we either take flight or stay and join the infantry." As for me, "having been in the infantry, I preferred flying over walking, so Irene would keep her tanks as full as possible at all times."

The setting sun was a tropical splendor. In the tropics the sun sets quickly with very little twilight. This was followed by the most beautiful big full moon that you could imagine. It was big and clear. It was the kind of moon that Hollywood would love to see. It was almost as bright as daylight.

We were returning from our aircraft and getting off the trucks with gear in hand when the first three warning shots came. Almost at once, the generators were turned off and the camp lights went out. It seemed as though total chaos over took by our own flight crews. For some of our group, it was pure panic. A few dropped everything and ran for the slit trenches where they cowered in the ditches. Some started sorting through their half dozen items to find something. I could never figure out what. Some of us ran with everything in hand to the closest empty hole, laid down our gear and jumped in. Search lights began to come on and criss-crossed the cloudless moon-lit night sky. High above, three Betty Bombers were caught in the lights. The first thing you noticed about the Jap bombers were that their engines were never in synchronization. The Aussie 40 mm Bofors ack-ack started firing. It appeared to me that all bursts were too low and behind the enemy aircraft. The planes held a steady course. Their bomb-bay doors opened and a string of many small bombs came tumbling out. The bomb-bay doors closed and the three planes continued on a straight line untouched. This was the first bombing or enemy action I had ever been in. It was Tuesday, 13 October 1942, at 2045 hours. Shortly we began to hear; 'whoosh, whoosh, whoosh, whoosh.' The sounds from above grew louder the closer the bombs got. Someone on the other side of the path yelled, "Hit the trenches, our "Little Friends" with their Daisy-Cutters are here!!" Once you hear that terrible sound of death and dismemberment you will never forget it.

Later we found out that these tumbling anti-personnel bombs, commonly known as "Daisy-Cutters" came in different sizes, ranging from 10-25 pounds. They were incased in steel pipes 3-4" in diameter and from 10-20" in length with a steel rod 10-30" long sticking out from one end. When the tip of the rod touched any object the bomb exploded and shoots out small scraps of razor sharp steel fragments in all directions. The radius of bomb damage is determined by the size of the cylinder housing the explosive. The height of the destruction above the ground or whatever the probe touches is based on the length of the rod. The purpose of this type of bomb was to seriously injure everyone within range and permanently disable the enemy from all future military service. Very likely a soldier standing, walking or running within range will lose both legs. It takes more personnel to support one injured patient than it does if he had been killed outright. It was easy to see that this kind of an environment was not conducive to a long and healthy life. I guess you could say, "For a flying organization this was front line duty in a real fire zone!!"

The alert lasted for one hour. Lights began to come back on and I looked for a place to hang my mosquito net that was near a slit trench. It is a wonder that many soldiers did not break their legs in their haste to get in a slit trench. Once more that night we spent an hour in the trenches. At a little before 0200 the alert was sounded and at the same time you could hear the sound of the incoming artillery rounds. I'd heard WWI soldiers talk about artillery attacks. They described it as a charging express-train. Just one time, and you can identify it the same as you can a Daisy-Cutter. The artillery rounds have a much different sound. Those 'Nips' did not want us to stay at Moresby that was for sure. They just wanted us to move out. We found out for sure that there were no atheists in the foxholes at Jackson Airdrome this night or during our stay in the combat zone.

5

The Enemy — Mosquitos, Weather, and Japs

AT **0400** HOURS THE NEXT MORNING when the CQ came to wake us. I was sound asleep dressed in my flight suit under the mosquito net. Then I reached out for my GI boots and shook them out. As I started to put my foot in the shoe someone asked what is in my boot? Then someone else asked the same question, "What is this green stuff in my boots?" I fumbled for the flash light under the pillow, turned it on to find that I also had a greenish mold in and on the outside of my boots. I shook them out again to be sure that there were no bugs or spiders inside or out. All our troops went through this same procedure every morning for our stay in New Guinea. I took one end of the towel and wiped the boots inside and out the best I could, then put them on. I visited the latrine which was nothing but a long narrow straddle ditch. Toilet paper was hanging over the end of a stake driven in the ground with a one gallon tin peach can over the roll of paper to protect it from the rain. Even so, the high humidity made the paper damp. At each end of the trench was a 55-gallon barrel with a steel lid on top. Inside were lime and a large metal grain scoop. A sign by the barrel read, "Use the trench, cover it up, signed Doc." Twenty feet away on tree stumps were two GI five-gallon gas cans of water for shaving, brushing your teeth and washing your face and hands. There was a posted sign: "Safe to use, your helmet is your wash pan." A few feet away were two eight-foot high well-constructed stands with six 55 gallon gas barrels on top each stand with a pipe and faucet coming out the bottom side of each. This was our shower. It had another sign: "Hot!! Test before using. Hot!!" Our last essential life item was several canvas Lister bags. The drinking water smelled and tasted very strong of chlorine. Near each water bag was a sign that read: "Drinking Water, safe, don't forget your salt pills, signed Doc."

Here we are in New Guinea. The enemy can look down from the hills and see us and the lights are on everywhere. Yet 9,000 miles away in San Francisco there is a black out. The same old story is that those who are not in war, play war, but those who are on the front lines forget to play. They just fight the war!!

All First Pilots were present for the 0445 briefing. Here I learned that Colonel Ennis, "The Menace," C. Whitehead, the Field Commander when I was at Luke, was here as a Brigadier General in charge of bomber command. How well I remembered the speech he gave on our arrival at Advanced Training. He said: "When I first got in the Army I wanted to be a cook and I became a cook; then I wanted to be a Corporal and I succeeded; then I wanted to be a Colonel and now I am a Colonel. Set your goals high, then go to work, and you can make it!"

Captain Lackey and an Australian Lieutenant were already waiting for us. Our Commander told us "that the weather should be flyable until at least noon with a little fog and stratus just after take-off. Today Australians will be pushing boxes out the cargo door of our aircraft on a hilltop named Myola. When airborne stay on the deck flying straight out on a heading of 130° for four minutes below the stratus until you are on the other side of the first row of hills. Then join up and we will climb out in formation to 3,000 feet on a heading of 50°. Pilots, keep a sharp lookout for the T-6. If it goes into a dive, break formation, spread out, get on the deck and head for the ocean. In your haste to get out of the area, do not get in the trees. When at treetop level keep changing headings. Don't forget, when flying on the deck and banking, not to drag a wing-tip in the trees and cartwheel into the jungle. We will fly over and back in close element formation. Brief your crew chief and radioman to go to the cabin after becoming airborne, and keep watch out both sides in all quadrants from ground up. Don't see things that are not there. For today only the lead Aussie pusher will come forward after take-off and point out the drop zone."

"For this first flight you should be able to follow me in and out where I drop. This will not always be the case and this is the only time your pushers have all been where we will be going. This is only to help us get started. It should take another five minutes after making the first turn out of the traffic pattern. At that time we should be at altitude and at the three 3,000 feet peaks. Keep an eye on the sky, the AT-6, my plane, the terrain, and where your pusher-navigator tells you to go. Once we get in the valley where the drop zone is we will let down to 2,800 feet in a left hand racetrack pattern and line up with the smoke pots. On the downwind, turn on the red light where you would normally drop your wheels. While in the pattern hold the airspeed at a 120 mph, auto-rich, 2200 rpm, cowl flaps trail, wheels and flaps up. When on the final at 2800 rpm slow to 90-100 mph. Just before you get over the first smoke pot, switch on both the green light and the bailout bell. As you approach the second flare pot, turn the light and bell off. Add power and make another circuit. Try to watch where your load goes so you can correct your aim on the next pass. It should take us 6-7 passes to empty the aircraft."

"To fit the ten aircraft we're flying this morning in the same small pattern may be expecting too much, but we will try it for the first pass. If there is not enough room in the valley the last two elements will pull up to 3,000 feet and hold until the first two elements are finished. Then we will switch places until all aircraft have finished so we can all fly back together in formation. Once everyone is finished and at 3,000 feet in trail formation we will descend to 50 feet above the trees and head for a point between 5-7 miles inland from the coast. This should take about seven minutes from the 3,000 foot peaks. Then we will fly back up the valley to Jackson. When on this side of those hills pull up to a 500 foot traffic altitude and enter a normal traffic pattern. Remember where you're parked because we are supposed to park in the same place each time. In this way the Aussies will be able to bring the assigned load to the correct aircraft and pick up the "Pusher" that flew with us. There is no Alert Crew so we have to find our own way back to the spot where you are now located."

"The last plane must be airborne no later than 0600. The reason is that the early morning strafers usually arrive after 0630 and hang around for an hour and then leave. We should not return before 0800. They have been coming in from the southeast and going out to the northwest. All we can do is hope that we miss them. In the event you should encounter aircraft trouble try to stay airborne until after 0800. Otherwise you might be trying to land during a bombing or strafing raid. That could be fatal."

"If we should return and there is no light signal from the tower or a red flag is hung out or worse yet no tower, you will know that the base has been taken over by the Japs. In that case escape as we were instructed last night. That is why we should have everything with us at all times until the situation either gets more stable, or we give up and leave New Guinea. There is one other important thing to remember and do not ever forget it. Always have a contingency plan for each flight. With no radios, poor weather, little or no fighter protection and plenty of enemy in the air, you must be prepared for any changes."

When I arrived back at NO 39 the Aussie truck was just driving away and Grassi was closing the cargo door. The crew chief said that we had full service and a 5,000-pound-load with four Aussie's aboard. I made a fast out-side walk around. Everything looked good. I prayed that she would bring us back after each mission. I talked to our pushers. None of them had ever been in an airplane before. They had some mock-up training on kicking out supplies. On this flight everything was in boxes inside gunny sacks. That was to hold the supplies together when the box split open on impact. They said that they stacked as much as they could inside the open door. It could not be higher than four feet high. It was to be aligned straight across from the cargo door to within three feet of the other side of the cabin. The three feet was room enough for one bloke to sit on the floor with his back against the cabin wall straight across from the open door with his knees up around his shoulders. Two of the men would stand in the tail section of the aircraft and the other one on the aisle side of the stack of boxes to be pushed out the cargo door on each pass. When the red light went on they would stack the boxes and sacks on the floor inside the cargo door then take their positions.

When the green light and bell came on all four would push as hard and fast as they could. Everything had to go out. They had to keep it from hitting either side of the door jambs on the way out or hitting, or going over, the horizontal stabilizer. If it hit any part of the tail section we would crash and all aboard would be killed instantly. There were no seats for the cargo pushers as the seats were folded against the cabin walls with the cargo stacked from side to side and at least four feet high the full length of the cabin.

I asked who had been to where we were going. One fellow said he had walked in and out twice and that he could point the way. I checked the ropes across the back of the load to keep it from sliding to the rear and getting the plane in a nose high position on takeoff. That would have caused the aircraft to stall. I told our pusher-navigator to come up front with me. The other three were to sit down across from the open door and to hang on. They were to stay away from that open door and on the way back they could all come up front. The two of us crawled over the cargo to the cockpit. I told him that he could stand between the two pilots while the crew chief was standing fire guard. When the chief gets aboard he had to stand behind him. I signed the Form 1 off. Then I fired the bird up and taxied forward into position so when the Commander moved out, I would be ready to follow. Our passenger was a sergeant in his late twenties. He had served three years in North Africa and was ready to return to Australia when the war in Europe broke out. He had just completed eight years of service. He was all eyes and watched my every move.

Captain Lackey started to move and we followed him to the run up area. After run up we received a green light and moved into position and held. Thirty seconds after the lead plane began to roll, I released the brakes and began to move as full power was added. When the wheels broke ground I leveled off with the gear up and stayed below the clouds flying between the row of hills for four minutes. Then I increased power and made a left climbing bank rolling out on a heading of 50°. The lead plane was where it should have been climbing to 3,000 feet. I could not see the T-6. Grassi was watching out the left side cabin window and Gregg had an extension on his headset and was manning the right side cabin window. The cockpit door was open and I could see the three pushers were looking out the cargo door.

Our pusher-navigator pointed out the "peaks" we were headed for. At 3,000 feet, Captain Lackey leveled off and we followed him in between two of the peaks. There on the other side was the DZ with the two flare pots smoking away. It was easy to see we could never get ten planes in trail formation in that small area at the same time. I hoped the last two elements would stay at altitude until we finished our drops. I sent our pusher to the back and told him to untie the ropes and that shortly the red light would come on. We immediately started descending and picked up a standard landing pattern. The downwind was at 2,800 feet. I switched on the red light, slowed down to 120 mph, turned on a 400 feet base and lost another 200 feet on the turn to the final. I rolled out on final at an indicated 2,400 feet, which was 200 feet above the DZ. On the short final with the two smoke pots lined up on our nose we descended to 2,300 feet altitude. When the first smoke pot disappeared under the nose of the aircraft I switched on the green light and bell. At that time we were 100 feet above the DZ indicating 95 mph. I could feel the load shift as the boxes went out the back door. As we approached the second pot I called to cut the light and bell and added take-off power. The dropping of the cargo reminded me of throwing a rock over a pond and watching it skip across the top of the water. I called it skip-bombing.

You could see that only the first six aircraft were in the pattern. The other four were in trail formation hugging the inside of the three higher hills. Still there was no T-6 in sight.

On the downwind for the second pass I could see that most of the boxes were in the drop zone. This time I dropped 50 feet lower to 2250 indicated and turned on the bell and light earlier. The boxes landed closer to the first smoke pot. Each pass the plane was lighter and you could feel the boxes leaving the aircraft. We made seven passes. When we dropped down in the DZ below the tree tops you could see that many of the mangrove trees were over 200 feet tall and were huge. Looking at the jungle-thick forest from this view point below the tree tops, the trees seemed to be matted with climbing tropical vines and ferns. The jungle was a mass of various shades of thick greenery. The canopy was so thick you could not see the ground or the enemy below.

After the seventh pass the Commander pulled up and we changed places with the other two elements. All four Aussies came forward and looked around. They talked mostly to Grassi and Gregg. This afternoon they were leaving with a patrol in the jungle. When the other four planes had dropped their cargo they joined us and we all headed back for Jackson Airdrome.

"Tokyo Rose" from "Radio Tokyo" came on the air and welcomed the 6th Transport Squadron to Jackson Airdrome. She said that Captain Lackey should take his thirteen C-47s and go back to Australia where they would be safe. How did he expect to protect them against the mighty Zero? She asked how we enjoyed last night's "fire works." This was followed by the latest American Hit Parade Music.

Once we got on the other side of the three peaks our Commander led us down to the treetops in the clear. The treetops were so thick that it looked as though an empty plane with gear up and with full flaps you could stall into the green foliage and it would hold the weight of the aircraft up. Then we could climb down and walk to the coast and then on to Moresby. How we wished that we had a good old "Stateside sectional topographical navigational chart."

In about six minutes we were below all the lower stratus. At that time we could see smoke from four big fires billowing up from the valley where we thought Jackson should be. Coming in from the southeast as we pulled up to enter a 500-foot traffic pattern we received a green light from the tower. Two of the fires were from different trucks hauling barrels of aviation fuel. The other two were aircraft. After landing at 0902 we were told that five Zeros had come in about fifteen minutes after our last plane was airborne. They flew up the same valley that we had departed from. The Japs had come in with all guns blazing. Two of their planes caught gas trucks full of aviation gas in the open and blew them up, killing the drivers and helpers. One of the Aussie's 2-engine Tiger Moth spotter aircraft was caught as it was getting airborne. The other plane was a taxiing P-39. Pilots of both planes died and their aircraft were destroyed.

As we parked 12-15 native men came out of the trees to help load our aircraft. The men had broad noses and thick lips. Most of them wore necklaces of teeth and shells. Some of the native men were dwarf pygmies. Then the native women and children appeared. Only one out of five children lived to the age of five. When you saw a family of New Guinea natives walking, first would be the father, then the oldest to youngest sons, then came the oldest to the youngest daughters and last would be the wife. They were all dressed, or should I say undressed, as the Aussie Captain told us. They would giggle, laugh, and point. Of course, we could not understand a word. The few teeth they had were all stained the color of dried blood from chewing betel nuts. Most of the women had big, coarse, frizzled, bushy hair. The Australians called the native women "Fuzzy Wussies."

A 6x6 gas truck came to refuel us at the same time two more truck loads of Aussie supplies arrived. We still used 91 octane gasoline. In a few months, it was increased to 96 octane, and later when we were stationed in Australia it was up to 100 octane. Our four pushers from the first trip, with rifles in hand, came up and thanked us for what we were doing, and for their first airplane flight, and told us that they would like to go with us again when they returned from patrol. I told them we'd like to have them and to just tell their chief, and remember plane number 39. Then I asked them where they got their rifles? They replied that they had stored them in the aircraft toilet. We wished them luck, and they drove away with the first lorry that loaded the boxes in our plane for our second mission. I walked over and spoke to Captain Lackey. He said

The Australians often referred to New Guinea women as "Fuzzy Wussies."

this would more likely be our last mission today due to the afternoon weather and when we returned we would go to eat. He still did not know what happened to the T-6. When we returned from this mission we were to take the same things that we had with us last night when the trucks picked us up. Tomorrow, we will be dropping at some other place.

We were on the ground a few minutes less than two hours. The reason for the hold up was because there were only two 6x6 hand-pump gas trucks. The clouds were now below 3,000 feet. Though we stayed on the trees after take off, you could see some puffs of gun smoke from the hills. It seemed to me that anyone in range that could not hit a C-47 should not be in the service.

On the second mission just after picking up a heading of 50° and starting to climb the co-pilot started pointing and yelling: "enemy, Japs, look!!" At about 10:00 o'clock high and perpendicular to our heading a flight of three bombers with fighter escort were heading towards Jackson. Between the broken clouds you could see the sun reflecting off their silver wings and fuselage with their big Meatball Insignias. Captain Lackey was still climbing. I added full emergency take-off power and pulled up off his right wing. His co-pilot, Staff-Sergeant Pilot McFarland saw us off their wing-tip. When I had his attention, I pointed up and looked in the direction of the enemy aircraft. Both pilot's heads looked up and out the pilot's side window. Within a second the nose of their plane changed from a climb to a dive. I pulled back into position. The Commander banked right to a heading of 80° staying on the trees until we were on the other side of the three peaks. This time we arrived at the DZ from the east. We used the same procedure to drop as before. The pushers worked like dogs to get the boxes lined up to push out on the green light and bell. These men had never been in an aircraft before either. Someone had given them good ground training.

It took one hour and thirty two minutes to drop fifty thousand pound of supplies. It looked like a high percentage of the sacks and boxes hit in the drop area. After the last pass we all joined up and flew between two of the 3,000 foot peaks and headed back for our home base. All heads looked up and to the west. We flew at treetop level from the pass to Jackson. Smoke rose from two off-base fires. When we pulled up and entered the traffic pattern we received a green light. On the downwind, the tower blinked us a coded message. I called for Gregg to come forward with his biscuit gun. He spelled out their message, L A N D - B O M B C R A T E R S. As we circled, it was easy to see three bomb craters in the runway. On landing we could dodge the bombed out holes, but on take-off with a loaded aircraft, if the runway were still in this condition it would be a real problem. It appeared that they had aimed to place three bombs side by side in the middle of the runway in order to close the field. Two of the bombs had hit in a slanted line half way down the runway on the left half of the strip with the third bomb landing 50-75 yards farther down on the far right edge of the strip. We made short field landings on the right side of the runway. By the time we were even with the two bomb craters our ground speed was slow enough so the aircraft could move to the left and miss the third crater. All of our birds got down safely, with the last aircraft landing at 1325 hours.

This time there were many more natives to meet us. It was interesting to see the different sizes and shapes of the women's breasts. Some were flat chested, some were big, round and sticking straight out, some were smaller ones, and some completely deflated hanging down. Some of the women were pregnant with their big stomachs showing, with filled breasts, black nipples, and dark rings around the nipples. A few were nursing. Never had I smelled such stinky body odor. When you were in the hot airplane and the natives were loading or unloading the plane, you had to hold your nose and get out of the plane. The stench was so strong that you wanted to go out and vomit. The smell was overpowering. On top of the heat and humidity, the odor was more than my nose could take.

Natives loading and unloading aircraft provided tremendous support to our military effort; however, the stench from their body odor was often over-powering.

The natives were all short. Few that I saw in the Moresby area were over 5' to 5'5". It seemed that one of these men could walk away with any load that could be put on their head or shoulders. Later when we flew gasoline, three or four natives would put a 55-gallon barrel of gasoline on the shoulders of one of the natives and he would stagger away from the aircraft with it. That is 360-380 pounds!! I never saw one of them stumble or fall. A thick pad of burlap was put on the native's shoulder and the barrel was balanced upright on top of this. They would carry it out beyond the wing-tip and lean over and the barrel would go crashing to the soft ground. Then the bearer would go back to the cargo door for another barrel.

The Aussie Pushers got out and walked away with their rifles. The crew picked up our gear and went out and waited under the shade of the wing for the gas truck. Refueling was all done by hand pump in the heat of the day. If we thought it was hot in the shade under the wing just wait until we got on top of the blistering hot aluminum wing. "Yes, I'M positive you could fry eggs." When we got back on the ground we were picked up and driven to the "mess hall." Captain Lackey told us to eat, then wait around where we had billeted last night. We were not to set up our cots and mosquitoes nets because we would more likely sleep at some other place. We feasted on such delicacies as canned bully beef and Australian mutton. When Captain Lackey finished eating he would go find out the latest and come back and brief us. He thanked me for alerting his crew to the enemy aircraft. That was, he said, "Good Airmanship." I told him that Sergeant Beaver was the one who first spotted them. He then thanked both of us for good fast teamwork.

At 1545 when the Captain returned most of us were stretched out either resting or asleep where we had slept the night before. The first thing he told us was that the two off-base fires we saw when returning to Jackson were two downed Jap Zeros that our ack- ack had shot down. The bomb craters on the runway kept our fighters grounded. He said that our drops had been excellent, with at least 85% in the target area. And at least 70% of the recovered airdrop was useable. The Australians were very pleased and thankful. They now have more supplies at this site than they could use. They had estimated that at least 60% would be lost or destroyed in the drop. The reason that we did not have fighter cover (our one and only aerial protection, the AT-6) was that the refueling truck backed into the aircraft's right wing-tip and aileron. They are waiting for parts to be located in Australia and airlifted to Jackson.

At tomorrow morning's briefing we will be told what we will carry and where we will go. If we keep up the good work there will be fewer missions and the ground forces will be able to push the enemy back and save Jackson Airdrome and the harbor at Moresby. We will sleep here for the next five nights. Then next Monday we will move to a new airstrip named Wards Airdrome. It is two miles from here, just on the other side of those hills to the south. The one runway at Wards is lined up in such a way that its traffic pattern will not conflict with Jackson. It is being built now and should be useable by then. We will be the first flying squadron to be stationed there. This last week the engineers started clearing for the field. One of the first things they did was to place several dummy camouflaged airplanes around the field. The next night when the enemy dropped real bombs on Jackson they dropped "WOODEN BOMBS" on Wards!!

We were off until wake-up at 0400 in the morning. At this time we were told that our squadron had been re-designated and our new name was the "6th Troop Carrier Squadron." The name change was effective as of 4 July 1942, but we were just learning about it three-and-a-half months later. We were not to go beyond the perimeter of the field. We must be back at least one hour before dark. We were to take our steel helmet, carry our guns, gas mask, and go with a buddy.

I asked Grassi if he would like to go for a walk on the flight line. He said "yes." I told him to get his helmet, mask, and gun. We caught a ride to the B-17 area. When the truck let us off, we started to walk in front of one of the Flying Fortress, "Suey-Q." The crew was making their pre-flight for a mission. One of the Officers yelled, "What are you two doing out here on the flight line?" I told him we had just arrived yesterday and that we were the pilot and crew chief on one of the C-47s, and we wanted to see the B-17s. As he started walking toward us we went toward him. I immediately recognized him and said, "Lieutenant Felix Hardison" and took off my helmet so he could see me. He began to smile, stuck out his hand and said, "Private Ford." I introduced him to Grassi, my crew chief. He then looked at my wings and said, "Another Stockwell." I replied that, "I'm afraid none of us will ever be half the pilot Sergeant Stockwell is." By this time his crew came up to join us. We were both introduced. One of his crew addressed him as Major. I looked and could see no rank. He turned the collar of his flight suit and there was a gold leaf. I said, "Wow, congratulations! I wish I had gone with you. What is a Major doing flying combat?" He said, "Remember, I like to fly. Besides I'm the Squadron Commander of this outfit, the 93rd Bomb Squadron, 19th Bomb Group." I asked, "How do I get a transfer to your organization?" He said he had two questions, "Have you ever flown a B-17, and how many missions do you have?" I replied that, "I had never been in a 17, and today was our first day of combat." Grassi spoke up and said, "Let him read the Form-1 tonight and then take him around for a couple of landings, and you will check him out." Everyone laughed. Then Major Hardison said that the Group was stationed in Australia. They would fly up and stage out of Jackson Strip, refuel and then go up and bomb Rabaul. He was sorry, but a transfer could not be arranged. But if I could get permission from my Commander, the next time we are up here and if I wanted to I could fly as his co-pilot on a mission. "When and where do I report?" "The next time, after tomorrow, you see the B-17s, bring your permission slip and look me up." My reply was, "Yes, Sir." He said that they now had to leave on a mission. He then asked if we would like to finish the "walk around" with him and get in the aircraft for just a minute. You know the answer, and away we went. I was all eyes and ears. It was most interesting. Grassi and I both enjoyed it. As we were leaving the aircraft the Major asked where I went to flying school. I told him, "Luke, 42-E in P-40s." He had to leave, so we got out of the plane and stood at a safe distance beyond and in front off the left wingtip until they started to move. We gave the Major a snappy salute as the B-17 taxied away. That was the last time we ever met. Then we returned to our camp area.

I set up my GI cot, hung the mosquito net tucking in three sides, and put my shaving kit under the net on top of the bed, and tucked in the net on the fourth side. The bed consisted of a GI Army folding cot, one Army blanket and pillow. The blanket served as a mattress and sheet. Gregg said, "If you aim to take a shower, now is the time. The water is scalding hot, but if you wait, the mosquitoes will eat you alive." He was right. The water was hot, and the bloody mosquitoes were never late in arriving in swarms.

When I finished chow and sterilized my utensils I kept an eye out for Captain Lackey. After he had finished and was walking to his cot, I walked up and asked if I could have a few minutes. He nodded. Then I told him all about meeting Major Hardison. When and if the 19th returned could I go with them as Major Hardison's co-pilot. He said, "Yes." Then he asked, "Was this the Lieutenant that was stationed at Fort Lewis and was grounded a year-and-a-half to two years ago." I told him that it was and that we were in the same squadron, and that once I had flown as his Observer in a O-47. The Captain said that he would like to see the Major for they had met several times. "Just keep me informed, and if the flying schedules permit, you may go with him." I thanked him and went to my cot. Grassi's cot was between the next two palm trees. I told Grassi what the Captain had said, and that he would like to meet the Major on his next mission to Moresby.

Tonight the enemy went all out for us and gave us a great show of fire works. First, for the evening meal came the strafers in two waves fifteen minutes apart. A slit trench is the only way that will save you with the bullets flying everywhere all at once. At 2130 and 2300 the bombers dropped demolition bombs and then daisy-cutters. Then, at 0200, two rounds of artillery came our way. The Aussies later confirmed that there were no more than three guns up there. After the second night I do not believe that anyone took his gas mask to the slit trench with him. It was always close by, but not in the hole with him. This kind of war will give you a real shot of adrenaline and keep you from sleeping. Then to top it all off, the CQ arrived at 0400!! Who said war was not hell!!

The next two days started out the same as the first day. Except most of the time only one element of three aircraft would drop at the same DZ. Each drop was at a different place. The drop zones were just small clearings in the jungle. When the Aussie ground troops could hear our aircraft they would light the smoke signals. We would fly over at treetop level to look over the "DZ" to see if it were Japanese or Australian. There was talk about having a strip cut out of the jungle in one of the valleys on the other side of the three 3,000 foot peak area. In this way, we could fly in troops, evacuate the wounded and deliver the supplies that we had been dropping with no damage or loss. It would save a three or four day walk for the infantry going to the front and be a lot safer. In that way we would be able to air-evacuate the wounded.

On 16 October 1942, while on the second flight of the day, the Squadron lost its first aircraft, flight crew and four Australian cargo pushers. They were on a combat mission dropping supplies in the area of Efogi. The C-47 was flying a 200-foot traffic pattern above the treetops when attacked by enemy fighters. In its attempt to evade the attackers a wingtip hit a tree and it cartwheeled into the jungle. The plane burned and all seven aboard were killed. The pilot was Second Lieutenant Wilson C. Cater, co-pilot was Staff Sergeant Pilot Glenn E. Webb and the crew chief was Master Sergeant Donald A. Mackey. Their radioman had severe diarrhea and they were flying without a radioman since no substitute was available. I was not with this flight group. It was flying to another DZ, but we heard many of the stories about the mission later that afternoon and for the next day or two. Having severe diarrhea when flying or during a bombing or strafing raid is very inconvenient. For some, most embarrassing, and right down dangerous for all. It usually requires a change of undershorts and pants.

The weather created its own special problems on the ground with the aircraft. There was so much moisture in the atmosphere in New Guinea that the electrical equipment soon acquired a corroded fungus growth. For that matter, all metal surfaces were subject to almost immediate corrosion. Ordinary lubricating oils in the hot temperatures seemed either to evaporate or simply run off.

The red alert sounded and shortly came three Zeros on the deck with machine guns firing death and destruction everywhere. Our defense forces, ack-ack and twin 50s, opened up, but hit nothing. The raids sure kept us on our toes. Fortunately, most of the time they made one pass and went home.

After our second mission on Monday, 19 October 1942, we landed at our new home base, Wards Airdrome, also known as 5-mile, APO 929. All Moresby bases had a second designation and that was the number of air miles from Port Moresby. The airstrip, taxiways, run-up, and all parking areas were covered with heavy gauged, Pierced Steel Planking. The PSP weighted 69 pounds. Each was made of 8'x 30" interlocking steel strips with many 3-inch holes evenly spaced the length and width of each strip. Landings or taking-offs on this surface was very noisy. Each aircraft was assigned a parking space called a revetment. Ours was No. 2, because we flew that position when in Squadron formation. The 6th Squadron's bivouac area was about a half a mile from our aircraft nestled in a very small valley between two knolls. Each of us was instructed to pick out a place to bed down. At this time we had pup tents. They would in the future be replaced with regular four-man tents. This was our bivouac area for the remainder of our tour of duty in New Guinea. It should take two to three weeks for our shipment of squadron household supplies to arrive from Brisbane. The first thing was to dig a slit trench and then a straddle trench and in that order.

For the next month until the shipment arrived from Brisbane, I planned to sleep on a cot under a mosquito net, under the left wing of our aircraft. It was more likely the safest place for that was what the enemy bombardiers were aiming for and their record was not very good.

This was the first time that we had seen any of the mechanics that we had flown up. They had been trying to set up shop and a camp site here at Wards. They had the first grass shack on the airdrome. They would do 1st and 2nd echelon maintenance on our aircraft. Fifteen of them were on flight status.

This meant that our own crew chiefs would not have to fly every day, which was a lot of help. Now, if we could get some radiomen and then some co-pilots, we would be in good shape. A consolidated mess was set up at Wards.

We also found out that the mechanics we flew up with when we arrived at Jackson were a Detachment of the 220th Service Squadron. They were to be our ground crew until the 6th's Ground Echelon arrived by ship. Disregarding hours, this Detachment under the supervision of Lieutenant Redford W. Chard, Squadron Engineering Officer, worked night and day to keep the planes flying. They did an excellent job. All aircraft maintenance was in the open, rain or shine, 1st, 2nd and some 3rd echelon maintenance. This included engine overhauling, repair of the aircraft accessories, and doing much of the sheet metal work.

Each afternoon after flying had been called off, due to the weather in the drop zone, all personnel were on a work detail digging slit and straddle trenches by our aircraft and in the camp area. Several lister bags were set up on the flight line and in the camp area. Four banks of showers, eight barrels to the bank were set up by the GIs. The officers erected their own. The hardest part was scrounging the plumbing. This was accomplished mostly by "moonlight requisition." One of the crew chiefs had been in supply, so he got the duty of trying to "Beg or Borrow" the plumbing fixtures. He also had to make the arrangements for toilet paper, soap, tooth paste and cigarettes. Each person was issued one free carton of cigarettes a week. He arranged for drinking and shower water to be delivered each morning. At first, I gave all my cigarettes to Grassi, but later I would use some of them for barter.

The Army Corps of Engineers, using two very small bulldozers, started clearing trees, scraping out and piling up a large, high, thick, 'U-shaped' mounds of earth around each of the squadron's aircraft. The top of the dirt was higher than the tail section of the aircraft. Each earthen revetment was large enough so the aircraft could taxi in, pivot around, doing a 180, and be headed back out. The purpose was to protect each individual aircraft from enemy bombs and strafing. It would require an individual direct bomb hit on each aircraft to do any damage. The mouth of the horse-shoe shaped parking bays was aligned so that a strafing enemy aircraft would have to make one pass on each aircraft and could not get lined up on more than one plane at a time.

Map of Port Moresby Area Airdromes
By January 1943 Port Moresby area had six airdromes

Open air canvas tent with a lister bag (water bag) hanging in front from a tree served as our engineering office for aircraft maintenance and repair. Most mornings an enlisted man added chlorine to the bag to kill contaminants, although the chlorine smell for the first few hours irritated men's eyes and lungs.

Next morning when we arrived for the briefing it was on hold because of low clouds and drizzle at the drop zone. Over the next year we had plenty of "Hurry up and Wait." In the Army you get plenty of it, and you never get used to it. Waiting is as old as the first warrior. I would like to have assumed that over the centuries the Army could have come up with a way to cope with this demoralizing problem. While waiting for the weather to clear, we were talking to the pushers. We wanted to know what we were hauling. We found out that the list went something like this: food (either dehydrated, canned, boxed, or dry), clothing, (mostly boots and pants), toilet articles, cigarettes, ammunition of different calibrators, depending on what was required, medical supplies, mosquito repellent, bed and head nets, steel helmets, and, of course, MAIL. Someone said, "It is the stuff that sustains life or takes life" that's what we flew.

After landing on 23 October, which was our 10th day in New Guinea, we were told that next week ten Australia co-pilots would arrive. They were assigned so we could get some time off. What about the radio operators? Headquarters was trying to fill that order. They should be here within ten days at the most. What about the aileron for the T-6? They are still looking.

It was time to clean my "45" for the first time. I removed my boots, spread out my one and only GI blanket, and reached for the cleaning kit and the 45. I ejected the magazine, pulled back the slide, and carefully removed the live round from the chamber. Being positive that at all times the gun was elevated to a 45° angle and not pointed toward anyone I made sure that the gun was now empty of all ammo. I then proceeded with a good cleaning. When completed, the gun was reassembled, and I slid the loaded clip into the pistol, and thumbed down the slide release. I pulled back the slide, placed one live round in the barrel and carefully slid the slide forward, and put on the safety. Then I removed the clip, added one more round, and replaced the loaded clip. I checked the other four loaded clips on the gun belt making a total of thirty-six (36) rounds. I needed to keep it better oiled as the rain, ocean air and humidity is a real problem in the tropics for all metals. From now on the 45 should be cleaned at least once a week.

On our next mission the T-6 flew overhead for the first time. We kept him in sight for the rest of the flight. After landing he came and talked with Captain Lackey. He said that on the way back when we were flying low on the treetops the only time he was able to locate us was when we crossed a clear spot in the jungle.

After debriefing we were told that "Major P.I. Pappy Gunn and his B-25" with a 75 mm cannon mounted in the nose was parked in the revetment at the southeast end of the runway. Pappy was the engineering-pilot who had perfected the flying cannon and modified the A-20 to carry the twenty-three pound fragmentation "parafrag" bombs. When we arrived, he and his crew chief were at the plane. He explained what he hoped the gun would do and how it worked. This was the forerunner of the aerial cannon that proved so effective against Japanese shipping.

After a few days we found that we could almost set our watch on the time when the strafers would arrive and from what direction. And yet our ack-ack never seemed to be waiting for them and seldom was able to shoot down one of the enemy aircraft. The Zeros always came in from the east, up the valley from the coast, on the deck with all guns blazing, spewing machine-gun death and destruction.

Next morning, at the briefing we were told that our drop zone would be ten miles north of where we had been dropping. There was a cleared area along the river in a big long valley. The Aussies were of the opinion that all Japs had been cleared out from the three peaks area to the drop zone. The plan was for the Allied Ground Forces to stop the pincer movement that the Japs had been trying to close in around Port Moresby when we arrived. Then they planned to continue on up the valley and cut off the main Japanese supply line on this side of the Owen Stanley Mountains. If they were successful, they would break the strangle hold the Japs had on Moresby and save our three airdromes in the Moresby area. This would permit more Allied Air Power to be moved into Jackson and Wards and stop the southward march of the enemy toward Australia.

Operations finally gave us the all-clear to go. The weather was to be low broken clouds until the destination. Once in the valley it should be clear with clouds covering the peaks. So we were to fly Contact Flight Rules (CFR) and stay below all clouds. If the weather closed in this would be our only drop today. We wanted to do our best to fly the necessities of life and the essential war supplies for the Aussies. These supplies were required because their ground supply line was stretched thin. It is very simple. The Army that gets their supplies and equipment when needed wins.

Take-off was as usual. When we came out of our valley we changed course and flew south of the three peaks staying below all clouds. Most of the way it was a solid overcast. Then we stayed in the valley on the east side of our first drop zone. We still had no air cover for the AT-6 could not defend or tangle with the enemy. It had to be just a matter of time before the Zeros caught us in the air. When we were on the deck over the jungle we should be safe from the air. When we flew over a cleared area or at altitude we were sitting ducks. When we arrived at the "DZ" it was a very small clearing in the jungle in a big level valley. The smoke pots were next to the trees at both ends of the drop zone. On the first pass we flew over to take a look, then got in trail formation and returned and dropped. It took ten passes to bail out two and a half tons of supplies from each aircraft simply because the clearing was so small. Some of the pilots over or under shot the drop zone and their boxes hit the trees at both ends. Pilots who had been through aerial and ground gunnery training were better at judging when and where to drop.

By the time we headed for home there was a solid overcast with a base of

800 feet at the DZ lowering to 600 feet at Moresby. The visibility under the clouds was three to four miles at the best with scattered showers. The flight back allowed us to practice flying on the deck below 100 feet going down to treetop. On occasion we would bring back tree leaves or kunai grass in the oil coolers. We were strung out in trail formation in the middle of the valley, which was no wider than the perimeter of the landing field when entering the hills just southeast of the base. Grassi shook my right arm and pointed up, saying "Japs". I could see two elements of enemy fighters in front and up at the base of the clouds heading for either Jackson or Wards. More likely the morning strafers had been held up due to the weather. Our leader must have seen them at about the same time because he made a right bank until we were near the hills on the northeast side of the valley. Then he made a 60° bank to the left and headed back down the valley for the ocean.

We flew out over the Coral Sea on the water for an hour at the very base of the overcast. We joined the coast at Hood Point by the sunken German ship, slowed to 120 with gear down, landing lights on and headed up the Military Corridor for Moresby. There we made a right turn over the ridge to Wards. At 250 feet over the middle of the field we made a 270 to land. The hilltop twin 50s gave us one blast. At that altitude and distance how could anyone miss?? Thank God, their aim at us was the same as when they fired at the enemy.

As soon as Captain Lackey was parked, he got in the alert truck and headed for the Anti-Aircraft's Headquarters. Their Commander was a First Lieutenant. We do not know what was said, but the gist was: learn your aircraft identification and learn how to hit your target. After the Australian Infantry, this was the first squadron stationed at Moresby. They were all trigger happy' and claimed that there was not enough time to check and identify an aircraft when it appeared. So they just started shooting. They must have had "Navy" ship training. A navy gunner's training is, "if you're a friend don't fly over our ship, if you're not a friend you had better not."

Then Captain Lackey told him the same story we were told when going through gunnery at Luke. "The ground school instructor would flash a silhouette of an aircraft on the screen at 1/100th of a second, and the students were to identify the aircraft. The student pilots were complaining that the slides were too fast. On the third day the instructor said that the next slide would be at 1/500th of a second and any student who could not identify the subject would be washed out. When the slide flashed on the screen there was a big laugh and everyone wrote down the correct answer. The instructor then told the students to study their identification books at least two hours a day until they knew all aircraft by heart, its dimensions, flying performance, capabilities and armament. You see the slide that was on the screen for 1/500th of a second was a 'Nude Blonde.' Not one student missed it. There is no reason that your men do not recognize the eight or ten different types of friendly aircraft that fly in this area. Your gunners need more aircraft identification practice. All of the fighter pilots have to recognize all aircraft in the South Pacific which are American Army and Navy, British, Australian and Japanese. They MUST know all their performances, armament and flight characteristics. If you do not have an instructor, I'll be glad to send some of my former pursuit pilots over to give some pointers. Stop treating us like hostile aircraft and do not shoot at us anymore." That was the last time we were shot at by our own troops when flying over Wards.

If our flight had been 20-30 seconds earlier or had we been flying at altitude, all ten C-47 aircraft, forty crew members and at least another forty Australian pushers would have been shot down and killed. Captain Lackey then got in touch with Brisbane and told them that the 6th was not a Suicide Squadron and that we needed protection and that we need it NOW!! If our planes were lost, there would be no support for the American and Australian Infantry. How long would the ground forces last with no supplies in the jungle during the monsoon season? They would not be able to walk, swim, or fly out for food, so you could forget the war in New Guinea. Within one week we had one P-40 for escort. What could it do against a flight of Zeros? More likely it would get all of us shot down. If the enemy spotted a lone P-40 flying, they would swarm all around it and certainly shoot him down. When they were directly over us, undoubtedly they would spot us and that would be our end. I made up my mind that my primary duty was to get my crew and aircraft back safely on every mission. Many times I wasn't sure that we were going to make it. I guess that this was the "freely chosen dangerous profession with flight pay" that the non-flying troops talked about.

Upon returning to our bivouac area we found that the Sergeant Major had made a trip to the beach at Port Moresby. He had picked up some boxes that Captain Lackey had shipped from the Army when we were on our way to New Guinea. After chow all First Pilots met with the Commander. He told us that when we were in Brisbane he was able to "Requisition" one 9" Case XX survival knife for each flight crew member, one air mattress for each First Pilot and twenty four-man tents. In time there might be more air mattresses. He told us to hand out to each crew member a knife and tell him to put it on his belt and keep it with him at all times. Then he explained that he was only able to get thirteen air mattresses. The scabbard I was handed was number "13," my lucky number. I secured the razor sharp knife in its leather sheath between the inner and outer leather holster of my "45." Now some sixty plus years later the knife is as shiny and sharp as ever.

Now we were getting rain and wind daily mostly in the afternoon and at night. Most of the flying was in the morning. Mosquitoes were always with us. The Atabrine may have kept us from getting malaria, but not the pesky mosquitoes. The mosquito head net was a nuisance, but it was essential.

Now that we had crew tents, I moved my cot from under the aircraft wing to the squadron area. All four of my crew moved into the same tent. We were in a banana field at the edge of a coconut grove. Before the war, this tract of land was farmed by Palmolive Soap of London. Bananas and coconuts were the only two crops that were commercially harvested on the Island.

At the next morning briefing we were told that we would be breaking the Squadron up and flying to more than one place all at the same time. My position for today would still be No. 2 wingman.

We will be dropping at "Supoto" in a large dry lake bed at 7,900 feet altitude. It is located just east of the Kokoda Trail and on the south side of the Owen Stanley Mountain divide near the summit Gap with a mountain peak within twelve miles over 5,500 feet higher than we will be flying. When on the final approach in the drop pattern we can't let our air speed fall below 100 mph. At this altitude the traffic pattern will be more spread out and we will have to add at least ten mph on all banks keeping an eye out for small arms fire from any enemy that may have evaded the pursuing Allied Ground Forces. Today we will have our first real fighter escorts. The reason is that we are so much closer to the Jap Air Bases, and more importantly the enemy cannot afford to let the Kokoda Trail be closed to their ground troops. In order for the fighters to protect us we must stay in close V-formation going and coming. If we should be attacked when in trail formation over the drop zone, we are to close back to V-formation and head down the mountain in a tight formation. If any aircraft should have mechanical trouble or get shot up, the fighters will have to stay with the main body of the flight. Captain Lackey said, "For any reason that I should fall out, Ford you and Weedin fall in the back of the squadron, and Lieutenant Wells your element is to move up and take over."

After take-off we flew in trail formation on the deck down the valley between the hills southeast of the airdrome where there were still snipers. So far only two of our squadron aircraft had been hit by the small arms fire. There was no major damage to a plane and no crew members or pushers were injured. The Squadron closed into

A coconut plantation near the air field reveals our makeshift clotheslines and a tin-can, warm-water laundry. Torrential rains and mildew were consistently a problem.

V-formation and flew tight stepped up javelin formation. Four P-39s moved in and kept close cover over the Flight Commander. There were at least four P-40s flying top cover. The weather was high thin cirrus clouds overhead with the lower clouds starting to build up over the mountains. Once in formation we made two wide climbing 360 degree turns to the left in order to gain altitude before picking up a heading of 045°, continuing to climb for the sixty-three mile flight to the "DZ".

At 8,300 feet we leveled off and immediately went into trail formation and started our drop. We lined up on the edge of the drop area. Parallel to the drop zone were rows of natives on both sides of the DZ. On my second pass, one native ran to catch one of the many boxes pushed out. The weight and

Flying in formation

velocity of the falling box drove him into the ground and he was killed on the spot. All planes continued to drop with the supplies falling all around the dead man. These were the only natives or soldiers I ever saw in the drop areas.

After the last pass we reassembled in formation and headed for Ward's Strip. At this time, 0810, broken clouds were already lowering down the sides of the mountains. Unless there was some other place to drop supplies this would be it for today.

From below the lower clouds we could see that the Japs had made their morning visit and had done their dirty work. Two columns of smoke were rising from both Jackson and Wards. Later we were told that one was a gas truck caught in the open and the others were supply tents.

We made one more mission going to "Gurney." This was the farthest from Moresby we had been since arriving. It was a round trip flight of 468 miles. Gurney is at the southeastern end of New Guinea near Milne Bay, which is also known as Fall River. Beyond Hood Point it rained like cats and dogs most of the way going and coming. From Hood Point down and back we were in trail formation flying very low out over the water hugging the coast line. We were able to drop without trouble. After landing back at Ward's Strip we could hear shooting coming from the hills off the end of runway 130. From about 1100 hours to 1700 there was a battle going on in the hills around the southeast perimeter of the airdrome. At the evening chow we learned that the Aussies had killed all the enemy in the take-off area. At this stage of the war in New Guinea no prisoners were taken. We made no more "Tree-top" take-offs and landings from Ward's Strip except for bad weather. It was still a 500-foot traffic pattern.

Today, being the last day of October, was pay-day. Troops were paid by their unit in cash. This was the first time any of us had ever walked up to the pay table armed with a loaded gun. We were paid in Australian Pounds. Each Pound (£) was equal to $3.80 American dollars. Now came the question, what to do with it? There was no place in all of Papua, New Guinea where you could buy anything. There was not one store on the entire Island. If you could not buy anything that only left five choices: sending it home in US Money Orders, buying US Saving Bonds, keeping it in your money belt where it turned green over night, gambling (which I do not, nor never did do), or a combination. It wasn't a big decision for me to make. As a Staff-Sergeant Pilot on flight pay I received $135.00 a month, less 25¢ a month for the Old Soldiers Home. So I sent $25.00 home, made out an allotment for two $18.75 Bonds and kept $72.25. That way if and when I ever got to Australia I would have some spending money. Many of the fellows gambled with three GIs in the squadron ending up with most of the money. At least two of the three were smart, for they sent their winnings home in money orders at least once a week. This seemed to be the pattern for the twelve months we were in New Guinea. The only way you could send money home from New Guinea was by U S Postal Money Order. That was taxable and the IRS had a perfect record. Later on some got into trouble for not declaring it as earned income.

On 1 November our aircraft was out of commission for a 100-hour inspection. So George and I did not fly. Of course Grassi, Gregg and some of the mechanics worked on Irene. George and I decided that if we could we would take a ride to Port Moresby.

I asked the Sergeant Major if there was anything to pick up in Moresby. He was not aware of anything. He offered us the squadron staff and command car until mid-afternoon. We thanked him and asked him to draw a map to Jackson Strip, Kookie Mission (the main island hospital) and on to Port Moresby. We also asked where we could get gas. After filling up by hand from a 55-gallon barrel, we headed for the coast about seven miles by road. Driving by the hospital we were dumbfounded to see so many tents with red crosses and a large cross in the center of the compound. You could see so much more on the ground because most of the tents were under camouflage nets.

Then we drove on to Moresby. There was nothing to the town. There were a few wooden buildings, quite a few grass shacks and more thatched overhead shelters on 12-14 foot poles. All they were for was to keep the sun out. They wouldn't stop much of the rain and were used mostly to stack goods under until they were moved. We met an American Army MP on duty at a fenced-in enclosure on the beach. I asked the directions to the docks at Port Moresby. He looked surprised and said that this is it. At night, one, maybe two, ships would come in and be anchored out in the harbor away from the beach. Then motor boats would ferry the cargo in and stack it here. The natives would load and unload the motor boats that ferried the cargo and troops form the ships to the beach. The organizations receiving the supplies would pick it up and have it moved out before daylight. All ships were in after dark and were out to sea before sunrise otherwise they would be an easy target for the enemy bombers and strafers. As long as there were no ships in the harbor, the docks, warehouses, or stacks of supplies were safe as the Japs seemed to stay away. It wasn't a worthwhile target. The troops being transported by water were handled the same way.

He then asked which field we were from. We told him Ward's Strip. He then asked, "What do you do?" We told him that we were both pilots. His reply was that all pilots are Officers. I asked if he would like to take a flight on his next day off. He said, "Yes, with real pilots." He said that he was off tomorrow. I told him that if he wanted a flight and would be at our aircraft at 0500 hours tomorrow morning, the real pilots would let him fly on one combat mission. Then I told him how to get there. You could tell that he wanted to go, but he did not believe that we were pilots. We thanked him and told him that we would see him at 0500 hours in the morning.

I drove a little farther down the beach road. All roads in New Guinea were either dirt or coral with plenty of chuck holes and either dust or mud. On the Island of New Guinea near the coast it rains all the time. It is either coming down as rain or its evaporating back up as steaming humidity.

We came to where several men were swimming in the nude. We asked why so many men on the beach were carrying their rifles and not in swim-

Village scenes west of Port Moresby. Native houses were built above ground to avoid flooding and to increase air circulation in order to provide some relief from the unbearable heat and mosquitoes.

ming. They told us that there were plenty of sharks and that they would come in almost to the waters edge. There was a posted rule that for every three men in the water, there had to be at least one rifleman on the beach, or one machine-gunner for every five in the water. As soon as a shark was shot everyone had to get out of the water for at least one hour.

I drove back down the hot, dusty, bumpy road to Jackson. We stopped at the same field kitchen where we ate when we arrived a fortnight ago, but we saw no one we knew and there were no B-17s on the strip. We stopped at our friendly barber shop. It was set up in the shade in a coconut grove. The barber chair was two ammo cases. The towel was a medical sheet. This was at the 101st Anti-aircraft Battalion Company area. It cost one half shilling, 23¢ for a haircut. Then we went back to Wards, refueled and returned the vehicle to the Orderly Room tent at 1312 hours. We had driven a grand total of twenty-two miles. The Sergeant Major told us that our troops had captured Kokoda this morning. That was great news. That meant that the main ground fighting would be on the other side of the Owen Stanley Range some sixty-three air miles away.

Then came the big news for our Squadron. Ten Australian co-pilots were

132

arriving that afternoon and would start flying on the 3rd day after today. We were asked to help get them settled in. We "volunteered" and wanted to know when and where they would be arriving. They should land at 1600 hours from Garbutt in an old C-39. We were to pick them up at Ward's Ops in the Squadron 6X6 and drive them back to the Orderly Room Tent. We needed to know where they were going to be billeted and we had to find out if supply had enough tents, cots, mosquito nets, and trench shovels. What about mess kits? After finding the answers we headed for the flight line to meet their aircraft. George and I met them. We introduced ourselves, welcomed them to the 6th, and told them how glad we were that they had come to help us. We told them what the Squadron's duties were and how many hours we flew. In our case, George and I each had flown 110:15 hours in October. They had just completed seven months at flying school and had a total of 200 flying hours. I drove them to the Squadron area and introduced them to Captain Lackey and the Sergeant Major. After a few words we took them to their "new homes" (their tents) that were being set up by the other squadron pilots. After the tents were up and mosquito nets were in place, we all walked a half mile to chow. Then we went back and everyone helped dig slit trenches.

Then Captain Lackey welcomed them to the 6th. He briefed them on the war situation, our mission, their work load, survival in the camp area, and how to walk out of the jungle. He told them that they were to be part of the Squadron and have the same rights, duties and responsibilities as all the other pilots. Tomorrow morning after chow go to operations and get on the flying schedule and be assigned to a pilot. He told them that across the field at this end of Wards were an Australian Beaufort Fighter/Bomber Squadron. They were flying American A-20s Havoc aircraft. When they were not flying, they should go over and introduce them-self and get acquainted. Their Commander's name is Captain Jack something or other.

Next morning at 0445 when we arrived at the aircraft there was our MP. I went over and introduced myself and told him that I was still the pilot. If he wished he could follow the crew chief and radioman around. I had to go to a briefing and should be back in about thirty minutes and that we were to be airborne no later than 0555. The co-pilot was to check the loading of the aircraft. Upon returning and making my walk around, I told the crew that we were going to Myola. The load was aboard and George was fitting and briefing the four pushers about the parachutes. Grassi had rounded up an extra parachute and had fitted and briefed our passenger.

The MP, a Private First Class, crawled over the cargo and followed George and me to the cockpit while Grassi stood fire guard. I told the MP that he could stand and watch us, but when the crew chief got aboard he would have to stand in front of him. We fired it up and followed the Commander to the warm-up area. He asked Grassi, "Are those two Sergeants actually going to fly this airplane?" Grassi smiled and said, "I hope so." On our first orbit after take-off the fighters joined up. George pointed out all eight P-40s to our passenger. We climbed to 8,400 feet in "V" formation heading for the Gap in the Owen Stanley Mountains. When over the drop zone we let down to 7,950 feet and out went the first drop. Grassi opened the cabin door and told him to watch the Aussies do their thing as we made another complete circle. Our passenger was all eyes.

Our passenger wanted to know why when the boxes hit the ground they did not smash to smithereens. We explained that from a height of 50 feet at a speed of 90-95 mph and the angle of release, the boxes would scoot along the impact area with a minimum of breakage. Everything is well packed and most boxes are in sacks. We told him to watch the cargo going out one of the other aircraft and he would see how it works.

The passenger asked me how long I'd been a pilot. I replied, seven months in flying school, six months since I received my wings, and before that I was a Private First Class, Third Class Specialist. He then wanted to know how he could become a pilot. George gave him the information and suggested that if he met all the requirements he should put in now. In that way, if he was accepted, that would be his next assignment after this overseas tour.

When we landed, he thanked us and said he'd like to go again. We told him that if we had the room, just look up No "39" and, if it was our day to fly, we would be glad to take him. He then said that some times when the ships unloaded they off-load empty shipping crates. These are good to make wooden floors to keep your tents off the ground. Anyone can have them just by hauling them away. All you need is a truck, claw hammer and pinch bar. Any of the MPs will show you where to go. It is all legal.

At our morning briefing on 3 November we were briefed that we would be landing at Kokoda Field, a wet, dirty, rocky and grass airstrip with plenty of filled in bomb and mortar craters. We had to be prepared for anything: all the way from mines in the landing field, artillery, small arms fire, to strafing and bombing by enemy aircraft. This airstrip had been captured less than twenty-four hours before and was still behind the enemy lines. The Jap's nearest fighter base, Poppendetta, was only twenty miles away. If we are unable to land we will drop our cargo at Myola and bring all the troops back to Wards. There should be some early morning scattered scud in the landing area. Now for the new crew assignment! I was assigned R.A.A.F. Sergeant Pilot C. I. Cox. He seemed like a nice enough chap. Later I found out that he was almost two years older than I was. That still made me the youngest in the crew.

George and nine others of the co-pilots that flew over with us got two days off and then went into a pool of co-pilots. George and I never flew together again.

When we returned from the briefing, I introduced our new co-pilot to the other two crew members. I told him that since we must be airborne and out of the area before 0600 hours, we would start his ground training after the last flight each day. For a few days he was just to sit and watch and do not touch anything. He was to ask any questions he wished and as often as he liked. Keep your eyes open for enemy aircraft, remembering flying school, "look out and glance in."

As we flew to the drop zone, I told Cox to take a good look at the terrain for we may have to walk out. If one does figure a Jap is behind every tree, of course there are a few hundred Yanks and Aussie infantrymen down there also. The trick is, if they are Allied troops identify yourself before they shoot you. Keep your gun holstered until you need it. A good infantryman can walk down the Kokoda Trail from the Gap to Moresby in three and a half to four days. Off the Trail it takes at least six weeks, if you're lucky. It will take us twice as long or more, that is, if we even make it.

Grassi and I kept up a constant chatter, calling out everything we were doing. I suggested that he mentally record the lay of the land, headings, and an estimate of the distance. We told him not to forget that he may have to walk out so keep a sharp eye out and remember the terrain and heading. Once we leave the traffic pattern here at Wards, the only way on the ground you can make it back on foot is with the aid of your compass. In the jungle you cannot even see the sun at high noon on a cloudless day due to the tall thick overhead jungle foliage. So keep your compass and signal mirror with you at all times and know the heading and the distance you must walk.

We made a normal take-off and joined up in formation with the fighters. We circled to gain altitude then continued to climb on course and headed for the Kokoda Gap. This was to be the first time we had been at an indicated altitude of 8,500 feet since arriving in New Guinea. We could see through the mountain pass to the other side of the Owen Stanley Mountains. From the lowest level of the Kokoda Trail in the gap it is sixty-eight air miles to Port Moresby. In order to get through the pass at this altitude we had to fly in trail formation. It was a calm morning with scattered clouds on the way to the top. From the pass to the landing field at an elevation of 1,260 feet it was almost straight down and a little to the west. Kokoda Strip is on the north side of the mountain range smack up against Mt Victoria, which is 13,440 feet. We made four tight spiraling diving circles to the right keeping between the Gap and the landing Strip. Two of the fighters went down and buzzed the field and drew no fire. The field was a clearing in the jungle with maybe 1,500 feet at the most from trees to trees. We three in the first element landed while the other seven circled overhead at 6,000 feet. Both American and Australian troops met us on foot. Captain Lackey flashed his landing lights and the other seven aircraft descended and landed. We throttled back keeping both engines idling as our troops and cargo were unloaded.

Sergeant Cox went out and talked to the Aussie Lieutenant in charge. They needed food and medical supplies plus everything else. Cox told them that we should return around noon weather permitting. Looking up high above was a flight of three Martin B-26 Marauders from Moresby headed to the northeast. The Martins at this time did not require an escort for they could fly faster and carry a heaver bomb load than any aircraft in the theater friend or foe. After the war, I read that this Squadron of B-26s shot down 94 enemy aircraft and the Japs shot down only six Marauders. What a record! This is almost 16 to 1 in our favor!! All our C-47s flew out air-evacuation patients. We had twenty-four stretchers (litters), and two walking patients. These were the first battlefield wounded patients to be air-evacuated from the jungles of New Guinea.

When the last plane was loaded the pilot flashed his landing lights and Captain Lackey took off. We had to stay back and parallel to the take-off path

Australian R.A.A.F. co-pilot C. I. Sergeant Cox and me posing in front of the right engine of the C47 "Irene".

in order to avoid the flying rocks, dirt and dust kicked up by the prop blast. It was a slow operation for ten aircraft to take-off one at a time as we waited for the dust to clear from the plane ahead. After the last aircraft was airborne we formed a V-formation in tight climbing 360 degree turns to the left and leveling off at 9,000 feet. The top of Mt Victoria was already covered with clouds and it was not ten air miles away. Off to the north and east was the Bismarck Sea with scattered clouds. Columns of smoke were rising from the B-26s bombing at Buna on the coast. After landing back at Wards, while watching the unloading of the evacuees, I observed that several of the patients had severe "jungle rot" in their feet. I also found out that these troops were the ones called "Swamp Rats."

We made one more mission to Kokoda Airstrip before the weather closed in. Irene was loaded down with thirty-two Australian infantrymen, all their gear, plus an Australian war correspondent. The newspaper man had flown with me on a dropping mission once before. Both times he stood behind the crew chief. He was all eyes and very talkative on both flights. We carried only twenty-eight passenger seats in a Gooney Bird. It is easy to see why Douglas called the DC-3 the "Skytrain." Two stood in the cockpit aisle and two sat on the floor with their gear in the cabin. Their Australian infantry Captain told us that the "War Plan" was to bypass and starve all the enemy on the south side of the mountains. If we could fly in enough troops and supplies before the monsoon started in earnest, the Allied ground troops would do the rest. The weather was marginal. Half way to the Gap we went into trail formation. We had slowed down to 120 mph and maneuvered our way up through the weather and the mountains. All our close P-39 escorts had full flaps and wheels down. They were in a nose high attitude in order to stay with us and were on the verge of stalling out. We were at an indicated altitude of 8,200 feet with not over a mile visibility and the gap is 8,000 feet, if we were at the lowest point. On the south side of the pass the mountains rose fairly steeply. The north side was close to vertical with a 13,440 foot peak within ten miles to the west and a 10,000 foot peak a little farther east. As soon as we could see clear sky on the north side of the mountains, the fighters took off and waited for us below the layers of broken clouds over Kokoda. We landed and all aircraft were unloaded and reloaded with evacuees for the return flight.

The return flight to Wards was one hairy flight. We took off and circled in trail formation up to 8,200 feet over the field. The escorts circled up to the base of the solid overcast with broken clouds below. The Squadron Commander then headed for the Gap which was within ten air miles from the east edge of the field. At this elevation the right wing was just feet from the trees and cliffs when a break appeared. Was this the Kokoda Trail or a dead end canyon between two of the mountain peaks? At flight level forward visibility was poor and not over a mile at the most. We were scraping the bottom of the clouds above us. This was only the second time any of us had ever been on the north side of the mountains and there were no maps. There were no mountains to the north with only broken clouds all the way to the Solomon Sea some twenty air miles away.

The Squadron Commander started to make a right turn as if entering the pass. Then at the last minute he made a steep left bank gradually decreasing the bank so as to be lined up straight into the pass. The flight of P-39s left us at this time letting down headed to the east. We did not see them again until the debriefing at Wards. Still, we could not see daylight on the other side of the Gap. We started another 360° turn to the left. Here we were at the very base of the clouds at 8,200 feet next to the mountains within 8-9 miles of the end of the airstrip. Cox began to shout and point down at 2:00 o'clock. He talked so fast I could not understand what he was saying. But looking down I knew. A flight of enemy fighters were strafing the airstrip. I told Cox and Grassi to keep close count on all the enemy aircraft. If we did not go through what appeared to be the pass this time, I would break formation, then climb in the clouds on a heading of 45° until reaching the top of the clouds or 15,000 feet, whichever came first. Then I would fly a heading of 180° for one hour, let down over the Coral Sea and return to Wards.

By this time our Leader was entering what we "prayed" was the correct opening. At 8,100 feet on a clear day, we did not have enough room to do a 180 and we were now committed. One hundred feet above the treetops, hitting the base of the overhead clouds with far less than a mile of forward visibility, mountains on both sides, enemy fighters strafing below us and our fighter escort having already left us, what do you do? PRAY, and FLY ON!!

We flew in close trail formation on a heading of 232. There was no room to be above or below the Leader, or on the left or right of his aircraft. So we just stayed in the prop wash, a river of turbulent air, kept following the leader and fighting the controls all the way. After five minutes we knew that we were through the pass but the clouds were still on the treetops. I moved up into V-formation, so if Captain Lackey should hit something I might have some maneuvering room on the right and I would be out of that terrible prop wash.

With each turn of the prop the funnel of mountains leading from the Gap became wider. Staying on the treetops we were descending in altitude. At 6,500 feet the visibility and ceiling improved so we could fly normal V-formation. There were two more broken layers of lower clouds. We circled down in the clear to the base of the lower deck at 800 feet and skirted around the fighter and bomber bases, and made a straight-in approach to Wards in rain and gusty winds.

At the debriefing, the P-40 and P-39 flight leaders were there with fire in their eyes. They claimed that we were stalling them out and then leading them into a boxed-end mountain canyon pass at stall speed with only 100 feet ceiling, a half a mile visibility, and no room to do a 180. Captain Lackey, said, "That is true, but my mission is to fly troops, food, medical supplies, ammunition, cargo, and air-evacuate the wounded, when and where needed."

"The Japanese first landed in New Guinea 21 January this year. The 6th Troop Carrier arrived 13 October, less than three weeks ago. When we arrived the enemy was at the door steps of Port Moresby only five air miles from Jackson. Now they are some eighty miles away and on the north side of the Owen Stanley Mountains. For the Japanese there is only one way for their soldiers and supplies to get to Moresby and that is by foot over the Kokoda Trail. We THE 6TH TROOP CARRIER SQUADRON simply stopped and cut him off by jumping over him with men and supplies. According to General MacArthur and General Kenney our Squadron, the 6th Troop Carrier, is responsible for making this turn around possible. The 6th stopped the enemy, turned him around and headed the Japs back north. This is war and we all must do our very best to feed the most bullets possible to the enemy. Without the 6th doing its part, it would not have happened. I rest my case."

This speech took all the wind and fire out of them. The P-39 Flight Leader spoke up and said, "I now understand why we must protect the transports at all cost. Please try to help us. When airborne, keep your airspeed up to at least 140 mph, a ceiling of 300 feet and two-mile visibility." That ended the discussion. The Briefing Officer said, "We can fight the war, but we cannot command the troops." He then told us that the enemy strafers at Kokoda Strip had shot up a lot of the supplies that we had just off-loaded from our aircraft, but that there were no reports of deaths or injuries. The ground troops had no way to protect themselves or the newly off-loaded supplies from the enemy air attacks.

At 1345 hours we had a tin can of C-rations, two bananas, which we each picked, a salt pill and all the hot canton water we wanted then went back to work. The engineer and radioman checked over Irene, refueled, serviced, tied-down and chocked the wheels for the night. The rain and wind both had picked up. There was no need to try to do a walk around, point out and explain the function of each part of the aircraft in this kind of weather. I told Cox that if we should get a break in the rain, I'd look him up and we could do some "Hanger flying" about the bird. If not, we would have to wait until tomorrow.

We went back to the camp area and listened to the rain coming down and the wind blowing the tent. We had to go out and enlarge the trench around the sides of the tent so the gushing water would not run under our canvas floor. Our "Home", an Army GI four man tent, was located on a slight rise at the edge of a banana field. There were coconut trees everywhere. However, we did not pitch our tent under one because, in high winds, when the coconuts fall they could kill you if they hit you on the head. There was a small ditch on the other side. Right now the ditch was overflowing its banks and was a raging torrent of water. In the monsoon season we had torrential rains and everything was rain-soaked.

One of our squadron C47s viewed from the cockpit window.

All our tents had canvas floors with mosquito nets on all four sides with a zipped up door and windows. They were still nothing more than a "hothouse". Each cot had a mosquito net strung out over it on a "T" bar at both ends of the cot. When we were outside before sunset and until after sunrise mosquito headgear nets were the order of the day. Still there were flies, gnats, insects and mosquitoes by the trillions. It was a constant swat, swat, slap, slap, and we would repeat it all over again. The only sure way to get away from them was to fly. Looking out you could see water running down from all four corners of the tent and gullies of warm water running every where.

Today was my day to clean and oil my "45". It would be nice to have a nice clear, dry, low humidity sunshiny day. But that is when we fly, not clean our artillery. I took off my GI boots, spread out my GI blanket, got out the cleaning kit and my gun, and went to work. Actually, the job only takes a few minutes. It takes longer to get out the cleaning kit, set it up, and put everything away, than cleaning the gun. When taking infantry training we had to assemble the 45 blindfold in 45 seconds.

I went to sleep and when I awoke it was night and my tent mates were hollering, "Ford, get in the hole, air raid!!" With one swoop of my arms I had the required equipment for an hour or so in the slit trench. It had slacked off from the heavy rain, but was still pouring. When I got in the hole, the water was level with the top. And this was to be our "Survival Escape!" I got out and went back to the tent, put my gun, boots and wet clothes on the back of the bench. I picked up two empty one-gallon peach cans and went back to the "Swimming hole" in my underwear, steel helmet and head mosquito net. I passed one of the cans to the other end of the hole. With two of us bailing the water out we were able to keep the water level low enough so our heads were below the top of the slit trench. The water was warm and that was the only good thing about it. It turned out to be a nuisance air raid, but the fifty minutes was not wasted. We decided to build a bank all the way around the slit trench, cover the top with PSP and a foot of sod, leaving an entrance opening at both ends. We created a large banana leaf rain shelter with a good overhang to keep the rain out. The thatched roof was to extend well beyond the water trench.

On the 5th, the Squadron was split up and dropped at several locations. I was sent out as a single aircraft without fighter escort. I was scheduled for two drops weather permitting. The first mission was to be at Skinewai, and the second one at a new location near Poppendetta. On the first mission to the Drop zone, there was a high overcast, with a middle deck of broken and lower scud just above the trees. In the lake bed where I was to drop, there was no lower deck and the ceiling and visibility were fair. I made the drop and returned to Wards.

When we parked, the next load was waiting and the gas truck was parked across from our revetment. I told Grassi to fill the tanks as we might need it. The Australian truck driver told me that we were going back to Skinewai again. Shortly after wheels up, we were in a light drizzle and low ceiling with a mile to a mile and a half visibility. This was strictly time, distance and heading navigation, but we got there. I knew that to the left and straight ahead was a rising terrain. Everything to the right was no higher than the sloping treetops all the way to the ocean. We flew till the river came in sight, then turned left and shortly came to the smoking fire pots. We made a 300 foot compass heading traffic pattern, pushing the cargo out below the treetops with all boxes landing in the DZ. I waggled my wings, disappearing over the treetops in the clouds to the southeast.

In the forty-five minutes it took us to drop the load of supplies, the weather had deteriorated to nothing and closed in down to the treetops. We climbed straight ahead in the clouds and had rain to 1,000 feet, turned right to 180° and headed for the coast taking note of the time. I told Cox and Grassi to sound off if there were any breaks in the weather below. After thirty minutes we started descending. At 300 feet in a rain squall we could see the churning waves below. I did a 180° and headed back for a land fall. We reached the coast somewhere below Hood Point turned left and followed the shoreline until we saw the beached ship on our left, dropped the gear, slowed to 120 mph and turned on the landing lights. I briefed Sergeant Cox on Hood Point and the ship. We continued flying up the coast. Both pilots had soaking wet shoes and feet. Just before Moresby at Bootless Inlet we turned right inland to Wards three miles from the coast and flew over the main hospital at 400 feet. We received a green light from the tower and landed. By the time we were parked, the squall line had pushed ashore and we were in heavy rain and high winds. I had Grassi get out and put on all the control locks, chocks, wing tips and tail tie-downs before cutting the engines. A few days before the Corps of Engineers had set anchors in the coral below the PSP for permanent wingtips, main gears, and tail wheel tie-downs. Each time the aircraft was parked it had to be at the exact spot in the revetment so it would match up with the tie-downs.

Cox and I went to be debriefed. Normally only the pilot would go, but Cox should see what it was all about. Other than the info about the flight and weather, I told the Briefing Officer that he might want to call the hospital commander and explain why I was so low when we flew over the hospital. It was either that or stop in for a visit and I did not see a welcoming mat so I continued to home base. He then told us that another of the 6th planes was missing and they were afraid it had been shot down. Our missing aircraft was going around the top of a small hill in the traffic pattern to make the next drop. The infantry reported seeing Zeros diving and hearing machine gun fire, then seeing smoke from the other side of the hill. Our aircraft had only made two drops and never returned to continue dropping. He then told us that it was Lieutenant Majure's plane. I asked what about search planes. He told us that the weather was too bad. The infantry was putting on a push to see what they could find and would keep us informed. If true, this was our second loss. This was the Officer who took me to visit his brother on the submarine in Hawaii.

Cox and I returned to our aircraft and told Grassi and Gregg that we should go eat, and I would talk to Captain Lackey. As soon as the weather cleared there would more likely be a search flight. So when you can, refuel. I went to the orderly room. The other eight First Pilots were already there. I expressed my sorrow, concern, and reported that our crew was ready to go on the search as soon as weather would permit. I also told them I had met Lieutenant Majure's brother and had been aboard his submarine while we were at Hickham. Captain Lackey spoke up and said that he knew I was going with "Harold" before we went to Ford Island on the third of October. I am sure that no other pilot in the tent would have believed me if the Commander had not spoken up. Over the next two to three days most of the pilots asked about the submarine visit, and why was I asked to accompany Lieutenant Majure. The only reason I could think of was that we had the same instructor at Milwaukee and had been several places together in groups. Many of the GIs also wanted to know.

Captain Lackey told us that the weather was too low now and that the American Infantry was keeping operations informed of their progress in locating the wreckage. If it was not located by daylight, weather permitting, to and from our missions, we would swing by the search area for a look-see. By the next morning the 126th Infantry had found the burned out wreckage with no survivors. On Saturday, 7 November 1942, there was a Memorial Service for the crew. All of the flight crews who had returned from their last mission of the day attended. The badly burned bodies had been buried at the crash site and the Grave Register will eventually, after the war, send the remains to a permanent resting site.

At the morning briefing on the 5th, my second flight had been scheduled to take the mission that Lieutenant Majure was shot down on. But since the Aussies needed more supplies at my first drop zone, I was sent back there for a second trip. When the word came back that the plane at Poppendetta had been shot down most of the squadron thought it was Irene. Several of the ground crew were surprised to see us. One of the sergeants even told me that they were about ready to divide up our things.

On the eighth of November, Dobodura Airdrome became operational. It was only five ground miles from the ground fighting and was a little less than four miles by air. This was one huge clearing on a flat level plain with nothing within fifteen miles that was over 200 feet above sea level, that is counting the tops of the trees, and many of them were 200 feet tall. If it was not blowing dust, it was blowing rain. When it rained, which was almost every day this time of the year, the field was nothing but muddy ruts, a real quagmire. All one had to do was to line up with the wind sock and land, at any one of 360°. That is, if your approach was from the south, west, or east, otherwise you were over the front line where a ground battle was raging. This was the biggest land engagement so far in the New Guinea campaign. We flew out a load of wounded. Some of the wounded combat infantry soldiers had cut the seat out of their trousers. When I asked why, they told me they had such severe dysentery, and were in such close combat, that they did not have time to drop their pants. I got to talking to one of the wounded Australian passengers, a Captain who had just come from Buna. He had several Japanese war souvenirs that he had picked up on the battle field. One was a Japanese Battle Flag, which he gave to me. I still have it.

Within one week our tent had the plushiest slit trench in the area, if not in all of New Guinea, thanks to George. He collected a carton of cigarettes from each of us. Then he drove to the port at Port Moresby, located our "MP" friend at the dock and traded one carton for eight PSP planks. We enlarged the slit trench so that the opening at each end was 20 inches and 20 inches of room in the trench for each of the four of us when under the PSP which was covered over with two foot of dirt. George then located the Aussie that had hired the natives to construct the banana leaf long-hut for our aircraft maintenance personnel. That cost two more cartons. A few days later there was no more water in our slit trench.

I wrote a V-mail letter home and it went something like this:

```
From where I am. On this date


Dear Mom and Dad,


   The weather is as usual for this time of a
year, in this part of the world.
```

We see the indigenous personnel here ever day
but we do not fraternize with them. That is a no-
no.

My duties are as safe as they could be. I do
a lot of what I was trained to do. It is always
interesting and sometimes very exciting.

Please, give me all the news from home. Dad
will tell you why I cannot write anything.
Hope all are well.
With love
Ernie

The next morning the rain and wind had stopped, but there was plenty
of fog. The question, should we try to take-off in the fog or wait until after the
strafers departed or would they even come? Well, they did not come and we
did not go. At 0830 we received a clearance to go and we were airborne by
0840. The Squadron broke up into flights and went to three different drop
areas. We, in the first element, flew back to Kokoda and dropped supplies.
The same tail numbered P-39s that were with us two days earlier were escorting us today, but I do not know if it was the same pilot. The smoke pots were
out along with a few troops and a large group of natives well to the edge of
the field. The ceiling and visibility was fair, and the Airacobras (P-39s) were
able to stay with us all the way, but we never did see the high cover.

By this time several of our troops had malaria and many had dysentery.
That is one thing that does not go with flying combat. The Medic again
warned us about the critical need to take our Atabrine and salt tablets. He
then stressed the importance of proper cleaning of our Mess Gear. I was
extremely lucky for I never got either. I did have a few head colds, but only
after returning from Sydney which was 2,000 miles to the south.

The 374th Troop Carrier Group was activated on 12 November 1942. It
was composed of the 6th, 21st, 22nd, and 33rd Troop Carrier Squadrons.
Lieutenant Colonel E. S. Nichols was designated as the Commander. Then
on 14 December, Major Edgar W. Hampton was appointed Commander and
Lieutenant Colonel Nichols returned to the United States. On 17 December
1942, Colonel Paul H. Prentiss, was assigned to the Group and assumed Com-

mand. In a few months, I attended his promotion party to Brigadier General. After the war, when he was Base Commander where I was stationed, I attended the party that returned all Generals in the Army Air Corps to their permanent rank, in his case full Colonel. During my military career I had the privilege to serve under Colonel Prentiss during four different tours of duty.

The next morning the weather was on the ground. There always seemed to be more waiting than doing. Cox and I spent most of the day on the flight line going over the various aircraft systems. In between the rain squalls we would go over the outside walk-around inspection. He was very eager to learn and had studied the dash one. He knew a lot of the answers, but not too many of the "whys" and "wherefores."

One of the first things we noticed about our Aussie co-pilots was that at 1000, 1400 and 1600 hours it seemed that they had to boil their Billie (tea). I actually believe, if the bombs were falling and it was tea time, they would have raise their hands, palm up, and the bombs would stop in mid-air until tea time was over. It seemed that on every mission Cox would point out and explain something about the interesting animals, birds, and vegetation of New Guinea. The Bird of Paradise is a protected bird, although that does not apply to the natives. The Natives use the Bird of Paradise feathers for part of their ceremonial headdress. There are eight species of the Bird of Paradise in New Guinea, of which the rarest is the "great emerald," or as the natives call them, the "sun bird." Each sun bird has many spectacular colors. It has two long thin, beautiful, tail feathers. On many flights we could see the birds flying in flocks and just above the tops of the trees. Along parts of the coast, at times, we could see clouds of waterfowls. At the most, I never walked over three miles into the jungle. I never saw any of the huge blood sucking leaches, big frogs, or pythons and I'm not complaining. The stories were enough.

A few days after the Aussie co-pilots arrived, our Australian Flight Surgeon arrived. A Dispensary Tent was set up next to our tent. The Doctor with his family had been a Medical Missionary in New Guinea for 15 years before the war. When the war in the Pacific started, his family was sent back to Australia and he was called back to active duty as a Medical Doctor in the Royal Australian Air Force. "Doc" told us many interesting stories about the natives and their strange customs. He was the only one in our outfit who could speak to and understand the natives.

Native men in full dress are pictured behind the wing of one of our aircraft.

For the next few days the Squadron flew in formation, three Vees of three each with heavy escort to a newly opened Airstrip at Popondetta. It was near Buna on the north coast, which at this time was the enemy's main ground base in New Guinea. On the north side of the mountains we flew below 300 feet down to a 50 foot traffic pattern. On almost every mission we observed flights of Zeros. Our escorts were able to keep them at a distance. At the same time B-17s and B-26s were bombing their airstrip so they did not have much time or interest in coming our way. We flew in mostly troops, for the big drive on Buna. The return flights were always full of wounded. On the next flight I flew in a jeep with five Australian troops. It was the first jeep I saw north of the Owen Stanley Mountains. An Australian Major and his Sergeant were the only two that I ever saw driving it. I was not the first to fly a jeep over the mountains.

For our next mission only a partly filled truck load of PSP arrived. The driver pulled away and four Aussies started to climb aboard. I told them to hurry up and give me a load because the weather was closing in over the mountains. The Aussie Sergeant said that was 5,700 pounds. I looked inside again and looked at Grassi. I then told the driver to bring another load. He signaled for another load and they put it aboard. That still did not look like much of a load to me. I had a talk with this driver and he said that we now had 11,400 pounds, which was two plane loads. Grassi and I looked at the oleo struts, they were both way down, almost on the bottom. As soon as we started to taxi I knew that Irene was way overloaded. We circled and circled to get over the pass. Dobodura was the only Air Strip in all of New Guinea where we could have ever made a safe landing with this load. We touched down at least 500 feet from the normal touchdown spot at 120 mph. No more two loads of one hundred sixty-five PSP planks at one time for me! We were very glad to see the PSP being laid. Landing in the churned up mud 4-6 inches deep is not the desired thing to do. You want to make sure that when landing in the mud the aircraft is tail low so as not to nose over. It takes a lot more power to taxi and take-off. On landing, the aircraft slips and slides around, and you have to use a lot of extra power to make turns for the brakes are of little help. The prop wash would throw mud all over the elevators and tail section. It never happened to me, but some of the aircraft would get holes torn in their elevators and flaps from the flying chunks.

For the next several missions we flew 14 barrels of 55 gallons of gasoline on each flight. We flew in troops, ammunition, gasoline (both 78 and 91 octane), bombs, food, a small medical hospital, medical supplies, and jeeps. In fact, if the army needed it, we flew it to them, as at this time and location this was the only way the ground troops could get anything. The Japs were putting up a terrific air and a savage ground battle to keep what they had. After we got fighter escort our air cover gave us the best protection they could with the limited number of fighters that were available. Most of the time our best protection was clouds and the treetops. Other Squadrons in the Group had more planes shot down than the 6th, and they flew far fewer missions.

One of our Sergeant Pilots was flying with the left starter motor out. When he taxied up to let his load of troops out, he just idled back the engines. The props stirred up clouds of dust. One of the troops on the ground who was getting dusted off was an American Infantry Major. He walked up in front of the left prop and hollered and moved his thumb across his throat to indicate cut the engines. The pilot looked down and pointing to the left engine, he shouted and tried to indicate that he could not shut the engine off. After the Major had tried several times without any luck, he took his right hand and put it on his oak leaf and again signaled to cut the engine. The Sergeant stuck his left arm out the cockpit window with his Staff-Sergeant chevrons showing and shook his head, "NO." It is a wonder that the Major did not either get in the cockpit or shoot the Sergeant. The only thing that happened at Dobodura about this incident was when the aircraft taxied away all the ground troops got dusted off again. For the next few days the Sergeant took a ribbing about pulling rank on a Major.

Flying an aircraft without a starter motor was not uncommon. During our year in New Guinea all of our pilots had to do it several times. Flying in New Guinea, aircraft parts were hard to come by and were at a premium. To start the engine without a working starter motor meant it had to be hand cranked from the ground. It is a very fast, tiring, laborious, sweaty job. In this heat it was very easy to flood the engine and that might take a twenty-minute wait before the cranking could start all over again. In case of an attack either by air, ground, or naval bombardment (Dobodura was not far from the Bismarck Sea), an aircraft with a dead engine and no functional starter motor would be a sitting duck. More likely the crew, passengers, cargo, and aircraft would all be lost.

A few days later, I flew a load of air evacuees and an Army Colonel back to Wards. The Colonel came forward, looked around and asked several questions. On the way back to the cabin, he told the crew chief that we had flown him and his men over ten days ago and that now he had to go to a meeting in Moresby. "On the way over your pilot was a Staff Sergeant. Now he is a PFC. Why was he busted?" Grassi smiled and told him that he was still a Staff Sergeant Pilot. There was a shortage of flying clothes so he was wearing an old pair of coveralls he had before he got his wings. The PFC stripes were dyed on and they would not come off. He gets some kidding, but he just laughs.

Now that we were flying on the north side of the Owen Stanley Mountains, at night and any time that the Airstrip was not in use, the ground crew would roll empty 55-gallon gasoline barrels out on the landing field. This would prevent the enemy from bringing in a landing force by air.

Today, the first Japanese POW that I saw was flown in to Wards. He was a young, bare footed kid, said to be twelve years old, clad only in a thin pair of black pajamas. He was blind-folded with his hands tied behind him. He was guarded by a 6'4" Australian Infantryman with a fixed bayonet. One of the interpreters was questioning him. The few times I saw a POW being questioned, it was always by a Japanese-American Nisei and they were always

Native men prepare to offload a tractor-bulldozer at an advance air strip, while Australian soldiers look on.

escorted by Military Police for their protection. Then three shots rang out, everyone jumped in a hole. The POW was put in a trench by himself. After the "All Clear" he was pulled out and was bleeding profusely from the mouth. No bombs or shrapnel came in our area and there was no ground fire. He was examined and it was determined that he had chewed off his tongue so he would not have to answer any questions. The Japanese military code forbade surrender under any circumstances. The Japanese regarded POWs as a disgrace, cowardly criminals, scarcely human. For a Japanese to guard prisoners was almost as dishonorable as being one.

The next afternoon, one of the Aussies' A-20s returned from strafing and frag bombing at Lae all shot up. Most systems of the "Havoc" were hydraulically operated. The pilot was unable to lower flaps or wheels. He came in and made a wheels-up landing on the grass next to the PSP and slid to a stop at the far end of the overrun area. The nose of the Douglas came to rest next to a bank in the grass and weeds. The name of the aircraft was "Lawn Cutter", its logo was a picture of an old hand-pusher lawn mower. After each mission a Jap's Head was painted above and behind the whirling mower blades so that it appeared that another Jap's Head came flying out. The "Lawn Mower" stopped in the grass positioned just like it would be if it were cutting grass. The plane was well shot up and looked like a sieve, but the pilot and gunner both got out without a scratch. In a few days it was back to flying again.

I told the Operations Officer that any time that I was not on the flying schedule, if they needed a pilot I'd like to fly. That at any time I was in New Guinea and was off for more than one day at a time, "Please, put me on the schedule, even if my crew does not wish to fly." I told them that I would be glad to fly with another crew.

Extracted from the 374th Troop Carrier Group Historical Report:

"Since attack by enemy aircraft was probable and expected during all flights in and around New Guinea, the Troop Carrier Pilots made maximum use of natural camouflage. We would fly as low as possible and choose the terrain which harmonized best with the aircraft camouflage, thus avoiding being silhouetted against the sky and making maximum use of cloud cover. The pilot, co-pilot, and engineer kept constant visual watch for enemy aircraft. All unidentified planes were considered hostile and evasive action was taken immediately. Both pilots and the radio operator maintained a constant radio watch."

"When letting down after crossing the Owen Stanley Range to the north, the pilot would loose altitude as fast as practicable until reaching tree top level. Approaches to the fields such as Dobodura were seldom made at altitudes of more than 300 feet above the tree tops. During the fighting in the Buna Area, transports were seldom more than 50 feet above the tree tops, even when making steep turns. Turns were made as close to the field as flying safety would allow."

"Landings at advanced airdromes in New Guinea were, as a rule, quite hazardous. Heavily loaded planes had to be landed on short fields that were often wet, muddy, slippery, very rough and with a surface of either grass, rocks or a combination. Of course, some had the added attraction of enemy ground fire and most had enemy aircraft. The ground troops said that is why we got our flight pay. Some of the strips were on inclines that at Wau rose one foot in twelve with a 12,000 foot mountain at the end of the field. This made it impossible to go around. The approach and landing at Bulolo was slightly downhill, on a hilltop in the bend of a river, the Airdrome itself being short, rough and always wet. The Bena Bena Strip was perched at 5,700 feet altitude on top of a sharp ridge with a sway-backed, curved, grass runway. Most landings in New Guinea were subject to cross and down winds, which were often quite violent."

"Weather over the Owen Stanleys was almost as serious a hazard as hostile aircraft. Vertical cloud development began rather abruptly and clouds often built up in front of a plane faster than the fighters could climb."

"Once Group Operations became functional, they controlled flight scheduling of all formations and individual flights. Special consideration was given to highly experienced pilots who expressed a willingness and eagerness to make additional flights after flying in general had been canceled because of weather. This concession by experienced pilots paid dividends in terms of thousands of pounds of extra freight, troops and evacuating wounded without a single mishap resulting. Experienced pilots sometimes completed two or three missions after the majority of aircraft were grounded."

While in New Guinea this was the main reason why Staff-Sergeant Pilot David C. Vaughter and I flew so many more missions than any other pilots in the 6th TCS, 374th TCG, and, later on, the 54th TCW. After flying was called off on account of weather for the day and the other crew members were tired, we would round up a flight crew on our own. Group was always happy for us to fly. Vaughter and I both just loved to fly although we never did fly together.

The weather briefings for our first five months of flying in New Guinea always seemed to call for torrential rain, clouds higher than the fighters could fly, with plenty of strong gusty wind. The Weather Officer would often say, "It will always stop raining before it clears up." Someone started calling him, "Stormy," and it stuck. For the most part, when flying in New Guinea, decisions on the weather were left to the individual pilot since the weather changed so rapidly. There are only two kinds of flying weather in New Guinea, "lousy or damn lousy".

There is only one negotiable air pass through the peaks in this area of the Owen Stanley Mountains. The "HUMP" was an extremely narrow, twisting gap at 8,000 feet. Peaks were a mile higher all around that are hidden in the clouds most of the time with mist and rain hanging down into the foothills. The expression was, "The clouds are filled with rocks!!"

NOTE: The Kokoda Pass was the original "Hump." This is where the expression "Flying the Hump" originated. It was not in the CBL, as some claim.

6

Kokoda

ON 17 NOVEMBER 1942, WE WERE SENT SOLO to a drop zone near the Wairopi River and Kokoda Airstrip without escort. The weather should be below enemy fighter flying. I was briefed that during the night the P-40 fighter squadron had run out of parachutes and they could not fly without chutes. The Group Operations Officer told them to borrow two chutes from the 6th TCS aircraft. How could we be so lucky? I went back to Irene and told the crew that we had no parachutes, and it was up to us if we wished to fly. The lead Australian Sergeant spoke up and said. "It is up to you, but I know that my outfit sure needs these supplies." I then asked Cox and he replied, "It is up to you." Grassi and Gregg both said, "You go, we go." I replied, "That's what we're paid to do. Let's go." On the way over there were many more clouds lower than usual for this early in the morning and the weather was building up fast. We were able to wind our way up to and through the pass and then let straight down below to the DZ.

I lined up in the small clearing with the smoke pots, headed west as near the sheer mountain cliff off the left wing as I dared and made six normal drops. On the seventh and final pass, I turned on the green light and bell. Within a second at 90 mph, 50 feet above the ground and well below the tree-tops, the aircraft swung violently to the left, shuddered, shook with severe vibrations and became all but uncontrollable. I added take-off power to the

Eastern New Guinea and New Britain

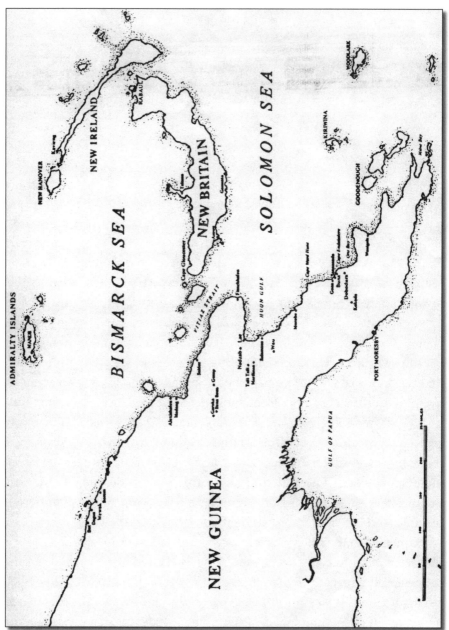

left engine, reduced power on the right engine, and called for a quarter flap. At the same time I applied full right rudder and aileron in an attempt to straighten out the aircraft, gain altitude, and kept from flying into the trees and the side of the mountain on my left. In gaining altitude out of the DZ area we flew through the tops of the trees at the end of the clearing. It did not seem to affect the flight characteristics of the shaking aircraft. I told Grassi to go see what was wrong. At 90 mph the aircraft wanted to spin to the left, below 85 mph it was shuddering and was on the verge of stalling. At 87 mph I could maintain directional control and climb at about 1-200 feet per minute. My arms were trembling and right leg was violently shaking totally exhausted from all the strength required to keep the "bird" in the air climbing out straight and gaining altitude. This gives you a real shot of adrenaline. By now we were above the trees and far enough from the side of the mountain for me to lean down and crank in full right rudder and aileron trim. I had better control with a half-needle right bank than turning to the left into the damaged elevator.

Grassi came back and said, "We have BIG trouble." I replied, "Tell me something I do not already know. What is it?" He said, "The main cargo door came off, turned about 45° to vertical and was stuck on the left stabilizer. During the last drop, all 700 pounds of the outgoing cargo hit in the middle of the door and bent it over the stabilizer. This widened the leading edge of the stabilizer to at least 18", cut the deicer boot in two, and more likely weakened the whole tail section and for sure the left stabilizer. Tree leaves and small twigs were stringing out behind both trailing edges of the flaps. This is from flying through the trees in our climb out of the drop zone." We were now at 500 feet and climbing. I sent Cox back to have a look to see if we might try to shake it off if we could climb to maybe 5,000 feet. Gregg came in over the intercom and said that Dobodura, 20 miles to the northeast, was being bombed and had heavy fighter escort. It was the only field on this side of the mountains that was long enough for us to attempt a landing. Cox could not fly, so I could not go take a look. When the co-pilot returned his report was basically the same. I told him about the bombing raid going on off to our right, and asked him to keep an eye out for enemy aircraft and clouds. Our Aussie co-pilot said, "This is a fair dinkum one-way ticket to immortality." I've never forgotten that and have repeated it many times over the years.

I told the crew that I did not believe the pass would be open. We should not even try with less than a 1,000-foot ceiling, and it was not that good when we came through on our flight over. My plan was to fly a 90° heading, try to climb to 13,000 feet or the tops of the clouds, which ever came first, then fly east for thirty minutes, staying close to the clouds at all times. Then I planned to turn to a heading of 180° for another thirty minutes. If there were any breaks in the weather south of the mountains we would then let down. If not, we would fly on to the Coral Sea and let down. How will Irene fly on instruments? In smooth air OK, but turbulence is another question. I sent Grassi and Gregg to go take another look to see if anything had moved. I asked that the Aussies be told to come up front because it will get cold back there. There was no way we could negotiate through the pass, so we continued on climbing to the east.

It took seventy-four minutes (one hour, fourteen minutes) to climb to 13,000 feet. On a course of 90° going around towering clouds we could not see the 10,000-foot peaks below. We were now in clear bumpy air, and after fifteen minutes I banked right to 180°. After another twenty minutes, Cox said he could see breaks between the cloud layers and the jungle below. Since we had some room to maneuver I decided to see how the aircraft would act with gear down. I told Grassi to drop the gear and to be ready to raise it if I could not control the direction. At a variance of over 3 mph, I was not able to control the direction of the aircraft. At an indicated airspeed of 87 mph it would climb at about 100 feet a "week," or at least it seemed to take that long. He pulled up the gear and we started spiraling down in a right turn. I changed heading many, many times to stay in the clear. At 700 feet and below most of the clouds, there were just scattered rain showers. We were somewhere northeast of Moresby so I continued on to the ocean. That was one long seventy-eight minutes letting down and skirting the weather. If the airspeed changed more than three miles per hour we would either spin or stall. That was the maximum tolerance I had. We came out on the coast somewhere west of Hood Point and headed back to Wards. I told the Aussies to go to the cabin and had Grassi put down the two front sets of seats, one on each side of the aisle. He was to be sure the five pushers were all buckled in. They were to stay in their seats until told to get out. Then I had him take another look at the tail section and out the back door. As soon as we landed, while still on the runway, he was to jump out and put the landing gear pins in. Then we would taxi to our revetment and park. All crew and passengers would get out and move away from the plane. Don't anyone touch the door, for the Commander and all the Big Wheels will want to see it. We flew over the field at 500 feet with the open door facing the tower, and got a steady green light. I made a wide, long, left hand approach. I could see fire trucks along the taxiways, four "Meat Cans," several other trucks, and a line of jeeps.

We touched down on the end of the PSP at 87 mph, a good smooth wheel-landing. We rolled to the end of the runway and stopped. I heard a shout from the cabin. Grassi said that the door had fallen off after we had slowed down to about 40 mph. I told Grassi to tell everyone to stay buckled up. He put the pins in and we taxied to our parking area. Sergeant Klotz drove up with our "cargo door" over the hood of his truck and said, "I think you lost this, I picked it up on the runway!"

It seemed that half of the base had followed us to our revetment. When I got to the back door, the Group Commander, Group Operations Officer, Group Maintenance Officer, Squadron Commander, Squadron Operations Officer, Squadron Maintenance Officer, Squadron Debriefing Officer, four field ambulances and most of the squadron were standing and looking over the left stabilizer. When I spied the Group Operations Officer I told him that he was responsible for getting us home. No one said a word. Everyone just looked surprised. I said, "If you had not given away our parachutes last night we would have bailed out on the other side of the mountains. Instead we chewed off our fingernails. The Chinese Laundryman will know for sure who this crew was!!" There was a big laugh. Then I explained the events of the last three hours and twenty-two minutes. There was a hole large enough to put your head and shoulders in the leading edge of the left stabilizer. Many rivets were popped all along the left side of the tail cone where the stabilizer joins the fuselage. It was a wonder that we ever made it back. This had not been a joyride. You could call it beginners luck, but GOD was truly my co-pilot.

The powers-to-be, decided that Irene would become the Squadron "Teck Supply" until it could be determined what it would take to repair our wounded bird and get the parts. What a sad day for the three Yanks on the crew. No more flying for Grassi or myself for the rest of the month. It was nearly one month before Irene was ready for the regular crew to test hop her.

On November 17th, the rest of our Squadron had been airborne, shortly after we departed on our near-fatal mission. They had troops for Dobodura. First due to the weather and then to the bombing at Dobodura they had to return to Wards. This was the first time the Squadron as a unit was unable to complete its mission after becoming airborne. They had to scrub the flight. Flying troops and supplies in a combat zone is challenging to say the least.

On a few occasions one particular squadron pilot would have a "Mag drop." It was generally known on what flights this pilot would "chicken out." One of the Squadron Officer Pilots told him that he wanted to see him in the shower so he could see how wide his "yellow streak" was. You talk the talk so why don't you walk the walk?? The "Slacker" said, "They pay me if I fly or not." The first Officer replied, "I'm paid to fly, not to like it. What are you, a pussycat hiding in tiger's stripes? Now get with the program." For a short time that cured his "Mag drops." This pilot reminds me of a Japanese Kamikaze Pilot I read about after WWII. "He was a cowardly pilot who shorted out his plane's spark plugs. He did not have a stomach for this type of flying." It has been said, "All successful Kamikaze Pilots commit hara-kiri!"

That afternoon I went to Operations and told them that I would like to fly as often as I could. I was told that the Commander was sending me to Mackay, Australia for a ten day leave. I asked "why am I being punished because the cargo door came off in flight?" The Operations Officer came to the counter and told me that there was no punishment to it. I should consider it an award for a job well done. As soon as Irene is flying you and your crew will be back flying together full time. When you return from Australia you will be on the schedule with the other crews until your aircraft is flying. I said that I'd still prefer to stay and fly every day rather than being sent to Australia. I then went to the Orderly Room and spoke to the Commander. I asked why I was being reprimanded. He said, "Why do you ask?" I told him that the Operations Officer had just told me that I would not be flying for a while and that I was being sent to Australia. The Commander said, "That is correct. I consider it is for a job well done and you should, too." I asked, "What about the rest of the crew?" I was told that Cox and Gregg would be flying with other crews so their crews could have some time off. Grassi would be finding what has to be replaced and repaired on your aircraft. Then he will order the parts. In the meantime he will be removing parts from Irene that are needed for the other flying birds if supply does not have that part on hand. When the stabilizer was hit, how much damage was done to the tail section, how many rivets were popped where the stabilizer joins the fuselage?" My reply, "If the rest of the crew stays and works, I think it only right that I stay and work. I could help the crew chief and fly so some of the other pilots could have some time off."

At this point the Sergeant Major came in and told the Commander that I would be flying out to Townsville at 0400 hours 19 November on the early morning courier. From there go to Mackay by train and return the same way departing there 29 November. I was to pick up my orders and tickets tomorrow afternoon. "All tickets have been confirmed and paid. This includes the resort where you will be staying." I asked, "How can I tell the crew I've been given a paid vacation and they have to stay here and work in the heat and mosquitoes?" The Commander stood up, shook hands, said, "Have a good time," and "Goodbye."

I walked to the flight line and found the crew chief and radioman both working in the heat. Grassi looked at me, then asked, "What is the problem? You look as if you had lost your best friend. You should be happy to be going to Australia." "How did you know?" "The Captain stopped and talked to us while you were at Operations." I said, "That it is not fair," and left.

I walked to Jackson Operations to see when Major Hardison would be returning, so I could get a flight to Rabaul, the "Great Milky Way." The only thing I was able to find out was that they had no schedule for the 19th Bomb. The only reason I got any information was that the sergeant remembered me as I was the first Sergeant Pilot he had ever seen or heard of. Later I found out that the 19th was getting ready to return to the States as a group and would not be flying any more combat in the South West Pacific. As critically short of bombers as the 5th AF was no one could figure why?? Again I told the NCOIC that if any of the bomb squadrons needed a Co-Pilot for a mission over "Simpson Harbor," and if I wasn't flying, I sure would like to go. He wanted to know if I could get authorization from my CO. I replied, "Yes, for he said if I was not flying he would sign for me to fly as Co-Pilot with Major Hardison to Rebaul."

In the afternoon, I picked up my travel orders, railroad tickets, resort reservations, and was told to be in front of my tent at 0300 hours on the 19th with B-4 bag in hand so Sergeant Klotz could drive me to Base Operation's grass shack. I told him I'd turn in my gun tomorrow afternoon. Then I went by the Doc's tent and picked up salt and Atabrine pills.

One of our planes landed and out came a POW, a Japanese Captain, the first Japanese Officer prisoner taken alive and brought to Moresby. His hands were tied behind his back with vines. A string was wound around his head with a 3" piece of burlap hanging down in front of his eyes. This only kept him from seeing straight ahead. He could look down where he was walking. He could tilt his head to one side and see a little to one side. Sergeant Klotz drove up at this point. While they were waiting for the interpreter, Sergeant Klotz asked the prisoner in Pigeon English if he understood English. The POW replied in perfect English, "Yes, thank you Sergeant, quite fluent. I graduated from UCLA." He had to relieve himself. The Australian guards were doubled and his hands were untied. When he was returned and they were still waiting for the Allied Interpreter, I asked if I could get his signature. He signed it in Japanese. I then asked him to spell it for me in English and he did: Captain Hayashida Yoshiwo. I still have it. Shortly, thereafter he was placed aboard an aircraft for Brisbane.

That evening, Cortez was sitting on the outdoor privy, pants down to his ankles. Up drove the first American female nurse we'd seen in New Guinea. She had stopped to ask directions. He made a date with her. She flew with him several times and was in our tent on a few occasions. Of course, Cortez was the first one in the 6th to have a date while in New Guinea.

Before supper I cleaned and oiled my 45 and wrote a V-mail to my sister. By the time I arrived for chow it seemed that everyone in the squadron knew that the Commander had awarded me a 10-day paid leave. Of course I was glad, but not happy that the rest of the crew was not going.

Back in our tent I told Grassi and Gregg that I hoped that they understood why I was going to Mackay by myself, for I sure did not know. The Sergeant Major had told them that I'd requested, if I go all four of the crew should go, but the Commander said that they had other things to do. He told them that I then suggested that I stay and fly so the other pilots could have some time off. The Commander had told me, "Go. Have a good time and good-bye."

I shined my GI shoes and polished my brass, knowing that by tomorrow morning the brass would all be tarnished and the shoes covered with mildew. I turned in my gun and got a receipt for it and my extra money equivalent to $900.00 US. The Sergeant wanted to know how come I had so much money, and how much was I taking with me. I told him that I was taking $247.25. I told him that if he would come with me to my tent I would show him my notebook where I kept a monthly record. When there, I handed him my notebook:

Date	$ Saved	$ Balance
prior to 20 May 42	610.00	610.00
May	65.00	675.00
June	100.00	775.00
July	100.00	875.00
Aug	100.00	975.00
Sept	100.00	1075.00
Oct	72.25	1147.25
Nov 18th	-247.25	900.00

After showing him my records I told him that, "I do not smoke, drink, gamble, or run around, so why shouldn't I save some of my money?" He said that, even before he looked at my record, he was quite sure it was my money. That I might not know it, but we do have a thief in the Squadron. Every week or so, someone has reported a loss to the Commander. He asked me not to say anything about it. Sometime the thief will be caught and he will "Fall down the stairs." That is an old Army saying that means when a barracks thief is caught the men in the barracks beat the devil out of him and then report to the First Sergeant that Joe, the thief "Fell down the stairs." If it does not occur again there is no record or disciplinary action. If it happens again he is out of the service.

The Sergeant Major wished that I would spend a few dollars and have a good time. I told him that I still did not feel good about running off to have a good time and leaving my crew behind. He said, "Don't forget that you brought back a crippled ship and nine men." I replied that, "Without Grassi we would never have got airborne to start with." He smiled and walked away.

That night we had the usual aerial night visitors. We waited in the "Hole," all ducked down because from the sound we knew that the "Daisy-Cutters" were landing real close somewhere in the Camp area. After the all-clear, we found out that our tent had been hit and had to be replaced. Shrapnel put many holes in the tent and wrecked my air-mattress. The palm leaf roof over our slit trench took a beating and had to be repaired.

Next morning the Ops truck took me to the mess hall at 0300. During hours of darkness an individual did not want to go walking around in this area. Australians guarded the outer perimeter and the American Infantry patrolled the base. In the truck we were stopped twice in less than half a mile. After breakfast Sergeant Klotz drove me to Base Ops. When I reported in I was told that a Captain from the 21st Troop Carrier Squadron was the pilot. When he arrived I went over and introduced myself. I told him I was one of his passengers, and that sometime before the coast at Townsville I would like to be invited up front. Our Squadron, The 6th T.C.S., have no maps and if I should get a flight into Garbutt it would be most helpful. He said, "When you get aboard come on up front with the crew. I doubt if you will get to see much because the weather will be down to minimums at Townsville." I thanked him and went back with the other twenty-five passengers. There was some fog and drizzle in the area or just morning mist. More than half of the passengers were Officers, of which two were full Colonels. There did not appear to be any medical patients.

As the crew came aboard, the Captain told me to follow them to the cockpit. The co-pilot was a young Second Lieutenant, maybe a year or two older than I was. I stood behind the Flight Engineer. This was called a C-53, a converted airline aircraft. We had several of them at Cudhay. It was actually a DC-2. After we were airborne and leveled off at 8,000 feet, we were just in and out of the tops of the clouds with a bright quarter moon and many stars. The pilot asked all about my flying background. He had seen a few of us around at Jackson and Wards but never had the opportunity to talk to a Sergeant Pilot. After a while the Lieutenant went to the back. The Captain asked if I'd like to fly. For the next two plus hours I hand flew the plane from the right seat. By this time the sun was up and we were in weather. It was nice to once again be flying in an aircraft with a full instrument panel that did not leak every time we were in rain. The farther south we flew there was more weather. Before long we were in solid weather with light turbulence. Eventually, the co-pilot returned and I gave him back his seat and thanked him. The Captain thanked me and asked how much time I had in the Douglas. When I told him he said that was more flying time than he had. When we were out one hour he called for weather and clearance for the Garbutt Airdrome. He made a normal instrument approach on the low frequency four-legged beam breaking out at 500 feet on the final in gusty wind, rain, and poor visibility. I was unable to see any of the coast or approach area.

After landing at 0825, I again thanked the crew and told them that if any wanted a ride with me just look up No. 39 at Wards. I fished through my B-4 bag and took out my rain coat. I then joined the other passengers and we all, including the two Colonels, had to walk to Operations in the rain and wind. I asked the NCOIC at Operations if the mess hall was open and if I could get transportation there. I also asked where to catch a bus to the train station. He said that I would have to walk to the mess hall and would have to pull KP before I could eat. I asked to speak to the Operations Officer. A Major came out from an office. I told him that I had just arrived on the courier from Moresby and that I wanted to eat before going to the train station for a twenty-three hours train ride. He said that the Base Commander had an order that all transient enlisted men had to pull KP before they could eat at the GI mess hall. I then asked if he had ever read AR 615-150. He said, "Sergeant, do not get funny with me." I replied, "Staff-Sergeant Pilot's only duties are to fly and that does not mean pulling KP." I suggested that the Major read the regulation because many Staff-Sergeant Pilots will be coming through, we are not going to pull KP, and we will eat at the enlisted men's mess hall. I asked for a copy of the base order. This made the Major so mad that I thought he'd explode. Operations could not find a copy. I then said, "Major what is your name?" He shouted, "What is your name." I gave him a copy of my orders and again asked for his name. He shouted, "I am the Operations Officer and my name is on my desk in that room, pointing to an open door." I stepped back, gave him a snappy solute, wrote down the time and date, then went to his office and copied his name. Then I went back to the counter and asked the sergeant when and where to catch an off-base bus.

While in Operations, I had missed the 0900 bus and had to wait another hour for the 1000 O'clock bus to the Townsville train station. I arrived at 1028 and checked in to reconfirm my reservations and store my B-4 bag. I had two hours and thirty-two minutes to spend before we were scheduled to depart. I stopped in and had breakfast, steak and eggs "staiik and aiiggs" as the Aussies call them, enough food for any farmer, and the food was very good. I don't remember the price, but it was very cheap.

We boarded the train at 1230 hours. All their antiquated cinder burners were much smaller than American trains. Their trains had seven priorities: 1st CLASS–fresh fruits, vegetables and dairy products, 2nd CLASS–first class passengers, private sleeping compartment with dining room accommodations, 3rd CLASS–second class passengers, community compartments and dining room accommodations, 4th class–third class passengers, coach fare, with no sleeping or dining privileges, 5th CLASS–live stock, 6th CLASS–military freight, 7th CLASS–civilian freight. I was a first class passenger, upper front pull-down bed. There were four in the compartment, two upper and two lower wall beds. Our little car had a long aisle down one side with compartments on the other side. There were no air conditioners in those days; all compartment and the coaches had electric fans.

Since it was the springtime (in Australia) all the windows were open with no screens except in the dining cars. Our adventure started on time with a series of jerks followed by many more before the clickety-click, clickety-clack got going from the rhythmic clicking of the train wheels on the steel rails.

After storing my B-4 bag in my quarters, I walked through the one first class Pullman car, the three second class cars, and eight coach cars. They were at the front of the train. Behind the passenger cars came the freight, fresh fruit and vegetables with the live stock and the caboose bringing up the end.

I then went to the lounge section of the diner. As I walked down the aisle it was easy to see how slow the train was moving even out on the flat coastal plain. In the lounge I found a seat across from an old Australian grandmother. She was talkative and very interesting. During her lifetime she had been on this train many times and had many stories to tell. Little did I realize that when speaking of railroads what the word "gauge" really meant. She said that in the early days of railroads in Australia an individual or company would lay down tracks and put a train on it and was then in business. Then someone would join up at one or both ends. One would think that the train would go from one end of the track to the other end. But that was not always the case. When talking about railroads gauge means the distance between the two sets of parallel rails and matching train wheels. In Australia, they are not all the same width. A train can only run when the wheels and the tracks are the same gauge (width) and match up. Originally in Australia there were many different gauges. At the start of WW I it was down to five. A few years back on this same trip one would have to change trains three times before arriving at the destination. Sometime before WW II, the Queensland Government said enough of this and directed that all gauges be the same by a certain date and so it was.

Another interesting story the Old Lady related was about when she was first married before WW I. She and her husband were making this same trip. It was in the springtime and the wild flowers were in bloom. One of the girls remarked about the beautiful colors. Some of the young men, including her husband, walked to the front of the train. When the train was hardly creeping up the mountains, as she referred to these small hills, the men jumped off the moving train and picked flowers. When the last passenger car came by they hopped back aboard and handed their bouquets to their ladies. At the snail's pace we were moving that would be easy to do. The rail distance between Townsville and Mackay was 240 miles and it took us twenty-three hours to make the trip. So one can see it was no breath-taking experience. We stopped at every siding for one reason or another. I had a coke. It was served without ice. Most of the people were drinking tall bottles of warm beer. I forget the alcohol content, but I do remember that it was much higher than stateside beer. At first, the American troops could not handle it. Since I do not drink, I can only say that one bottle in this high temperature and humidity was more than most Yanks could drink at one time.

The second class compartments were mostly filled with American Army GIs. They were in one group on their way farther down the coast to Rockhampton. After listening to their war stories for a while it was time to go eat. Later I found out that all these GIs had just got off a troop ship at Townsville from the States and were on their way south. None of them had ever seen any action, but could they tell some wild war stories! That is one thing I soon learned that the biggest braggers and spinners of war stories were usually the ones that had seen the least or no combat. It was now time to eat. The three meals on the train: supper, breakfast and dinner were excellent with a lot of good food and all of mine were paid for in the cost of the ticket.

Just before 2200 I returned to my compartment. The lower two passengers already had their curtains pulled and were not making a sound. By the time I went to sleep no one else came in. Several times during the night we had to pull over on a siding and waited while another train would pass. During this journey I never did see my traveling mates.

I was up and in the lounge car before the first rays of sunlight cleared the eastern horizon. I watched the sky change from a purple to a clear light blue and then there was a fiery red sun rising out of the Coral Sea. It was one beautiful sunrise. It looked like the Aussie Grandmother had not moved all night. She said that she always got up with the chickens. As time went by a few more were in the dining car. Breakfast was not served until 0600. She was first and I followed her into the diner. The Aussies have a big meal for breakfast.

From our dining car table we could see the Coral Sea. She said that just off the coast and parallel to the shore line was the Great Barrier Reef. It turned and twisted from just off the south coast of New Guinea in the Torries Straight area to a point out from Rockhampton, Australia. There are just a few openings in this winding coral reef that are wide and deep enough for an ocean going ship to pass from the Coral Sea and the Arafura Sea. In a straight line on a map, from the northwest to the southeast, the Reef is 1200 miles long. But following it by air as it twists and turns it is over 2,000 miles. Some months later when our Squadron was stationed at Garbutt Airdrome, we would spend hours flying over the Great Barrier Reef. On a clear day from 2,000 feet up the beauty is indescribable. Fifty-one years later Etta and I visited the Coral Reef in a glass bottom boat. It was just as spectacular as I had remembered it. Most of the morning was spent listening to the armchair commandoes tell war stories. At 1100 those of us getting off at Mackay were called for dinner. We had another good meal.

At 1200 hours we arrived at Mackay right on time. I caught a military bus to the resort. It was located at the edge of town in a palm grove on a slight rise above the beach with some of the most beautiful manicured grounds I had ever seen. In the midst of this setting was a very large white single story hotel. It was completely surrounded by a screened-in veranda. There were many small cottages behind the main building. I asked the bus driver if he was sure this is where I was to go. He said "yes," but if I like, I could go in check, and he would wait. I checked and found out that he was correct. Seated on the porch were several men who had crutches and canes with them.

As I was checking in, the desk clerk asked if I was on any special diet. I said, "No, why, do I have a choice of what I want?" She replied, "No, but many of the patients are on special diets." I said that I was not a patient. She asked to see my orders again. I handed her a second copy. She read it and then left the room. She and a much older one-armed American man returned. He asked, "Why were you sent here? This is a rest resort for ambulatory American enlisted military patients that will be returning to duty?" He asked, "What do you do?" I told him I was a pilot and that I flew combat in New Guinea. He said, "Oh, so we now have Sergeants piloting military aircraft?" I said, "Yes, look at my orders." He said, "Take a seat. I'll be back." He took the orders and left. I could hear him on the phone, but could not understand what was being said. After several calls, long delays, and much talking he returned. He said, "Yes. Brisbane says there are Staff-Sergeant Pilots." I asked if he was going to let me register or not? "Unless the Army tells me differently you may stay," he said. Being a healthy looking specimen I would be quartered in the last cottage farthest from the dining room. I was briefed on a few things and headed down the path with my B-4 bag in hand. When I got in the back of the main building I could see that there were at least twenty-five small cottages.

The room was large, airy, two beds with built-in closets, a ceiling fan, bath, blinds, and screens on all windows and the door. The view of the grounds with the Coral Sea in the background was what you would expect to see in *National Geographic*. It appeared that each cottage was divided into four units. My bed was the second one in from the door. I hung up my B-4 bag and put toilet articles and a few other things in the dresser drawers.

Then I took my camera and went for a walk around the grounds and down to the beach. This was one beautiful tropical setting, but there were no bathing beauties on the beach. The weather was comfortable while in the shade of the palm trees, but once I got to the beach it was hot even with a light breeze. There was no wide sandy beach from the trees to the shore line. It was not like the beautiful snow white sugar colored sandy beaches along the south coast of New Guinea west of Port Moresby. The trees were up on a low bank. The coast line is not long and straight for a mile or two but twists and turns unevenly with a very narrow strip of sand.

After walking for at least two miles in the wet sand near the water's edge, I came to the entrance of the ship channel leading to the city. A short distance inland there was a dock with a lone, old fisherman. He was just standing there as if trying to decide if he was going to fish, stare at me, or go back home. As I approached he called out, "Welcome down under, Yank. Where you from, the Sugar Resort?" The sugar company owns it. Before the war in Europe they would entertain prospective customers and company officials and their wives. When the war started the Australian government leased it, and turned it into a recuperation camp for their Army. Once the Yanks came, they took over. I asked him how the fishing was. He said "good" when he fished. He didn't feel like it just now. The Australian Army had just notified him that his grandson had been killed in battle up north. Last year his son, this lad's father, was killed in North Africa. He was all alone now. His wife died several years back and his one daughter was working in a war plant in the big city. He told me that there were very few able-bodied Blokes left between 14 and 70 that are not off to war. He said to take care and thanked me for coming to help, and then he walked away. I felt so very sorry for the old Gentleman.

I walked on into the city. It was closing time. Within an hour the business section was deserted. They had "rolled up the sidewalk." I caught a bus back to my billet and washed up and went to eat. We were assigned tables, because most were on some kind of a special diet. The majority of the men were either on crutches or using a cane, and the waitress needed to know where to bring their food. One would never know that there was a war based on the menu and the amount of food that was stacked on each plate. Each bite was more delicious than the last. The Army was still using the Sugar Resort's Chef.

There were 183 patients plus one, which was me, who were being billeted and served meals. Most of the tables seated eight. All seven of the American Army Infantry soldiers at my table were from the 126th Regiment. When I heard that, I told them that their Regimental Commander was shot down and killed in a C-47 on 5 November while on a re-supply mission. That was the mission that I had been briefed to fly as my second flight of the day. By the time I had returned from my first mission, another infantry unit had a higher priority for equipment and supplies, so I was sent to that unit. When I returned from the second mission the weather was too low for another mission. That is when we found out that Lieutenant Majure and his crew were missing. By next morning your people had located the wreckage.

One of the Sergeants said, "You are correct. I was on the search team that found the aircraft. That is when and where I got hit in my left side just below the heart by a Jap 6.5 mm. Later the doctors in Moresby told me that I was very lucky, for if it had hit one inch higher, it would have been in the heart and the rescue party would have buried me with the burned bodies at the crash site. I will spend eleven more days here and if all goes well I'll go back to duty." The Sergeant said that after eating, if I would come to his room and could identify it he would give me something from the wreckage. When we got to his room he reached in his duffel bag and among his things pulled out a white business card. He asked, "What was the name of your Officer aboard?" I said, "Second Lieutenant Harold B. Majure." He handed me the crumpled card and said, "It's yours." I thanked him and told him all I knew about Lieutenant Majure. He then wanted to know how I was wounded. I related the long story of how I happened to be here. I then told him that instead of me being injured it was my aircraft that took the beating and there was no other available aircraft to fly until mine was repaired. He thought that was funny! Then I asked about his background. After all these years I can remember only that he was a Tech Sergeant, had a Polish name and was from Pennsylvania. Most of the GIs in the 6th at that time were from his home state, and many were Polish. He knew none of them, but had been in most of the states as a trucker before joining the Army in '35.

It seemed strange to be in a town as large as Mackay with so few single girls my age. They were either in the military, working in a Defense Plant somewhere, or home with children. I spent eight days there and had only one date. That was a daytime boat ride to one of the small offshore islands the US Army had for excursions and picnics. It was nothing to write home about. I spent most mornings walking the beaches. The afternoons I spent talking and listening to the wounded soldiers talk about their experiences. At night there were movies in the Dining Hall.

One morning at MacKay I read a most interesting article about General MacArthur's thoughts and description of the environment and natural hazards of War in New Guinea. It was entitled, *The Green War*.

Other approaches to Port Moresby having failed, the Japanese now attempted the incredible, an offensive over the Owen Stanleys. At first the small rear guard of the digger militiamen, who remained in the range until August 8, assumed that the enemy soldiers climbing toward them were merely patrolling. To their astonishment, massed infantrymen, manhandling mortars, machine guns, and field pieces, crept slowly up the slimy, zigzagging, hundred-mile Kokoda Trail. In four weeks Major General Tomitaro Horii's sixteen thousand men had crossed the raging Kumusi River at Wairopi and struggled over the thirteen-thousand-foot Kokoda Pass. Five jungle-trained battalions leapfrogged one another into Isurava village, one hundred and fifty-five miles from their starting point, and pushed down the precipitous southern slopes toward Imita Ridge, twenty miles from the bluffs around Port Moresby. How many men died in this heroic endeavor will never be known. Many perished in the Kumusi, and others disappeared in quicksand or plunged into gorges. In places, the winding trail, a foot wide at most, simply disappeared. It took an hour to cut through a few yards of vegetation. The first man in a file would hack away with a machete until he collapsed of exhaustion. Then the second man would pick up the machete and continue, and so on. In that climate the life expectancy of those that lost consciousness and were left behind was often measured in minutes.

MacArthur had sent two of his best Brigadiers, Pat Casey and Harold George, to survey the Papuan terrain. They returned to Brisbane shaken. Until then they had assumed that Bataan and Samar were covered with the densest jungle in the world, but New Guinea was unbelievable. They told the General that they didn't see how human beings could live there, let alone fight there. From the air, whence they had first seen it, Papuan's most striking feature had been the razorback mountain range, stretching down the peninsula like the dorsal vertebrae of some prehistoric monster, its peaks obscured by dark clouds swollen with rain. It wasn't until they had landed and ventured into the rain forest on steep, slippery, root- tangled trails that the full horror of life there had struck them. Blades of grass seven feet high could lay a man's hand open as quickly as a scalpel. The jungle was studded with mangrove swamps and thick clumps of bamboo and palms. Often the trail was covered with waist-deep slop. The air reeked with vile odors—the stench of rotting undergrowth and of stink lilies. Little light penetrated the thick matted screens of overhead vines, but when the rain stopped and the sun appeared, vast suffocating waves of steam rose from the dark marshes.

This was the setting of the Green War: the green of slime and vegetation, the green of gangrene and dysentery, and the green-clad enemy, whose officers smeared yellow-green, bioluminescent micro-organisms on their hands so they could read maps at night. The diggers, and the GI's, who were now joining them, called themselves 'swamp rats.' The hideous tropical ulcers that formed on their feet, arms, bellies, chests, and armpits were known as 'jungle rot.' Waving away the clouds of flies and mosquitoes that swarmed over mess gear was called 'the New Guinea salute.' Bugs were everywhere: biting ants, fleas, chiggers, poisonous spiders, and brilliant colored enormous insects that would land on a sleeping man and, like vampires, suck his body fluids. Twisted vines swarmed with vivid colored birds and great winged creatures with teeth, like gigantic rats. Pythons and crocodiles lurked in the bogs and sloughs, waiting for a man to stumble from the mucky trail. At night a soldier would rip away blood-glutted leeches from his genitals and his rectum. Bug bites, when scratched, turned into festering sores. Since native bearers were reluctant to help him, especially near the front line, the average soldier had to carry as much as a hundred pounds on his back, and he always ran a fever. It was a rare infantryman who wasn't afflicted with yaws, scrub typhus, blackwater fever, ringworm, malaria, amoebic dysentery, or bacillary dysentery. For every man suffering from a gunshot wound five were laid low with illness, and that is not a true measure of the extent of the sickness, because no one was hospitalized unless his fever rose above 102 degrees.

MacArthur heard all this while treading back and forth in his Brisbane office. Then he stopped, turned to Sutherland and Dick Marshall, and said in a low, trembling voice, 'We'll defend Australia in New Guinea.'

Historian Ronald H. Spector's book published in 1985, *EAGLE AGAINST THE SUN, The American War With Japan*, pages 189-190.

"General MacArthur left Melbourne for his new headquarters aboard a special train on July 21 (1942). Behind MacArthur's maroon-colored coach, built for the Prince of Wales' visit to Australia and still bearing the royal crest, were two flatcars. The first carried MacArthur's limousine, gleaming in the afternoon sun; the second bore General Sutherland's slightly less grand Cadillac. As they rolled into Brisbane early the next morning, Signal Corps men were waiting with an urgent message: the Japanese had landed at Buna.

The Japanese forces, 16,000 men of General Horii Tomitaro's elite South Seas Detachment, quickly consolidated their position on the coast and struck out across the Owen Stanley Mountains for Port Moresby, the prize that had eluded them in the Battle of the Coral Sea. Between Buna and Port Moresby lay some of the most rugged, forbidding terrain on earth. Jagged mountain peaks rising to a height of over 13,000 feet, steep gorges, turbulent rivers and streams, all covered by thick jungle, dominate the interior of the Papuan peninsula. The rainfall is heavy and, in some seasons, almost continuous. A single overland route connected Port Moresby with Buna: the Kokoda trail, a primitive track of slippery mud and rock. In places it was almost vertical; in other places it was so narrow only a single man could pass at a time.

It was the sort of terrain that would have challenged even the most enthusiastic out-doorsman. But the Australian, Japanese, and the American soldiers were not enthusiastic outdoorsmen. They were loaded down with up to seventy pounds of gear, in the steaming heat of the low-lying jungle and swamps or the chilling cold of the higher mountain passes, plagued by malaria, dysentery, and a particularly virulent form of typhus; they were usually short of food, always near exhaustion. 'There are mists creeping over the trees all day and sometimes you can't see your hand in front of your face under cover of the jungle,' reported one Australian soldier. "'Most of our chaps haven't seen a Jap! You don't see the Jap who gets you!' Seventy-five percent of the troops fighting on the Kokoda trail had never seen a single Japanese soldier.

Australian forces along the trail, badly outnumbered, fought a stubborn retiring action against Horii's advancing forces. By mid-September, they stood on the Imita Range in the southern foothills of the Owen Stanleys, the last defensible barrier before Port Moresby."

A few decades later I read a LIFE-TIME book titled *WORLD WAR II, ISLAND FIGHTING* by Rafael Steinberg. Page 60, JUNGLE COMBAT WITH A FANATIC FOE.

"In the summer of 1942, the jungle-clad region of southeast New Guinea known as Papua suddenly became one of the most important pieces of territory in the Southwest Pacific. For six months, what historian Samuel Eliot Morison would later describe as 'certainly the nastiest' fighting of the war surged back and forth over the narrow strip as Australians and Americans struggled to repel Japanese forces attempting to take the Allied bases at Port Moresby."

Much of the worst fighting occurred around the Kokoda Track, a narrow precipitous path over the 13,000-foot Owen Stanley Range that was drenched almost daily by rainfalls of as much as one inch in five minutes, and was so steep and slippery in many places that troops crawled single file and clung to vines to keep from sliding down mountainsides. 'The few level areas,' said Australian Colonel Frank Kingsley Norris, were 'pools and puddles of putrid black mud.' It was, said Norris, a 'track through a fetid forest grotesque with moss and glowing phosphorescent fungi.'

Yet the Japanese moved along the track to within striking distance of Port Moresby in October 1942, before the terrain—and stiffening resistance—stemmed their advance.

As Australian troops, assisted by Papuan carriers, drove the weakened, starving Japanese back to the Buna-Gona coast in November, they passed human skeletons picked clean by jungle rats and found evidence that some desperate survivors had cannibalized the dead. Meanwhile, American units had landed at crude airstrips near Buna to join the combat. In two months of savage struggle at Buna, the Allies lost 3,095 killed and 5,451 wounded—an even bloodier fight than the better-known Guadalcanal campaign."

It was nice to know that the Top Brass knew how the troops had to live and the environment they fought and died in.

Yet, I would be glad to get back to New Guinea. With nothing to do after the fast pace of the previous two months this was just plain boring. On the morning of the 29th I caught the bus to the train station for the 23-hour ride back to Townsville. Then I took a military bus out to Garbutt Airdrome. I reported in and was scheduled for the 1000 hour flight to Wards. I had an early breakfast on the train but I wanted to check to see if they still had the rule that I had to do KP before I could eat. I went to Operations and asked to see the Operations Officer. The same Major came to the counter. I asked if the Base still required transient Sergeant Pilots to pull KP before they could eat in the GI Mess. He then looked me over, got red in the face and very loudly replied, "Sergeant, this is insubordination." I replied, "May I eat at the GI Mess Hall now and not pull KP?" He turned and walked away. I walked to the PX and bought some snacks for the flight north. I flew back to Ward Airdrome in an old C-39, landing at 1530.

I stopped at the 6th Operations and asked to be put on the flying schedule for tomorrow. I was informed that I would not start flying until the 2nd. I signed in at the Orderly Room and asked for an appointment to see the Commander tomorrow morning. I picked up my mail and "45". It seemed that while I was gone the mosquitoes had doubled in numbers. The mosquitoes, humidity and stifling heat were the first things you noticed upon landing.

While on leave I had spent $60.25. I asked the Sergeant Major to add the $187.00 to my savings, making a total of $1,187.00 that was now in the Squadron safe. I reported to the Commander, and thanked him for the paid vacation. Then I told him about the GI's from the 126th Regiment I had met and their finding the crash of Lt Majure's aircraft. I then gave him a copy of my complaint about Garbutt Airdrome requiring Sergeant Pilots to pull KP before they could eat at the GI Mess Hall. He promised to forward it to 5th Air Force and that he would to speak to the Group Commander about it.

The Commander told me that the 6th had its third combat loss. The aircraft was shot down in flames on 26 November just as the wheels were coming up after take-off. It crashed and burned about five miles south of Dobodura. A Jap Judy dive bomber machine gunned them down. The crew was: Second Lieutenant Earl B. Lattier, co-pilot, Staff-Sergeant Pilot Franceses D. Milne (R.A.A.F.), flight engineer Tech Sergeant Joseph E. Paul, and radio operator Arthur Believe. Sergeant Pilot David C. Vaughter was next to take-off and saw the whole affair. Vaughter had been Lattier's co-pilot flying over from the States and they were good friends.

The 6th had just lost twenty-five percent of their aircraft in the first six weeks of combat. We could not afford this high a loss rate. If it continued the Squadron would be out of aircraft and flight crews within six months. From all indications there were no more aircraft or crews in the pipe line.

While I was gone several of the drinkers in the Squadron had conjured up and made a concoction they called "Guinea Rot Gut". They had cut down two coconut trees, stripped them, laid them side by side about two inches apart with one end raised about two feet higher than the other end. They drilled the eyes out of the coconuts, added sugar, plugged the holes and placed the coconuts in the "vee" between the two slanted dead palm trees. Every day the coconuts were shaken and turned. In a few days they were fermented and the "brew" was ready to drink. It must have been potent for one of our Mexican radio operators drank a canteen of this mixture and passed out on the spot. The Medics put him on a stretcher in the shade next to the Medical Tent, which was next to our tent. A few hours later he came to and staggered back to his own tent and slept for a few more hours. The next day he said, "Man, this has more kick than Tequila!!" After that I knew I was glad that I was and still am a teetotaler.

The next day I helped Grassi do repairs on Irene. The sheet metal men were scheduled to start repairing the tail section within the week. Many parts were still on back order. The crew chief was pulling the 100-hour inspection early. Gregg and I were "helpers." I'm sure that I was more in the way than helpful, but at least I was there in the heat and I tried to be helpful. Within sixteen years I would be The Chief-of-Maintenance for all Air National Guard and Air Force Reserves Squadrons in the United States that in case of mobilization would be assigned to MATS.

That evening as we were sitting on a downed coconut log eating and swatting mosquitoes T/Sgt Klotz drove up and asked if I'd still like to fly on a B-17 for an early morning bombing mission to Lae. The reason was that their co-pilot and one of the waist gunners became very sick on the flight over the Coral Sea. The Medics grounded them until their temperature went down and they stopped vomiting. It must have been something they ate. They were sure it was not malaria. There were no Flying Fortresses stationed in New Guinea at this time. If a co-pilot could not be rounded up, the mission would have to be scrubbed. Captain Lackey heard the conversation and spoke up, "If your not on the schedule and want to go, this is your chance." That was it. Operations notified Jackson that I was available and T/Sgt Klotz had me at Jackson's Operation at 0315. In the two mile ride the Army Guards stopped and checked us three times.

When I reported in with all my flight gear the Pilot looked me over and questioned me about my flying. I was not sure that he was going to let me go. The Ops NCO came up to the counter and thanked me for filling in an emergency. He asked me how flying was going and how many missions I'd flown. That must have satisfied the Captain for from then on I was a member of the crew for this early morning high-level bombing mission, my first. We went through a routine pre-flight with extra attention being paid to the .50 caliber ammo belts by each gunner.

We went back to Operations for the briefing. This was to be a three ship, high level, 28,000' bombing of AAA gun emplacements and ships in the bay. Intelligence said to expect moderate flack over the target and 4 to 6 Zeros before and after the bomb run. Now for the cheery side, if you should go

It is a long climb up the tree to gather fresh coconuts. Coconut milk fresh from the tree tastes sweeter than the milk of mature coconuts that have fallen to the ground.

down or bail out, the Japs are not ONE bit friendly. After a brutal interrogation the best you can expect is a quick death by a single shot in the back of the head. The cannibals will put you in a pot, boil you alive and then eat you. The headhunters will cut off your head and put it on a pole for religious ceremonies. Each of us was to be positive that we were wearing our dog-tags and had no personal effects or military documents. This is the same briefing we always received in the 6th. The weather was forecasted on take-off to be 800-1000 feet with broken visibility 5-miles and broken to scattered clouds to 6,000 then above all weather and to target. The Lae area, at 0658 drop time, should be scattered below 10,000. On the return flight clouds will be solid over the mountains up to 15,000 to 18,000 and climbing with 800 to a 1000 feet ceiling in the Jackson area with blowing rain.

All twenty-seven of us rode back in three 6X6s to the three B-17s. Our bombardier was a M/Sergeant and I think the oldest member of the crew. It was interesting to note that he kept a close eye on the Norden Bombsight, but nothing like some bombardiers I've since read about. While the Captain was making another fast walk-a-round inspection I double checked my parachute and adjusted it. Next, I was getting into the regular co-pilot's high altitude flying gear: pants, boots, jacket, helmet, nylon inserts, and gloves. They were all a little large but would do. It was time to climb aboard with a parachute, oxygen mask, 45 in its shoulder holster and all survival equipment on my web belt. I removed my gloves and helmet and placed them in the knee pockets of my flight pants. Then placed my chute in the co-pilot's seat, got in strapped the chute on, and cinched the lap and shoulder harness up tight. I released the shoulder harness, and hooked up and tested my oxygen mask. I adjusted the seat and rudder peddles. Now I was ready to watch the Pilot and Flight Engineer go through the check list and start up the four engines.

Since we were the lead ship we were the first to taxi out with the other two 17s following. After run up and a green light from the tower, we took the runway at 0525 and started to roll. Everything moved so slowly with two minutes between take-offs. We climbed straight ahead for four minutes. Then we took three very slow shallow 360, 10° banks before picking up a heading of 336°, and we continued climbing out on course. At 10,000 feet we went on oxygen, at 20,000 feet, still climbing, all guns were checked out and fired a few rounds. The pilot leveled off at 28,400 feet then a gradual 400 foot let down to pick up airspeed. Sure glad that their co-pilot had left his winter flying gear or I would have frozen. This B-17 formation is so far apart that it is nothing but vicinity flying.

Thirty minutes before our ETA the Pilot called on the intercom and told us, "wake-up time for from now on we could expect enemy fighters from here on to the target." The bombardier was all set up and ready to start the bomb run on command. The crew chief told me that the bombardier had been a bombardier instructor at Lowry Field, Denver, Colorado Bomb and Gunnery School before being transferred to their outfit.

The lower ball turret gunner was first to call in, "two enemy pursuit aircraft climbing below at one o'clock." Shortly another flight of two was seen climbing off our left nose. At this altitude it took some time for the Japs to get above and behind us ready to make a diving pass. The sky was clear at this altitude and visibility was unlimited. The gunners were able to keep all their twin .50s fixed on and leading the enemy aircraft just waiting for them to come in range. Looking out my side window I could see that the guns of the No 2 Fort were at the ready and moving with the approaching Zeros. Being a clear day at flight level, no clouds to dive out of, and the sun was not high enough to blind our gunners, it could be a "turkey shoot" for our shooters.

Here they came diving from 5,000 feet above and behind the three ship formation. This was not a surprise, but was very helpful. The three Forts stayed on course and the gunners waited for the enemy aircraft to come into the gun rings. At this moment everything went into fast motion. One minute the only sound were the four engines and then ten .50s firing altogether. With the shaking of the "17" you became wide awake and there was plenty of noise.

Twenty seconds later all was quite once again. One of the enemy Zeros exploded off my right on the far side of the No 2 Fort. Don't know which or how many of the gunners were involved, but plenty of tracers were converging on this one doomed plane before it disintegrated. By this time we were on the bomb run and the remaining three pursuits peeled off to meet us on the other side of the ack-ack. No injury to flight crews or reported hits on any of our three aircraft.

The four known Anti-Aircraft Artillery were throwing up plenty of black balls of exploding flack. The tops of these "black clouds of death" moved and dissipated very slowly. It appeared that each burst of shrapnel was just waiting for one of the aircraft to fly into it so it could cut the plane to ribbons. Thank God, it was below us. The bomb run was a straight and smooth flight. Shortly after bombs away one of the batteries of flack stopped. Then the bombardier announced: "one less AAA to contend with." The enemy navy must have gotten the word we were coming for no vessels were in sight. Our Captain made a 180 and we flew back over the same gun emplacements. It appeared that their gun crews had not expected this. One more unit hit the dust before we headed back to Jackson.

Once the ack-ack stopped the Zeros were back in position coming in high and on our nose. This time they had the advantage of the sun being behind them and the closure rate was several hundred miles per hour faster. All gunners knew where to expect the fighters would be diving from. This time we could see their tracers before our guns opened up. One of the Zeros took enough hits to loose altitude and was trailing smoke. Only one confirmed kill on our way to the target and a possible one on the way out. Our No 3 wingman took several hits, but was able to hold his position. All three aircraft returned to Jackson Airdrome.

I believe this bombing mission was successful because this was a very cool, old-time bomber crew with clear weather and at the altitude we were flying. At 28,000 feet, the Zero was close to its operating ceiling. As we first approached Lae, the closure rate of the enemy pursuit aircraft when diving from the rear, was so slow that they were over exposed to the Fort's concentrated fire power. When leaving the area their fighters had double advantages as the sun was higher allowing for a head on attack and a vastly increased closure rate.

After parking and the crew was out of the aircraft a jeep and the refueling trucks arrived. Then up drove a staff and command car with a Major as the driver. He spoke to the Captain and wanted to know how the mission went. He informed us that crew replacements were on their way from Australia and should be here in time for the flight back to home base. The Major instructed the Captain to line his crew up in front of his aircraft as the CO wanted a picture. A picture was taken and the Major thanked me for filling in and making it possible to complete the mission. When I returned to Jackson's Operation, they got me a ride back to Wards. For the next two or three days there were a lot of questions about my bombing mission.

Years later I read that the first aerial bombing took place in 1849 over Venice, Italy when the Austrian Army dropped bombs from hot air balloons. The first aerial bombing from an aircraft was in 1911 by the Italians during their war with Turkey. The bombs were dropped by hand over the side of the aircraft. The accuracy and damage by both methods were very poor. This was the beginning of aerial bombing.

That was all there was to my first bombing mission, until fifty-nine years later on the 12th of December 2001 on my 80th birthday. Then I had a real surprise as our daughter-in-law, Linda, had found a picture in the January 1943 issue of *THE NATIONAL GEOGRAPHIC MAGAZINE*!! There was a picture showing me wearing my pith helmet, which was a copy of the picture taken with the crew I flew with in 1942.

The 6th TCS ground troops arrived by ship on 1 December 1942 with 11 Officers and 155 enlisted men. There was a big work party to help set up tents, and showers, and to dig slit trenches and straddle ditches. That evening we had a big party and a lot of visiting to catch up on the latest news from both sides. This meant that the radiomen and crew chiefs would be getting more time off as all our flight crews were now here for duty.

Today the 6th TCS took over all its own 1st and 2nd echelon aircraft maintenance. This was the first time since July that all of our own Squadron was back together, which led to a more efficient and cohesive organization. Maintenance crews made it a practice of prowling through dumps and salvage yards in the vicinity of Port Moresby to salvage batteries and other items from wrecked aircraft. When any ship crashed the crews would engage in good-natured rivalry in bartering for the much-needed parts and equipment

American Bombers Attacking from Australia 51

Tojo's Physic and Crew of Nine Americans Return from a Visit to a Jap Base

Unshaved, unwashed, and weary after hours in the freezing substratosphere, they cheerfully line up and grin for the photographer. Yes, A. E. F. morale in Australia is excellent. Off duty soon, they'll have time to think up more insults to paint on Flying Fortresses. Note that the gasoline drums are widely dispersed.

probably have fought to hold my place.

Six Flying Fortresses in two flights of three, both in V formation, approached the Japanese-held base of Lae in New Guinea.

"Open your bomb bays," Captain H. ordered calmly over the interplane phone.

Through a side window I watched the bomb bay doors open on the ship off our right wing. At the same time those on the Fortress off our left opened. I could not see the three planes in B flight, for they followed directly behind us (page 54).

As we drew nearer the target area, I felt remarkably confident from the knowledge that six Fortresses in tight formation made up the attacking force. Contemplation of even one of these ships with its bomb bay wide open, all guns ready, and the four engines droning on a steady course through the frigid substratosphere is mighty comforting over enemy territory.

Antiaircraft guns began firing as we flew

in at 28,000 feet. Their shells burst below us. A few seconds before Captain H.'s bombardier released his load, the Japanese gunners fled for shelter.

Looking out of the side window, I saw bombs fall away from the Fortress off our right wing. They seemed to float through the air as in a slow-motion picture.

An Enemy Airdro...

Interested to see what ... I nearly fell out of the ... fire blazed on the edge ... huge masses of black ... from two other fires i... cause of the straight ... had only a few seco... down on the target. ...

For almost ten ... bombs we sailed on ... ground gunfire or e... stood by an open wi...

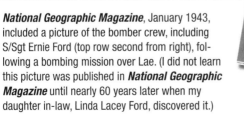

National Geographic Magazine, January 1943, included a picture of the bomber crew, including S/Sgt Ernie Ford (top row second from right), following a bombing mission over Lae. (I did not learn this picture was published in **National Geographic Magazine** until nearly 60 years later when my daughter in-law, Linda Lacey Ford, discovered it.)

as they stripped the downed aircraft. When the scavengers were through there was nothing usable to pack away.

Almost anything had to be better than sitting around doing nothing just slapping the mosquitoes and accomplishing less!!

On the 2nd, I was back on flight schedule and flew for the next nine days. On the 5th we flew two P-40 Allison engines to Garbutt. They still demanded that we pull KP before we could eat. I filed a flight plan for Charters Towers with the two engines still aboard. There we had the engines off-loaded and RONed. We had supper and breakfast there without one word about KP. Next morning we flew over to Garbutt, picked up our load and filed for Wards. Once we got airborne and on our way, I called Garbutt Tower and told them to notify Base Operations that two priority P-40 Allison engines from Port Moresby were dropped off at Charters Tower. Arriving at Wards, I filed another complete written report and requested it be forwarded to 5th Air Force. Within one week this problem was corrected and no more flight crews and Staff Sergeant Pilots were required to pull KP.

I went over to the 8th Photo Squadron. The Photo Joe Squadron took all the aerial pictures for photo intelligence and maps for the Allied Forces in New Guinea and the surrounding islands to the north and east. They flew F-5As and stripped down P-38 Lightning's. One of the first persons I ran into was the Commander, Major Karl Polifka. He was at Gray Field in the 2nd Photo squadron when I was stationed there. He immediately stuck out his hand and said that Felix had told him that I was now an Enlisted Pilot flying Troop Carrier out of Wards. After talking some, I told him that I had come over to see if I could chisel some 35-mm gun film and equipment to develop and print all my own film. He called in his Photo NCOIC and told the sergeant to fix me up. When I needed more I was to come back.

I took plenty of pictures everywhere I went. A few months later when I returned to the ZI, all pictures were checked by the Base Censor Office at Garbutt Airdrome where I was stationed. Nearly all were approved, wrapped in a sealed box, stamped with the Censors Seal, dated and signed by the G-2 Censoring Officer. When at Brisbane on the way home, once again all pictures were individually checked and were stamped, signed, sealed in a G-2 package and released.

After completing my tour of duty in December 1943, I returned to the states through Hickham Air Field. At Hickham, once again the seal was broken and 601 pictures were confiscated. I blew my stack and demanded to see the Officer in charge. I demanded that the pictures were not to be touched until he arrived. Here came an Army full Colonel. We had some pretty strong words. Among other things, I told him that he and his men were trying to steal my pictures and negatives. He said that was for the Army to decide. The only conceivable reason that he was stealing my pictures was so he would be able to show and tell his family and friends about his war experiences. That must have hit a raw nerve because he said, "Lieutenant. That is enough!!" I told him if he took any of my pictures, for him as the Officer in Charge to sign for them and print his name, rank, serial number, organization and APO, so I'd know who to complain about. After he had signed I told him that if within two months from that day I had not received all 601 pictures and negatives, I would have my Dad talk to a friend, the Governor of Colorado. He would suggest that the Governor ask why an "Arm chair Colonel, thousands of miles from the front lines had confiscated 601 of my pictures and negatives which were of no military value. All these pictures had already been approved for release by two other Commands that knew what was of value to the enemy." I believe that I left only one step ahead of the MPs. Forty-five days later this Unit mailed to me, in care of my parents, 307 pictures and their negatives. I never did anything about it and never received any more pictures.

At the end of the morning briefing, it was announced that the Commander had put me in for another Distinguished Flying Cross.

On the 10th of December 1942 the Air Echelon of the 33rd Troop Carrier Squadron arrived at Wards Airdrome with their ground troops scheduled to arrive on the 28th of December. The 33rd had been held up to support the US Marines fighting in Guadalcanal. While flying co-pilot in a C-47 on 4 December 1942, Staff Sergeant Pilot Robert C. Dillman, my first flying school classmate was killed in action. He was shot down by ground fire just at dusk on take-off from Henderson, Cactus Field. The aircraft had just got airborne when hit and crashed with no survivors into the Solomon Sea a mile or two from the shoreline.

With the arrival of the 33rd TCS this completed the four Squadrons in our Group. This was the first Troop Carrier Group stationed in News Guinea, since the 22nd TCS and the 21st TCS were still operating out of Australia.

The 22nd moved to New Guinea on 14 February 1943 and the 21st moved on the 18th. Before the war was over there were nineteen (19) Troop Carrier Squadrons in the 5th Air Force.

To make us a little more independent, the 6th opened its own Mess Hall and the 33rd took our place in the Base Consolidated Mess. When the air echelon first moved to Wards Airdrome, our meals were C-Rations out of a tin can with all the bananas and coconuts we wanted to pick and eat. For bananas, all you had to do was reach up, pull and twist one from the stalk. To get a coconut, someone had to climb a palm tree and cut the coconut from the cluster. Once it was on the ground it had to be husked, and the eyes had to be drilled out. Then we could either drink the milk from the coconut or pour it into our canteen cups and drink it. Under no circumstances were we to pick up and eat or drink the milk from a coconut found on the ground. After four or five hours on the ground in the hot tropical sun the fruit would spoil and make you very sick. Very few Yanks ever climbed a palm tree to get a coconut. I never tried as it was just too hard. We would pay a native one cigarette to climb up and twist off a dozen coconuts and then husk them. They could go up the palm trees like a monkey in nothing flat.

Once the 6th had it's own Mess Hall there seemed to be as much "Bully Beef" (Spam), mutton, canned peaches, chicory coffee, tea, powdered milk and eggs, to which you added water, canned peas, string beans, and corn as anyone wanted. About this time the Aussies opened their bakery. Oh, what a blessing! Later we were issued dehydrated eggs which could either be scrambled or be used in cooking. I could not eat the powered eggs fried in Australian mutton tallow. Then came canned orange juice, but it was rationed. In January we were issued our first K-Rations for snacks or in-flight meals. They were a change and not too bad.

That night for chow we each had one double helping of fresh fish. One of the ground crew mechanics who we had flown up from Townsville had gone fishing and brought back enough for 300 men. Someone asked how. Where are your poles or nets? What did you use for bait, and so on. Finally, after the Commander asked for the sergeant's secret to his success, he stood up and said that before he joined the Army in 1935 he was a commercial fisherman. Yesterday he had asked Cookie, the Chef, if he were to bring in enough fish to feed everyone tomorrow morning would he cook it for supper tomorrow night. Cookie said that if the fish were here by 1000 that he would cook it, but after 1000 he'd go with the scheduled Army Menu. "I borrowed the squadron 6x6 along with two tarpaulins, then stopped by the infantry and got three dozen hand grenades and drove to Bootless Bay. I went to a sheltered inlet where there is very little wave action and covered the bed of the truck with one of the tarps and stretched the other one over the top of the sideboards around the two sides of the truck-bed. I backed the truck up to the water's edge. I was now ready to go fishing a little before 0600. I threw in a grenade, waded out and started picking up fish that were floating on the top of the water. I was back here before 1000. If there had been another two or three men to pick up the fish, we could have brought back a truck load. If there were four of us, the fish would have come back all gutted, cleaned and ready to cook." Cookie was an excellent Army chef, but with all of his culinary skills he could not turn our GI rations into a 5-Star restaurant. But we gave him an "A" for trying.

After supper I went over and thanked the sergeant and told him that I had tomorrow off and would like to go. He said to be in front of the orderly room at 0500 in the oldest long pants and heaviest boots I had. Three of us went fishing. It was real fun. We could have easily filled a whole truck bed. There were all kinds of fish from three small sharks on down in size with many different shapes and colors. Our fisherman told us that when the grenade exploded under the water the concussion stunned some of the larger fish and killed the small ones. It would rupture the gills of the smaller fish. When the fish was either killed or stunned, they would turn over on their back and float to the surface. We had to be extra careful when in the water for the coral was razor sharp. Not only would it cut you through your boots, but if you do get a cut you would get a serious infection. We stood on the sandy beach and only one of us, (we took turns), would pull the cotter pin out of the grenade and throw it as far out in the bay as we could. Then the three of us would wade in and pick up the floating fish and bring them back to the truck. We were where the water was no more than waist deep. We got back to the kitchen before 0930.

That night everyone had all the fish they could eat. I do not know the names of the different fish, just where they came from, how they were caught, and that they were good. From then on for the rest of the year while in New

Guinea, our mess served fresh fish at least once a week. During our year at Wards I went fishing at least a half dozen times. When four of us would go, we gutted the fish on the beach. Sometimes big sharks would get in pretty close to the beach, but we never were able to kill one. By the time we'd get to the cab of the truck to get a rifle the shark would be gone.

I did not fly on 12 December 1942, my twenty-first birthday. The day before I was old enough to vote, I had flown as a Pilot ninety-one (91) combat missions. Two months before reaching my twenty-second birthday I flew an additional two hundred seventy-three (273) combat missions. As a combat pilot this made a total of three hundred sixty-four (364) combat missions in New Guinea during WWII.

About this time, a Squadron logo appeared on the bulletin board. It was titled BULLY BEEF EXPRESS. It was a round circular patch. Centered at the top, parallel to the outer edge of the patch, were the words BULLY BEEF. Directly below, at the bottom of the logo, parallel to the outer edge, was the word EXPRESS. In the center of the logo was a picture of a tin can of bully beef. On the top of the can were the words "6th T.C.S." Superimposed on the face of the can was a Walt Disney head of a ferocious, Texas long horn bull with curved horns extending to the edge of the emblem. Smoke was coming out of each nostril and the bull had fiery red eyes. The new logo was designed by one of our pilots, Lieutenant Frank C. Libuse.

At dusk we flew 30 miles and delivered a load of supplies. On the final approach, at the end of the grass field, running perpendicular to the landing field was a good-sized river. There were dozens of natives with many camp fires scattered along the west bank of the approach side of the river. There were three natives in each of the small native dugout canoes. With both pilots windows open and throttles back, just before flare out, you could hear the shouts of the natives. Upon landing I asked why the natives were so restless. The Alert Driver asked if we had a few minutes so that he could show us something that we would never forget.

The four men in our crew piled into the jeep and the driver drove us to the river. Every year many of the villagers were either killed or badly maimed for life by the thousands of crocodiles in and around the river. Periodically the local villagers would go on the warpath and kill a few crocks. This was one of those times. The natives had made charcoal fires all along the river bank.

Straddling a bicycle, I posed next to the "Bully Beef Express" sign posted at Wards Airdrome in New Guinea that welcomed visitors to the 6th T.C.S. (Troop Carrier Squadron).

Near each fire in the fast moving river were two to five small wooden dugout boats. The canoes had been chiseled and hollowed out of long tree trunks. These vessels were kept upright by two bamboo pontoons in the water with one pontoon on either side of the craft. Two men would be poling (rowing), one in the front and one in the back. The third "savage" was standing in the middle of the dugout holding a long pole which he would probe in the river for crocodiles. Once the native had stirred up a crock he would try to herd it to shore near one of the beach fires. The natives on the shore had husked coconuts placed in the glowing hot charcoal embers. When the crocks were close enough, two men on shore would take long poles which were forked at one end. They looked like a long capital letter "Y". The natives would hold the stem of the Y so that the V part of the pole would interlock under a glowing hot coconut. With one man on either side of the fire, they would toss a red hot coconut in the air over the crocodile—just like tossing a ball to a dog. The crocodile would jump and try to catch the glowing coconut in the air.

Every now and then one of the crocks would catch the missile of death in its mouth and swallow the glowing red-hot ball of fire. Later Doc told us that when the crocodile was in the water and had his mouth open the back of his throat was closed. The reason was so no water could go down his throat and he would not drown. Once the mouth was closed everything in his mouth would pass on into his stomach. The natives on the beach would go wild with excitement, waving their arms, jumping, shouting, running around, slapping one another on the back, and dancing with joy. In the meantime, the crock would go berserk, thrashing in the water, diving, shaking and doing everything possible to get rid of that red-hot ball of death it had just swallowed. All the time the river current would be moving the reptile down the river and the natives would move along with him on the beach near the edge of the river. After many gyrations the crocodile in a death throe would jump straight up in the air with only the tip of its tail touching the water. He would make a last violent shake of its body and fall into the water on its back. The dead crock would float down the river, belly up, with steam coming out of its stomach where the hot coconut had burned to the rib case. At this point one could hear some of the most bloodcurdling yells that a human could make. All pandemonium would break loose and the natives would utter the most mournful shrieks, howls, and cries that sounded more like a wolf than a human being. The jubilant natives would then go back to their fire and start all over again. When the crock first swallowed this lethal fireball the three natives in the boat were in danger of being hit or swamped by the thrashing of the doomed reptile.

On 14 December, I test flew Irene and released her for flight. She had been grounded for twenty-nine days. It was very good to have the same crew and aircraft back together. We each knew one another's abilities, limits, likes and dislikes, and had a mutual respect for each other, which made for a smoother and safer operations.

While on leave I came up with an idea that I wanted to present to the crew. If we would have bailed out on our last mission (remember we had no parachutes) it could have been either over the Japanese side of the ground fighting. With neither side taking prisoners, how could we get together without being shot or captured. My plan would only work to identify crew members to crew members. It would not work with the fighting ground armies. The intent of the plan was to get our crew together on the ground as soon as possible with the minimum risk and with minimal sound. The idea was that

I often thought that I could learn so much if only I could converse with the native men I met. Many valuable lessons about the New Guinea culture, their primitive lifestyle, and jungle survival could have been learned.

after a crew member landed and disposed of his chute, look around and if he could not see or hear anyone, then he would call out any number from "1 to 100." Say the number was "39." If a crew member heard the call he would answer by calling out "49." Regardless the number called out the replay would be ten higher. The crew accepted the idea and from time to time while flying someone would call out a number and everyone that heard the number would answer correctly. This was just for practice. Each time we had a new crew member he was instructed on our "Escape and Evasion Plan." Emphasis was placed on not to keep calling, but to get out of the area to keep away from being captured, tortured, interrogated, and then killed.

We had one officer in the 6th TCS, First Lieutenant Merle H. Scheffey, who could not get along with anyone, Officer or enlisted, rated or non-rated. He could not get along with anyone and he was one lousy, paranoid pilot. He was even required to go overseas with the ground support personnel aboard the troop ship. He was the only Pilot Officer in the squadron who did not fly over. He was the third or forth ranking Officer in the Squadron. No Officer wanted him as a co-pilot and thank God he would not "Stoop so low as to fly co-pilot for any Enlisted Pilot. This is something that no Officer should ever do or be expected to do," unquote. The Commander was in desperation as to what to do with him. The Commander, Operation Officer, and the Engineering Officer had each talked to him about his attitude and treatment of the men, all to no avail. An answer finally came from 5th AF.

A Dutch C-40, 42-1302, aircraft was assigned to the Squadron to fly a daily mail run, from Wards to Fall River on the far southeast tip of the Island

CFR weather permitting. This plane required only a pilot and a crew chief. No engineer could get along with Lt. Scheffey. After a few flights each crew chief would report to the Engineering Officer and then the Operations Officer that they could not take anymore of his verbal abuse and caste system, another engineer would be ordered to fly as his crew chief always with the same results. Eventually every available crew chief and assistant crew chief in the Squadron had his turn with the same results. After a few weeks the Dutch came for their C-40 and Lieutenant Scheffey was back in the Squadron for regular flight duty. While he was flying the mail run we got some new squadron flight crew members to replace the crews that had been killed. Lt. Scheffey had never been checked out in a C-47, so there was still a problem. "The Powers That Be" decided that he would only be scheduled for flights between Wards and Dobodura, only in good weather, and only with the new crews, so that he could be checked out. If this did not pan out he would be grounded and sent to the front line in the Infantry. For about two weeks, Operations was able to schedule him for a minimum number of flights always to Dobodura and back, seldom for more that one flight a week, and always in good weather.

On the 16th, all flight crews were late in getting to the flight line and we were going to be late for rendezvous with the fighters. Aircraft were loaded in minimum time, control locks removed, gas sumps drained, and safetied and props pulled through. The pilots would do the run-up on the way for take-off. Irene was very difficult to start. Some of the Birds would not start, some conked out while taxiing. That's what happened to us. Only one of our ten aircraft that were scheduled to fly got airborne. They had to make an emergency straight-in landing at Jackson only two miles away.

The Engineering Officer, realizing something was drastically wrong, had Operations notify Fighter Command. A maintenance check found that someone had cut the spark plug wires to several of the cylinders on both engines, and then had poked the cut wires back into the harness ring. As soon as the problem was discovered, a Squadron muster was called and all Squadron personnel fell in, in front of Engineering. Four of our Squadron Sergeants stepped forward and talked to the Commander for a few seconds. Each Sergeant showed the Commander something. The Commander seemed as surprised as everyone else. He then announced that these four G-2 Agents were in charge of the investigation. We were to co-operate 100%. There would be no flying today. As the Investigators released the aircraft they were to be towed back to their revetments and repairs started. Upon completion, there would be a test hop on each aircraft before being released for flying. The next day all planes flew, but the investigation lasted for four days. Everyone was questioned and cross-checked. The conclusion was that the Japanese must have penetrated the outer Australian parameter defense and the inner defense guarded by the US Army.

There were two big surprises, one that it ever happened, and second that we had undercover G-2 Agents in the Squadron. One of the men worked in Operations, one in Engineering, one in the Orderly Room, and one in the Mess Hall. All but one had been with the 6th since Camp Williams. They just blended into the Unit and were one of the GIs. This was the only sabotage while I was with the 6th TCS, or for that matter, with any Unit I ever served while on active duty. They were transferred out of the Squadron within the week as soon as the investigation was through. To my knowledge, from then on, we did not have any undercover G-2 Agents in our outfit. Of course there may have been other ones all along. Was this internal sabotage or external penetration by the enemy? Either way, the result was not good and we never found out.

We were briefed that it was no longer essential that after each flight we refuel since it no longer appeared that we would have to walk out of New Guinea. We were just to use good common sense, keeping in mind where we would be going, the load, weather, need for a good reserve, and always refilling each night.

Colonel Frederick H. Smith, Deputy Chief of Staff for the Fifth Air Force, expressed his opinion of the battle for Papua when he declared that "In view of the bad weather and bad terrain, the handling of ground units was the key to the final outcome. It was in the transport of such units and their supplies that General MacArthur paid tribute to the work of the airmen in a typical summary of the campaign. "To the American Fifth Air Force and the Royal Australian Air Force no commendation could be too great. Their outstanding efforts in combat, supply, and transportation over both land and sea constituted the keystone upon which the arch of the campaign was erected. They have set new horizons for air conduct of the war."

"Bloody Mac" as he was called after the Buna Campaign, would fly up to Moresby in his B-17. He would then strut around in his perfectly knife-sharp starched khaki trousers, many rows of pretty ribbons, sunglasses, and his corncob pipe while the photographers took pictures. The Four Star General then would climb aboard the "17" and fly back to Brisbane. On one occasion he came to the 6th Troop Carrier Squadron Operations and paid tribute to the 6th. After watching the loading of a small bulldozer aboard one of our C-47s, he turned to an aide and asked, "What kind of aircraft is this?"

The following was extracted from a three page article in *Collier's Magazine* dated December 4, 1942 entitled "ARMY BY AIRMAIL", by George Johnston, Official Australian War Correspondent in the Southwest Pacific:

"The 'bully-beef bombers' started something when they flew an army into the jungles of New Guinea and kept it fighting. Theirs was a pioneer achievement. It rolled back the Japs and it opened a chapter of military history that is still being written.

They were up at 4 A.M. every day, in the air by 'first light,' and flying right through until dusk if the weather was 'reasonable,' that is, by Papuan standards. It took guts and stamina, morale and will power to fly as they did in unarmed aircraft with only two .45's and two Tommy guns against the cannon and machine guns of the Zero. -it just added to the fun. The advance and the initial defeat of the Japanese had been made possible only by the bully-beef bombers.

If the planes failed to get through, the troops could not fight. No air transportation-no campaign. One day a storm of cyclonic dimensions swept the Owen Stanley's. All day the transports tried to get through, but none succeeded. That day the Australians took Gona Village at bayonet point. Next day there was no supply. They fought on without food, but when their ammunition was gone they had to get out. It was to be another seventeen days before Gona was again taken. Everything depended upon support from the air. And the support from the air was magnificent.

I flew several times across the range in these transports. But I can't remember any trip when my stomach didn't feel as if it were doing slow rolls or when the hair at the nape of my neck was not bristling with fear. I never could get accustomed to diving through a gray rain cloud, seeing a vaguely darker shape ahead, realizing sickeningly that it was the side of a mountain wall just as the plane lurched violently, nearly rolled over as it turned to get out of trouble.

Our transports never came back empty from the battle field. Always there were wounded to be flown out. Without aircraft it would have taken more than two months to transport a wounded man from the Buna front to Moresby, and many would have died on the way. With air transport it was possible for a man wounded in a dawn attack at Buna to be in a modern operating room at Moresby by mid-afternoon."

"Within a month the fresh-faced kids from Maine and Florida, from Oklahoma and Texas, from Nebraska and Michigan, had lines carved round their eyes, and the set of their jaws had stiffened. Most of them had accumulated between 180 and 200 hours flying time in combat areas. The fact that their planes were virtually unarmed-what are two Tommy guns and a pilot's .45 against the cannon and machine guns of a Zero-added to the fun.

"We had seen them, day after day, as briefly seen specks scooting through the gaps in the giant jungle trees. Occasionally, when we were in an area cleared out of the jungle for use as a drop zone, we would see them come banking in with motors throttled back, great wings almost scraping the trees. As they circled, you could see the men in the open doors frantically hurling and kicking out boxes. The black specks streamed down.

"Once, with another Australian war correspondent, I was leaving the front-line positions near Buna to bring some dispatches back to Port Moresby. Clouds were down over the entire range. There was a dogfight between Zeros and P-40s in full swing over Buna as we circled endlessly to gain sufficient height to cross the summit. Each agonizing circle took us almost into the middle of the whirl of Japanese and American fighters. Eventually we popped out of the cloud, came into sunshine above a rolling cumulus through which the high purple peaks protruded majestically. My colleague and I breathed profound sighs."

Australian War Correspondent, George Johnston flew with me twice. Once we flew on a dropping mission and the other time when the 6th made its first landing at Kokoda. He and Cox got out of the aircraft and that was the last time we talked together. A couple of months later I saw him talking with an Australia Infantry patrol at Wau. Later a news clipping appeared with a picture of Irene No 52 unloading Aussies and their mortars at Wau.

One of the C-47 pilots stationed in Australia taxied into a coconut tree at Jackson Airdrome. The impact was so forceful that the right wing of the aircraft had to be replaced. There were no C-47 or DC-3 spare wings in the Theater. Maintenance crews went scrounging through all the aircraft salvage dumps in the Moresby areas and came up with an old wrecked DC-2s right wing. It was removed from the fuselage minus wing tip, aileron, wing-flap, landing light, and with plenty of dents in the leading edge of the wing and holes in the underside. The sheet metal, hydraulic and electrical shops went to work. At this time in New Guinea all aircraft maintenance was still outside day or night, sun, wind, heat and/or rain. To add to the there discomfort there were always plenty of mosquitoes. In time the smaller wing was attached to the "wounded bird." Then the plane was test hopped. An enlarged right aileron trim tab had to be added to compensate for the different size and length of the wing. After several ground adjustments the "DC-2½" was approved and released for flying.

Christmas Of '42

25 DECEMBER 1942 IS ONE CHRISTMAS I shall never forget. It was raining, windy, with sheets of blowing rain and a solid low overcast. I flew one mission over the mountains. Then flying was called off for the day. Shortly after noon Sergeant Klotz came and informed me that there was a "hurry up priority flight" to Australia and asked if I would take it. Operations were trying to round up a crew and we would be RONing. My crew turned out to be a 2nd Lieutenant for co-pilot, crew chief Sergeant Ernest C. Wooten and Sergeant Gregg, our radioman. This was the first flight for the Lieutenant since leaving the States straight out of flying school. We were to fly two RED TAGGED P-40 Allison engines and seven passengers to Garbutt Airdrome. I briefed the passengers and told them that this was a priority flight and the weather was lousy. It was going to be a long, rough flight and if any or all did not wish to go that was up to them. All climbed aboard the truck and we headed for the aircraft. On the way I asked the co-pilot if he had ever flown in a front or through squall lines. He replied, "No." I told him that we would be earning our flight pay today and briefed him just like Sergeant Cox: "Fold your hands in your lap, hold on and ask all the questions that come to mind as often as you wish. Sergeant Wooten and I will try to make it fly." I gave all passengers a briefing and told them if we had any calm air the crew chief would let them come up front a couple at a time, but otherwise they should

stay strapped in at all times.

We were airborne at 1458 hours. The weather was foul, not fit for "man or beast or aircraft either." The forecast called for solid clouds all the way. We would be crossing two squall lines before reaching Townsville with a cold front at Garbutt. We estimated 4:20 hours en route. That would put us in there at night. They were predicting 500 feet and one mile visibility or less with no other place to go. These were the days before in-flight Radar, TACAN, VOR, ILS, GCA, Ground Positioning System, or any of that wonderful navigation and landing aids of today. Of course, there was no IFF. No alternate field was available and none was required for First Pilots flying in and out of New Guinea. The field minimums for each flight were whatever the clearing authority thought that particular pilot was capable of making safely. We had no maps. I was able to copy the tower and the radio range frequencies and draw out the four radio range legs and let-down instructions.

Before leveling off the Lieutenant and I were both soaking wet from our knees down. Irene as always leaked like a sieve in the cockpit when in heavy rain. With no auto-pilot or artificial horizon flying was work with total concentration. The weather was almost as bad as it had been between Fiji and New Caledonia. One hour out John called Townsville with a position report asking for the weather and let-down instructions for Garbutt. He was unable to raise anyone. After several more calls he fired up the Collins with the same results. All we could get was thunder, lightening, and sheets of blowing rain. We were unable to tune in the radio range or any commercial radio stations. The CFR's approach procedure was, before reaching Magnetic Island to let down to 1,500 feet or below the base of the clouds, which ever was lower, drop your gear, slow to 120 mph on a heading of 150° with landing lights on. A fighter escort would escort us in.

I switched to the main fuel tanks and let down on time and distance, breaking out just below 200 feet, still in heavy sheets of blowing rain. The waves were very high and rough with spray and white caps and it was as dark as midnight. Shortly, during a flash of lightening, I could make out land maybe a quarter of mile or less. Except for the lightening it was pitch black with no lights, ships or coast line in sight. Both the co-pilot and radioman were calling on all frequencies to no avail. The only thing over the radios was ear splitting static. The co-pilot, crew chief, and I had our eyes glued on looking outside. The cockpit lights were dimmed to almost off. After flying around for some time unable to pick up the range or a local commercial radio station and not being able to find any landmark, I decided to climb up to 3,500 feet to see if we could raise anyone on the radios. I raised the gear, turned off the wipers, left the landing lights on, and made right single needle turns until leveling off. I could not figure out what was wrong. Why no one was answering us. We knew that the Collins was blasting them out of their headsets for at least a thousand miles.

I told Wooten to keep a sharp eye out looking ahead in the landing lights at all times. The highest peak I could remember in the area was 2,200 feet. If he saw anything he was to let me know immediately even if he only thought he saw something to just let me know! I kept on more power than normal just in case we had to climb all of a sudden. I made many circles trying to correct for the wind drift hoping to keep over the spot we first reached on our initial let-down. I got on the "Coffee Grinder," the pilot's cockpit radio 396kc to the tower, and requested that they have the anti-aircraft people shoot up some flares in front of us so we could let down on them. There was not a word, only static after at least an hour of fighting the weather in circles. The airspeed varied between 90-235 mph, which is above the red line. Due to the violent up and down-drafts it was one hairy tiring elevator ride. I glanced up and there in the landing lights right on our nose were trees on the side of a mountain cliff!!! I gave it full power and did a steep climbing Immelmann. Cross checking I found the altimeter was now reading 4,300 feet and climbing at 95 mph. Where did those trees come from?? That was more likely the most stress I'd ever put on a C-47 and yet it seemed not to affect its flight characteristics. I yelled at Sergeant Wooten, "Why did you not call out? We almost got killed!" The Lieutenant asked, "What was that?" I told him that we had trees in the landing lights. The trees were growing out of a cliff on the side of the mountain. I had made an Immelmann to get away from them. He said that he did not know that a Douglas could stand that many "Gs". I did not know it either. That was what we were taught to do in P-40s as the quickest way to reverse direction and gain altitude. An Immelmann is a climbing half-inside loop, and when on your back in an upside-down inverted position fly a half roll back to a normal upright in-flight position. This maneuver will gain altitude and make a 180° change of direction. We leveled off at 7,500 feet which I knew to be higher than any peak within 1,000 miles. When I pulled back on the wheel and added full power we were on one of those elevator up rides indicating over 235 mph. This airspeed and with the violent updraft and full throttle was all that kept us from stalling out and crashing head on into the face of the mountain. The strong updraft kept us from mushing into the trees.

I sent Wooten back to check to see if everything was still tied down and in place. After checking the load, he was to look to see if all the passengers were strapped down good. I did not want to scare them anymore than they already were.

All mountains in this area had to be to the southeast of the Airdrome, so I flew fifteen minutes on a heading of 340° ± holding at 7,500 feet plus or minus 1,000 feet. I told the co-pilot that I was going back down to the Sea and then make a landfall and fly down the coast to the southeast until we either found the Airdrome or we would land on the beach. With this much wind the visibility and ceiling should not be any lower than it was when we were down there before. I asked if either of them had any better ideas to speak up. There were no suggestions. It seemed like the cockpit was a swimming pool. The overhead pilot's escape hatch seal did not hold, creating the problem. It always leaked when it was raining, and it seemed to always be raining.

It was now 2325 hours and the gas was all but gone. We had been in the air for 8 hours 27 minutes. The rear tanks were empty and we were running on the mains. At minimum cruise, smooth air, and an empty Gooney Bird, you can stay in the air for ten plus hours. But we were overloaded and constantly changing altitudes. The mixture control was between "Auto-Lean" to "Emergency Rich," and we had been using a lot of high power settings.

In a few minutes, still at 7,500 feet, here came the flares, and lightening blazed at the same time. Then came the black puffs and you could smell the gun smoke. This told me that it was ack-ack, and now the "bloody bastards" were shooting at us. We went into a steep spiraling diving power descent indicating 2,000 feet a minute, on top of the anti-aircraft fire. We reversed direction of turns several times on the way down. All explosions were leading us. A few were close enough that I thought I could feel the concussion even in this turbulent storm, but we took no hits. It was nerve-wracking for if one piece of shrapnel had hit the fuel tanks we were goners. I was glad to see that they could shoot no better here than at Moresby. I was trying to keep over where the ack-ack was coming from. That way we'd be a smaller target and I'd have a better idea where the Airdrome was. At 500 feet I turned to 0° and kept descending until we broke out just below 200 feet. I did a 180° and my best estimate headed for the coast where the anti-aircraft fire had been coming from. It was still pitch black and raining like a hurricane in the movies. The sea was whipped into a white fury and sheets of lightening were all that made any visibility possible. If anything, the storm was worse with curtains of pouring water. Thank the Lord for the lightening. I slowed to 120 with landing lights and windshield wipers on with a heading 150°. There was no forward visibility and we had to look out the side storm windows to have any forward visibility. If it hadn't been for the flashes of lightening we would have never made it. The weather was far worse than the "Weather Guesser" had forecasted.

When we crossed the coast line at the very base of the overcast under 200 feet, the co-pilot called out that we were over a cemetery. I knew right then where we were. If only we had enough gas! I told Wooten to stand by on the Wobble Pump and I would handle the cross feed if need be. We were now over a darkened runway which ran perpendicular to the coast. What a relief! If only the gas would hold and there were no high wires or towers I knew we could make it. I flew straight down the runway with no drift, just sheets of blowing rain coming straight in from the Coral Sea. I was holding a steady 120 mph flying level at 200 feet. When over where the landing touch down point should be the right fuel warning light began to flicker. I made a right 45° for 30 seconds and then a tight left 225° back for the runway. Two-thirds around the level bank the right engine began to sputter and lose power and at this time the left engine fuel light started flickering. Sergeant Wooten was on the wobble pump with smooth even strokes. I could get no more power out of No. 2 so I dropped the nose, pulled the right throttle back and touched the feathering button. There was no time to crank in any rudder or aileron trim or to try any fuel management. We were too close in and I was sure that all tanks were empty. I lowered the gear. All this happened on a very short banking turn to final. I was just leveling the wings from the close-in proce-dure as we crossed the end of the runway. As we rolled down the runway No. 1 died and I feathered it. The co-pilot was pulling up on the hydraulic pump handle with his left hand and the crew chief was pushing it back down with his right foot to keep an even 6-800 psi. This was the only time in my twenty-three years of flying as a pilot that I ever ran out of fuel. We had been in the air for 9:21 hours. That was excellent considering the many different high power settings, altitude changes, and the gross weight of the aircraft.

After touch down the airdrome lit up like a Christmas tree and the Alert Truck came to meet us. Wooten went out, put the pins in, chocked the wheels and put on the control locks. I had only touched the brakes to come to a full stop and to put the parking brakes on. All that time I was keeping a close eye on the hydraulic pressure. I called down to the Alert Driver and told him to get transportation to the mess hall for eleven hungry men. He was to tow the Bird in. We ran out of gas and no maintenance was required. We just had too many hours of flying. We have two RED TAGGED P-40 engines for the Depot. I told him that we are going to RON and will depart for Moresby at noon tomorrow. Notify the Airdrome Officer that all of us are combat troops so "No KP" and after chow I'll be back in Operations looking for a lot of answers.

By the time the Form 1 was completed transportation and a tow bar to tow the aircraft to the flight line were there. All passengers thanked us and two kissed the watery tarmac when they got out. One of them asked Wooten, "Why was the Sergeant doing all the talking and the Lieutenant was saying nothing?" Wooten told him that the Sergeant was the pilot. When under the wing, still in the blowing rain, I told the passengers that all who wanted chow were to stay on the bus. After a short stop in Operations we would go to the mess hall.

Sergeant Wooten turned Irene over to the Alert Crew, again, telling them about the two Allison engines for the Depot, and that he would be around in the morning to fuel it up. He told them to tow it in, park it, no work or inspection, to just park it and off-load the two engines and close the doors.

I told the bus driver to take us to Operations, wait for me while I closed our flight plan, and then drive us to the mess hall. He could either have coffee and wait for us or come back when we were finished. Then he was to take the crew back to Operations and the other men to Transient Quarters. When the crew was finished in Ops our Lieutenant was to go to the BOQ, and we three GI's were to go to Enlisted Crews barracks. I told him that if he stayed with us we would leave our gear in the bus, otherwise, we would unload it at the mess hall. The driver said that if I could get him a cup of coffee he'd stay. It seemed like all ten sounded off a good loud, "Stay."

On the way back from chow, I told the Lieutenant that when we get to Operations it might be best if he just listened, for the conversation might get pretty heated. I told him just to remember what is said on both sides of the counter. When we get back to Wards for him to report it to our Commander and to the Operations Officer. If the AO, OD and whoever else is there make any kind of a fuss and do not answer some questions it could get very interesting. They cannot do anything to a Staff Sergeant Pilot unless I get insubordinate and that I will not do.

I told the driver to take our passengers to transient GI barracks. Then I told the passengers that if anything was said about them doing KP before they could eat in the morning to tell them that they were from combat units in New Guinea. Combat troops are not supposed to pull KP. Then I told the driver to come back and pick us up here at Operations. We would leave our bags aboard.

When the crew walked into Operations at 0140 hours we had a reception party waiting to meet us: the Officer of the Day, the Airdrome Officer, and the Base Operations Officer. The only one of the three to speak was the Base Operations Officer. He was the same Major I'd had a run-in with over KP on my way to Mackay, and the time I'd off-loaded the Red Tagged engines at Charter Towers on the 5th. "Well I see we have another visit by THAT SERGEANT PILOT. I might have known. Sergeant, the last two times you stopped in here you caused a hell of lot of trouble and now you caused all northeastern Australia to be blacked out for over six hours." I looked him in the eye and said good and loud, "Major, those were just warm-ups for tonight. I see the Base is now up and doing business. Where have they been since about 1800 hours when we needed help? Major, which side of the war is this Base on?? I've been informed that the Base no longer requires combat crews and Staff Sergeant Pilots to pull KP. Sir, is that correct?" He was so mad he did not speak. It looked as though he was about to explode, but he did nod his head up and down. His face was a bright red and he was highly agitated. "Major, what happened to Base Communications? Why would no one answer No. 118539? I'm positive every station in Queensland heard us dozens of times. Why was there no help?" There was dead silence. Then in a calm controlled voice he said, "We had no flight plan." My reply, "In that case where were your fighters? Why did they not come up and investigate?" He said, "The weather was below flight minimums and too bad for them to get up." My response was, "Do I understand that Garbutt only has fair weather fighter pilots? Is that what I'm to tell General Kenney?" The Major's facial expression confirmed that he knew I knew the General's address and that I would write him again within the week. "By the way, I flew No. 118539 from the Factory in the States to New Guinea plus an additional 300 hours since arriving in the Theater. I flew every single hour as the First Pilot. When I picked up No. 118539 at the Factory it did not have an auto-pilot or an artificial horizon, just the seven basic flight instruments and neither has been installed since. If a Sergeant Pilot can fly halfway around the world with only half an instrument panel you'd think your pilots could fly in their own backyard with a full instrument panel. I received my pilot wings in P-40s at Luke. Someone around here must have tracked us after our original position call one hour out at 1820. They must have known that we were coming from the north. New Guinea is the only land to the north so if no clearance, why not query Moresby to see if No. 118539 was heading your way?" No answer. "Tomorrow at 1200 we will be returning to Wards. If you have anything for Wards or Jackson we will take it. We are now going to bed. Please notify the Anti-Aircraft Commander that I congratulate them on their marksmanship!"

I did a snappy salute, about faced, and the four of us marched out to the waiting bus. I told the driver to drive the Lieutenant to the BOQ and let the three of us off at the GI Transit Quarters. Then I told the crew to eat breakfast and to find their own way to Operations and to be there by 1000 hours. This Christmas Day of 1942 had been one very long tiring, fatiguing day. I was simply exhausted. I firmly believe "that the hand of Providence intervened and delivered all of us safely." "And I might add with no gas to spare!!"

Next morning the four of us arrived in Ops before 1000 hours. Sergeant Wooten and Gregg went to refuel and pre-flight Irene. When the co-pilot and I walked into Operations the NCOIC came up to the counter and said: "Serg, I heard you were here." The co-pilot spoke up and said, "I'll bet you did." At 1200 we departed for Moresby with a full load. We saw none of our adversaries from the night before.

On our way back from Garbutt Airdrome in perfectly clear, calm weather, approximately midway to Wards out over the Coral Sea, we flew over a single palm tree. There was no land in sight, just a tree growing out of the sea water. Over the fifteen months on this tour I flew over and looked down at this unusual sight several times. In order to see it you had to be exactly on course with a calm sea. Later I learned that it was called Bougainville Reef. It should have been called The Bougainville Tree.

Arriving back at Wards, I made a full oral report to the Operations Officer and then to the Commander. Two days later, I turned in a written complaint to 5th AF about Garbutt. Then I was told that on the night of 24 December two of our Second Lieutenants, Jerome L. Simpson and Edwin R. Heyboer were both killed in a fatal jeep accident here at Wards Airdrome during a bombing raid.

After making my report to the Commander I asked how the Squadron Christmas Party had been and then asked, "Why did we not go to England last summer?" He then told me. About the time we had started for Europe the FBI found out that during July a German POW pilot escaped from a POW internment camp in Canada. It was believed that he was headed for Detroit. The FBI for a long time had wanted an excuse to raid the Detroit German-American Bund, and this was their chance. Among other things they found was a copy of a our SECRET General Order and Flight Plan showing date, route, call signs and radio frequencies for our Squadron to fly to England. There had only been five copies of the General Orders. Each copy was numbered and assigned to a different General. However, the number on the copy found at the Bund had been cut off. There was no way to find out where the leak was. If the Germans had this information they might have had Me-110s, submarines, and/or a pocket battleship waiting for thirteen unarmed C-47s. So the Army immediately canceled our orders and within two months we were on our way to New Guinea. It was our good fortune that it worked out this way and we did not meet up with the Messerschmitts or the German Navy out over the North Atlantic.

A very strange twist about the German POW came on 25 June 1999 when my wife, Etta, her two sisters Ruth and Jane, and I were on our way to Germany. This was Etta's and my fourth flight to Germany to visit where her Father was born and lived as a young man. On this flight I talked to three

Germany Air Force Pilots. They had just completed a special upgrading fly-ing class at Luke in the latest USAF Fighters and were on their way back home. When they found out about our aborted try to fly to England in July 1942 all three at once started telling me about this POW. He was one of their leading Aces at that time in WWII. When he escaped from the Canadian POW Internment Camp he did find his way to Detroit. The Bund smuggled him to Old Mexico and from there back to Germany. He was sent to most of the German Flying Squadrons telling of his experiences and about how to "Evade, Escape, and Rescue." Three weeks later he returned to flying combat and was shot down and killed. All three signed my Short-Snorter on a 1920, 100 MARK bill that Etta's father gave me some fifty years earlier.

8

Jungle

TODAY IT WAS BACK TO DOBODURA, and we had more than the usual number of fighter escorts. While on the airstrip unloading at Dobodura, we watched one big hairy air battle. Something happened to one of the P-38s, and the pilot landed and parked close to us. The Aussie Major met him and they talked for at the most a minute. The pilot walked around his "Bird", inspected it, and then got in the jeep with his parachute. They drove up to our aircraft and the Major yelled up and asked me if we were going to Moresby. I told him: "Yes," that all of us will be going to Wards and we would be leaving in about fifteen minutes if our Fighters can keep the Japs away from us. The little blond-headed Second Lieutenant asked if I'd give him a ride. I told him "Yes," and to get in and come up front. He was very excited and told us that he had just made his first "two kills." He could not see anything wrong with his Lightning, but it would not do over 200 mph. It was working fine until the last Zero got on his tail. He saw tracers go by him but did not think that his aircraft had been hit. The 38' had not lost its cooling system so the engines could not be damaged too much. The plane just lost power and he could not dog fight at that speed. He was one happy, excited young Flyer. I told him that in just over a week I'd be flying to Sydney for ten days. I'd be glad to give him a ride down and back. He thanked us and that was it.

From a news release by General Kenney, "As the year 1942 ended, the

374th had two full Squadrons, the 6th and 33rd, operating in New Guinea, as well as air echelons of the 21st and 22nd Squadrons. They had successfully carried into the front lines more than 40,000,000 pounds of airborne supplies with a loss of 15 planes."

At the end of 1942, Lieutenant General Robert L. Eichelberger was ordered to the front to take command of the 32d Division. "Go out there Bob and take Buna or don't come back alive!" This was MacArthur's cheery send-off to General Eichelberger as he left Brisbane. From then on, General MacArthur was known as "BLOODY MAC"!

On 1 January 1943, I flew The Allied Commander of Ground Forces, Southwest Pacific, Australian Chief of Staff, Field Marshal Sir Thomas Blamey and Aide back from Dobodura. Just as we landed two things took place. A heavy rain shower soaked the Field and as we were turning off the PSP 250 pound bombs began hitting the Field. I pulled into the nearest empty revetment and rang the bail-out bell. Grassi put down the stairs, put in the landing gear pins, control locks and chocks. Grassi, Gregg, and Cox directed the twenty-eight passengers to slit trenches. By the time I had cut all switches, shut down the aircraft, got out of my parachute, strapped on my "45", Bollo knife and helmet, gas mask, and worked my way down the aisle stacked high with their gear, only two of us were left aboard, General Blamey and myself. He was standing in the rear of the aircraft on the flat heavy aluminum loading platform entrance watching the rain and waiting for transportation. As I hurried to deplane, the General stepped forward to get a better look outside just as I reached the wet loading surface. I tried to pivot to keep from colliding with the General, fell and slid into the sharp aluminum rear door jamb and cut a bloody gash in my right leg. Some sixty years later I still have a scar. I told the General that if he did not get out as of now he had just assumed command. I then limped out with my bleeding leg as another stick of 250s began exploding. An A-20 in the next revetment was hit, exploded and began to burn with shrapnel and flaming pieces of aircraft flying everywhere. After that Havoc blew up the General abandoned ship. It was another forty-five minutes before the General's Aide arrived with a Jeep.

There were no navigational aids or maps at any landing strips or drop zone areas in all of New Guinea. All "strips" and "drops" had to be located visually by the pilot from the verbal instructions either from the briefing officer or an Aussie that had been there. Going into a new area involved a lot of guess work. The first three months we were in New Guinea, the Japanese had air superiority and there was a lot of "dodging and dropping" on our part. With the mountains, clouds, wind, rain, low ceilings, and short narrow clearings in the jungle, maximum proficiency was required for each landing and on every mission. In combat there are no weather minimums, decisions were up to the Squadron Operations and each pilot. A few of us flew regularly and solocal when the rest of the Squadron was grounded because of weather.

Litter patients were delivered by native carriers direct from the battlefield to the nearest cleared jungle field for air transportation back to Wards. During December and early January the 6th flew out an average of more than 100 patients daily achieving a peak of 280 on 8 December. Every possible plane was thrown into the service. When the battle was over, the record showed that the 374th TCWs flew out 2,530 sick and 991 battle casualties from the 32nd Division and its attached troops. This does not count the dead, for they were buried on site. At a later time the Grave Registrar would find the graves and relocate any remains that could be found. These are impressive figures for that time and place, but they represent only a part of the Troop Carriers' work load. War is an awful bloody business. To see grown men, who for the most part were only 17-21 years old, with gaunt faces and sunken red eyes, cry like babies though not physically injured is something you will never forget.

We flew two missions to Dobodura. Then the weather turned sour and dropped below flight minimums. At debriefing we were told that our aircrafts were now being loaded for Dobodura as that was where the squadron would be going as soon as the weather cleared, hopefully in the morning.

Another one of our P-38 fighter escorts ran into mechanical difficulties and made a forced landing at Dobodura and was unable to make it back to Moresby. The 8th Fighter had the parts and two mechanics standing by. They were here and ready to go if anyone would fly them to Dobodura. We need to get that Lightning and pilot back on this side of the mountains before the weather clears and the Japs caught them on the ground. No one sounded off and there was no show of hands. I caught the eye of the Commander. He asked if I would take the flight. I replied, "If my crew will." The Debriefing Officer then told me that there would be no fighter escort and in this crappy weather there should be no enemy fighters up. He said to take the load of ammo that is now on your plane and the four Aussies that are loading Irene. They would see about unloading on the other side. The two fighter mechanics will meet you at your aircraft.

By this time the weather was well below safe Squadron formation flying conditions. There was plenty of rain and thunder storms over the mountains and strong gusty winds. This was just the normal weather for this time of the day. Underneath the thunder storms over the mountains the ceiling and visibility were so that if the pilot knew his way he could find his way up and through the Kokoda Pass. Today those wind draft below

An aerial photo of the "First Aide Hut" at Kokoda (on the north side of the pass). We often carried medical supplies to the front lines and evacuated wounded troops from the battlefield. Over the course of my 364 combat missions in New Guinea, I transported more than 1,500 medical evacuees, both American and Australian, from front line combat zones.

the thunderstorm would be called wind shear and no sensible pilot would dare, or be allowed to, file a flight plan into such an area. But in New Guinea we were not that smart and some of us did it several times a week. Once we were on the north side of the mountains we would be able to spiral down below the base of the clouds 50 to 100 feet above the tree tops. We dodged the rain showers and found Dobodura. Even from that altitude it was easy to see the ground fire from the raging battle in the Buna area.

I landed and taxied next to the Lightning, parked and cut the engines. The fighter pilot was very glad to see us and we met at the back door of the plane. He was afraid that he was going to have to spend the night with his aircraft. The two mechanics immediately started to work on the plane and the Aussies went to round up four "lorries" to unload ammunition. By the time the P-38 was being run-up and ground tested we were ready to crank up. The fighter pilot had told us that if they got his bird fixed he would test it below the clouds. If it checked out he would climb straight out on a heading of 90°

till on top or 25,000 feet, and then head for Moresby. I told him that would not put him on top and to be careful in flying in and around thunder storms at that altitude because of wind shear, lightning, hail, and severe turbulence.

I told him if he would fly back over the field below the clouds on a heading of east, we would wait to see him out of the area and on his way. If his aircraft did not check out he was to come back and we would be waiting with the mechanics. I then told him that we were going to fly under the clouds on the north side of the island to Fall River, refuel, then fly under the clouds on the south side of the island back to Moresby. Those thunderstorms, mountains, and aircraft do not mix. I asked him if when he got back to Moresby to have his Ops call the 6th TCS at Wards and give them No. 39's flight plan. If the weather closes down before we get to Fall River we will pick out a clearing, land, and wait out the weather. He thanked us and went to his plane. Shortly, he was airborne and in no time, back over the field. He wiggled his wings and disappeared into the eerie overcast heading east.

There were ten of us. We had a little over four hours of gas for a flight of little less than two-hours. With this weather and the mountains, we would not be able to go back through the pass or fly over the mountains with this line of thunder storms. I planned to fly down the north side of New Guinea below the weather to Fall River, then land, refuel and fly up the south coast to Moresby. I had not been along the north coast line and we had no maps. I'd studied one in Townsville. As long as we had 200 feet altitude, one mile visibility, and had the coast in sight off our right wing, we would be OK. But Dobodura was not the place to RON. There were plenty of enemy ground troops in the area and when their fighters and bombers arrived that would be curtains for us. I had a little talk with all aboard and told them the plan and risks. If anyone wished to stay and join up with whatever Allied Ground Force they could find now was their chance. Then tomorrow they could report to the pilot of the first C-47 that landed and get a ride back to our Unit at Moresby. I had no takers. I told Cox and Grassi to keep their eyes open in front of us and to their right for any clearings large enough to land in. There was only water on my side, the Solomon Sea.

Now it was our time to depart. The ceiling could not have been over 350-400 feet with a couple of miles visibility at the most and scattered rain squalls. We pulled the wheels up at 1635 hours turning right and flew down the coast to the southeast. About forty minutes out, Cox spotted a very large level field. It had a native village with no red roofs in the trees at the edge of the clearing and a good-sized meandering stream parallel to the south side of the clearing adjacent to the forest. He and Grassi both said that the clearing was larger than the Wards area. The surface appeared to be a level plain covered prairie with short grass with no kunai grass in sight. We continued on down the coast for another fifteen minutes. At this time with thickening, darkening clouds, the ceiling and the sea seemed to become one. There was no forward visibility with sheets of blowing rain. It was a real torrential downpour. There were many off shore islands with an irregular coast lines with cliffs higher than our flight level. With such a low ceiling and visibility in the monsoon season plus rugged terrain it was time to turn around. I made a sharp left 180 out over the sea.

I told Cox and Grassi that it looked like we would be RONING at their field even if the village did not have red top roofs. If we make a safe landing, when the weather clears tomorrow, we will have enough gas to fly back to Wards. Or during the daytime we can always fly to Dobodura and have the 6th fly over a few barrels of fuel if Dobodura is unable to spare a few gallons. But if we continue on down the coast for another hour and cannot land at Fall River we've had it. There are not supposed to be any headhunters or cannibals in this area. That doesn't mean that the natives will not try to kill us. We will have to post guards. This is in the area that is controlled by the enemy and should be considered a kill zone. But we were not to shoot at anyone or anything unless it was a life and death situation. I told them, "leave your safeties on, but if you see it's the enemy, un-safety your gun and be ready."

"Grassi, go tell everyone to get a drink and then refill their canteens to full. Better take our gas masks just in case and besides it is "Bloody Mac's" orders. Get their guns, have them with them at all times, and keep them on safety. Practice all safety rules. Then explain to the troops our situation and plan. Ask the Aussies if any of them have ever been in actual ground combat. If so bring the trooper with the most combat up front." Shortly Grassi was back with one of the Aussie Sergeants. He said that all four of them had been in combat in North Africa and for the last ten months in New Guinea. I told the Sergeant, "You are the only ones who have been in actual ground combat. So we're asking you to give us a defense plan until we get airborne, hopefully sometime tomorrow around noon. I'll park out in the open lined up so we can take off without taxiing into position. The first thing is to protect all ten of us and then the aircraft. You stand up here behind the crew chief. I'll fly over the cleared area so you'll know how to set up your defense plan. When the engines are cut and the crew chief opens the back door and put the stairs in place, you and your three Aussies jump out and set up the perimeter defense. Take all your equipment with you."

"Grassi, you and Gregg tie down the aircraft and get out the water barrel and all the C-rations. Cox, you collect, control, and hand out all food and water, stretch it as far as you can for at least three days. Divide it up evenly among all ten of us. Serve out one meal at a time. Any water we collect we must use the water pills before we drink it. Bring all the water, salt and Atabrine pills we have and the Aircraft First Aid Kit. Gregg, get the trench shovels, fire axes and anything that we can dig with. If Irene is strafed or enemy ground troops explode her we don't want to lose anything we need. Be sure everyone is wearing his dog-tags, steel helmet, head net, and gas mask. Have your rain gear with you for it will start raining by the time we're parked. I'll try to park up close to the trees, but from the air the plane will stand out very clearly and be easy to spot."

I slowed down to 120 mph at an indicated altitude of 360 feet at the very base of the ragged overcast. I could see no stumps, rocks or holes, only a large grassy plain. Some of the trees to the south edge of the clearing had gigantic trunks and were at least two hundred feet tall. From the ground up there was a solid wall of various shades of greenery. The co-pilot and crew chief both said it looked OK to them. I then asked our Aussie if he'd been able to see the area. He said, "Yes. In the night when it is dark we should have a pass word." He suggested "DOBODURA as that is a very hard word for the Japanese to pronounce and the natives cannot." I told him that upon parking, the crew has to secure the aircraft, collect the water, food, aircraft medical kit, digging tools, and personal gear. Then we will report to you for instructions. Expect us to be there within fifteen to twenty minutes. I pointed out where I planned to park. It was out in the clear about half a mile from the village and lined up for a take-off. "Sergeant, go tell your troops and the two Army mechanics to keep a cool head with guns on safety. Do not pull the trigger until you see what you're shooting and then only if you aim to kill. Each of you take all the ammo you have with you. And one other thing, after dark don't anyone get amorous and visit the native village girl's hut. That is a no-no!"

Grass is the smoothest surface to land on. I spun around and parked at the spot we had picked out. Grassi had the door opened before the props stopped turning. The four Australians were out and ran out about 100 yards from each quadrant of the aircraft. They hit the grass in a prone position facing out from the aircraft. They were now ready to fire at any inbound enemy. The time was 1805 hours.

I assigned each crew member and the two mechanics their guard posts and duties until the Senior Australian wished to give us other assignments. I told them that I would take the post in front of Irene. That would relieve the Senior Aussie to move around as he chose and to have a better control of the situation. I said, "Grassi you and Gregg go to the right wing and you two mechanics take the other two posts. Sergeant Cox, you take care of all food, water and any other equipment we have and don't forget the toilet paper. Remember the Army says 8 sheets per man per day! Cox, when all is calmed down and the Aussie Sergeant has us in place you can start serving each of us our rations for the evening meal. No one is to get near the food and water except Sergeant Cox. When we get out everyone is to help carry all the supplies out about 50 yards at a 1030 position to the back door of the aircraft. Cox you stay there and the rest go to your assigned post. Don't see who can stand the tallest, for you might be a good target for any Jap in the area. But at the same time, unless I see or hear someone I'm not planning on crawling around in the mud on my stomach at least at this time."

It began to rain as I was getting out of the cockpit. We six Army Air Corps Airmen had it better than the other troops for we had oilskin raingear, while they had ponchos. When the wind blew the poncho did not afford much protection from the waist down. The crew and two mechanics rounded up everything that we were going to take with us and then divided it up to carry away from the plane. There was only one problem and that was the 20-gallon water barrel. It was full of fresh water when we left Moresby this morning. The only time it had been used was within the last fifteen minutes. At this time it must have weighed at least 180 pounds. How do we get it out of the aircraft and on the ground? There was no ramp or way to make one. One of the mechanics came to the rescue. He took two of the long wide cargo tie-down webbed belts, secured each to a cargo floor "D-Ring" across from the main cargo door. Then he rolled the barrel to the back door, turned it parallel to the cargo door, laid it on top of the two straps which were evenly spaced in from the ends of the barrel. Then with two men holding the ends of both straps, which had been looped under and over the topside of the barrel, and with one man on the ground on each end of the barrel it was eased out the door and lowered to the grass below. From there on it was just a matter of rolling the barrel where you wanted it to go. While this was going on, Grassi dropped and anchored eight litters for the off duty troops to sleep on.

When the cargo door was being closed, I realized that I might need the field glasses which were in the pilot's side map case. As I was reaching for the glasses I noticed the compass. When I got to the back door I pointed out the direction to the north shore of Dobodura and Moresby. I told them not to forget just in case we had to walk out. Grassi put up the steps and closed the door. Cox took the lead, walked out, and set down the two cases of C-rations he was carrying. He was followed by three other airmen and the last two of us, pulling up the rear by rolling the barrel of water. We covered all supplies, top and bottom, with the two 12 X 12 foot tarpaulins that were standard equipment in the "Tie-down, Load, and Lash Box," which is stored in the aircraft under the main cargo floor. One side of the canvas was camouflage and the other side bright orange. The orange side is to be turned up for Air Rescue in the event the aircraft went down in friendly territory or at sea. This time only the camouflage side was to be visible. The enemy had at least one fighter base within 100 miles of here, and their bombers should be expected to fly over this area once the weather clears.

Once all the gear was in place on one of the tarps with the other tarp over the top and tucked in around all sides so it would not blow away or let water in, each of us went to our post. When I reported in, I brought the Aussie up to-date. Then I told him that he was relieved and for him to make any changes needed and to keep me informed. As soon as all the guards were in place he was to let Sergeant Cox know so he could start handing out the evening meal. "You figure out if Cox is to deliver the C-cans or someone from each post is to go to him. You and your troops eat first, then the left wing, tail, and right wing. I will be last in that order."

Shortly, the "Lead Sergeant" with his rifle and fixed bayonet left to inspect the other three posts. In about 30 minutes he returned with my evening meal. At this time we were getting blowing rain. He told me that as soon as it was dark he was pulling our posts in so we would be about 10 feet from the nose, tail and both wing-tips. He doubted that the natives would attack at any time and especially not at night, "For the spirits of the jungle are very hostile at night." An attack by the natives would only be in daylight, and then only if we went into the trees. I do not believe that they would come out in the open area and attack. Now the Japanese could attack from any direction and at any time. An enemy squad could take us anytime they wanted to. We did not have the firepower or skill to repel them or hold them off. We might be able to handle a few snipers.

I'm now going to pull out my three "Blokes" and go down to the stream and collect a bucket of small rocks, some long vines and sticks. When we return all posts will be moved into our night positions. Then I will set up an outer defense. We'll string the vines all around the plane and on the outside of the guard posts. The vines will be stretched about a foot above the ground. On the vines between the posts will be hung the little tin C-cans we eat from with two small rocks in each. Once it gets in place, if the rope (vines) or can is touched the rocks will rattle. Then the guards will know that something either a man or animal is trying to go through the staked-out area. When, and, if it stops raining each post will dig a fox hole. But now it would only fill with water faster than we could dig it.

The four Aussies left and we saw them disappear into the jungle. About an hour later, just as it was getting dark, here came the four Infantrymen. They were loaded down with green vines and a big arm load of forked sticks. The sticks were about three feet long with a short "Y" at one end.

The four Aussies deposited their loads equally spaced around Irene. Each of the guards was then brought into our new night positions. Each of the four Australians picked up a steel rod from the "Tie down Box" that was used to anchor down the aircraft wing-tips. They pushed, twisted and turned the rods a couple of feet into the ground. The Lead Aussie and I laid out the vine ropes in a circle ten feet outside the guard posts all around the airplane. When the "Y" sticks were in the ground, the vine ropes were strung out all around the aircraft on top of the "Ys" and then we tied the rope in place with a short piece of vine. Each of the tin cans was turned upside down, and with their bayonets, two slits were punched through the bottom of the can so the rain-water would run through. The tin cans were turned back over. Two small rocks were put in each can and they were tied, evenly spaced, on the vine rope around the perimeter of Irene. The reason the vines were one foot off the ground was so a man could not crawl under the vine. If a man or animal walked through, their legs would hit the vines and the infiltrator would sound the alarm. This would cause the rocks in the cans to move around and make a tingling sound. This would alert the guard even if he could not see the invader. This should aid in preventing anyone from penetrating our enclosure without us knowing it.

"If at any time you think that you should shoot at an intruder, be positive you are firing away from the aircraft and away from the native village. Stay down on the grass. Do not stand up or walk around in the dark. Also stay at your post. If you see or hear anyone moving around challenge him. Say only one word and say it only once, "password." The reason for calling only once is that you do not want to give away your position. If you do not hear 'Dobodura' loud and clear shoot to kill when you see him. If you do, or do not shoot, stay still and be quiet at your post. I'll be there as soon as I can." He handed me two small rocks about two inches across. He told me to keep the two rocks on me where I could get hold of them really fast if I should need them. "When anyone within the vine rope enclosure needs to go to another guard post when it is too dark for us to recognize one another, gently tap the two stones together and say 'Dobodura.' Do not wait to be challenged. Just tap the rocks together and say 'Dobodura.' We four chaps are now going in the aircraft to try to get some sleep. At 0100 hours, we will take over the guard duty for the rest of the night. Do not go to sleep on guard duty. In my Army in a combat zone if a soldier on guard duty goes to sleep or leaves his post it could mean the firing squad."

After the four Australian blokes slipped out of sight we never heard a sound from them, not even the opening and closing of the aircraft door. The only sounds I could hear were the blowing wind, the rain, and on occasion a dog barking or howling from the direction of the native village. Other than flashes of lightning it was pitch black. Otherwise there was not a speck of light. It was one long, horrible, terrible, lonely wet watch. It was the first time I'd been out in the unrelenting torrential rain while in the tropics. It was no cup of tea. We could not stand, walk or lie down. I had to crouch down under my slicker and rain hat, hold my 45 and the two rocks inside my rain gear to keep the gun dry and immediately available, if needed. My Australian fleece lined flying boots were warm and dry. But in a crouched position my legs and ankles were killing me with cramps. I was unable to turn on a flashlight to check the time. It was just one long, long, four-hour miserable watch. I wondered if the P-38 pilot had made it back to Moresby. Even now I am glad that I had decided to fly out of Dobodura. If we had stayed overnight the chances of all of us getting out of Dobodura in one piece were pretty slim. If the enemy had known that only one C-47 was on the field they would do everything possible to destroy it. That was the one aircraft that was giving them the most trouble at all times.

In this torrential rain and wind rain-soaked malarial jungle pitch dark night on guard duty on the outer perimeter, I remembered the stories that my grandparents told of my Great-Grandfather Albert Alfonso Levi Martin and the American pioneers. Martin told how they would circle the wagons around the night camp sites to protect them from the Indians. Our number-one enemy was the Japanese and then the natives. Thank the Lord we had no visitors during our stay.

After an eternity, I heard two solid clicking of rocks followed by the pass-word, "Dobodura." That was like music from heaven. I told my relief that I hadn't heard or seen one thing except the elements and a few barks and howls of the native dogs. I was surprised that such a big man could be so quiet. With fixed bayonet and his large brimmed hat pinned up on one side, in true Aussie tradition, it just made him look all the bigger. I was all slouched down and he was standing at least 6' 3" and all of 13 stones (182 pounds).

I waited inside the back door of Irene until the last Yank and Sergeant Cox were in. I whispered and asked if anyone had heard or seen anything. No one had. I told them to be positive that their guns were on safety and to pick out any litter they wished except the lower one across from the back door and "let's get some sleep." It was raining in rain squalls as hard as it had all night. No sooner had I got stretched out than here were the mosquitoes. Grassi must have been attacked at the same time for he said that he wanted to spray the inside of the aircraft. The idea was great but it meant that all of us would have to get up, put on our rain gear, and go outside and wait under the wing for at least fifteen minutes. We all agreed only because there were no mosquito nets and we had to sleep. Grassi got out the hand spray gun and a can of mosquito spray. As he was filling the spray-gun the rest of us went out to stand under the left wing of the aircraft. He must have got them all, for there were no more insects. We all slept like logs till daylight.

The next morning there was a solid overcast. The weather was ominous looking with blowing wind and plenty of rain. From the cockpit, the field looked just like a lake. The ceiling was 2 to 300 feet at the most down below the top of some of the higher trees with a quarter to half mile visibility at the most. On take-off with the rain on the window shield visibility would be considerably less even with the wipers going. I briefed all in the aircraft. If the weather completely cleared we would fly directly to Moresby. If the weather cleared to 1,000 feet and 3 miles by mid-afternoon we would fly back to Dobodura and have them notify Moresby that we were all safe. We would fill up with aviation fuel, 91 octane, if we could find it. With an empty aircraft, low power settings and a two-plus mile field to take-off in mud, we wouldn't have to worry about detonation if we can only find jeep fuel at 72 octane. Then if the weather was safe we would fly over the mountains or east of here on down to Fall River, refuel, and fly up the south coast to Wards.

I told everyone in the plane to stand by while I talked to the Lead Aussie about guard duty now that it was daylight. I put my two rocks in my hand and went down the stairs. The guard on the left wing and the nose each nodded as I came in view. I asked the Aussie NCOIC if anything had happened during their tour. The only thing that they had seen were several natives in the trees off our right wing looking our way. He was sure that they meant no harm, but were just curious. I told him what I'd told the others about flying out. Then I asked him if he saw any need to keep guards out here in the weather during the daytime. Maybe one or two standing under the wings just to keep a lookout would do. He agreed, since we had a clear field of vision. "Have Cox bring my rations so I can eat on post." We divided the day's watch into two hour shifts. I would take the first, followed by Grassi, Gregg, and then the two P-38 mechanics. We hoped that it would not go that far and we would be gone before too long. As soon as the thunderstorms are over, we will fly to Dobodura. We do not want to tangle with them unless we have full tanks of at least 91 octane.

Sometime after eating, I was sure natives were peering out from the trees. Even though the right wing-tip was no more than 100 feet from the nearest trees with the blowing rain and thick foliage, it was still hard to be positive. I'd keep circling the plane and on occasion reverse directions all the time I was keeping watch out across the large open space for any movement. In the clearing there was no enemy within range of their 6.5 mm rifles. If the enemy did not attack from the trees we were safe from a ground assault. But any break in the clouds and we could be in real danger from the air.

When Grassi relieved me, I asked if the four Aussies were asleep. He said, no, that they were telling the Yank Airmen about capturing Buna. When I got in the aircraft it was most interesting to listen to them tell about the campaign. Listening to real infantrymen talking about actual combat, I believed what they had to say.

Looking out the co-pilot's side window, one could clearly see at least a dozen nearly nude native men. There were no spears, bows and arrows, clubs or slings in sight. I went back into the cabin and told the others. Then I asked the Lead Aussie what he thought about going and trying to talk to them. He said, "Let's go." Everyone put on their rain gear. He exchanged his rifle for Cox's pistol. In that way we would not look so aggressive. He briefed all the troops on where to go and what to do. Gregg was still on guard duty. He was to stay under the left wing-tip and watch for enemy action from the open field. The other seven men were to get in a straight line, single file, about ten feet apart, facing the edge of the trees and standing at parade rest. The line was to be parallel to the south side of the aircraft fuselage and 90° to the right wing-tip. The Aussie and I were to move out very slowly and casually, not acting aggressively. Do not shoot unless we shout "Shoot or fire," or you see the natives are attacking us. He designated one of the Aussies as the only one to shoot, and to only fire once into the trees above their heads. If this does not scare them off, do whatever you must. Just injure as few natives as possible. Do not shoot to kill, if it can be avoided. One single shot will attract any enemy in the area. Then we would be in real trouble.

The troops lined up, and the Aussie and I sauntered over toward the natives trying to look as friendly as we could. The natives stayed where they were and did not run. When we were about twenty feet from the trees with the natives behind us, the Sergeant began speaking to them. There came back some words from them along with laughs and giggles. We took a few more steps toward them. Two of them moved out from behind the trees and walked a few steps toward us. After many smiles on both sides and words between the Sergeant and what I assumed to be their Medicine Man, both sides walked toward one another. The Sergeant extended his hand and so did both of the natives. I then did likewise. We held hands and pumped them up and down for at least a minute. All the natives I could see came out and we had to repeat the same hand-shake with each one. The Sergeant told me that he thought we should have his blokes stack their rifles under the right wing and come on over. Shortly all nine of us and the natives were standing out in the pouring rain jabbering away in pigeon-English. We moved in under a leaf canopy that blocked out the rain just like being under a huge umbrella. From where we had been standing we could not see their overhead protection. It seemed that our new friends were trying to invite us to their village. I knew that all of us would like to go.

It was now 1350 hours. Time for Gregg to be replaced on guard duty. If it did not stop raining very shortly, we would be here for another night. I was very concerned about the Squadron not knowing for positive our status and whereabouts. I spoke up and told them that I and one of the Army P-38 Sergeants would stay and stand watch. We would send Gregg back. The other eight could go and have a good time. If the weather started clearing they should come back on the double, but in any case, they should be back in a couple of hours. All watches were synchronized. If we didn't fly out before 1700 hours I'd like to go visit the village before it gets dark. The four Aussies came and picked up their rifles, then Grassi, Gregg and the whole group disappeared into the jungle. One of the P-38 mechanics, a T/Sgt, and I were left alone under the wings of Irene with our thoughts. With the blowing wind and rain, the other guard was drenched from his knees down. In my case, my Aussie flying boots kept me dry and warm. For the next two hours we just moved around under the aircraft, always facing outward and watching for any thing or any movement. All I ever saw were sheets of blowing rain.

At a little before 1600, here came all eight of our group and many more natives than had been here when they left. Grassi brought them up to the plane. They looked, touched, laughed and giggled. Grassi asked what I thought about blowing the landing gear warning horn. I thought it would be

OK, but the Lead Aussie should explain first and try to tell the natives that the airplane would make a loud noise for them. The Sergeant explained several times and then tried to make a racket like the horn. Grassi moved the gear handle and the horn let out a blast. All of the natives jumped, got scared and ran to the trees. Grassi stopped the horn from blowing. The natives slowly returned and they wanted to hear the horn again. The Aussie Sergeant told me that he found out that over the last few days several enemy troops had come through on their way to the mountains. The last group had been here yesterday morning. Apparently they were trying to escape from Buna. He was informed that Australian Missionaries had lived here before the war. There was one old woman in the village who could speak pretty good English. She had worked for the Preacher's wife.

I told the troops that I'd like a couple of them, at least one of the rifleman, to walk with me to see where we would be taking off. I wanted to check the surface of the area. I told Grassi to hold down the fort until we returned and to keep an eye on us. We would keep in the clearing of open grassland at all times. Then once again I pointed out the various headings if they should have to walk out of here. The three of us must have walked at least a mile before we turned around and headed back. The surface was strong enough to support Irene. It looked like tough prairie sod from back home in the Midwest, only it had a much better ground cover and it was all green. Halfway back to the aircraft I could see many naked children out in the rain watching us. We waved and continued on back to our own troops. I told our people that the surface was satisfactory for take-off. We would go when it stops raining and the weather clears.

It was a little after 1700 hours. We set up the guard schedule for the night and up to 0800 in the morning. I asked if anyone wished to go back to the village. "At least half of us should stay here. We need one of you who can talk to the natives. The P-38 mechanic and I will make three. At most, two out of the rest may go." Cox and Grassi were the only ones who held up their hands.

The five of us went with maybe fifteen native men leading the way down a narrow, primitive jungle trail. In the dense tropical rain forest it was very damp, muggy, and gloomy. The ground was soft and slippery from the steaming undergrowth. You could hardly hear the wind or rain. Off the beaten trail there was a mass of tangle, impenetrable long hanging intertwined vines, thickets, bushes, and underbrush. The trees were so thick you could not see more than two feet in a straight line. It was just one wall of dense greenery. This is one jungle that Tarzan could not swing from tree to tree on a vine for it was a solid wall of vegetation from the ground up. White orchids flourished around the base of many of the trees. Ferns, palms, and bamboo grew everywhere in abundance due to the moist, steamy, humid atmosphere. Off to the edge of the path the ground was saturated with rotting, moldy vegetation. We could hear many strange weird screeching bats, birds, screaming cockatoos, parrots, macaws and several other different kinds of birds. Wild pigs were rooting and fighting along with other wild ground animals. It seemed that all were very close, eerie, and scary. This was not a silent forest. Looking up high we could see and hear the singing birds as they flitted from tree to tree. Even though we were not in the rain it was damp, humid, and sticky with intense heat and the air just reeked with the terrible order of the rotting foliage. This was a haven for mosquitoes and all kinds of flying insects. Several times the trail skirted around bogs of green smelly slough. The barefooted pygmy natives walked faster than I thought they would, and you could not hear them or our rifleman who brought up the rear. It was some time before this little trail ran into a wider well-traveled path. Every soldier in the line was dripping with sweat and our uniforms clung to us.

We began to see little heads and eyes peering around the tree trunks but not making a sound. The dogs began to bark and make a terrible ruckus. Shortly we came to a clearing. There was one large long thatch-covered structure and maybe another thirty family thatched-roof huts. All were about six to seven feet off the ground on poles. Smoke from the cooking fires hung like fog in the humid heat just hanging under the thatched roofs. They were very primitive dwellings. Under most of the huts were barking dogs, squealing pigs, playing children, and the native women preparing the evening meal over the smoking, eye-stinging fires. There was a musty smell and a stench from it all. We found out that the smokey fires were not only used to cook with, but also to help control the mosquitoes in the sleeping quarters. It was questionable which was worse, the biting mosquitoes or the stinging, blinding smoke in your eyes, mouth, and nose. When we first arrived, it appeared that at each grass hut the women were around the fires making the evening meal. Once we entered the village, all activity ceased and all eyes were on us.

I judged there to be possibly 150 natives in this village. At least one third were totally nude. All females had nothing on from the waist up. There was every shape and size of breast imaginable. Many of the women were pregnant, and some were very pregnant. Several of the babies were having their evening meal by suckling their mother's breasts. All parts of the men were totally visible, with only two twisted bananas leaves to hold them in place. Most of the older women had few if any front teeth. There was one old snaggle-toothed, withered, flat-chested woman who just kept her eyes on us all the time. Two young couples walked by and the old women went wild with laughter and kept pointing. I felt sorry for the two young men for both had erections. Later we were told that they were married couples. It was not the natives' custom to date before they were married. The marriages were family prearranged. These natives seemed to be at ease in their state of nudity as we would be when fully dressed with our close friends. As one of the fellows said, "They are all hung out!" The average life expectancy of a New Guinea native was 29 years if they should be fortunate enough to live past the age of five.

In the village where the trees had been thinned out it was almost dark and rain was coming straight down with very little wind. It was now time for us to leave. Our Aussie interpreter told them that we would walk back in the clearing. By the time we were out of the jungle we were once again in a drenching, blowing, downpour. The only thing that kept all of us from getting sick or pneumonia was the hot, humid temperature. When we got back to the aircraft, the rain was beating a steady tattoo on the fuselage.

While walking back to Irene I remembered the briefing we had the night we arrived at Jackson Airdrome. This was the first time I had been off the beaten path in New Guinea. It is easy to see that when an aircraft went down in the jungle the foliage would close in and swallow all sight of the downed plane from the air by search aircraft. After three days there would be no traces of the plane on the ground due to the massive growth of the fast growing impenetrable rain forest.

That night we posted only two guards and they stayed under the wings of the aircraft. Sometime during the night I awoke. It had stopped raining. I looked out the side window and could not see anything. Next morning it was all clear, and I could not see a cloud in the sky. I woke everyone. I told Grassi to dip-stick the tanks, drain and safety the sumps, and then we did a pre-flight inspection. I asked Gregg to help me pull No. 1 Prop through and asked the two P-38 mechanics to get No. 2. After measuring the tanks, Grassi said that we were just short of three hours of flight time. I announced, "We were heading for Moresby. Cox, serve everyone one your special breakfasts." I then told Cox, "You, Grassi and I will eat in the air. The rest of you can start eating as soon as we load all of our supplies aboard." Within fifteen minutes we were on our way.

We would have liked to buzz the village, but for two reasons I did not. One was to conserve fuel and the other was to hug the treetops all the way to Kokoda Airstrip. I wanted to circle up the side of Mount Victoria through the Kododa Pass and down the other side to Wards. I told Cox and Grassi to keep an extra sharp look-out for any and all aircraft especially on their side of the plane. The enemy was more likely over Dobodura bombing and strafing right now. It was 0520 hours and you could see for ever with not one cloud in sight, just a clean washed jungle. When Grassi came forward from checking in the back after take-off he said that the P-38 Mechanics told him that on take-off the prop wash threw sheets of water out from both sides and under the wings.

After take-off we made a right turn and stayed on the deck keeping well to the south, getting as far away from the coast as possible and as close to the Owen Stanley Mountains as we could. The three of us up front could tell that Dobodura was taking a beating from the columns of smoke and the reflection of the enemy silver aircraft in the early morning sun. No aircraft that we could see was close. We made tight spiraling, climbing 360's, keeping close to the north side of the mountain to get through the Kokoda Pass. I told the co-pilot and crew chief, "Now look out not only for the Japs but for our own fighters. For if their aircraft identification was no better than the 101st Ack-Ack, our own fighters might think we were a Betty Bomber and fire away." We went through the Pass in the tree-tops at 8,100 feet. This was the lowest an aircraft could fly through this break in the mountains. It was only a few minutes before we could see the transports climbing out from Wards forming into formation with the fighters getting into position. I elected to fly at their altitude with landing lights on. This way we would pass them very close and on their left and they would be able to see our big Field No. 39. As we approached I flashed the landing lights and waggled the wings and then went into a dive for the jungle below. We came over Wards at 100 feet and pulled up, entered a 500-foot traffic pattern and received a green light.

I told Cox and Grassi that we would be flying when the Squadron returned. "Get full service, go eat, and be back as soon as possible." I told the rest of the troops to come with me. I'd get them breakfast and arrange their transportation back to their Organization and tell their people where they had been. When Grassi opened the rear cargo door the first thing to meet us was the stifling hot, humid heat. There was a large reception waiting for us. Group Operations Officer, the 6th Commander, and most of our squadron that was not flying were there. Colonel Adams, Group Ops, spoke first: "Welcome back! Where have you been? I know your plane doesn't have enough gas to have been in the air for three days?" Big laugh by all... All our troops got out and I stood in the cargo door and told the reception party of our whereabouts. I told them that we would be ready to go out on the next flight when the Squadron returned. We needed transportation to the mess hall and then to Ops so we could get these troops back to their units. Someone will need to explain to their Organizations why it took so long to get back. "Tonight I'll make out any written report you may want from me." Colonel Adams said, "You just made your report for a job well done."

Captain Lackey called to Grassi who was already up on the wing refueling and asked the status of Irene. The crew chief said, "It will be ready to fly as soon as we finish with the gas and oil. I hope we will have time to get a hot meal." The Commander said, "All of you will eat as soon as you finish servicing Irene." He told the Ops Officer to get on the line with the 8th Fighter group. Have them pick up their two Sergeants. Let them know where they have been and that they were both safe. "We knew that the sick P-38 returned safely and we had an idea that you were in a clearing on the north side of the mountains." An Aussie truck load of ammunition for Dobodura pulled up and was waiting to unload. They were from the same unit as our four Aussies and were very glad to see one another. Our Aussie Leader said that he would like to go back to his outfit with them, and he would be able to eat there. These four Aussies were true "Jungle Soldiers." This was the only time I stayed in the jungle other than at our home camp site while in New Guinea. Years

Over the three months since we first arrived loading and offloading supplies became more organized allowing aircraft to deliver more military supplies to the front lines in less time.

later I realized that I had spent two days and nights behind the enemy lines. Of course, practically all of our flying missions were behind enemy lines. We did not know it, but we were working our way to Japan by leap-frogging over the enemy, cutting them off from supplies and thus in most cases starving them out. What made this possible was the C-47 and its crews. We made two trips to bombed out Dobodura that day. I was off the next day.

While we were "on the other side of the mountains," one of our newly arrived ground echelon troops went to the Commander with a complaint. He did not believe that he should be forced to live under such primitive conditions and demanded his "inalienable rights, as set forth under the constitution." The Commander told him that the Army would grant him "Life, but liberty and the pursuit of happiness must wait until he was discharged."

In December 1942 the Squadron had only nine aircraft, including Irene which was out of commission for the first 14 days of the month for major repairs. I still flew 98:50 hours. During this period the 6th officially flew 5,110 combat troops and 2,162,100 pounds of supplies. All of this was over the Hump. Their records do not show how many air-evacuations we returned to Wards. We were one busy Squadron. The ability to move and supply troops in a combat zone, on both side of the enemy line by air, was a priceless asset to the Allies for which the 6th TCS had no peers.

Relative to the Buna campaign the following is quoted:

From Vol. 43, No 4, Page 5, August 1999 — *POLARIS SUBMARINE VETERANS PUBLICATIONS*:

"IN AND UNSUCCESSFUL ATTEMPT TO RESUPPLY THEIR TROOPS IN NEW GUINEA, THE JAPANESE EQUIPPED THEIR SUBMARINES WITH PLYWOOD TORPEDOES WHICH THEY FILLED WITH RICE AND FIRED ASHORE."

9

The DC-3/C-47

TWO DAYS LATER I WAS ASSIGNED A NEW CAPTAIN, fresh from the States, as my co-pilot until Sergeant Cox returned from leave in Australia. This was his first flight in New Guinea and also his first flight in a C-47. We went through a hurried pre-flight. I told the co-pilot to fold his hands and keep them in his lap and watch both the crew chief and myself and ask any questions he wished and as often as he liked. The weather was broken scud 300-800 feet high with a light mist. We had maybe two miles visibility. We rolled out on the PSP and I gave it full power. At about 80 mph the Captain began to shout and point to the instrument panel in front of me. I could see nothing wrong and we were already committed with not enough run way to stop. I told him to keep his hands in his lap and to touch nothing. I told the crew chief to raise the gear then milk up the flaps. When on top and pulling into position I asked what was wrong. He was white and shaking. He stammered and shouted, "Sergeant, you took off with the artificial horizon caged. We could have all been killed." I replied that, "If I had tried to use it, we would have all died." Grassi handed him the Form 1, pointing out that we could not use it, that we could fly only on the seven basic flight instruments. When we landed at Dobodura, our co-pilot, "Two Tracks," as Captains were often referred to, was still not calm. For the next ten days we flew together with no problems. I spent many hours showing and explaining the systems. The best way to learn how to fly is to teach it. From Camp Williams, Wisconsin, in July 1942, for the rest of my twenty-three-plus-year military career I was an Instructor and Instrument Check Pilot.

We had just landed from a mission and parked when there were three quick shots. Engineering, Operations, and the Orderly Room all sent jeeps to transport all flight crews away from the aircraft and to the bivouac area. Three revetments of crew and the Aussie Loaders ran for the nearest jeep. All loaded in on top and were hanging on. Later we added it up to be twenty-five (25). If this was not a record it must be close to it. Thank God, it had been raining all night and most of the morning, and the ground was wet and soggy with standing water everywhere. We must have been moving 15 mph when a 250 lb bomb landed not more than 50 feet from the side of the vehicle. Most of the explosion was absorbed by the water, soft mud, and the depth to which the bomb penetrated before it exploded. The concussion turned the jeep over on its side. All of us hanging on the outside were thrown clear and skidded along on our bare hands, face and upper torsos on the rough coral road surface. We had a terrible roar in both ears for the rest of the day. No-one was seriously injured, but all of us ended up in the Medics to get cleaned with alcohol and painted with iodine. In my case the palms of both hands and right shoulder got clobbered. Someone asked if we would receive Purple Hearts. We all laughed. From then on there was no longer a top or hood for that jeep. The shop never did get the hood straightened out and no spare parts were available.

For the period of October to December 1942 our Group lost eleven aircraft. This was almost equal to one Squadron of crews and aircraft. This was nearly one fourth of all the transports in New Guinea at this time. Our Theater could not stand this kind of loss. If the enemy did not get you the weather would. General MacArthur is quoted in William Manchester's AMERICAN CAESAR, "Kenney's most significant contribution that year ('42), was his ingenious use of the C-47 transports." After hearing that, we began to understand why the Japs were being pushed back. Our Squadron received the War Department's, Presidential Distinguished Unit Citation with cluster. It's worthy to record two quotes of the highest authority in the US Military that were made after World War II. General Dwight D. Eisenhower, when asked about the C-47 and its value in WW II, said, "One of the most important weapons for victory in World War II." When asked about the C-47, Former Air Force Secretary Harold E. Talbott said, "Unquestionably ranks as the best single airplane ever built. The only thing that could replace a C-47, was another C-47!!"

When General Kenney was asked about the value of the Troop Carrier Squadrons, he stated that they are, "The Third Tactical Arm of the US Army Air Forces in the Southwest Pacific."

The reasons this aircraft was so good was the design, the Ground Crews that maintained them, and the flight crews that flew them. Of course when speaking of New Guinea, when you throw in enemy action, the short unsurfaced runways, the mountainous terrain, the weather, no maps, and no navigation aids, the loss rate was very, very low. With few exceptions the weakest part of the Gooney Bird was its pilot. As long as everything was running as designed it was easy to fly and very forgiving. But when you lost an engine you were in trouble. With the gross weight we flew, only the very best of pilots ever made it. If an engine failed on take-off with our overloads you were in the trees. The only fault with the C-47, it was underpowered.

The DC-3 made its first maiden flight on 17 December 1935. This was thirty-two years to the day after the first flight of an heavier-than-air aircraft. There were a total of 10,629 civilian DC-3s and military C-47s manufactured by Douglas Aircraft in the United States between 1935 and 1945. Many hundreds, if not thousands, were made during this same period by foreign Allies, as Douglas gave them the rights to manufacture. Hugh Raymond, the Chief Engineer for Douglas Aircraft Corporation, designed the DC-3. I have his signature on my Short-Snorter and a one hour Video tape on the design, test, and maiden flight of the "The best and best-loved airplane that has ever been designed and put into production."

Someone in the Squadron received a news clipping written by the Editor of the Washington Post who had interviewed Lt. Gen Kenney the Commanding General of the 5th Army Air Forces in the South-Western Pacific:

> "A high capacity for improvisation went into the air-borne attack
> on Buna. It is Kenney's objective opinion that the New Guinea
> troop-transport job was in some respects more remarkable than the
> Nazis' conquest of Crete by air." As Gen. Kenney described it: "The
> Nazis took off from modern airdromes in Greece, less than a hun-

dred miles away. They had short supply lines. Our troops we carried from eight hundred to a thousand miles. As General MacArthur, Australian General Blamey, and the rest of us saw it, the Japs at Buna, Sanananda, and Gona on the north coast was, in effect, on an island. His island was surrounded by water perilous to us and by an all impassable jungles and roadless mountains. The Australians and the Japs fighting on the trails, already had shown the impossibility of conducting decisive operations with land transportation. You could not put a jeep on the trails, not even on the best one from Moresby to Buna by way of Kokoda. Hunting parties took three weeks to traverse that trail, depending on native bearers who could only pack forty pounds per man."

"Kenney continued, "To attack the Japs from Moresby was possible only by air or by sea around the coast. General MacArthur chose the air. While the Australians were holding at Ioribaiwa, only twelve miles up the trail from Moresby, we launched the air offensive. We advanced from jungle strip to jungle strip, reconnoitering flat strips from the air, then sending in light planes to land, belly-buster, in the clearings. The pilot, having attracted crowds of natives by his landings, put them to work cutting a runway strip through the grass. We made runways a couple of hundred feet wide and three to four thousand feet long. The strips were pretty bumpy. This work began at the end of the dry season. When the wet season came on, bringing rainfall as heavy as six inches in one night, the strips were quickly churned into mud. That meant cutting new strips."

"Into the completed strips, we ferried troops and supplies to hold the neighborhood. The troops moved over native trails to other designated flat spots, cutting new strips. Soon we had the ferrying service on regular schedule. Because of the rapidity with which equipment could be flown in, there was no necessity for establishing large dumps of supplies and food. The ground forces carried enough for three days' need on their backs, and before the three days were up we gave them another ration. Similarly we flew in light and medium artillery, including one-fifty-five millimeter guns, scores of jeeps, horses, mules and a field hospital of two hundred and fifty beds. When we settled down to it, we brought in a thousand tons of stuff a week. One day we handled two hundred and sixty tons by air."

"I asked about the problem of evacuating the wounded. Said Kenney, "In addition to bringing men and supplies in, we carried men out as fast as they became disabled by disease or wounds. During December we ferried seven thousand people back to Moresby, bringing in another seven thousand. Hundreds of natives were flown from point to point to serve as porters and laborers for construction gangs working on airdromes and improving the trails."

"All this time we were effectively blocking Buna and Gona from the air preventing the Jap from bringing in reinforcements. Our air bombardment destroyed supply lines to his advanced troops in the mountains. Soon we had him out numbered on the ground - - finally by five to one. Our troops were comparatively fresh, had enough to eat and were evacuated as fast as they became sick. His were exhausted, undernourished, and ravaged by disease. Our troops were getting supplies while his were getting none. The job took a lot of good navigation and hard flying. I classified the transport crews as combat crews and they received decorations on the same basis as the fighters and the bombers."

"Our main reliance was upon approximately twenty-fives standard cargo airplanes, chiefly C-47, capable of carrying two and a half tons of supplies or troops over the range. They ran on schedule. Many of the pilots, Americans and Australians, had never seen the north side of the mountains when they were first called on to undertake this job. They certainly delivered the goods."

The Aussies opened a bakery for all the Allied Forces in the Moresby area. They had no bread slicer or paper wrapping. As soon as the hot bread came out of the oven it was packed eight loafs in a gunny sack and stacked in fresh air racks. Each unit had to pick up their own issue no later than 0400 hours each morning. When the fresh new hot bread arrived at the Squadron Mess Hall the gunny sacks had to be stripped from the bread. Many of the burlap strings were stuck to the outer crust of the bread. This was from the sack being pulled over the hot bread and the weight of the bread stacked in piles to dry and to wait to be picked up. In the hot humid climate; mosquitoes, insects, worms and other bugs would crawl into the "Staff of Life." In the Squadron when the bread was ready to be sliced by hand often one or more of the uninvited guests would be cut in two. You could either pick the "critters" out or eat them. After all it was just protein. Both ways did happen. More often the bread looked like Swiss cheese after being debugged.

10

Sydney

EARLY NEXT MORNING I WENT TO OPERATIONS to file a clearance, because I was on my way for ten days in Sydney. This would be my first leave in the Big City. I was sorry that Grassi and Gregg were not part of the crew. They had returned within the fortnight from ten days in Sydney. All but three seats were filled with 374th Group personnel. There was the little blond-headed P-38 fighter pilot we had flown from Dobodura last month. I walked over to him and said. "I see you are going with us." He looked up in surprise, smiled and said, "Yes, Sir. My turn to be surprised." I told him that I was a Sergeant Pilot. My flight suit had no rank on it. I told him that we would be boarding in about fifteen minutes. "If you'd like, when the crew gets aboard, come up front with us. There is no seat, but you can stand behind the crew chief and stay as long as you wish."

We were airborne at 0450 for Townsville with 4:25 enroute. We had lunch, refueled, refilled, and were in the air for Brisbane by 1045 with an ETA of 1530. We departed Amberly Airdrome for Sydney at 1645. We arrived at Mascot Airdrome at 1930 hours in the middle of their summer. This was a good day's flight of 11:55 hours flying time.

Two buses came for the passengers. We never saw any of them again until time to return to Moresby ten days later. A bus picked us up and drove us to a small Military Office next to the main passenger terminal. It was used only for US Military flight crews with questions, problems, and for their transportation on and off the airdrome. The crew chief and radioman went off on their own. I gave them the address and phone number where I would be staying. The 374th Group Sergeant Pilots had a flat where I would be billeted. This billet had been arranged by the 21st Squadron's Pilots before the 6th left the States. Sergeant Cox gave me a number and said that in case of an emergency they could get in touch, for he had several family members in the city.

Three of us started out in the same civilian cab. It was a wood burner, just like the one I rode in at Brisbane when we first arrived in Australia. The other two got off on the way and the driver took me on to Ithica Flat, Bondi Beach, King's Cross. This is the cosmopolitan center of Sydney, the spot that stays open all night with something going on every minute. This was the suburb where most of the American R&R military flight personnel stayed when in Sydney. The billet was a large four-story apartment building. The "Lady of the House" walked me up to the third floor, knocked real loud then put her key in the door and opened it. She called out, "Here's another Yank that came to join you," she handed me the key and left. In this suite there were four bedrooms, two baths, a kitchen, dining room and a large family room. This suite was used only by the Enlisted Pilots of the 374th TCG. There were two other Staff Sergeant Pilots when I entered. They were from the 21st TCS. This crew would be flying out in the morning in the aircraft we flew down. We had seen each other at some of the Group Briefings, but we did not know one another. They were going out for their last night on the town. They asked if I wished to join them. I'd been up for almost twenty hours and was dead tired. I thanked them and told them that the aircraft was in good service. I undressed and took the best, long, soapy, hot bath I'd ever had and was sound asleep before I hit the sheets. Yes, two clean white sheets and a pillow, how nice. All this and NO MOSQUITOES!!

The next morning I was up and ready to go eat by 0830. I found a place for breakfast a block and a half from the front door. Most of the clientele were Yanks, I think all were Fly Boys. There were two tables of pilot Officers with their crushed caps. This was the first time I'd ever seen such beat up military caps. I was the only Enlisted Pilot in the room. One of the Officers came over to the table where I was with three Sergeants. He asked where I was stationed and asked what do you fly. Then he asked when and where I got my wings. When I told him he must have believed me for that was about all he had to say about a Sergeant wearing pilot wings. His group was from a B-24 outfit at Darwin. I asked if I ever got out that way with some time off could I come over and fly co-pilot on one of their missions. He replied that the Old Man, Operations, and the pilot whose aircraft I'd be flying with would all have to agree.

Later that day I ran into First Lieutenant Lakeman. We had been class-mates and had the same Flight Instructor at Moffett. Lieutenant Lakeman went through in grade as an Officer. I asked him where he was stationed and what he was flying. He said at an Air Depot at Port Moresby. I asked if it was the new Depot that had just opened at Jackson. He replied, "Yes, where are you stationed?" I told him two miles away at Wards. He invited me to come over and help him test hop some of the aircraft. He was the only pilot assigned and it was keeping him too busy. I promised that I'd be glad to fly all I could and would be there within ten days after returning to Wards.

In the afternoon I ended up at the Australian Hotel. This was the num-ber one hotel in all of Australia. It was very nice and a hang-out for Ameri-can Troops. It had one attraction on which the management and the Yanks did not agree. The Hotel had a very large, beautiful, expensive, crystal chan-delier hanging in the middle of the Hotel Lobby. The Yanks liked to toss the large Australian pennies up in the center lighting fixture. The Hotel man-agement was afraid that eventually the weight of the coins would bring their chandelier crashing down. I saw a sign that I thought to be very appropriate: "Don't steal, the Government hates competition!" The Australian people liked the Americans, but most of the older ones had a saying: "The Yanks are over-paid, over sexed, and over here." I understood that this was a saying from WWI, but of course it was the first time I'd ever heard it.

That evening I met an Australian girl by the name of Toni. I bought her a coke and asked what she liked to do. She replied, "Roller skate." I said, "Let's go. For that is my favorite pastime." We took a ferry to the rink. When we arrived many of the young people said, "Hi, Toni." She went to put on her skating togs. I went to rent a pair of skates and found out that the only rentals were clamp-ons. I'd never had anything on except shoe skates and mine were back in the States with my parents. When she came on the floor I was out in the center showing off. The moment I saw her I knew that she was a really good skater and that I was not in her class. Everyone was talking to her. She was well known and well liked. Then I saw a life-size cardboard silhouette of her. It was capped, "Our Toni, Champion Figure Skater of New South Wales." There were pictures, banners, plaques, and trophies of her. Of all the Aussies I could have asked to go skating, I had picked her. I had told her how much I liked to skate and led her to think I was pretty good. We stayed till the rink closed and I did have a good time even though we were not even in the same league.

From the ferry I took her home in a cab and made a date for the movies two evenings later. She seemed like a very nice young lady. She had all her own teeth and did not smoke or drink. She had a full time job with the telephone company. She was one week younger than I was. Her father and two brothers were in the Infantry, and all three were in New Guinea. We had three dates during my ten days on this leave. I asked if when I returned on my next leave in Sydney in a couple of months I could call. She said, "Please, do," and we parted. While in Sydney I first heard the saying, "Queue up" which means "Line-up" or "Stay in line," or "Close the gap."

Between January and November 1943, I had four more ten day leaves in Sydney. From the second leave on, Toni and I wrote regularly and when I was in the City we had many dates. We went to most of the tourist attractions, movies, Church, and roller skating on most of the nights she was off work. I had a wonderful time and she must have, too, for she wrote and asked that we get married. If she had been an American, or was permanently living in the States, I would have jumped at the chance. But being a foreigner, I could not see it. We did have a lot in common, and she was a very nice young lady. But either she would want to live in her country or would want to travel back and forth a lot if we lived in the United States. Besides all that, I sent her letter home more as a joke. It seemed as if everyone in my Little Home Town wrote and all said, "NO, NO, ERNIE!" Now some sixty-two years later, I know that I made the correct decision. Some time later, after returning to the States on a 30-day leave and another 30 days at Redistribution Center, I was on Bond Tours for the next six months. On 17 March 1944, St Patrick's Day, I met and had a date with a young lady in Minneapolis, Minnesota by the name of Esther (Etta) Marie Trautner. For my part from that one date she was going to be my wife. On 9 April 1944, Easter Sunday, after church we became engaged. We married on Memorial Day, 30 May 1944, on our 13th date!! This last May we celebrated our 65th anniversary and we'd love to celebrate many more.

Teri and I visited most of the sights in and around Sydney and had a very good time, but I was anxious to get back to flying. I saw no other Sergeant Pilots, but was stopped several times by Officer Pilots and asked why a Sergeant was wearing pilot wings. Most knew of Enlisted Pilots, but had not met one. One non-rated First Lieutenant demanded that I take those Pilot Wings off. I tried to explain that I was a pilot, but he would not believe me. He said if you do not remove those wings, I'll call the MP's. I told him let's go for I am not going to remove my pilot wings. I showed him a copy of my orders. That calmed him down some. That was the only time anyone ever "DEMANDED" that I remove my pilot wings.

On the day of departure from Mascot Airdrome, everyone was present and on time. During the flight back, I talked some with Lieutenant Bong, the little fighter pilot, and found out that he was now an Ace. I never met him again. He turned out to be the number one all-time America Ace of Aces with forty-three confirmed kills to his credit. On 6 August 1945 while test-flying an experimental P-80 aircraft at Edwards, Major Richard I. Bong was killed. It is interesting to note that was the very day that the first A-Bomb was dropped. On this flight he was so much quieter than when I flew him over from Dobodura. The trip back was just a long routine flight. When we landed it seemed that we were in one gigantic steam bath with the stifling heat, humidity, and mosquitoes waiting to greet us.

While Sergeant Cox was in Sydney he stopped by his Organization and was issued another pair of Australian R.A.A.F. knee-high fleece-lined Military leather flying boots. I liked them so much that he offered to give them to me. I would not take them, but they were very nice.

Topography of Wau Airstrip

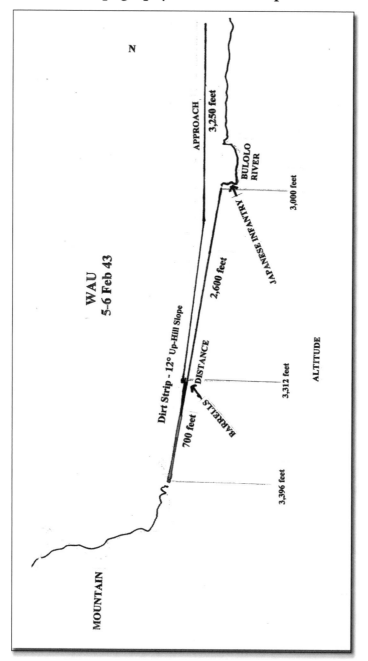

11

Battle Of Wau

The 317th TCG arrived at Wards Airdrome in early January 1943. For various reasons they had a series of accidents, mostly by inexperienced, "Stateside" pilots. All their flight crews outranked ours by one to two ranks. They had no Enlisted Pilots, less than half the flying experience, and all that was stateside time. Within two weeks they were ordered to exchange their new, more up-to-date aircraft for the old, war-weary C-47s of the 374th TCG. Then the 317th was sent back to Australia for further training.

On 21 January 1943, C-47, serial number 41-18539, field number 39, Irene, was exchanged for serial number 41-18646, field number 52. F/O JAMES W. LOCKLEAR of the 40th TCS had flown this aircraft over from the States. The new Irene, even though only a few serial numbers different, was the latest off the line. It was in a different block of serial numbers and was manufactured after Irene No 1. It had all the latest features and was a much better aircraft with a full workable instrument panel, Hamilton Standard Paddle Props, high blowers, a Navigator's position up front, driftmeter, astrodome, radio altimeter, and two Pratt and Whitney R-1830-90C engines. With the new paddle blade props it could take-off and land in a shorter distance. The new Irene had portholes in each of the twenty-eight passenger windows in the cabin. We were told that in the event of an enemy air attack, the rubber plugs should be pulled out to fire M-1 rifles through the holes. I never heard of anyone being so dumb as to try it. Irene No 1 was great, but

In front of the new "Irene" are crew members S/Sgt Ernest Ford, Sgt C. I. Cox (Australian R.A.A.F.), T/Sgt Amerigo Grassie, and S/Sgt John Gregg.

Irene No 2 was a much better aircraft. It even had a workable artificial horizon and an auto-pilot. Later, when we were stationed in Australia, the auto-pilot was great for flying over the Coral Sea, but we could not use it in New Guinea. What a pleasure it was to fly the latest equipment and not get wet in every rain storm.

Here is some new information about Irene. On 19 August 2001, I received an e-mail from JEFF MORGAN in Australia, jeffmorgn@lm.net.au, the present owner of Irene, 41-18539.

At the morning briefing on 24 January 1943, we were told that, "We will be landing at an old gold mining field, one of the richest goldfields in the world. The Germans had hacked out an airstrip on the north side of a 12,000-foot mountain. There are both headhunters and cannibals in nearby villages at the upper south end of the field, and a branch of the Bulolo River is on the north end. The clearing is 3,300 feet long, but only the last 700 feet of the strip is usable do to the many bomb and mortar craters. Do to the constant enemy air and ground attacks on the airdrome, the unexploded bombs and mortar shells have not been removed and the many craters filled in. The Aussies have barrels along the side of the dirt strip at the touchdown point of the usable part of the landing strip. We will have no trouble landing in that short distance on this field! When the Allied Forces are not using the airstrip the barrels are moved across the clearing so enemy aircraft cannot land. There will be NO, REPEAT, NO ATTEMPTED GO-AROUNDS. Either you make it on the first and only try or you WILL crash and all aboard will be killed. This is one short uphill landing field. Now listen and I'll tell you how the German's landed and took-off in their Junkers. Oh, I forgot to tell you that the useable part of the strip we will be landing on is a rocky, grass field with filled in bomb crater holes and is on a 12-14° uphill slope! That is over a 84-foot rise in the 700 feet of usable landing space. As if this is not enough, at the very end of the uphill side is a 12,000-foot mountain!"

"Now pay attention or you will not make it! We come in over the river at 1600 feet indicated altitude in a very long loose trail formation spaced out at least half a mile apart. The landing plane has to have time to taxi clear of the end of the dirt strip before the next plane can land. There is very little space at the upper end of the strip for a turn-around. The north end is the lower end of the field at an elevation of 1,200 feet and is next to the Bulolo River. Just to make it even more interesting and to keep you on your toes the Jap Infantry are dug in on the approach end of the landing strip by the river taking pot shots at us. The trick to landing a fully loaded C-47 in this short uphill strip is to touch down where the barrel markers are. All approaches are headed south straight into the mountain at 90 mph with gear down and with full flaps. When we cross the river at the very end of the dirt strip, aim for the touch-down point where the barrels are. At that time pull up the flaps and the nose of the aircraft at the same time to compensate for the sink and add full take-off power. If you touch down by the barrels with full power you will have no problem in stopping in the next 700 feet. On take-off at the far south upper-end of the strip, if you were to release the brakes at normal taxi power, 800 RPM, the airspeed will be 90 mph before reaching the barrels. Of course all take-offs are with normal take-off power."

After parking do not cut the engines, but stay at the very upper end of the field clear of the landing area. Until the Aussies are able to push the enemy farther away from the perimeter of the field we can never have more than four aircraft on the ground at one time for three reasons: not much room to maneuver after landing, the enemy controls three sides of the dirt strip, and the headhunters and cannibals are on the mountain side. We must be ready to take-off in a ten-second notice. On landing, when the aircraft has cleared the landing strip and has come to a full stop, the pilot is to pull the left throttle back to a slow idle and switch on the green light and the bail-out bell. The crew chief will put down the stairs and hold the door open from the inside of the aircraft long as the green light is on and the bell is ringing. When the light turns red and the bell stops ringing, the crew chief will pull up the steps and close the cargo door whether all the troops are out or not. You are to stop unloading the second the red light comes on and the bell stops ringing, and you get the hell out of there as fast as you can with maximum take-off power. All landings are uphill into the mountain and all take-offs are down hill to the river. The Japanese Infantry will be shooting at you and trying to knock you out of the sky."

"Remember, no pilot has ever lived to make a go-around at Wau. At least one Junker, one B-17, a B-24, a P-38, two AT-6s, two C-47s and two Bettie Bombers are permanent land marks to remind you that one cannot go-around. This is why we are paid FLIGHT PAY, so let's go and earn our pay."

On this mission on 24 January the flight was as briefed. No one can believe the required approach and landing until you have made one landing at Wau. The approach and landing was far more scary and dangerous than the enemy at the end of the field firing at you. Each time you landed at Wau you did earn your "Flight Pay."

At this time our Squadron had sixteen Officer Pilots and twenty-two Enlisted Pilots of which thirteen were American and nine Australian. It is my opinion that at least 85-90 percent of the American Enlisted Pilots were highly motivated pilots and were as capable as the upper two percent of the Officer Pilots. However, we had two Staff Sergeant Pilots who seldom flew as First Pilots. Both were checked out and it appeared both were fair pilots. It seemed that one did not care if he ever flew or not. The other one had lost all interest in flying as a pilot and wanted to become a navigator. On clear nights he would spend hours looking at the stars trying to identify them and locate them on charts. He was always pointing out the Southern Cross to anyone who passed near his tent after dark, weather permitting. He had a Lieutenant navigator friend in the 43rd Bomb Squadron. The Lieutenant spent hours instructing our pilot how to read the almanac and charts, and use the sextant. His "friend" loaned him books, charts, and a sextant. Many nights our pilot-navigator, while sitting on the hill behind his tent gazing at the stars, would call out that we are now in Port Moresby Harbor or at Jackson Airstrip. Sometimes his readings were accurate and he would be at Wards. If my memory is correct we were located 9°28'24" South and 147°10'7" East. After several weeks of his self training "Ground School" he would go on night flights to Australia. That way if the weather was clear he would be able to practice celestial navigation by the stars. He would spend hours when flying trying to center and hold the sextant bubble still while bouncing around in turbulent air.

After the war he got out as soon as he could and got a job with a non-scheduled Airline that flew between Shannon, Ireland and Boston, Mass. On the night of 5 December 1947, while flying navigator on a civilian DC-4 the weather at Logan Airport was below minimums. On the third approach the pilot came in to low and hit the seawall shearing off the landing gear. All aboard were killed in the burning wreckage.

The night before Buna fell all enemy soldiers who wished could spend a few minutes with a Korean "Comfort Woman." While the party was going on, their Japanese Commanders were escaping by submarines. The next day when the Aussies and Yanks captured Buna, the women's nude, bloated, maggot infested, smelly, fly-ridden bodies were found lying on their backs, cut open from the crotch to the throat. We were told they had been killed with a long Japanese ceremonial sword.

We made another Red Tagged flight to Garbutt. Upon landing we were told that many changes had taken place and a few transfers had been made in the Base chain of command. From then on flight crews were treated as they should be. That afternoon on the way back to Moresby at 9,000 feet, above most of the broken clouds, there were a lot of bang, bang and black puffs. Between the breaks in the clouds we could see a convoy of ships. We could not get an accurate count, but from the wake of their ships it looked like they were headed for Moresby. We had not been briefed of any ships or naval activity enroute. We did not hang around to count or observe the type of ships or number or type of escort. There is an old Navy saying, "If you're a friend do not fly over us, if you're not a friend, you'd better not." Thank the Lord this Navy was no more accurate with their ack-ack than the 101st at Wards or Townsville. Upon landing I made a full report.

During the first part of February the 6th TCS got a real break. Stateside fuel, gas, and oil trucks arrived and the aircraft no longer had to be fueled by hand pumps from 55-gallon steel barrels in the back of GI 6x6s. Hydraulic fuel, oxygen, and drinking water were still delivered by 6X6 trucks.

On the 5th of February we flew desperately needed supplies and troops into beleaguered Wau. In a two-day period we flew in over two thousand armed infantrymen and artilleryman with all their equipment, ammunition, supplies, and personal gear. The only opposition on the 5th was small arms ground fire by the Japs surrounding the airstrip on all three sides. As the Aussie Infantry jumped out of our C-47s they would run only a few yards, fall down and start firing their Bren Guns. There always were plenty of targets to shoot at. This was the only way we were able to get in and out without being hit. Flying in and out of Wau was truly "bush pilot flying." It required more guts than good sense.

On the next day, 6 February 1943, the mission was back to Wau. We were briefed to expect strong enemy action from the air and ground as the airdrome was under heavy siege and was about to be overrun. The Japanese were making an all out maximum drive to take and hold Wau. There was so much enemy fire that we could not have more than three aircraft on the field at any one time. The other planes were to stay in the air two miles north of the river below 200 feet above the trees, and circle while our close air cover fighters shuttled back and forth between the aircraft in the air and those on the ground. "The purpose of this mission was to deliver the on-board infantrymen, artillerymen, their supplies and to air-evacuate the wounded. This was not a rescue or evacuation mission. It was to fly in ground troops so they could go into battle at the very edge of the landing strip." Almost as soon as the Aussies left the aircraft they were in actual ground combat exchanging rifle and mortar fire with the enemy! Later we were told that many of the Aussie mortars were firing in less than five minutes after being off loaded.

This was one of those days when we had a mix of more than one squadron's aircraft flying in the same element. The reason, every available 374th TCG plane was required for this mission. Our flight of three had just landed and here came another Gooney Bird and landed right behind me. Who and where it came from I did not know. At the same time an Australian Wirraway touched down and very shortly bombs began to fall down the center of the dirt strip. The two Aussie Crewmen bailed out of their "T-6" on the run. They were only a few yards distant away when their plane was hit. Both crew members were able to get up and run from the burning, exploding aircraft with shrapnel flying in all directions.

The best thing for us to do was to try to get airborne for there was little or no chance on the ground. The sky over-head was thick with enemy fighters and bombers with many being shot down. Our top fighters were engaging their bombers. The Nipponese Infantry were on three sides of the field with headhunters and cannibals in control of the mountain side. It seemed that every enemy rifleman was firing straight at us. We were now the second aircraft in line for take-off. Due to the limited turn-around space at the uphill end of the dirt strip, we had to take turns to get in line for take-off. There was no other way around this unknown aircraft in front of us. The aircraft that landed last was now in position to be the first aircraft to take-off. This Gooney Bird was not one of ours. It had just followed our flight of three in and now was the lead aircraft for take-off.

The pilot of this unknown C-47 was now first to take-off and it just sat there. It seemed that the pilot could not make up his mind on what to do or how to do it. He had three planes behind him and all three of us were hemmed in and he would not move. The pilot must have panicked for he just sat there. There must have been a "short circuit between his head phones!" He could not assimilate all the options and his indecision seemed like an eternity before the aircraft started moving. At last he applied power and the aircraft began to roll. As the gear came up, the aircraft began to climb as fast as the overloaded bird could climb. At around two or three hundred feet the aircraft was hit by ground fire. Flames and smoke could be seen and something either fell off the plane or out the back cargo door into the river. On impact it broke up and exploded. Theory has been advanced since this flight carried ammunition. It is possible that a box or two of hand grenades may have been rolled out the cargo door and that was what we saw explode on impact. I do not know and did not stay around to take a second look.

Before the explosion we were rolling down the east side of the bumpy, rutted, dirt, rocky strip with full throttle trying to dodge the new bomb craters that had been made since we had landed within the last five minutes. At the same time a line of mortar shells came walking down the center of the dirt strip. We were able to get airborne, between impacts with mortar rounds bracketing the nose and tail of our aircraft. When our gear came up we dropped down a foot or two and hugged the down hill sloping ground, still at full power, until at least a mile north of the river. We then joined the formation that was still in a holding pattern. The other two C-47s followed suit and none of the three of us were hit. Our Squadron's top fighter escort engaged the enemy fighters and were keeping them busy. It was not until 28 October 2002 that I positively learned that the unidentified C-47 was Serial No 41-38658: EARLY DELIVERY from the 33rd Troop Carrier Squadron.

When the air show was over and our P-39s had cleared the area of enemy aircraft we returned from across the river and landed at Wau and off loaded our troops and equipment. There was still plenty of enemy ground fire and many more bomb and mortar craters in the dirt strip.

The only reason we made it out was that we stayed on the deck roaring straight toward the enemy infantry soldiers at over 200 mph. In the fifteen to twenty seconds after releasing the brakes until on the north side of the river, with those two big eleven foot six inch whirling propellers racing towards them, and with the ever increasing roar of the engines and all the ground firing around them, it must have un-nerved the enemy ground troops. So instead of rising up above the river bank and firing at us they ducked for cover and three aircraft got away. By taking off and staying on the deck with full throttle three C-47s, three flight crews, eighty-seven ground troops, and all their equipment and supplies were saved. It is easy to be wise after a mission, but I still think that was the only way we were able to fly out and escape that murderous air and ground fire.

The hesitation and wrong decision by the pilot of the first aircraft to take-off and climb was fatal with a terrible loss of life, equipment, and a desperately needed aircraft. By climbing, the aircraft was directly overhead and within easy range of the enemy ground troops lying in wait behind the river bank. Their concentrated fire power hit the low, slow flying aircraft. Much later, I learned that this aircraft crashed about two miles from Wau. Pure cannon fodder! My plan was to be exposed to enemy ground fire for the minimum time and to make as much noise as possible. By staying on the deck this would give the enemy troops below the river bank the minimum time to shoot at us. There is no substitute for combat experience. I have a news clipping photo of Irene No 52 at Wau at this time. If I had realized that my picture was being taken I would have stuck my head out the pilot's side window, smiled, and waved.

In a few days I was told that I had been put in for the Silver Star for leading three fully loaded aircraft out of a "death trap" at Wau while under a bombing, mortar, and infantry ground attack. As I was clearing the Squadron to return to the ZI many months later, I was told they still had not heard anything. When clearing 5th AF at Brisbane where I was awarded my sixth DFC, I asked the status of the request for the Silver Star. They knew nothing about the recommendation for the Silver Star, but if it came through approved the orders would catch up with me later on. From time to time over the next twenty years of active duty, I queried Personnel and always received the same answer, "Don't know anything about it, and have no orders."

When my Mother died on 25 April 1978, my sister Anna Lorene Scarbrough, Manzanola, Colorado settled Mother's estate. She came across a civilian book titled *AMERICAN HEROES of the WAR IN THE AIR*, Volume One, by HOWARD MINGOS, published 1943 by Lanciar Publishers, Inc. New York. On page 293, listed under THE FIGHT FOR ISLAND AIR BASES, appeared the name "Staff Sgt. Ernest C. Ford, Air Corps, U.S. Army, Manzanola, Colo. Silver Star"

In "The Story of Kenney's Fifth Air Force," as it appears in *The Flying Buccaneers* by Steve Birdsall, Published by Doubleday & Company, Inc., Garden City, New York, 1977, on pages 46 and 47, General Kenney had this to say about our day at Wau:

> "The Japanese had already reached one end of the uphill strip and mortar fire was thumping into the vital field. The C-47s had only enough room to land, and as the doors opened the troops jumped to the ground and raced into battle, bullets and shrapnel whining around them. Some transports were even forced to wait above until the Australian grenaded the Japanese out of the way, but fifty-seven landed at Wau, unloaded with their engines running, then took off to make room for the next planes. The following morning the Japanese again tried to take the strip but by noon they had been driven back and Wau would hold out. When the Japanese

bombers arrived over Wau on February 6, 1943, there were four C-47s on the field and five more circling to land. One stick of bombs fell right along the center of the runway, but all except one transport escaped harm. This (a picture of a wrecked burning aircraft) Australian Wirraway had just landed, and the pilot and observer were only a few yards from the aircraft. They dived to the ground as a bomb exploded alongside the plane and demolished it."

Flying combat did not worry or bother me and it certainly did not keep me awake at night. My ability to take "Combat Naps" at any time or place was a real asset. That was not true for some of the flight crews. But this type of flying wears you down physically. When flying combat, fear is always a constant companion. After a flight like Wau it was easy to see who the "worry warts" were. There were some whose nerves were about to crack. There were two, possibly three of the Squadron pilots who, in my opinion, were terrified of dying, and some who itched for battle. I believe that when my time comes I'll be there. Once a mission is over remember what you learned and what you did right or wrong. Then it's time to forget it and go on to the next mission. "Remember what you learned, gain from the experience, but do not keep thinking, what if —. We have a war to win so let's get on with the program." It can truly be said that flying into Wau was hazardous duty. At this time the entire airstrip was a "killzone" from both the air and ground not to mention the hazardous landing conditions or the "headhunters and cannibals." Fear is always there, but training and experience are a pilot's best weapon coupled with plenty of prayers.

One thing that the Troop Carrier pilots did learn was how to maneuver the clumsy C-47s as though they were fighters. Most Troop Carrier Combat Pilots in New Guinea during the period of 1942 and the first couple of months in 1943 had no psychological problems about flying combat in C-47s. However, it was a real problem when fighter or bomber pilots had to fly combat in C-47s. After being protected by flak suits, armor plating, machine guns, cannons, self-sealing fuel tanks, and good fighter escort, it was so scary and life-threatening. When flying the unarmed, unprotected transports in combat, in all kinds of weather, landing in very small unpaved, dusty, dirt, wet, muddy, grassy, rocky strips, dodging bomb and mortar filled craters, uphill

C47s lined up to take off after unloading supplies

strips, few could make the transition. With few exceptions, all our combat missions were flown behind enemy lines. A few months later when the Allies had gained air superiority and we had good fighter cover it was different. The "Gooney Bird" was one of the most vulnerable of all wartime aircraft. I guess it is mostly what you start out in. Like I told the Navy submariners at Pearl Harbor, "I would not want to be in one of your little tin sardine cans, but thank God we do have you and your submarines."

From page 121, *CHRONOLOGY OF WORLD WAR II, The Day by Day Illustrated Record 1939-45*, Compiled by Christopher Argyle, Marshall Cavendish Books Limited Exeter Books, New York, New York.

"SATURDAY, FEBRUARY 6 (1943) Air War: Pacific - 26 of 70
Japanese planes shot down by 37 Allied fighters over Wau."

My sister, Lorene Scarbrough sent an article by Mr George Johnston, the Australian War Correspondent who had flown with me twice before.

"The victory was won by Australian artillery and infantry, but
without the eleventh-hour support of the American transport planes
it would have been a disastrous defeat. Often the Americans who
manned the transports grabbed their revolvers and Tommy guns

and sprinted down to the front line 500 yards away, to empty magazines at the Japs in the few minutes they had to spare while their
planes were being emptied of supplies and loaded with wounded."

"Out there today they are still on the job. The bully-beef bomber
just can't be done without. The war in the Southwest Pacific is just
beginning. There is a lot of tough, bloody fighting ahead, fighting in
which airpower is going to be the trump card. And when the curtain
goes up—as it will go up—and when you read of jungle fighting and
aerial warfare, remembering the unsung heroes behind the scene:
the kids from Maine and Florida, from Oklahoma and Texas, from
Nebraska and Michigan, the kids who became men overnight in the
toughest campaign of the war—the kids who fly the bully beef
bombers in New Guinea."

Sorry, I never got to play "John Wayne" and stick my gun out the pilot's
side window and take a few shots at the enemy. During these days we were
not on the ground that long. We were too busy supporting the Australian
Military who were doing the ground fighting. At this stage of the war no
flight crews were out of their aircraft and the engines were never stopped.
But this would be great for "Hollywood." During the period from January to
July 1943 as First Pilot I flew twenty-nine (29) missions into Wau, thirteen
(13) as an Enlisted Pilot and sixteen (16) as an Officer. I received a "Battle
Field Commission" on 8 April 1943.

After returning from Wau to Port Moresby on the 6th, I was sent to Coen
Field in Northern Australia to pick up Aussie troops and supplies. I returned
to Wards the next day.

On pages 27-30, *374th TROOP CARRIER GROUP, 1942-1945* by Col.
EDWARD T. IMPARATO, Turner Publishing Company, Paducah, KY
42002-3101, Copyright 1998.

Colonel IMPARATO was 374th Group Operations and had full
knowledge at the time of the Wau Missions on 5 and 6 February
1943. He writes of this and other missions I flew while under his
command in New Guinea that were just as dangerous, or more life
threatening.

Later I learned that Colonel Edgar W. Hampton, then a Captain, in the 21st TCS, was the first C-47 pilot to fly a combat mission in New Guinea on 22 May 1942. I saw him often during this tour of duty and many times later in the States as we were stationed twice on the same base.

Test Flying

A DAY OR TWO AFTER THIS, A CRIPPLED LIBERATOR with several dead and wounded aboard was on a long final approach at Wards when a C-47 cut in on a tight pattern and landed in front of the disabled B-24. The tower held a steady red light on the Gooney Bird from the downwind to touchdown. From the point where the C-47 turned on base leg the tower began shooting off red flares. The bomber, in attempting to go around, crashed and exploded. All eleven aboard were killed. The C-47 pilot claimed that he had a green light, but many testified they saw a solid red light and many red flares. The pilot was sent to Brisbane where he lost his wings. Later we learned that he ended up as an Infantry Officer in Alaska. Fortunately, he was not from our Group.

Returning from Wau on 10 February 1943, we learned that the 90th Bomb, known as the "Jolly Rogers," a B-24 Squadron, was to be stationed at Wards. We soon found out that our Squadron could take-off or land, fully loaded, in less time than it took two Liberators to either get in the air or land. With twice the horse power and less than twice the maximum take-off weight of our Birds, they should not take so much time. This Squadron should have been stationed at some other airdrome for they slowed down our operations. But, there was no other airdrome for them.

The Australian (Diggers) Infantry were having a lot of trouble with the Headhunters at Wau. The "Wheels" in Brisbane came up with the idea to fly the Native Chief, Witch Doctor, and one or two other members of the Tribe to Moresby. The plan was to wine and dine them, give each a box of trinkets, try to convince them to harass the Japanese, and to stay away from all Allied Patrols. The natives in their war paint were all decked out in their finest headgear bird of paradise feathers, ostrich plumes, (flown in from Australia,) or with a parrot wing on top of their head, a shark tooth, and mother of pearl necklaces, long bones sticking through their nose, and another long shiny bone going through the skin of their chest. When it was all agreed on, each of the group received a large 12" X 15" picture of himself and another one of the whole group. The Papuans went wild over the pictures, the first they had ever seen. It seemed they were more excited over the pictures than they were over the plane ride. We were told to get them in the plane, and seated and to keep them seated. That was a real job. After a two-day affair in Moresby, they were flown back to Wau. The Australian interpreters went over the agreement several times before taking the Chief and party back to their village.

The next time an Aussie Ground Patrol was in their village the natives were up to the same old thing—trying to eat the outsiders, namely the Aussie Patrol. The only thing is these visitors came armed. Fifth Air Force made a bombing raid against the end of the Airstrip and wiped out the entire village. That was the end of cannibalism on the north side of this mountain. These were the only natives that I ever heard of who were deliberately bombed while I was in New Guinea.

A member of our Squadron stole an Italian motorcycle from an Australian Military Police Unit at one of the other Airstrips in the Moresby area. When he brought it back to Camp, most of the fellows wanted to ride it. The oldest man in the Squadron, in the 30s prior to joining the 6th, had worked for a circus and had rode a motorcycle in a barrel. He gave us several demonstrations on how to ride the bike. This cycle did not have "crash bars". To show us how fast it would go he would race out of camp with a roar in a cloud of blue smoke throwing up dust and bits of the loose coral from the road. When he returned he would point out that the speedometer was reading anywhere from 90 to 120 mph. After doing this several times he showed us the trick. While sitting on the bike talking to us, he would back the bike up and take all the slack out of the chain. This would be only half an inch at the very most before giving it the gun. The average layman would not even notice what the rider was doing. The rider would then gun the engine wide open, the rear tire would spin on the loose gravel and the needle on the speedometer would fly to the peg indicating the maximum speed of 120 mph. He would then press the button and stop the speedometer needle which would be reading 120 mph. If he wished he could bleed off some of the indicated reading to any speed below 120 he wished by pressing the stop button to stop at the desired indicated speed.

I took my turn at it. I had never been on a bike before. This was a very light weight motorcycle and easy to push and move around by hand. After two or three safe and sane slow rides in the camp area I tried his trick, backed up the machine and took all the slack out of the drive chain. I put my left foot on the ground and gunned the engine. The plan was to pivot around on my left foot throwing gravel and dust with a loud roar and a lot of smoke, then take-off out of camp for the flight line. The plan may have been good, but when I gunned the engine I lost my footing and the bike fell over with me underneath. The bike spun around on top of me for a couple of circles grinding me into the sharp coral road. My flight suit, new Aussie high-top-boots, left leg and hand came out losers in this stupid maneuver. At this very moment, the Squadron Commander drove up in his jeep. He looked down at me under the bike, got out of his jeep, came over, turned the bikes engine off, and lifted the cycle up so I could crawl out. He helped me up with many of the Squadron members looking on. He asked how I felt, then told me to never ride a motorcycle as long as I was on flying status and never to get on one of those things again. He turned to the group and said to return the bike to its rightful owners. He then told me to go to the Medics and get patched up. That was the end of my motorcycle riding. In a couple of weeks the Supply Sergeant gave me a new pair of flying boots in exchange for the ones I had beat up.

At the next morning's briefing we got some new information in addition to the usual: when, where, what, route, weather, enemy activity, and escort information. Most of us had heard about the Early Warning System that General Chennault was using in the CBI. Until this date we were using the same "poor man's radar:" with spotters located along the coast and in the mountains with binoculars and a radio. Today, we were starting with one big improvement, IFF, Identification Friend or Foe. It was an electronic radar means whereby a ground tracking station could identify each individual aircraft. Last night while we slept a small black box was installed in the tail of each of our aircraft with a control box in the cockpit. This little unit transmitted a coded signal. By dialing in the correct code into the control box at the correct time, the ground controller could identify you as Friend or Foe and know your exact location. Before each mission the pilot would sign for a secret code sheet to cover the duration of the flight and make a time check. Each Pilot was issued a rough outline (map) of Papua, New Guinea showing the coast, Owen Stanley Mountains and the Air Strips. The sketch was divided into equal grid lines top to bottom and from side to side. The vertical grids were numbered numerically, and the horizontal lines were lettered alphabetically. At set times the pilot would dial in a different code into the IFF control box. At any given time, if an aircraft was not squawking (transmitting) the correct identification it was considered as foe, and fighters were scrambled to investigate. At first there appeared to be many foes, but after a while everyone put in the correct code at the correct time and it became a very useful aid. It was not only used to find the enemy but to help steer lost pilots to their base. Basically here is how it worked: Moresby Radio would come on the air when a Boogey came within the square next to you. They would give all known information such as: altitude, heading, ground speed, and a guess as to the number and type of aircraft and destination. If the IFF was on, it was said that the "parrot was squawking." While flying, if the pilot was requested to turn the IFF off, he was instructed to "strangle the parrot."

Once, when we were flying a P-38 fighter pilot over the mountains to his base at Dobodura, Moresby Radio came on the air and gave the location of two fast moving targets approaching our square. The fighter pilot got on his knees between us and was looking out. We were at 12,000 feet, letting down at 1,000 feet a minute. The crew chief in the dome called out, "A formation of two above and closing in on us fast." At this time we were in the clear. With no clouds close enough to dive into there were only mountains. I added power and made a tight left diving 180° spiraling turn. We were over Kokoda Air Strip and I was trying to get as close to the vertical north side of the mountain as I could. Below was the same place I had lost the cargo door a few months back. About this time we got a real good buzz job with plenty of prop wash when the buzzing aircraft pulled up in front of us. Our brave Fighter

Captain named off all the Jap Fighters in the Theater. Of course, none of their aircraft look like a twin-tailed Lightening. It is no wonder he was not an Ace, because he could not even recognize the aircraft he flew. Those were two of his own Squadron's aircraft. He was one scared pilot. With a crew of all Sergeants, we did not say a word.

During the twelve months I spent in New Guinea I did not speak once on the radio. In Australia yes, but not in the war zone. Once we added this new capability, most of the time the radioman would be monitoring the IFF set. When Moresby would report that "Bandits" were in the adjoining square, the crew chief would stand on a stool and look out of the Navigation Bubble. The radioman, with the aid of an extension cord, would go to the cabin and look out both side windows. The two pilots would cover from wing-tip to wing-tip and from the ground on up. The four of us never relaxed. We kept our eyes moving all the time specifically looking for enemy aircraft diving out of the sun. There were very few stiff necked pilots flying combat!!

The natives had no metal or paper, therefore they had no paper money or coins. The natives near the coast used sea shells for their money. One of the American nurses gave her maid an old bra. This native female was overly endowed. The next day when the native returned she was wearing the bra but not in the normally accepted, designed way. Instead of having her breasts in the pockets of the bra and covered, her attachments were pointing straight out as usual. The bra pockets were hanging down under her breast with her new "money bags" filled with sea shells!!

My good friend Dave Vaughter, one of the best pilots in the Theater, came in to land at Wards. The Aussies were working on the airdrome filling in the bomb craters and replacing the badly twisted and wrecked PSP strips. Dave came in for a normal landing approach but the workmen would not clear the Strip. He swung around and buzzed the Field, but they still would not move. He made one more normal pass with wheels down. This time he was so low that all the Aussies had to hit the deck. But as soon as he passed overhead the Aussies got up and started back to work. On the next pass they cleared the Field. Just prior to this pass, he opened his front storm window and poked out the crew chief's "Grease Gun" with a 20-round clip. He sprayed the landing strip with 45 caliber machine gun fire where the Aussies were working, made a tight close-in pattern, landed and parked in front of the Operation's

Grass Hut. The Tower had been giving Operations a blow by blow account even before the strafing. All the time the Tower had been giving the work detail a steady red light. By this time most of the flight line personnel were either at Ops or Engineering, the next grass hut over. Immediately Dave got out with the loaded machine gun hanging from his shoulder and his 45 on his hip. Dave was one of those rare pilots who did not have any fear in his make-up. Fear was simply unknown to this man. He walked up to the Operations Officer and made his complaint. Shortly the Aussies arrived by jeep, armed with their rifles. The Operations Officer became a diplomat and settled the problem without it turning into a gun battle. From then on incoming aircraft always had the right-of-way.

A very amusing article appeared in the Guinea Gold. It was dated Stateside, 26 Feb 1942. The notice was one year old at this time. Navy pilot, Ensign Donald Frances Mason, while on submarine patrol in the Atlantic sighted an enemy submarine, dropped two bombs, then radioed the following message to the Navy, "Sighted sub, sank same."

In 1980 all living former West Coast 42-E Staff Sergeant Pilots and wives celebrated our 38th Year Anniversary. This was our first get-together since graduation. General and Mrs. Doolittle paid us the honor of spending the entire evening with our group. Most of us had individual pictures taken with the General. The General introduced me to Mr. Mason of Navy fame, "Saw sub, sank same," and they both signed my Short-Snorter. Mary Tarnish, our Primary Navigational Ground School Instructor, was there and called out each of us by name from memory as we arrived for the last night's banquet. What a surprise that she was there. It was more surprising that after nearly thirty-nine years she would remember any of us let alone each of us by name. There was no Class Book or any pictures to go by, just her memory. She told us that we Aviation Students were the best of all the Students that attended King City, and that we received the worst treatment of all.

Prior to arriving, we were told that each of us was to give a two but not over four minute story of our life since graduation. The first part of my speech went like this, "Ladies, Mr. Mason and Ex-Sergeant Pilots and wives: As far as I am concerned, the highest tribute that could be paid to us Ex-Sergeant Pilots is the honor that we have been paid this night by having Mr. Aviation himself come to us. What can be said of this man of Letters that Kings,

Queens, Presidents, the man on the street, or pilots have not already said? Sir, You were my idol long before The Tokyo Raid. My Grandfather used to say Jimmy Doolittle can fly in the clouds, and not even the birds can do that! Thank you, Sir, for coming."

One morning just after breakfast a single Jolly Rodgers B-24 was returning from bombing Simpson Harbor at Rabaul. The Liberator was so badly shot up that the only way the pilot was able to fly it back was on Auto Pilot. All manual systems were shot out. The pilot had nursed it back at 11,000 feet and had been able to get over the mountains but would not be able to land. When near Jackson heading for Wards, the crew members who were able started bailing out. Our Squadron Adjutant, First Lieutenant Robert W. Loder, was returning from Jackson when he saw one of the parachutes slowly oscillating back and forth and losing very little altitude. After a long time the 130-pound tail gunner landed. Lieutenant Loder pulled up to where the young Airman was folding his chute. The Lieutenant asked, "Are you one of those that bailed out of the crippled B-24?" The gunner answered, " No, Sir, I'm one that my Lieutenant kicked out." Later we learned that five of the eleven crew were either dead or too injured to jump before the bomber ditched in the Coral Sea and all aboard went down.

One night I had just dropped off to sleep when here came the Japs. It had been two nights since they had made their last visit. I started to dress, had my boots and shirt on, when I could hear whoosh-whoosh from a daisy-cutter. I grabbed my pants, put on my steel helmet and dove into the hole. With the exception of the two ends the slit trench was completely covered by PSP and had a couple of feet of dirt on top of that. The trench was not deep enough for any of us to stand upright with a steel helmet on. It was a cozy arrangement. In the trench I bent over and put one foot in one of the legs of my trousers and then my other foot in the other trouser leg. I had just started to pull up my pants when "All hell broke loose." At the time I did not know what it was. Something was in my pants running up one leg, over and around my "privates," then down the other leg reversing course and repeating the same maneuver all over again. All this time I was jumping up and down trying to get away from whatever I'd scooped up in my trousers and at the same time trying to get out of my pants. With each rise of my head, my steel helmet was hitting the underside of the steel PSP. After nearly knocking myself out, I finally got out of my pants. The other three guys were hollering and yelling "Ford, what is the matter?" "Stop it." When I did get my pants off, one of the fellows lit a match and discovered the problem. It was a small field mouse. Even under the PSP and with a thatched roof over the top of our slit trench he should not have lit the match. Three weeks later the Doc could still see black-and-blue marks on my neck and shoulders where my helmet had banged into me. With all the varmints in New Guinea I was thinking of most of them in that "Hour long" ordeal, which in reality must have lasted less than a few minutes.

From the night we arrived in New Guinea until the middle part of March, night raids by enemy bombers were all too frequent. What a wonderful relief it was to get two or three nights in a row of uninterrupted sleep! Intelligence later told us that during our stay in New Guinea, the Squadron had been in over 100 air raids. Yet only two of the 6th Squadron personnel were killed on the ground at Wards due to enemy action.

A few days later another Jolly Rodgers B-24 was returning from a lone Photo Mission at Rabaul when attacked by a flight of Zeros while out over the Solomon Sea. Photo-Joe shot down two of the enemy and lost No. 4 engine in exchange. While making for a bank of clouds one of the attacking fighter's rounds hit a safety latch on top of the bomber. The huge yellow life raft flew out of its compartment on the top-side of the B-24. In doing so it inflated, and one of the attacking Zeros flew into it. The prop of the fighter must have hit one of the CO_2 bottles in the raft and they both exploded. Immediately, the other fighters all turned tail, abandoned the attack, and headed back to their base. The Liberator was able to make it back to Wards without further enemy action. The next day Tokyo Rose came on the air and said that the B-24 had some kind of a new secret weapon.

On my first day off after returning from Sydney I drove over to see Lieutenant Lakeman at the Air Depot at Jackson. Almost the first thing he wanted to know was when I could fly... what sweet music! I told him today and any other days I was off, which was usually one or sometimes two days in a ten day period. In most cases we did not know until the night before. Sometimes I might be able to arrange it so that I would know a day or two ahead. It was agreed that in three days I would try to be back to fly co-pilot on a B-17F test hop. He took me to Quality Control and checked me out a Dash-1 Pilot's

Flight Hand Book. I was to study this between now and the time of the flight. Then he introduced me to the crew chief and went back to his office. This would be the mechanic that would be flying with us for the test flight. The Sergeant gave me a very detailed walk-around inspection and cockpit familiarization introduction to the aircraft. This old Master Sergeant took me under his wing as he would any new pilot. He gave me three hours of very good and interesting instructions. He told me that on "Test Day" I should just listen and keep my eyes on what Lieutenant Lakeman and he would be doing and ask all the questions I wished.

Three days later I arrived at the Air Depot at 0700 with a well read and studied Dash-1, and with oxygen and gas masks in hand. As Cox once told me, "I know the answers, but I'm still looking for the questions and how to apply them." I had spent all my spare time since Tuesday studying, getting acquainted in the cockpit and going over the aircraft systems. Grassi spent several hours explaining things and answering questions. This B-17F was assigned to the 63rd Bomb Squadron. The aircraft was named "Black Jack" and had been shot up pretty badly while over Rabaul. It had been thoroughly ground checked since being released by the Depot. Last evening it had a good run-up by the enlisted mechanics whom I would be flying with and was signed off for a test flight. Before I arrived this morning another pre-flight had been completed. When Lieutenant Lakeman, three other GIs, and I arrived, it was our turn to flight test this Flying Fortress. It was a flight test of the engines and flight controls, but no firing of the guns. From there on it was just a normal 1:45 hour flight. I sat in the right seat, watched and listened as the pilot and flight engineer went about their duties.

When the air test was over I was able to hand fly back to the down-wind. Then the Lieutenant took over and made two landings, and that was it. The radio operator made an extract copy of the Form 1, and the pilot signed it.

When I turned in the extract copy of the Form 1 our Operations NCOIC wanted to know where it came from. When I told him he said that I was not on flight orders to fly with the Depot and could not get credit for the flight. I told him the whole story and that I would be flying with the Depot when I was not flying with the 6th. He asked, "What if you should get injured, killed, or missing in action, then what?" I asked to speak to the Operation Officer. The NCOIC advised against it. Group does not have the authority for one of their pilots to fly with another Command without a written request from the Unit and approval from 5th AF. He told me if I ever flew with another Unit not to talk about it and not to bring back an extract of the flight. If I should get hurt, killed, or missing, there would be all hell to pay, so just be careful and not talk about it. That night I told all my "Hut mates" not to talk about it. Of course, I believed every GI in the Squadron already knew.

Over the next three months I flew seven more flights with the Depot. I was co-pilot once more in a B-17, and another time in a B-24. The other five times were in fighters: once in a P-38, another time in a P-39, and three flights in a P-40. Two of the P-40 flights were normal one hour test hops with no problems or write-ups, and I signed them all off for combat duty.

The last P-40 test flight was the most fun and required the most planning. I knew the day before the test flight that the 8th Fighter Squadron would be escorting the 6th on their early morning mission. I made arrangements to test hop P-40, Field No. 13, one of the 8's Fighters. Irene would also be flying. I went to Operations of the 8th Fighter Squadron and asked to see the Ops Officer. I told him that I was assigned to the 6th Trooper Carrier Squadron as an Enlisted Pilot. That I would be test hopping their P-40 at the Air Depot at Jackson tomorrow morning. There was a big laugh by all the pilots in the hut. They had heard of Staff Sergeant Pilots, but had not heard of them flying their aircraft. I told him to talk to his last two crew chiefs of his P-40s that had just returned from the Depot and ask them who test hopped and signed them off. He took me next door to Engineering. Of course, Engineering knew nothing about it. I suggested that they get out the Aircraft Form 43s on both their aircraft and see who signed off as Test Pilot at the Depot. There was my signature, S/Sgt Pilot. They could not believe it.

The Operations Officer said, "Yes, you did, now what do you want?" I told him that I would be test flying their No. 13 tomorrow morning. The 8th would be flying escort for the 6th and that C-47, 41-185646, field No. 52, named Irene would be flying. That is the Douglas that I'm regularly assigned to fly. He said that he did not know that the 8th would be flying escort to the Troop Carrier in the morning. I said, "You are." Again he asked, "What do you want?" I told him that while in the local area after the 47s get in formation on their way out, I'd like to pull up off the right wing of Irene No. 52 so my crew chief could take a picture. Everyone laughed and he said, "No." I told him I received my wings at Luke in P-40s and all my class had been sent to transports. At first I did not like flying C-47 transports, but now I've accepted it. I would like a picture of me in a P-40 off the wing of my aircraft. "How do we know that once you get in close you won't fire on the transport or on our aircraft?" "That's easy. Your crew chief is at the Depot with your No. 13 when I take-off and land. He can see that the plane is unarmed. Besides, when I approach the flight of transports, surely your pilots can keep an eye on me and keep one unarmed P-40 in its place." He smiled, extended his hand and said, "You win. You've already figured out all the answers." I replied, "Thank you, Sir." Time, altitude, heading, airspeed, and location were all worked out.

I could not get back to the Squadron fast enough to make sure that Grassi would be flying and that he would take my picture. After that, I went back to Jackson to see Lieutenant Lakeman. I told him what I'd planned and to make sure the Kittyhawk would be ready. The next morning the plane was ready even before I arrived. I was airborne 1:15 hour before time to join up in formation with Irene. I completed the flight test and was in position on time.

I was dressed for war, had on a Flight Suit, Mae West, parachute, helmet with built in headphones, throat mike, a hanging oxygen mask, sun glasses, and was wearing gloves. I had the canopy open, gear down with full flaps, barely creeping, waiting for Irene to pull into formation so I could close in on her right wing. Two of the Fighters buzzed me and gave a "Thumbs Up" signal. When the C-47s were in formation and climbing out I pulled in very close below and just in front of the right wing of No. 52. I saw Grassi aiming the camera in my direction. All the crew waved, and when I dropped down and back I could see waving hands at all the windows on the right side of Irene. This was the only time I ever saw Irene in flight when I was flying in another aircraft. I pulled out of formation and returned to Jackson. That evening several in the Squadron asked Irene's crew, "Why was the P-40 off your wing?" Grassi said, "I guess the pilot wanted to look us over."

Flying an Airacobra was like the one flight I had in a P-64 at Luke. By this time I had nearly 1,000 hours twin engine time. The P-38 was the easiest of the four fighters that I was fortunate enough to fly.

I went back to the Depot on my next day off. A Captain was sitting at Lieutenant Lakeman's desk. I asked the whereabouts of Lieutenant Lakeman.

Returning to Wards, flying low over the jungle just off the Southern New Guinea coast

The Captain said that he was no longer with us. He was killed while testing a P-39. I told him that I had come over to help flight test anything he needed help with. The Captain looked at me in total disbelief and asked me to repeat that again. I said, "I came over to help flight test your aircraft." He said, "Sergeants DO NOT FLIGHT TEST MILITARY AIRCRAFT." I said, "I've been test hopping this Depot's P-38s, P-39s, P-40s, B-17s and B-24s since the first of the year. Check your records. There is the Line Chief ask him." At that moment the Line Chief saw me and came in and said to me, "Glad to see you, Sarge. I hope you can test a 38 this afternoon so it can be released back to its Squadron." The Captain spoke up, "He may have come over, but he is NOT GOING TO FLY WITH THIS DEPOT FROM NOW ON, SO GOOD DAY!!" I saluted, did an about face and marched out. That was the end of my Depot flying, sorry to say.

About this time Captain Thomas M. Ridley was assigned to the 6th. He had a very interesting, but a very sad background. He was in pilot Flying Class 40-E. Upon receiving his wings he was assigned to B-26s, the clipped wing Martin Marauder, at Langley Field, Virginia. While on take-off on his very first training flight the aircraft had a runaway prop. The "Widow Maker" was not yet airborne and going far too fast to stop. The Martin crash landed in a very large drainage ditch beyond the end of the runway. The aircraft was "Class-26ed," destroyed. The pilot was killed and co-pilot, 2nd Lieutenant

Ridley, spent several months in the hospital. From there he was sent overseas to the 19th Bomb in the Philippines. When the war started what was left of the 19th Bomb was to evacuate to Darwin, Australia. Enroute his plane was shot up and the crew bailed out over the South China Sea. He spent two plus days in the ocean in a one-man Dingy. An American submarine rescued him and eventually let him off at Darwin. He was then assigned to a P-40 Squadron. After training in the Kittyhawk in Australia, he came to New Guinea for duty. Shortly after arriving at Moresby once again his aircraft was shot down and he had to make a "nylon letdown." It took him eight days to walk out of the jungle. This Officer should have been sent to the States for Rest and Recuperation, but instead he was sent to us. When holding a cup of coffee, if it was over half full it would slosh out of the cup. He could not hold his hands from shaking. Yet, he was still on flying status. He flew with me twice as a co-pilot while I was a Sergeant Pilot. He was the most watchful co-pilot I ever flew with. He kept his eyes going in all directions at the same time. It seemed he could see an aircraft before it came over the horizon. He was the best radar we had and a real nice, quiet fellow.

For the next day's mission the crew list was posted the night before as usual. Lieutenant Merle H. Sheffey was scheduled to fly as First Pilot and Captain Ridley as co-pilot. That meant that we would be flying to Dobodura. During the night the battle situation changed. We had to rush troops and supplies to Bulola the first thing next morning. Bulola was a very short, grassy, rocky, wet, down hill strip located on top of a hill in the bend of the river near Wau. This was one hairy airstrip and no field for an unqualified pilot to even try to land on.

At 0750, 8 March 1943, when we arrived the grass and rocks were slick from the morning dew and the spray from the river. Lt. Scheffey was sixth to land. He made three passes, each time touching down too far down the strip and going way too fast. We had been briefed to touch down in the first few feet on the approach end, no faster than 70 mph, with full flaps and a lot of brakes. The briefing officer said that, "any pilot that could land on an envelope and not cancel the stamp was qualified to land at Bulola."

On the fourth pass he was determined to land. All other aircraft had landed and were being off-loaded. His wheels touched down near the middle of the field going much too fast. Realizing he could not stop and that he did not have enough room to take-off, and if he continued on they would go over the end of the strip into the river some 20 feet below, he ground-looped to the right into an Aussie gun emplacement. In doing so, the right landing gear collapsed and both props were torn off. The right prop ground up sand bags around the trapped Aussie Antiaircraft gunners and their 20 mm AA guns. The scalding hot engine oil spurted over the entombed Australian gunners and all three were scalded to death. Their cries and screams from pain and for help were most pitiful and heart breaking. There was nothing any of us could do. The right engine and wing completely covered their tomb. The 25 gallons of 80°C to 100°C hot oil squirting over them eventually drowned out their pleas for help. To add to the disaster, the aircraft was smoking and looked as if it would explode and burn any second.

The left prop went through the cockpit. All of the crew escaped uninjured except for the pilot. The No. 1 propeller went through the pilot's seat. Lt. Scheffey could not get out and was screaming for help. Sergeant Pilot Johnny Meeks was the pilot of the closest aircraft. He ran to the smoking wrecked aircraft. He jumped up on the left wing onto the No. 1 engine and on up to the top of the cockpit. He reached down, got hold of the pilot and pulled him up and out. Meeks was a tall thin muscular Sergeant. Two other crew members came running and carried the injured pilot to a safe distance from the smoking aircraft and the screams of the trapped gunners. They laid the pilot face down. His back was bleeding like a stuck pig. He asked to be turned over. When they turned him by his shoulders face up, his lower body did not turn over. The prop had cut through most of his lower torso. A crew member got a stretcher and a stack of blankets. An Army Medical Corpsman gave him morphine and tried to put some sort of a tourniquet around him. Meeks placed him in his aircraft and took off alone with maximum power for Wards. The evacuation flight took a little over an hour and a half at treetop level.

Up until this time Lt. Scheffey had been "Trouble City" for all who came into contact with him. He was a lousy pilot and never should have had pilot wings to start with. He should never have been checked out in a C-47 let alone for combat duty. "Why let rank lead, when others of lessor rank with the ability can do better?"

The officer spent a month at Kookie Mission Hospital at Port Moresby, and a few more months at Brisbane Army Hospital, before returning to a stateside VA Hospital. The Moresby Hospital Chaplain came to our Squadron and read off a list of men that Lieutenant Scheffey said he had unjustly treated. He was begging forgiveness. He said if he lived he would write each of them a letter of apology. Years later after the war, I heard that he did. He was in a wheel-chair from then on.

When Captain Ridley returned to Wards he was given a medical examination and returned to the States for combat fatigue. The poor man's nerves were completely wrecked. He'd had four major aircraft accidents all in less than twenty-two months.

One morning Sergeant Dial and I went Wallaby hunting. We both took our crew chief's carbine with plenty of ammunition and I brought my camera. There were no roads west of Moresby, only a native foot path in some of the places. Most of the time we drove on the beach. We knew that if we got stuck, or if the jeep broke down, or if we got lost, we would have to walk back. All we had to do was follow the beach from the way we came or continue on to the west until reaching the river at 30-Miles. We drove up the coast west of Port Moresby and went through a native village. All the huts were off the ground, seven to eight feet on high poles. This was to keep wild animals, snakes and crocodiles out of the sleeping quarters. They built fires under their huts and burned wet and green wood with green leaves to make smoke to help control the mosquitoes in their hut.

We drove on up the beach until we came to a large clearing at least a mile wide and a mile-and-a-half or two miles long. With the exception of a few isolated scrub trees nothing was over waist high. Most of it was short prairie-like grass. We took our stubby rifles, plenty of ammo, and the camera. After walking a short distance we saw several wallabies in the distance. As we got closer, they stayed put, raised up on their hind legs and tail with ears cocked, looked at us and chewed their cud. When we were no more than 100 feet away each of us picked out one and fired. Both went down and stayed. All the others bounded away, and we fired no more. Two clean kills in the head, but what would you expect at that distance with a rifle in broad daylight with no wind and the target sitting still? It seemed to me that the only difference between a kangaroo and a wallaby was size and color. Dial saw the pouch of his kill kicking and moving around. Then out poked a baby wallaby's two front feet. Dial waited until it was almost all the way out then picked it up and held it. Not knowing what to do he watched all four feet, claws, tail, and teeth. Dial held his "baby," and I carried both rifles as we headed back to the jeep. We then drove back to Moresby. The medics gave the baby a clean bill of health. Doc gave us instructions on what and how to feed it. Later, Doc told us that it was a year to a year-and-a-half old. Dial decided to keep it and make it the Squadron mascot. It would follow most of us around the camp. But whenever Dial showed up, his baby would always go straight to him.

A few nights later we were in the hole waiting for the bombing to end so we could get back to sleep. On this night after a bomb would explode, we could hear a lot of movement and thrashing around in the near-by banana grove. We had been instructed to keep our heads down below ground level during all bombings. So immediately after the next explosion Sgt. Klotz fired several rounds with his rifle in the direction of the noise. No more sound from that direction. After the all-clear when the lights came back on, Sgt. Klotz went over with flashlight in hand and brought back his "kill," a four foot iguana.

We flew a load of Navy personnel solo with two P-40s as our escort to NAS Goodenough Island. When off the northeast coast of New Guinea out in the Solomon Sea we were intercepted as scheduled by the Navy Defense Force Fighters for their area of operations. They escorted the three of us to the Naval Air Station. Upon landing, a Navy Airdrome Officer picked up the pilots of the two fighters and our crew. On the way to Operations he invited the four pilots up to the Officers Club for a coke. In the meantime our aircraft was being unloaded. The three aircraft were refueled and ours was loaded for the return flight to Wards.

When I told the Navy officer that the two C-47 pilots were both Enlisted Pilots, he said that he would let us off at the Chief's Mess. One of the fighter pilots asked if I was the pilot who flew P-40 Field Number 13 off the right wing of Irene when on a test hop. Grassi spoke up and said "yes" and that he was the one that took his picture. The four of us had a good meal and the first coke we had north of Australia. It was served with ice. While waiting in Operations for our aircraft to be loaded, we were talking to the two P-40 pilots. One who had recognized me as the Staff Sergeant Pilot that had flown one of their aircraft in formation with Irene. They asked if I could come over and fly with them on some escort flights. I told them that would be great. Just let me know, and I'd try to be there. It never panned out, but the offer sounded good. I told them that if they came my way, I WOULD give them a ride.

That night a single enemy bomber came over and dropped a load of Daisy-Cutters. In the search lights, it looked as if the bombs were coming straight down to hit on top of us. Many hit in the trees above the camp area of the 101st Anti-Aircraft Artillery. There were many causalities. Shortly after the "all clear" sounded our Medic's received a call for blood type "O" Positive. One of our Medical Technicians drove three of us in the "Meat Can" to their Dispensary. When we arrived our Dog Tags were checked. Then we were escorted to where the wounded were still lying on the bank of their slit trenches. The Doctor, looking at my Dog Tag, asked me my name and serial number then looked at the Dog Tag of the unconscious wounded soldier. He said that our blood matched. He told me to lie down on the ground next to the injured patient, to keep still, and do not move. He swabbed both of our arms and stuck a needle in both our arms with a small long connecting tube, and pumped blood from me to him. I had to lie there for forty-five minutes. Then we were driven back to our Medic's. Our Doctor gave me a 48-HOUR EXCUSE SLIP for not flying. He called and notified Operations that I was grounded for the next two days because I gave a direct blood transfusion. I got to sleep through the next two mornings' early wake-up calls. All we ever found out about the fellows we gave blood to was that they were still living when they arrived at the hospital in Australia.

At mail call I received a copy of a letter from General Kenney stating that I had been awarded the Distinguished Flying Cross, the first of six that I would receive.

13

Battle Field Commission

ON 8 APRIL 1943, I FLEW THREE MISSIONS TO DOBODURA. I was the only member of my regular flight crew. Today's crew was good, but I still preferred my own men. Returning after the last flight, Grassi met us, wanted to know how everything went, and if we had any write-ups. When I told him "no problems," he immediately started giving me a bad time just making no sense, saying a word or two on one subject, then changing to something else. I could see Gregg standing in front of the left prop he was smiling and almost snickering. Finally I said, "Grassi, you've been in the New Guinea sun too long. I'm going to talk to the Doc and then the Commander about sending you on leave to Australia." He could no longer keep a straight face. He stuck out his hand with a big Grassi smile and said, "Congratulations, Lieutenant." He then pinned two Gold, Second Lieutenant, bars on my flight suit collar. Gregg also shook hands and congratulated me. What a surprise! I suppose everyone in the Squadron knew that we thirteen Staff Sergeant Pilots were going to receive Battle Field Commissions except us. That night the Squadron had the biggest party with Officers and Enlisted men that I had ever attended while overseas on that tour. As a GI Pilot I had flown 225 Combat Missions. That is the night most of us started our Short-Snorters. A Short-Snorter is primarily signatures of aerial combat crew-members. They sign on your collection of bills (currency), from the different countries you've flown in.

My flight crew Wards Airdrome, Port Moresby New Guinea (April 1943). Left to right front row Corporal Ernest Wooten and T/Sgt Amerigo Grassie; top row 2nd Lt. Ernest C. Ford, 2nd Lt. Cortez Houston, and S/Sgt John C. Gregg.

Three days after being Commissioned each of the Ex-Staff Sergeant Pilots was recommended for the Good Conduct Medal for being good GI's, I guess??? The actual orders were issued on 25 June 1943.

A few days later 5th Air Force in Brisbane discovered that they had no IQ scores for those of us who were Ex-Sergeant Pilots and ordered all of us to come to Brisbane to be tested. Our Commander got on the horn and asked if they wanted all flying shut down for three days. The answer was, "of course not." He said that he would administer the test to his new Officers and forward the scores within three days. It was agreed. The First Sergeant put thirteen numbers in a helmet. In reverse alphabetically order we each drew one slip of paper. My official military IQ is 132!! I didn't know I was so smart. I only wish it were true.

The first Ground Officer duty I was assigned was to censor the mail of my enlisted crew members. I told Grassi and Gregg when they had mail to send out, bring their V-Mail to me sealed and I would sign on the back that I had read and censored the letter. Just don't get us in trouble. I think all of the Ex-Sergeant Pilots did the same for their regular crew members.

For the next few days Tokyo Rose was telling us that we should all leave New Guinea, and be out before 18 April. That was the first anniversary of that treacherous sneaky bombing on their beloved homeland in Tokyo by Jimmy Doolittle and his gang of B-25s. On the 18th, the Rising Sun would bomb us off the face of the earth. We did not leave, but shortly before noon on the 12th they came with the largest force of enemy fighters and bombers assembled so far in the Japanese war. There were 46 bombers and 60 Zeros. The noon-day sky had broken clouds over Moresby and their silver aircraft just glistened in the sunlight. From the slit trench on the flight line we could look up and see the most enemy aircraft we had ever seen in one formation. Our Ack-Ack was going wild. We could see no Allied Fighters before or after the enemy reached their target. It was a very destructive raid. Five of the Group's planes based at Ward's Airdrome were damaged and others were sprayed with shrapnel. The bombs landed so close that the very earth shook, and yet no one in our Squadron was hit. Several supply tents, open storage, military office huts, and GI quarters were destroyed. They put on a good air show!

On 18 April we had to be back from the second mission by 1400 hours. At that time the Squadron dressed in Class As, such as we had, and lined up on the flight line. The reason for stopping all flying and playing soldier was so General Kenney, General Whitehead, and all Group Staff Officers could see our Squadron's Flight Crews being decorated. Alphabetically by rank each flight crew member was called forwarded to be personally decorated. General George C. Kenney pinned the Distinguished Flying Cross on my shirt. He gave me a few words of congratulations and said "keep 'em flying." He told me to keep up the good work, and then we shook hands. I stepped back one step, saluted, about face and marched to my position in ranks. General Kenney then congratulated all Ex-Enlisted Pilots for having been promoted to Second Lieutenants. On this occasion there was no military fly-by, but there were more than the usual number of fighter aircraft in the air both high and low coverage.

On the late afternoon of 20 April, after regular flying had been cancelled due to weather, I returned solo from Wau. We were at 14,000 feet on top of

Ten days after Staff/Sergeant Pilot Ernest C. Ford received his Battlefield Commission (was promoted to 2nd Lieutenant) an awards ceremony was held at Wards Airdrome on April 18, 1943. All in the squadron dressed in their Class As and lined up on the flight line for the ceremony.

big fluffy, billowing clouds. When off my left wing at 90° was a Jap Navy Float plane. Immediately after seeing him, here came a burst of tracers. Thank the Lord we were out of range. I made a sharp diving right 45° turn into the clouds. Thirty seconds later, still in the clouds at 13,500 feet, I leveled off, picked up my original heading, and increased the indicated airspeed by 15 mph. The two aircraft both had about the same maximum airspeed so if I'd stayed in the clear he should not have been able to overtake and shoot us down. You still do not like to see tracers whizzing by. It isn't the ones you see that kill you.

On Easter Sunday, 25 April 1943, a group of us took the Squadron 6x6 and drove three miles to Church Service at Kookie Mission, the largest hospital in New Guinea. This was the hospital that I had flown over at 400 feet the day Lieutenant Majure was shot down. The hour service was once interrupted by a strafing attack. The only place to take cover was lying on the ground on the other side of the coconut logs we had been sitting on. I was as close to the ground and log as I could get all hunkered down and stretched out as straight and as long as possible. There must have been at least four hundred of us at the Church Service and no one got hit or injured. Many of the coconut logs were chewed up and loose coral gravel was thrown into the air. Near by Ack-Ack went wild and as usual there was a lot of noise. There

General George C. Kenney awarded 2nd Lieutenant E. C. Ford his first Distinguished Flying Cross. This ceremony marked the first of six Distinguished Flying Crosses Ernie Ford received in World War II.

were many expended rounds and no downed aircraft. The hospital was well marked and not within a mile of any military installation. It had been there for at least eight months. It is against International Law to strafe or bomb a marked hospital. Who says that, "God does not take care of HIS people?"

On 9 May, I flew to Merauke, Dutch New Guinea, on the southwest coast of New Guinea. This was the farthest west I had ever flown in New Guinea. The Advanced Air Echelon of 5th Air Force was exchanging Advisors with the Dutch and I was the ferry pilot for both parties. I flew the Yanks up and brought the Dutch back. We followed the coast and stayed on the deck going and coming as there was no fighter coverage.

On 20 May 1943, the 54th Troop Carrier Wing was activated with Colonel Paul H. Prentiss as Commander. Major Fred M. Adams became the temporary 374th Troop Carrier Group Commander. On 22 May, Captain William D. Wells became our new Commanding Officer. Three days later on 25 May, Lieutenant Colonel Lackey was promoted to full Colonel and was transferred as Chief of Staff to the cadre that was forming the 54th TCW.

I flew down to Hood Point and landed on the beach. The crew walked to the nearby native village. It looked like all the other villages we had seen. The reason for the visit was to take pictures of Errol Flynn's daughter. Her facial features and hair were much different from any of the other Papuans.

Shortly thereafter Colonel Lackey, went flying in the Wing's PBY Air Sea Rescue aircraft. He buzzed a native sail boat hitting the mast and knocking the boat over with all aboard going into the sea. It ripped the bottom out of the aircraft and he had to land on the grass. Later he told us that he lined up on the boat and had planned to come in close, pull up so the prop wash would blow their sails. Instead, when he pulled back on the yoke the aircraft just continued mushing straight ahead. The PBY was too slow in reacting.

A few months later Colonel Lackey became the Commander of the 317th Troop Carrier Group. On 5 September 1943, this Group led by Colonel Lackey made the first and most famous paratroop drop during the Pacific War in the Markham Valley behind Lae. Years later I learned that one of the paratroopers was a very good friend, a high school classmate from Manzanola, Colorado by the name of Kenneth H. Houston. He was in the 11th Airborne which fought in New Guinea, Leyte and Luzon and traveled to

Colonel John H. Lackey, an officer and gentleman of the highest caliber, rose from 1st Lieutenant to Colonel during the 4-year period of World War II.

Japan landing at Atsugi on 31 August, 1945. He was in Mac Arthur's honor guard on the USS MISSOURI for the signing and the surrender of the Japanese on ending WWII 2 September 1945.

Colonel Lackey was the first pilot to land in Japan after hostilities ceased. That was even before the Peace Treaty was signed. The purpose for his flight was to pick up and deliver to Washington D.C. the US Army Signal Corps's 16mm and still pictures that they made showing the destruction by the two Atomic bombs that were dropped, one on Hiroshima on 6 August 1945 and the second bomb three days later on 9 August on Nagasaki. Once he had the pictures, a Navy stripped-down B-32 flew into Atsugi, Japan, picked up the Colonel and the pictures and made a record-making flight to the States. The plane made three refueling stops enroute before arriving in Washington D.C.: Okinawa, Kwajalein and Honolulu.

My wife, Etta's oldest brother Wes, was a member of the first cadre of fifteen Army Signal Corps cameramen including two Nisei soldiers who were their interpreters. They were put ashore in a LST landing craft in the harbor at Hiroshima, Japan on 18 August, 1945. This was three weeks before the Peace Treaty was signed. Their pictures were the first that the world was able to see of the destructive power of a nuclear device. When the pictures were released by the United States Army Signal Corps in Washington they made worldwide news. They show the destructive force of an atomic bomb. The destruction of these two cities left a life-long impression on Wes.

As destructive as the Atomic Bomb was, just look at what the Hydrogen Bomb would do.

ATOMIC BOMB	IMPACT POINT	HYDROGEN BOMB
1 mile	Total Destruction	9 miles
1¼ miles	Severe Damage	11 miles
2 miles	Moderate Damage	18 miles
3½ miles	Light Damage	30 miles

Incidentally, in 1946, Colonel PAUL W. TIBBETS, Jr. signed my Shorts-Snorter. Just in case you forgot, he was the pilot of the Enola Gay Dimples 82, the B-29 that dropped the first atomic bomb over Hiroshima, Japan on 6 August 1945, at 08:15:17 from an altitude of 31,060 feet. The bomb detonated 1,890 feet above the ground and killed outright a minimum of 80,000 people. Major CHARLES SWEENEY was the pilot of the B-29 named Bock's Car that on 9 August 1945, dropped the second and last atomic bomb on Nagasaki, thus ending WWII.

Since speaking about "other family members" who served in WWII, my brother Otis served 16 months in the Infantry in the Philippines, Japan and Korea. His Corps was in ships off Japan getting ready to land on the beaches south of Tokyo when the second bomb was dropped. It is my firm belief that those two atomic bombs saved my brother Otis and hundreds of thousands of other Americans, let alone a million or two Japanese. My sister's husband Glenn W. Scarbrough served in the Ordnance Corps in the ETO for 24 months. Etta's brother Phil was in the Navy in the Pacific aboard the USS Destroyer REMEY No 688, Flag Ship of the Red Devil Squadron in Admiral Halsey's 3rd fleet. This was picket duty for the invasion of the Philippines and on to the end of WWII. In 1948, at the University Minnesota-Navy football game Phil was sitting in the stands behind Bob Hope. Phil told Bob Hope

The second time comedian Bob Hope signed Ernie Ford's "Short-Snorter" he also signed the accompanying photograph, "To Ernie, Here we go again, Bob Hope." In 1948, when Bob Hope was asked if he recalled a pilot by the name of Ernie Ford he replied, "Yes, he was the pilot that had been flying combat since the Civil War."

that his brother-in-law was Lieutenant Ernest C. Ford and asked if he remembered him. Bob's replied, "Yes, he was the pilot that had been flying combat since the Civil War." This was the same remark he had made four and a half years earlier when he interviewed me on National Radio while I was on one of my many Bond Tours. Fifty some years later he signed the picture the Army took of Bob Hope and me when I was on his NBC program. This time he wrote, "Second time around" and then signed, BOB HOPE. He is the only person that has signed my Short-Snorter twice.

14

The Great Milky Way

ONE OF THE WARD-BASED JOLLY RODGER' B-24s got caught in the search lights over Simpson Harbor, Rabaul, New Britain, while flying the Milky Way. It was called the Milky Way because it had the most concentrated ack-ack in the world, including the Island of Malta. The pilot tried to dive out of the lights with no success. He then tried to shoot the search lights out with the same negative results. Eventually the pilot managed to make it back to Wards with both wings so badly buckled that the aircraft was "Class 26ed" beyond repair and had to be taken apart and used for parts.

I flew as co-pilot-navigator for the Squadron Commander of a new B-25 Unit. There were ten Mitchells (B-25s) in the formation. This was their first flight in New Guinea, and all on the radio at the same time. Since there were no maps, someone had to show them the way. We went on a bombing mission over the jungle near Wau. Every time they saw an aircraft, one of the gunners would call out the name of a Japanese aircraft. Then all the gunners that could see the "Yanks" would start firing away until I thought that their gun-barrels would melt. Fortunately, the P-39s were so far away they could not have hit them if the gunners had been on target. We did not see one single enemy aircraft all day. I told the Commander that his troops should go back to Aircraft Identification Class and learn their aircraft and then learn how to shoot. Don't start firing when the aircraft first comes into view. Wait

At times when there was no active fighting in the immediate area, the arrival of supply aircraft attracted many natives who would otherwise be "invisible." At many airstrips in New Guinea offloading and loading aircraft became a social event for the natives.

until the aircraft is in range and in the gun sighting ring before firing. The effective range of a 50 Cal is only 600 yards. One flight was enough for me with those cowards. The Commander's name was Captain Ford. Within two weeks he flew into a mountain and all aboard were killed.

Over the next few months I made several flights to Bena Bena at Mt. Hagen. It is located 250 miles northwest of Moresby in the highlands about 60 miles south of Madang, a large enemy fighter base. The grassy, sway-backed, 1,500 foot long airstrip had a 10% grade with a hump in the middle of the field. The strip was located on a ridge of a high plateau with a 300-foot wide gully at the very end of the landing area. Touch-down was at 5,100 feet altitude. There were always severe to violent cross-winds over this gully. All landings were into the hills and takeoffs away from the hills. The aircraft was at its most critical airspeed at the end of the runway during takeoff and land-ing. This was where the wind shear was encountered. At a mile high, with the runway slope and an over loaded aircraft this could be a real problem. One of our aircraft apparently came in too slow, got caught in the downdraft, stalled out, and hit on one wing. Fortunately, the crew escaped without injury and the cargo was off loaded safely, but the aircraft was washed out.

Within minutes after our landing, hundreds of natives appeared out of the jungle and surrounded our aircraft. Most of the men were carrying spears and shields or bows and arrows. Many of the warriors had a net webbing sack hanging around their shoulders filled with stones. The natives could hurl these stones from their slings with deadly accuracy just like "David and Goliath" in the Bible. None of them were brandishing their weapons or looked hostile. The natives there were much taller than the coastal natives. The natives wore more jewelry, shells, wild boars teeth, and polished stones than the coastal tribes. They had beads on their arms, fingers, ankles, nose, ears, and hanging around their neck.

Daytime temperatures were cooler with far less humidity than on the coast. The Doc said the winter nights could get down to the high 60s or low 70s. The Missionaries called Bena Bena, "The Garden Spot of New Guinea." They had taught the natives how to grow tomatoes, sweet corn, head lettuce, potatoes, yams, and squash. The Squadron was always glad to have a mission to Bena Bena since there was a good chance of picking up some fresh vegetables. We always brought back as much as we could get, but we never could get enough.

This native tribe had some very strange customs. Instead of shaking hands in the traditional way, the natives would take one hand and hold your crotch. Remember, when the natives did this to another native they were touching bare flesh. Then both parties would laugh and giggle. We Yanks would get the same "Hand shake." In my case, it was no more than a very light touch. Of course, all of us had our flight suits on. By the time we started going to Bena Bena we had American Nurses in New Guinea and some of our pilots would on occasion get a nurse to go with them. When the natives felt us, it usually would only be two or three natives at the most. But when the nurses came almost every native would feel her crotch at least once. Of course, the "gals" had been well briefed on what to expect and what they would see. They were dressed in regular flying suits. When the women were there the natives paid no attention to the male flight crews. After making their "hand shake" the natives would laugh, giggle and point!

Some of the native men had a very, very strange and most unusual body attachment. It was a long, curved, and tapered white gourd attached to their penis. It started at the base of their organ and extended out for four to ten inches beyond the end of the penis. Some of the extensions were straight and some would curve up and back to the native's body. The end of the tube was held in place by a vine around his waist. It looked like a permanent erection. This sure got the attention of the American nurses. This was the only tribe that I saw that was so adorned. Our Australian doctor said that it was just to draw attention to their "manhood."

About six weeks after we received our Commissions, the Wing Commander made an inspection of our camp area. When he discovered that most of the new Officers were still living in the same tents with the rest of our Enlisted Crew, he hit the ceiling. He shouted, "You're dragging the bar through the mud. Don't you want to be Officers?" In unison all thirteen of us shouted back, "Hell, no!!" He said no more, and left. I doubt if any General had ever met such a raunchy group of young Second Lieutenants. As Sergeant Pilots about the only regulations we paid much attention to concerned flying. Now as Officers we came back to the real Army and all that goes with it, including religiously obeying all directives and orders. At that time the only good thing about being an Officer was the increase in pay. That afternoon the Squadron Commander gave us THE WORD TO MOVE, and we moved.

Eddie Silsby, Cortez, and I decided we would get one other pilot to go in with us to build a tent-house. By this time all the other new Officers had joined together. In a day or two the Adjutant told us that a new replacement, Lieutenant Wilbur J. Grisbeck, was assigned and could move in with us if the four of us were agreeable. We were the four of us got together and all expressed our views on what our new "Home" would be like. I explained that I wanted a dark room. We all agreed to build and became roommates. By 2001 I was the only one of the four still alive.

The four of us started scrounging material for our American style hut. We set forth building our new two story castle. First, we picked out a spot on one of the low ridge-tops in the camp area. Then we went to the Port to find our MP friend. He was no longer there, but we found another Buddy. We were able to scrounge such items as: nails, screws, window screens, two bathroom wash sinks, four water faucets, three light sockets with four electrical wall outlets, a shower head and a medicine cabinet with mirror. We picked up eight telephone poles fourteen feet long. The lumber was no problem. It was just a matter of driving five miles to the sea port, pulling the nails out,

Eddie Silsby and I pose in front of "Irene" during a break. Building our new "officer's quarters" consumed most of our free time in May 1943 and proved to be a great diversion from our war concerns.

loading, taking it back to our new "home stead," and unloading. From Squadron Supply we checked out a 20 X 20-foot tent.

We checked tools out from the Engineers and started leveling off a 25-foot square area. This was for our two-story tent-house. The ground was on a slope. We leveled it off, dug holes in each of the four corners of our cleared area and squared them up the best we could so that the center of each pole was twenty feet apart around the perimeter and each hypotenuse of the square from corner to corner was 28.28 feet. All four telephone poles were leveled on top with the pole that was at the lowest point in the clearing. On the northwest side we set another pole with the opening between the two poles thirty inches apart. This was for the only outside door. Straight across on the north and south sides, six feet from the east side, two more poles were set in the ground. Between these two poles, three feet north of the south pole, the last telephone pole was planted. This was to support the stairs to the second floor. One of the Army Corps of Engineers came over with his transit, level, and plumb line. He leveled and plumbed the top of all eight poles. We nailed a frame all around the top of the upright poles. We shoveled in and tamped the earth with a mixture of dirt, rocks, and coral in the holes around each upright.

This was the most time consuming and exacting of all our work. Next was the second story floor with all its supporting joists. When the second floor was finished, the Commander came by and asked if we were going to have a dance. All we would need were the girls and the music. The floor was strong enough to support a good-sized crowd. Then in went the ground floor

I finally had a desk upon which to write letters home. Of course, since letters home could not include any information on my whereabouts or what I was doing, they were short. On the right is a picture of me smiling as I lounged in front of my new two-story officer's quarters.

and the stairs to the upper level. Up till now we had used a ladder to get up and down. The ceiling in the lower room was seven feet eight inches high. The roof of the top floor was an eight-man GI tent. All four sides on both floors were screened in seven feet above the wooden floor.

For the second floor each of us made a wooden cupboard that had two shelves with a cross pole to hang our clothes on. It was made in such away that nothing was over forty inches off the floor all around the room. That way when sitting we could see out in all 360° and when in bed we would be able to see out at ground level from our side. In the middle of the room we had a 4 X 6-foot, 7/8 inch thick sheet of plywood for a table desk standing on two sawhorses. Eventually we acquired eight chairs. We had four upstairs and four below. Hanging in the middle of the tent over the table was a 100-watt bulb under a dark green gambler-type light shade. On the ground floor behind the stairs we installed one of the sinks and the medicine cabinet. The lower floor was divided into three areas. Whenn entering the hut we walked into the "living room" where we had our four chairs. Across from the door were the stairs with the wash basin behind them. In the northeast corner was a 4 X 6-foot darkroom for my photography. This is where the second sink was installed. In the southeast corner was the shower. Think we now had a screened in shower, no mosquitoes, but plenty of scalding hot water. On the outside about twenty feet away, were two 55-gallon barrels on a heavy wood rack. This was our hot water. We never were able to figure out how to get cold water when we wanted it. The toilet was still an outside open air four holer with plenty of lime. It was covered by a seven foot thatched palm roof with a four foot overhang to reduce the rain and sun. The two-story tent was where we lived from May to 2 October 1943, when the Squadron was transferred to Australia.

We had hardly moved into our new home when in came the mice. Supply had no traps but we were able to borrow two from the Mess Hall. As soon as we made a kill we would stencil a white mouse on the outside of the hut above the door and around the house between the first and second story. I do not remember the number of "Kills," but we were able to control the mice. Next week when the regular R&R flight went to Sydney they brought us back six traps. We returned two new traps to the Mess Hall. We now had six mouse traps for our own "trapping" and we never ran out of "Game." We soon had more "Kills" than any fighter pilot in the theater.

On 20 May 1943, one year to the day after I received my Pilot Wings the 54th Troop Carrier Wing was activated. Colonel Paul H. Prentiss was relieved as Commander of the 374th Troop Carrier Group. He was promoted to Brigadier General and made Commander of the 54th TCW. There were eight Officers in the new Wing, of which one was our own Colonel John H. Lackey, Jr. He was a very deserving and qualified gentleman. Before too long we celebrated a promotion party for General Prentiss which I attended. Three years later at Sedalia, Missouri I attended his demotion party back to his permanent rank of Colonel. My next tour in his Wing was at Donaldson AAFB where I went through Glider Pilot School. Two years after that I once again had the privilege of serving under the Colonel at Great Falls, Montana while I was going through C-54 pilot up-grading for the Berlin Airlift.

On 14 June two of our young soldiers were killed when the "Lead Ship" crashed on take-off killing Corporal Marlin D. Metzger and Private First Class Frank S. Penska. The plane was not an aircraft from the 6th.

Flying back from Townsville to Moresby on 25 June 1943, while we were out over the Coral Sea, Grassi came forward and said: "We have a million dollars aboard." I said, "No one said anything to me and I saw no guards.

How do you know?" He showed me the manifest. It read: Lt. so and so, US Army, Finance, $1,000,000 (cash) June payroll. I sent Grassi to bring the Lieutenant forward. Shortly he returned and said the Lieutenant was asleep. I told him to wake him up and ask him to come up front. Shortly a sleepy young 2nd Lt. without a side arm came forward. I asked if he was the Finance Officer. He replied, "Yes." I asked, "Is it true that you have $1,000,000.00?" He grinned and nodded his head in the affirmative. I asked, "Where are your guards?" He said, "You are." I said, "What do you mean, I'm the guard?" He said, "Where can you go except to Wards, where we will be met? If the seals on any of the Finance Bags are broken all aboard will be held until the money is found and then the thief will be shot, maybe!!" I'd been Squadron Finance Officer for the month of May but never a Finance Guard. All of us and the MILLION DOLLARS arrived safely at Wards, and on time.

Thinking back over the years it was seven years later to the day, 25 June 1950, that I spent the night the Korean War broke out in Korea. At that time I had left my wife and two sons who had just arrived in Tokyo and flew off to another war in Asia. But that was another war, so now let's get back to the Southwest Pacific and WW II. Between these two wars I served another overseas tour flying for the State Department in Central and South America. Fifty-six years later, 25 June 1999, I was on my way to Berlin. A few years before going to Berlin I had been in Rome several times. The only reason to mention this was to note that I have been in all three of the Axis's Capitals. All three visits were after WWII was over, thank GOD.

I had met Lieutenant Green, a Navigator, from the 43rd Bomb Group several times. He knew that I loved to fly and wanted to go on a mission to Rabaul. One night he told me that if I really wanted to fly an early morning mission to the Great Milky Way to come over and talk with his pilot. That night Sergeant Klotz and I followed the Lieutenant back to Jackson. I met his pilot. He wanted to know how much flying time I had and what I'd flown. At that time I had over a thousand flying hours, had flown twelve different types of aircraft and had flown on one B-17 bombing raid over Lae last year. His next question was, "How come a Second Lieutenant had so many hours?" When he found out that I had been a Sergeant Pilot, and had just received a battle-field-commission, he told me that I had more pilot time than he did. He said that his co-pilot only had two missions in the "17" and was right out of Flying School. He promised to ask his Operations if I could go. Lieutenant Green would let me know within the week.

It took another week from the time I got the word until our schedules matched and we were set up for an early morning mission. I told Grassi what I was going to do. If I did not get back or got shot-up, he was to go immediately and tell Colonel Lackey in Wing and ask him if he would try to take care of the paper work. The Colonel already knew that I had been flying with other Flying Units on my off-duty time. Grassi said to have fun and come back and tell him all about it.

I arrived in the 43rd's Operations one hour before I was scheduled to be there carrying my parachute, oxygen, gas masks, compass, 45, and knife. The Operations Officer came over and talked for a few minutes and thanked me for wanting to fly with them. He told me to go to Engineering in the next hut over, so I could go out with the pilot and flight crew to pre-flight the aircraft. The crews arrived in about thirty minutes. Then we rode out to the aircraft. It took another forty-five minutes to look over the aircraft, oxygen system, bombs, and all the machine guns. Each ammo belt was inspected very closely and slowly. The bombardier and gunners were double checking their hardware to be sure that it was all there and ready for action. We then left for the Flight Briefing. The flight would be twelve B-17s, four elements of three each, in "V" formation. Our ship was the second element leader and second in command. If anything should happen to the Squadron Leader we'd take over.

The targets were waterfront docks, storage areas and docked ships. The bombing would be from 28,000 feet. Simpson Harbor was forecasted to be clear with clouds most of the way up and back. Take-off was scheduled for 0538. We were to be over IP at 0820. Intelligence believed that most of the enemy fighters and bombers would be out of the area making raids on us. Their ack-ack was expected to live up to it's name, the Great Milky Way, with one of the most concentrated and deadly anti-aircraft fire in the world.

All nine of the crew rode back to our aircraft with the bombardier holding his little black canvas bag containing the Norden Bomb Sight, between his legs at all times as if one of the crew was about to steal it. After another quick pre-flight we all got aboard. The flight engineer asked if I had any questions on getting set up in the right seat. I told him to keep an eye on me and if I did something wrong or was going too slow to help me out and see that I did not goof up. I followed through the oral check list with the pilot. The flight engineer and I covered the right side of the cockpit. After all four engines were running each crew member checked in over the intercom. When the pilot called for the co-pilot, he gave a little of my flying background and welcomed me aboard. Instead of thirty second take-off intervals it was two minutes. Then we climbed straight out in a very loose trail formation. We never did get in close formation like we did in 47s. We leveled off at 28,000 feet over Dobodura. At almost that time our fighter escort first came into sight. I counted ten P-38s. On command from the pilot all gunners test fired their machine guns. At this time we were out over the water. All the clouds were below us as we crossed the Solomon Sea. As we approached New Britain, our fighters had to turn back for that was as far as their radius of action. It was 160 miles on to Rabaul and 160 miles back to where we were scheduled to have fighter cover back to the coast.

The pilot called over the intercom that we were now on our own and to stay off the air unless we saw enemy aircraft. He told us to stay awake, keeping our eyes open in all quadrants, especially for diving enemy aircraft that came out of the sun. The bombardier called in that all bombs were armed and the bomb sight was set up ready to go. The navigator informed us that we were on course at 28,000 feet with a ground speed of 178 mph. We were now 150 miles from the IP. In 20 minutes at 0746 we will start letting down at 200 feet a minute until leveling off at 24,000 feet. By that time we should be over the IP. At flight level the clouds were broken over the ocean. Once over the coast line the clouds were broken to scattered with build ups over the mountains. The tops were already 8,000 to 10,000 feet and growing and it was only 0726.

No quicker said than here came the first flight of Japs and Zeros from up high at 2:00 o'clock with all guns blazing. They must have been on their first mission for before they came within range of our gunners, they stopped firing and broke off their attack. All eyes were on them. Then off our left wing, high and at 10:00 o'clock, came the main attacking force. They dove straight through the formation firing all the way. No bombers went down, but there were many hits. Now that everyone was awake and on the ball the fighters had lost their surprise. The pilot asked for a report. Each gunner called in, with no injuries or hits. The fighters Battle Plan seemed to be for the fighters on our right to make a diving pass, break-off and climb back to altitude, re-group for another pass. Then the flight on our left would make the same maneuver as before. This went on for at least fifteen minutes. Three fighters were shot down with several others being damaged. None of our crew claimed any hits or kills. I think that the B-25 I had flown co-pilot-navigator for actually fired more rounds at Allied aircraft on the distant horizon than this one B-17 fired when under actual enemy attack for thirty minutes. This was one cool, efficient crew.

It wasn't long before the fighters stopped diving and shooting at us and pulled away. Then the real fireworks started, black puffs of thundering clouds of exploding steel with smelly gun smoke. It was a blanket of fire works below us from all the exploding shells. The black flack seemed so thick that you could have walked on it. They threw up a cone of black exploding shells with red dots of fire, but most of it was below us. They were on target but, just too low. Thank God for that! It was 0820 and the weather was clear for the bomb run. This started at the IP and lasted the whole bomb run and until after "bombs away." As the bombs were jettisoned from the bomb racks you could feel the attitude of the aircraft change. After the bombardier turned the air-craft back over to the pilot, he told us that this was just like practice bomb-ing while in school back in New Mexico.

When the ack-ack stopped the enemy fighters returned. There were a few less than before. All the other fighters must either be on a mission or out for maintenance. They stayed with us until we left the coast. From that point on to Moresby most of the talk over the inter-com was about, "What a Milk Run, the easiest mission they had ever flown." I had expected a lot more activity with determined fighters. If the ack-ack had raised 1,000 feet we would have been boxed in because the sky was all but covered below us and the clouds were marching right along with us. The P-38s met us at the beach of New Britain and stayed with us till over Dobodura. That was my third of five actual bombing missions and it was not as bad as many of our missions. At least they had twelve 50 caliber machine guns in each aircraft to defend them-selves. On this day we had 144 50-caliber machine guns to protect us and to discourage the enemy fighters. The attacking enemy fighters on our right must have been inexperienced beginners, but the ones on our left were old hands and good at that.

15

Jimmy Doolittle, "Wrong Way Corrigan," Dick Ratan, and Jeana Yeager

WHEN ON OUR WAY SOLO ACROSS THE MOUNTAINS late one afternoon after Group flying had been called off, we were trying to find a hole between the billowing white clouds. At 14,500 feet, we broke out in the clear between two cells of towering thunderstorms. The aircraft began to bounce around and seemed very strange. I couldn't see anything wrong up front, no ice on the wings, engines running normal, so I sent the crew chief to take a look in the back. In a second he was back in the cockpit laughing. We had a load of thirty-four Aussie Combat Infantry Troops all dressed in short sleeves and shorts. They got cold in the forty-some minutes we had been weaving our way between the clouds and mountains. Their Captain had them up doing calisthenics. We turned on the cabin heat and the erratic maneuvers stopped.

We had our first nighttime nuisance air raid in some time. I was asleep when the first warning shots were fired. Everyone except me ran for the hole. "Photo-Joe" was flying high when the search lights first picked him up. The ack-ack started firing, but as usual, it was too low and behind the target. Occasionally he would drop a few Daisy-Cutters. This night he made several passes. Pretty soon the whole Squadron began yelling, "Ford, get in the hole." Then the "Old Man" sounded off, "Lt. Ford get in the hole, now." At that minute I could hear a swish, swish, and I hit the hole on the run and a slide. This was the second and last time my tent was hit by bomb fragments. Next morning one of the Squadron GI's found a bomb fragment. It was a piece of scrap steel marked "FORD." It appeared to be from an old Ford car or Fordson tractor. I tried to buy it, but he would not sell it. It must have come from one of the many ship loads of junk steel the Japanese bought from the United States prior to the war.

The 5th Air Force was trying to get more C-47s and flight crews from Washington. The War Department was reneging on their crew promises, which were far too low to start with. General Kenney wrote directly to General Arnold, (extracted from page 173, Volume Four, *THE ARMY AIR FORCES In World War II*):

"In the case of troop carriers, I figure I can get five hundred hours of New Guinea operation out of them. It is asking a lot, for the figures show that between weather and the Nips a man lives longer in a P-39 than he does in a C-47 flying the troop carrier supply runs in New Guinea. These kids get a hundred hours a month, so that if I replace them at the five hundred hour mark I will need twenty per cent per month for that reason alone, instead of the seven and one-half per cent your staff has promised me. The replacement rate per month for troop carriers should be twenty-five percent. The troop carrier group working between Australia and New Guinea is averaging over one hundred hours per month, per crew. The great part of their haul is over the 750 mile over water hop from Townsville to Moresby on schedule which they keep regardless of weather. I don't know how much of the grind they can take but with a replacement rate of seven and one-half per cent I cannot think of sending them home before fifteen hundred hours."

It was a nice try. But, as usual, if Washington could find another Theater to send their crews and aircraft to, that's where they would go. There were no replacements in the pipeline. The Southwest Pacific always had the last priority, and so it was in this case. The Pacific War was truly a step-child to the war in Europe and Africa.

I was the first Troop Carrier pilot in the Southwest Pacific to be returned to the ZI for flying combat who was not injured either physically, mentally, or returning for some special assignment. Before I was rotated back to the States I had flown 1,244.50 combat flying hours and 364 combat missions. This was the most combat missions for any pilot in the Unites States Army Air Forces. During Korea I flew another 21 missions making a total of 385 combat missions.

I did not fly on this date, but I remembered that five years ago on 17 July 1938, American Aviator Douglas Corrigan (DOB 22 January 1907), "Wrong Way Corrigan" as he became known, made his famous flight to Ireland. Before WWII, when we were in Primary Flying School, our Navigation Instructor told us that she had told him how he could make this flight and get away with it. All he had to do was to follow her instructions and keep his mouth shut. Over the years before his famous flight, Corrigan had repeatedly requested in writing to the CAA for authorization for him to fly from New York to Ireland. Each time the response was: "Request Denied."

One night during the second week of July 1938, he took off in his second-hand Curtiss-Robin monoplane. He flew nonstop from Long Beach, California to Washington, D.C. Next morning he went in person to CAA's Main Office and requested authorization to make a nonstop flight from New York City to Ireland. He was again refused. He asked, "Why?" He was told that his aircraft was not equipped for over water flight: no radio, no navigator, no celestial navigation equipment, no room for a navigator and his equipment, no over water survival gear, not enough gasoline, no de-icing equipment, and further more the government could not spend time and money searching for him when he went down at sea. He told them that last night he had flown nonstop from Long Beach, the same distance, without all that extra equipment and he had gas left over. Request denied. He left in disgust and flew to Floyd Bennett Field, New York City. There he had his aircraft fully serviced, including the extra cabin gas tanks he had aboard.

He rode the train to Connecticut to visit his sister. For the next eight days he studied the weather reports day and night from the radio, newspapers, and visits to the local airport weather station to see what the teletypes reported. Finally, the weather met his needs so he went back to Floyd Bennett Field. Early the next morning he filed a flight plan, non-stop, direct to Long Beach. The weather was at the very minimums for flight. There were low scattered clouds, poor visibility, and he was scheduled to fly between the two decks of broken to scattered clouds arriving after dark. His aircraft was equipped with an Earth Inductor Compass. The procedure for setting this compass was, after becoming airborne, to fly over the field or a known heading, and set the compass. This was usually accomplished by flying over a marked runway at a thousand feet or below the clouds. The danger with this compass was that it would always be on course or 180° off the desired heading. In a few minutes after take off, he broke out with a solid undercast below and a high overcast. He was to fly between these two decks of clouds until it was time to let down and land in "Sunny California."

"Wrong Way" died 9 December 1996 still claiming that he flew by his filed flight plan and that at no time during his famous flight did he ever see the sky above or the land or water below. When his ETA was up he let down, found an airport, and landed. It was a strange coast line with "No palm trees." He had been airborne 28 hours and 13 minutes. The 3,150 miles averaged out at 111.8 mph. That is when he supposedly found out that he was in Dublin, Ireland. There was a "Little" investigation and that was it, except that from then on he was known as "Wrong Way Corrigan." All good pilots and navigators knew what he did. He would never admit that he purposely entered the reciprocal heading and was therefore 180° from his filed flight plan. There was no way the CAA could prove it,, so he got away with it.

Forty-nine years later Etta and I visited "Wrong Way" at his home. After a while I point-blank asked if he deliberately set the compass 180° off course on purpose. He said, "No," with a twinkle in his eye and a big smile. He signed my Short-Snorter and gave us clippings about his famous flight. We talked for a little over two hours. Later he wrote us and sent us signed pictures of him and his famous aircraft.

Some time later our oldest son, Steve, picked Wrong Way up and drove him from his home in Santa Ana, California to Mojave, California. The pur-

Record of Combat Missions for Ernest C. Ford

EVENT	Arrived New Guinea	21st Birthday	Battle Field Commission	Departed New Guinea
Year:	1942	1942	1943	1943
Day and month:	13 Oct	12 Dec	8 April	2 Oct
Days in New Guinea	0	49	145	291
Days not in combat zone	0	11	32	63
Combat missions	0	91	225**	364
Korean War June-July 1950				21

Total Combat Missions flown as Pilot during military career: 385

**As a Staff Sergeant Pilot, on 22 September 1942, I signed for IRENE, my first aircraft, C-47A Serial No 41-18539, Field No 39 at the factory in the USA and flew it as First Pilot until January 1943. At that time our Group 374th exchanged aircraft with the 317th TCG and I was assigned a different aircraft, C-47 Serial No 41-18646, which I also named IRENE, and continued to fly it as First Pilot until December 1943. I left New Guinea on 2 October 1943, and continued to pilot IRENE completely encircling Australia until just before Christmas 1943, when I returned to the States. I received my Battle Field Commission upon my 225th Combat Mission on 8 April 1943.

"Wrong Way" Corrigan personally autographed this photo when Etta and I
visited his home nearly 50 years after his famous flight.

pose of the celebration was to honor the Flight Crew of the Voyager, their
ground support and all their financial supporters. Steve was one of their advisors. He was responsible for securing all their around the world diplomatic
clearances for the countries they flew over in their record breaking first round
the world, non-stop, non-refueling flight. Etta and I were financial contributors to the cause as they had to make their own airframe for the flight. We
made several trips from our retirement home in Sacramento to Mojave
before and after the big flight of 14-23 December 1986.

A few days prior to their flight Steve asked the pilots, Dick Ratan and
Jeana Yaeger, if there was anyone in aviation that they had not met. They
both spoke up and said, "Yes, Jimmy Doolittle." Steve told them that he could
arrange a meeting. They wanted to know if he knew the General. He told
them that he had never met the General, but his Dad knew him. I received a
call to arrange a meeting. I told Steve that was ONE big order, but I would try.
The result came several telephone calls and a few letters later. It was all set.

On 14 August 1987, Etta and I had a luncheon for twelve at the Fishery

A 1987 photo of General Jimmy Doolittle, Etta Ford (my wife), Dick Ratan and Jeana Yeager (the Voyager pilots), and Merle Strauch (a flying school classmate of mine).

A 1982 photo of the author, General Jimmy Doolittle, Mary Tarnish, and Etta Ford (the author's wife).

Restaurant in Monterey. This was the General's favorite restaurant in the area. The party consisted of General Jimmy Doolittle, Dick Ratan and Jeana Yeager, the Voyager Pilots, Merle and Jane Strauch, my Flying School Classmate, and the General's civilian aide, Steve and his Step-Son Robert Tabor, Forbes Simpson, the pilot that flew Steve and Robert up and back from San Diego, Dan Card, one of the Voyager Advisors, Miss Alyisha Ball, from President Reagan's West Coast Public Relations Office in Los Angeles, Etta, and myself. The Restaurant was closed to the public for this special occasion until after 1600 hours. Special souvenir Menus were made and all twelve in the party autographed a copy for each of us. Etta and I picked up the tab and have the Visa receipt to prove it. After the meal there was a press conference and pictures by the press. Then we drove to the General's home. There we spent two plus hours seeing his many awards, trophies, and taking more pictures. That day we were in some mighty select company. It was most interesting.

In 1962, President Kennedy announced that before the end of the decade we would have men on the moon! Mary Tarnish, my navigation instructor at King City, was appointed to be in charge of plotting the navigational course to and from the moon. Much could be said about this, but it was well covered in the one hour ABC National Network Documentary Program.

16

Lost Both Wingmen

ONE DAY, AS WE RETURNED FROM A MISSION, we saw a strange looking black, twin-tailed stubby aircraft fly over. It looked like it was going to land at Jackson. Later, Operations told us that it was a Northrop P-61, Black Widow, radar night fighter. That night at about 2200 hours we had an air alert all of us got in the holes. We could hear only one fighter take-off. Search lights came on and caught all three enemy bombers in the lights. There was no ack-ack firing. Shortly, we could hear the distant whine of a diving aircraft. The three Betties were continuing on in a straight line. Then we began to see tracers converging on the lead aircraft. We could hear machine-guns firing and we saw the lead enemy bomber explode. Still we could not see our fighter even though he must have been in the search lights. There were many cheers from the ground. The whine of engines, more tracers, fire, smoke and the second Bettie began to loose altitude. The Black Widow was staying and pumping more rounds into the falling and burning bomber. At about 8-10,000 feet the second aircraft exploded. By this time the third plane had jettisoned its bombs over the jungle and made a diving right turn, and was out of the range of the search lights. Then came the distant whining sound of the fighter climbing for altitude to make another kill. We never were able to see or hear anything else. It did not appear that the bombers ever fired a single shot, or at least we never saw any tracers. This was the first time we had ever

"Hells Bells" parked at Wards Airdrome prior to the accident.

seen a radar aircraft in action. At the next morning's briefing we were told that the third bomber was shot down and crashed about fifty miles northwest of Moresby. "The Knight of the Air" (P-61) had landed safely without having ever been shot at.

Our Commander Major William D. Wells, while taxiing his aircraft Hells Bells No. 63, taxied into a tree hitting the right wing. The wing-tip, deicing boot and navigation light had to be replaced. Of course, there were no spare parts. It took a week to scrounge up the parts in Australia and get the bird back in the air. From then on he was known as "Hells Bells, Wing-Tip Wells."

My good friend Eddie liked to study the dictionary. Quite often he would say, "War is nothing more than legally authorized murder." One day the Commander heard Eddie say it, and they got into a heated discussion. Finally Eddie told him, "Sir, you may go and take an aeronautical copulation of a celestial satellite." Wells said that's enough and walked off. About an hour later Wells came back with fire in his eyes. He gave Eddie the devil and told him if he ever cussed him out again that he would get a written reprimand.

On 15 August 1943, we were briefed that we would be flying in Group formation with full fighter coverage. The mission was to Tsilli-Tsilli located in the Markham Valley area behind Lae. I was flying as Tail-End-Charlie in the Squadron formation. When we joined in formation climbing out from

Wards, two other 47s from the Group closed in, one on my left and one on the right wing. When ever we flew with two or more squadrons we were always briefed to close in all gaps for better fighter protection. This was the same way as when flying formation by the individual squadrons. Both the top and close cover fighter escorts on this mission were P-39s.

As we entered the Markham Valley Japanese fighters caught us just as we were pulling up to enter a 500 foot traffic pattern. Grassi was standing on his little stool looking out the Navigator's Dome. He began to shout, "A Zero is diving and firing at us." We were already on the base leg in an extended right echelon with the gear down and a quarter flap. One of the enemy Zeros came diving from high and behind. On the first pass he shot down both of my trailing wingmen. When Grassi first started yelling I chopped the throttles back. The airspeed dropped below 100 mph as I pushed the nose for the trees. 200 feet below I raised the gear and flaps. As the fighter over shot and passed overhead, the "Meatball" of the Rising Sun insignia never was so big or so close. Then I pushed the throttles to the fire wall flying straight ahead. No. 3 wingman went into a graveyard spiral. He crashed and burned near the edge of the grass air strip. The right wingman was last seen heading for the mountains on fire, trailing smoke and vanished into oblivion. The Zero did a sharp 180 and came back head on for me. By this time I was just above the trees at full throttle. Here came his tracers. How they missed, only God knows. Not one single bullet touched Irene. We skidded, banked and reduced airspeed, flying too low and slow for the Zero to line us up in his gun sight. What evasive tactics can an unarmed fully loaded transport take against an armed, attacking enemy fighter? From the first firing of his machine guns at my trailing wingmen until the head on pass at me could not have been over three to four minutes by the clock. These few seconds went into slow motion and the compressed time seemed to be hours. There was nothing I could do about it, except to only depend on training and instinct. In my memory some sixty plus years later, it was an eternity. I can still see the tracers and the Jap fighter pilot's big flying goggles as he pulled up from a head-on attack to avoid a mid-air collision at tree top level.

He was not a Kamikaze Pilot, one of the "Divine Wind Boys," for he did not ram us head on. Our closure speed was as high as 550-560 mph and 230 mph on the low side. At this time in World War II that was fast, that is, if one aircraft was a transport and the other one a fighter. Most fighter pilots arrange their ammo belts so that 1 to 5 or 1 to 7 are tracers. The tracers are so the pilot will be able to see where he is shooting and correct accordingly.

In my case, I was sure he was aiming for my No. 1 engine for all the tracers were off and below the left engine. After many changes of heading, airspeed, banks and skids, here came two of our P-39s, and that is all that saved us. Our escape literally defied all odds. You don't have time to think if you want to stay alive. It's all by reflexes. This took place over the jungle to the side of the newly cut, lush grass field where we were to land. All transports that had not landed, cleared the area as fast as we could, making a crooked zigzag path just above the kunai grass all the way to the mountains.

All the airborne C-47s were clearing the area and heading back for Moresby. As fierce air battles were going on all around and above us, fighters, bombers, and transports were being shot down. All of this was taking place over and near the grass strip which was nothing but a clearing hacked out of the kunai grass. We could see that several of our fighters were shot down as the enemy had many more aircraft than we had. While in that valley most of the flying was "in the weeds," then at treetop level, while changing course at least every minute. We headed for Wau. When we were well out of the area we climbed up over and through the mountain passes, in and around the towering thunderstorms, and returned to Wards without escort. Each aircraft came back on its own not in formation. All we were interested in was getting away from the enemy fighters.

The only way I can figure that we were not shot down was that initially the attacking Zero was so high, going so fast, that when he first started firing and with the relatively short distance between the three C-47s, Irene's reduced airspeed and flying in the actual tree tops, he simply overshot us. If the Zero had continued its dive and firing there would be insufficient time and altitude to keep from crashing into the jungle. He had to pull up and make another pass.

The enemy fighter made a 60° hard left bank and a 180° change of direction and came back for a head-on attack. At the same time Irene was going straight towards him at full throttle to shorten the time for him to shoot at us on this pass. All the time I was flying as low as I dared. Grassi was yelling that our P-39s were diving for the Zero. The enemy fighter pilot had to reckon with the short time he had to get us in his sights, avoid flying into us, or if we exploded flying into the wreckage. Since both our aircraft were on the deck he had very little maneuvering room and only three of four seconds at most to act. He may have also seen our diving fighters. Whatever the reason, on this pass he only got one short burst and all tracers went into the trees below and to the right of our No 1 engine. The Zero passed over and just off our left wing-tip. By now our two P-39s were after him and we left the area at full throttle. Who said, "that THE GOOD LORD won't protect you!!" This was another mission where, "GOD was my CO-PILOT!!"

This is the kind of mission that will pump a shot of adrenalin into the blood stream. In flight training we were told that training reduces fear, and that you do what you've been taught to do without thinking. I would say that is correct. If you stop to think about what you should do, you're dead. Even before Colonel Robert L. Scott published his famous book *GOD IS MY CO-PILOT* I knew that GOD was MY CO-PILOT. Later we heard that more than one of the "Fly Boys" was so scared that some voided in their flight suits. Fear, horror, fatigue, and anxiety are all demoralizing. Combat has all of these, whether it is in the air, on land, at sea, or under the ocean. As it has been said about war, there are hours and days of pure boredom and then minutes of shear terror and that is so true. Pilots are not trained to get shot down, but trained to fly another day!

Later that day, there were several different counts of how many aircraft were lost by both sides. There were the official 5th AF, the *Guinea Gold Newspaper*, the enemy's count, Tokyo Rose's number and what I saw in my small view of the whole air battle. The only C-47s lost were my two wingmen. But I know for a fact there were many other aircraft and crews lost. We got clobbered. An unusual part of this near fatal mission was that our crew was transporting 5,000 pounds of food stuff, mostly fresh vegetables.

This was the first day for the Republic Thunderbolt P-47s to fly combat in the Southwest Pacific. In relationship to the other fighters in the Theater at this time, the P-47 was one very fast, "Hot" aircraft. From the time they scrambled at Moresby, climbed to 31,000 feet, weaved their way around and between the towering thunderstorms, and flew 182 miles, they were over Tsilli-Tsilli in twenty-six minutes at an overall ground speed of 416 mph. In those days that was real speed!

The next morning we were told that the two downed aircraft were from the 21st Troop Carrier Squadron. A few days later I learned that the Co-Pilot of the C-47 that went into the mountains was Flight Officer DARWIN REED HAMILTON and that he was missing in action. We were classmates in flying school. As of August 2004, the wreckage had not been located. This was my second classmate to be shot down in this part of the world since we arrived in New Guinea. On 4 November 1942, Staff Sergeant Pilot ROBERT C. DILLMAN was shot down on take-off from Henderson Field in Guadalcanal and all aboard were killed. DILLMAN was a member of the 33rd Troop Carrier Squadron. Half of the 33rd had been "SHANGHAIED" on their way to Port Moresby and forced to fly support for the Marines.

The following appeared on page 177, Volume Four, *The Pacific, The Army Air Forces*, August 1942 to July 1944.

"The first attack on 15 August caught the troop carriers as they were flying in the ground echelons of the first fighter squadrons to be based at Tsilli-Tsilli. One flight of the C-47s had just landed when twelve Sallys, escorted by an equal number of fighters and flying low enough to have avoided the Allied radar, roared in through mountain passes. Japanese shells riddled one airborne C-47 of the second flight and caused it to crash killing all occupants. Another transport vanished into the surrounding mountains and was never found. The remainder of the second flight turned back to Port Moresby making their getaway by some skillful flying at treetop level. Fortunately, the escorting P-39s engaged the attention of the Japanese fighters. When the fight was over four P-39s had been lost, but three of the four pilots saved themselves and claims showed eleven Sallys and two or three of the fighter escort were shot down. Damage on the ground had been slight."

Sometime later, I received a news clipping saying that I was now in the Hall of Fame for the state of Colorado.

Eighteen months later I was a Flight Commander at Sedalia, Missouri, training Combat Flight Crews in C-46 aircraft. At the end of a six hour night training flight at 0130 hours, the flight was returning to Base in a fifteen ship formation. As the formation leader, I lead the flight over the field as scheduled. Being the Flight Leader I peeled off to enter the traffic pattern. The right wingman followed as had been briefed and as was in the written SOP. No. 3 wingman immediately peeled off and up into the No. 2, C-46. The two aircraft had a mid-air collision, crashed, burned at the edge of the field and all eight crew members were killed. It was 0620 the next morning before I got home. Etta was sitting up in bed reading, waiting, and wondering why I was so late. When I told her what had happened she got very scared. She knew one of the pilot's wives. This was the first time my wife began to realize that there was danger in flying. Before this, it had always happened to someone else and at a distance. This time it came close to home.

A few months later, at Sedalia Army Air Base, Sedalia, Mo. I was able to give Etta the first flight that she ever had in an aircraft. It was in a C-46. On this flight, we had an electrical fire in the circuit breaker junction box. The crew chief was able to extinguish the flames. There was plenty of smoke and electrical burning smell. Etta was in the jump seat and her big brown eyes were getting bigger every second. She was watching everything. The electrical junction box was located below and within two foot of her left foot. We had to turn off all electrical power and return to the Base. We landed on their green light. Alert met us to see what the trouble was. She was not very impressed. I was in hopes that she would get some of the thrill out of flying that I did. Two years later, at Lawson Field, Columbus, Georgia, I was able to talk her into going up again. This time it was an uneventful flight in a C-82. Flying up front was not her cup of tea.

17

Colonel Charles A. Lindberg

THE SQUADRON RECEIVED A HURRY-UP EMERGENCY medical request from Kookie Mission. It was the largest hospital in all of New Guinea. They needed a plane load of medical supplies to be picked up at Garbutt Airdrome. Operations sent one of our youngest, most bashful 2nd Lieutenants and crew. An American Army Nurse went along to expedite the pick-up and sign for the Hospital supplies. Upon landing, the crew went to Operations to debrief, eat and file for the return flight. The nurse went about her duties. At the appointed time all met back at the aircraft. The load was very light, just bulky. In fact there was not enough room for the crew to get up front through the back cargo door. They had to enter by way of the crew ladder to the cockpit. It turned out that this emergency flight consisted mostly of Kotex!! What kidding this young officer received over his flight to Australia. From that day on he was known as the "Kotex Kid."

This brings to mind another Squadron flight with an Army Nurse aboard. While returning from a ten day leave in Sydney on a five-hour flight over the Coral Sea the nurse had the urge to relieve herself. The standard relief tube was the only equipment provided in the cabin toilet and was not suitable for her needs. Since the aircraft was not equipped to accommodate female passengers, she came forward and expressed her urgent and immediate needs to the pilot. As usual the crew chief was summoned to handle the situation. He came up with a 14-quart mechanic's bucket that was used to clean the aircraft and wash parts in and around the plane. The pilot "requested" the crew chief to place the bucket in the rear cabin toilet. The crew chief assigned the assistant crew chief the duty. There were many smiles, snickers, and laughs as the mechanic carried out his task. But all hell broke out after landing and all passengers had departed. The crew chief told the pilot that the nurse's bucket was waiting his attention. The Captain said, "Empty it." The crew chief replied, "It is not my duty or my assistant's duty to play nurse maid to a female passenger." The Captain said, "Just go ahead and empty the bucket." The crew chief said, "Sir, put it in writing." This went on for over ten minutes. Two good friends parted with a strained relationship with the pilot doing the honor. From then on the crew chief was known as "Slop Jar Shorty" or words to that effect.

On the 2nd of September, First Lieutenant Richard B. Stanton went on a test flight in a B-24 of the 90th Bomb Group. The aircraft never returned. In time all aboard were officially reported as missing. There were no known enemy aircraft in the area. It was assumed that there must have either been an on-board explosion or they tried to act like the Troop Carrier Pilots flying low and flew into either the jungle or the Coral Sea. No "May Day" call was received. One year later on 2 September 1944, the missing crew was officially changed to killed in action.

On 4 September 1943, I returned from leave in Sydney and was unpacking when Grassi came up to our hut. After some small talk he congratulated me on being promoted to First Lieutenant. This was the first I'd heard of it. He handed me a pair of home-made silver bars. There was no place on the Island to buy them and none of the Officers had an extra pair. He had hammered them out of two Australian silver florin coins. He must have spent hours hammering and shaping silver, soldering the clasp on the back and then polishing the face of the two matching shiny silver bars. Some sixty-six years later I still have them.

Several times when flying across the Coral Sea in clear weather Grassi would be the only one awake in the cockpit. He would be hand flying over the ocean as good as any pilot. What he did not know about a C-47 is still not in the books. As I write this some sixty plus years later there are many DC-3s and its versions that are still flying throughout the world. A few years ago

Etta and I saw twelve C-47s lined up on the ramp at Tel Aviv, Israel. This is the largest fleet of Douglas planes that I know of that are still in daily use as of this date. As of March 2002, Douglas claims that 1 out of every 5 DC-3s and C-47s manufactured are still flying somewhere in the world. What more could be said about a wonderful flying machine sixty-eight plus years since the first one rolled out the factory door and fifty-nine years after the last DC-3/C-47 was manufactured. When Grassi would climb aboard it was time to go and not before. He was a Master Mechanic among his peers.

I received a letter from my mother with a Denver Post newspaper story and picture dated Tuesday, August 24, 1943, by Art Cohn, International News Service War Correspondent. He had interviewed me sometime in July. I'm sure he flew up from Brisbane interviewing pre-selected individuals at several bases in the Port Moresby area. He then went back to Brisbane to write and file his stories. Later I met one of the 90th Bomb pilots he wrote about. It seemed that the printed article was not the way the interview went. He got my name and home town correct. He said that I was, "A Baby-Faced, bashful boy of 21." I guess that part was true. Anyhow, the picture in the paper was taken when I was a Private at Fort Lewis, Washington. In essence, the article said that I held the record for the most combat missions, 325. That was as of 30 June 1943.

Our Group with heavy fighter escort returned to Moresby from Nadzab. When over Jackson we broke formation to land at our home base. Turning on the downwind at Wards we got a steady red light. There in the traffic pattern was a C-47 pulling another aircraft. The second plane was kind of square and had no engines. It appeared that the second plane broke loose from the Gooney-Bird. This airplane made a very close-in pattern and rolled to a stop in front of an Alert Man standing with raised hands in front of Operations. After landing, all First Pilots went to Operations for debriefing. There we looked at this strange looking engineless aircraft and were told that it was a CG-13 Glider.

Little did I realize then that within six years I would have made two hundred forty-one dead stick landings in these little flying boxes and been awarded a pair of "SILENT WINGS", Glider Pilot Wings. A glider was the only aircraft that I ever had an accident in. It nearly killed me. I really got clobbered. The yoke hit me in the face and chest. The rudder pedals jammed

MANZANOLA FLYER HAS RECORD FOR MISSIONS IN SOUTH PACIFIC

Coloradan Has Flight Record

Lieut. Ernest Ford, With 325 Flights and 600 Hours in Combat Zone in Troop Carrier Service, Is Baby-Faced, Bashful Boy of 21.

Lieut. Ernest Ford of Manzanola, Colo., with 325 missions and more than 600 hours in the combat zone to his credit, probably holds the record for missions and hours in his branch of the service in the southwest Pacific, according to Art Cohn, International News Service war correspondent. After living several days with a troop carrier force at a New Guinea base, Cohn asked which pilot had made the most missions, and learned that Ford was the top man.

"I expected to find a grizzled veteran, possibly a retread from the last war, a husky, blustery fellow with a weather beaten face and a personality to match," Cohn wrote.

FINDS BABY-FACED BOY OF 21 YEARS.

"Instead, I was introduced to a baby-faced boy, age 21, a modest, bashful kid who claimed he was five-feet-seven and weighed 150 pounds, but who appeared to be giving himself the best of it."

Out of 325 missions, Cohn said, he expected to find a book of heroic experiences, but Ford quickly dispelled that notion.

"I have never been injured," Ford

is a branch of service seldom written about, an unspectacular but no less vital branch of the army air forces.

No headlines and few medals for the troop carriers, but they carry the mail . . . and he mules and the ammunition and the food to the men who will make headlines because of them. An occasionally, like Lieutenant Ford they receive the Distinguished Setice Cross for delivering the good frequently within rifle range of he enemy.

TROOP CARRIERS IS VITAL BRANCH.

"I don't suppose I'll be a lieutenant in the regular army after the war, but that's all right. I'm ready to go back as a sergeant . . ." Cohn wrote that the troop carriers

LIEUT. ERNEST FORD Of Manzanola, Colo., transport pilot with the south Pacific troop carriers, whose 325 missions and 600 hours in the combat zone make him the record-holder in his branch of service for missions and hours in that area.

Denver Post article, August 24, 1943 noted that I had flown 325 combat missions. Before I left New Guinea, I had flown 364 missions.

into both of my feet. I received a broken nose, two black eyes, four broken ribs and both arches broken in my feet. I had heat treatments for months for the pain between my shoulder blades. It occurred while in glider training school on a night training flight. We were being towed by a C-46. In the landing pattern when the 'Tow-Rope Release Handle' is to be pulled, the tow rope would not release and separate the two aircraft. The pilot of the tow aircraft is supposed to have his crew chief watching out the Navigator's Bubble to be positive the glider has released and is free. After the release the pilot of the tow aircraft is scheduled to lose altitude, increase speed, and clear the area so the glider pilot can make his landing. All we know for sure is that the tow crew fouled up and it came close to killing both of us in the glider. It was as dark as pitch and the tow plane airspeed got up to 185 mph. It was surprising that both wings did not fly off our "little shaking box." The CG-15 is red-lined at 150 mph. Both of us pilots had our knees pushing forward on the yoke trying to keep from gaining altitude so that the other end of the tow rope would not hit the rudder of the tow ship. At the same time we were trying to get the co-pilot's storm window open so we could cut the tow rope with our knife. This is the recommended SOP, but the window was stuck in the closed position. When the "D Ring" finally came loose on it's own from the glider, we were at 700 feet over the Greenville (South Carolina) city hydro-electric plant five miles from the end of the runway.

The airport was the only clearing in the area. There were homes, factories, trees, and hills, and it was a pitch black night. The approach end of the field was up on a fifteen foot embankment. With 15° flaps we stretched the glide for every inch that it would go. When our glide path dropped below the runway lights, we hauled back on the wheel, dropped full flaps for the elevator lift and crashed landed at 40 mph on the crest of the embankment. The nose of the glider broke at the trailing edge of the wings. The cockpit stayed on top of the runway undershoot area with the tail section hanging below on the face of the embankment. The "Meat-can" was there to meet us. They had seen our landing lights go out of sight below the runway surface and were sure that we were both killed. Needless to say the glider was a total wash-out. No "Report of Survey" or investigation is made on a glider crash unless there is a death. They were designed to be expendable. The history of the gliders revealed that a high percentage of the pilots were expendable also.

It took more guts to fly a glider than good common sense!! I'm referring to the American Military gliders of WWII, not the soaring planes we see today that most people call gliders. The war gliders carried pilot, co-pilot, fifteen combat infantrymen, or a jeep and five infantrymen, or a small bulldozer and operator, etc. Gravity forced gliders down like a rock. Soaring planes soared on the air currents. The record for a soaring plane to stay in the air is 38 to 39 hours!! Glider passengers were referred to as "Glider Riders."

We landed at Lae on the 12th and 13th of September 1943. This was the Airdrome that Amelia Earhart departed from on her last leg of her ill-fated flight in July 1937. The Operation tin-roofed building had one blade of a Hamilton Standard Prop from an old F-2 aircraft hanging above the entrance which read, "Lae-In" with just one "n." The strip was on a large grassy level plain with the east end of the grass runway ending at the beach right at the

The author (far right) standing in front of the Operation's building, the "Lae In", at Lae Airdrome on the north New Guinea coast. Lae was liberated by allied troops on September 12, 1943. In July 1937, this may have been the last building Amelia Earhart was in prior to her ill-fated last flight into the Pacific.

water's edge. This and Wau were the only two fields that you could tell had ever been used prior to the war. Wau had an old wooden shack at the south end of the strip next to the mountain. Both Lae and Salamau were recaptured by Allied Troops on 12 September 1943.

On the second day we landed at Lae, the Operations Officer asked if we had a few minutes. When we said: "Yes," he told us to keep an eye on the "Black Widow" parked on the grass out front with the pilots standing nearby. "Please, do not talk to any of them." All I could see were twelve to fifteen pilots in a group talking near the parked P-61 with a guard on duty walking back and forth in front of the aircraft. The guard slowly walked to the right wing-tip, stopped, looked all around and he would then reverse directions. At that moment a tall, slim young man dressed in civies came running from around the back of Operations. He ran up and climbed into the cockpit before the guard or the group of officers noticed him. It was all so quick. It seemed that as soon as he was in the cockpit the left prop began to turn and the aircraft started moving. The guard was hollering and trying to un-holster his gun. The Operations Officer ran out to the guard. The guard then holstered his gun, ran and hopped in one of the several jeeps parked near by. In

FACES IN THE POST GALLERY OF FAME

preciation for Some Public or Private Act or Benefaction Performed in the Current Week

VALL,
rd of ener-
movements
ce Denver's
advantages
on as presi-
er Automo-
ciation, now
y wartime
which is en-
ations while
trade con-
sible.

BARRY M. SULLIVAN,
Chairman, who, with the willing and patriotic support of
thousands of workers and
contributors, helped m a k e
Denver's Red Cross war fund
campaign a magnificent success, with $838,286, or $65,000
more than the city's $773,000
quota, donated by 111,979
subscribers—a fine addition
to Denver's wartime record.

W. M. WILLIAMS,
Executive secretary, highway traffic advisory commit-
tee to the war department,
for public service in direct-
ing a statewide survey which
showed, he said, many Colorado motorists are "sabotag-
ing the war effort" on the
home f r o n t by excessive
speeding, flagrant overuse of
cars and by creating accident
hazards.

LIEUT. ERNEST C. FORD
Of Manzanola, Colo., pilot
with the army troop carrier
command, who, at 22, holds
what his buddies believe is
the top record of this war for
number of combat missions.
Now back in this country for
well-earned rest, he has completed 360 such missions, carrying troops and supplies in
dangerous Pacific war zones.

SGT. ALFRED BARNETT,
Denver marine, for a grand
fighting record at Tarawa.
Shot thru the left eye just as
he reached the beach after
having waded 800 feet thru
the surf, he slapped a patch
on the wound and then, without further medical attention, fought seventy-three
hours, as marine mates fell
all around him, till victory
came.

On April 1, 1944, my name was added to *The Denver Post Gallery of Fame* in recognition of the record number of combat missions I had flown in the South Pacific campaign. At the time, the tribute appeared in *The Denver Post*, I had already been redeployed stateside to represent the Army Air Corps on a U.S. Bond Tour to raise morale and funds for the war effort.

this heat and in his haste to start the jeep he must have flooded it, for he never did get it started. He then jumped into another jeep and got it running. The Operations Officer was waving frantically and hollering for the guard to drive the jeep out on the grass strip to stop the aircraft from getting airborne.

Just then the aircraft only partly down the runway, with only the left prop turning, did a 180 on the grass strip and the pilot gave it full throttle. The aircraft headed towards the beach gaining speed all the way. The airplane was in the air before the sergeant could get into position. Before reaching the edge of the water, up came the gear and the aircraft made a climbing 60° bank into the dead engine. It looked as if the pilot stood the aircraft on its right wing-tip. On the field there were many excited pilots knowing that at any second the plane was going to crash. It appeared that the pilot was going to make a close-in pattern and come back and buzz the field. At the last minute down came full flaps. The gear hit the full down position as the wheels rolled on the grass at the far end of the strip. The right prop began to turn. By the time the aircraft was back in front of us the left prop was feathered and the gear was retracting. The pilot repeated the same steep climbing turn into the dead left engine and this time made a close in left hand traffic pattern. The airplane taxied up to where it had been parked before the "show started."

The pilot climbed out on the left wing and sat down. The Operations Officer motioned for all of us to stand below and in front of the left wing of the parked Black Widow and listen to the pilot. By now there must have been at least fifty of us. The "Major" told us that this had been a Confidence and Demonstration Flight to show the maneuverability and safety of single engine flying of the Night Radar Fighter. All three of them, the "Pilot," "Major" and the "MP", were civilian employees from Northrop Aircraft. Now I would like to introduce our Test Pilot, Colonel Charles A. Lindbergh. The applause and shouting drowned out all take-off and landing aircraft noise. It turned out that the group of pilots that had been standing in front of Operations were all P-61 pilots. The "Show" was for them for some of them were afraid of the aircraft. This was a test flight that none of us would ever forget.

Twelve years later at Brownsville, Texas, when Etta and I were stationed on the Mexican border we saw Colonel Lindbergh. Then in 1990, Etta, her sister Ruth, her husband Larry, and I drove to his grave site on the 52-mile "Road to Hana" on the Island of Maui, Hawaii. The road to Hana is known for its 56, one-lane bridges and 617 curves. We can assure you that they are all there. It was a most beautiful slow ride in the rain. We even stopped at Black Beach.

Blood Plasma

The Wing must be going "Stateside" because I came out on orders to be the Squadron Chief Instructor Pilot and Instrument Check Pilot. On the same order I was issued a Green Instrument Card. A Green Card meant that the pilot had his own clearing authority to fly in any weather. He could take-off, fly, and land at any field that he thought he was good enough to give it a try. This is a license to kill yourself and all aboard, if you're not on the ball and use good judgment. Remember familiarity breeds contempt. The reason I was appointed was because I had the most flying time of any pilot in the Squadron. I had trained and checked out the most pilots and had the most instrument time. And I still had not reached my twenty-second birthday!

There was only one month while we were stationed in New Guinea and I was not on leave that I did not have the most flying hours of all the Squadron flight crews. That was in November 1942, when Irene was out of commission for half of the month.

The Wing Commander had a farewell party for the 6th TCS Officers and our Australian Pilots. At this party I had my only coke on the island of New Guinea. The General told us that, "Port Moresby was the starting point of the road back to the Philippines." One of the many things that General Prentiss said, "Forde," that is what he always called me, "I do not know if you are a brave pilot, a crazy pilot, or both, but we are sure going to miss you. I just

After the enemy had been cleared out of New Guinea in September 1943, I was assigned a "Special Services" mission to fly "Hollywood types" around the island to the various Airdromes captured during the offensive. (The author viewed this assignment as a real boondoggle.)

wish we had a whole wing that would fly like you." He remembered that statement for I was under his command three more times before he retired. Each time when I reported in to a new station where he was in command he would make a remark about my flying in New Guinea. Somewhere I read, "One can only be courageous when one has something to fear." In New Guinea there was plenty to pray for and to be afraid of, but it was not something that I ran from. Some of our missions were "routine milk runs," but you never knew that until the flight was over and the Form 1 was filled out. Then there were the missions of pure terror. At long last it looked liked we might survive enemy action, the mountains, and the very worst of the weather, and get home before 48!!

```
HEADQUARTERS
54TH TROOP CARRIER WING
APO 929
24 September,1943
TO THE OFFICERS AND MEN OF THE 374TH TROOP CAR-
RIER GROUP:
```

It is with real regret that I realize that the close association with you over a period of almost a year in New Guinea is about to terminate. It has been an honor and a pleasure to have commanded such an organization.

I believe I am correct in saying that the personnel of your group have received more decorations than any other organization of similar size in our services and it is rightly so as the records of deeds done will testify. You can leave here for your new assignment knowing that your work was well done, and that you have brought comfort, supplies, and aid to thousands of our own troops and to those of our Allies and much discomfort to our enemies.

I feel sure that you will continue your brilliant record and hope that the relief from the strain of combat flying and air raids and with some of the comforts of civilization available, that those of you who are war weary will soon regain your former good health.

The friendships and association made here will always be a pleasurable recollection and I hope that those of you who fly up here from time to time will make it a point to come by and see us and give us all the good news from down below.

So long, good luck, and happy landings.

s/Paul H. Prentiss
t/PAUL H. PRENTISS
Colonel, Air Corps,
Commanding

This seems the appropriate place to make the following entry:

From Vol 43, No 4, page 5, August 1999, *POLARIS, WWII US SUBMA-RINE VETERANS* Publication.

"In an unsuccessful attempt to re-supply their troops in New Guinea, the Japanese equipped their submarines with plywood torpedoes which they filled with rice and fired ashore."

This is all I know about this. When and where this took place I do not know. As I have noted before the Allies were trying to starve the abandoned troops. There was plenty of evidence of cannibalization on their part on the Kokoda Trail.

The 6th Troop Carrier Squadron was transferred from the war zone to Garbutt Field, Townsville, Queensland, Australia APO 922 on 2 October 1943. It took the better part of a week and several flights by each flight crew to transport all the Squadron's personnel, personal effects, and Squadron equipment. Townsville did not have as high a humidity and it had fewer mosquitoes than New Guinea. One of the first things we noticed at our new duty station was the ants. They were everywhere in the "slate" billets we were housed in, mess halls, Medics, and even in the hangers. Cows, horses, and dogs would wander out on the runway. Day or night you had to be positive that the runway was clear before taking-off or landing. It was just like the old west back home before "herd law" went into effect when "free range" was the law of the range.

The primary mission of the 374th TCG was to take over the flight schedule of the 317th TCG making thirty-two daily round-trip flights between Australia and Port Moresby. With these orders we were relieved of combat flying.

The 6th had another mission and that was to ferry troops and supplies all over and around Australia. This was a "Fat Cat" deal for me, as I got to fly all over and around the outer perimeter of Australia. I could pretty much pick and choose my flights, but that was not so for the new crews and many of the older pilots. As the Operations Officer told me, "Why shouldn't you be able to get your choice? You have the most flying time in the Squadron, the most combat, the most decorations, you flew the roughest missions, and you always wanted to fly more." During the year our Squadron was in combat I flew 364 combat missions. During this period I was in Australia for sixty-seven days, either on official flights or on leave, now called R&R. If I'd spent the entire period in New Guinea flying, and if I'd flown at the same ratio as when I was there, I would have flown a minimum of 445 combat missions. This would have been further increased if Irene had not been out of commission for twenty-seven days from 17 November 1942, to 14 December 1942. So one can see that when I was in New Guinea and on flight duty I got to do what I loved to do, FLY.

To get some idea of what the 6th Troop Carrier Squadron did for the war effort in its first year in combat, we were the first TCS to be permanently stationed in New Guinea making us the third TCS in the Southwest Pacific at that time. The 21st and 22nd TCS were stationed in Australia. They would fly up and stage out of Port Moresby for a day and then fly back to their home base in Australia. By the end of WWII there were nineteen TCS in the Theater. For the period 13 October 1942, to 2 October 1943, the flight crews of the 6th Troop Carrier Squadron were awarded a combined 408 Medals: Distinguished Flying Crosses (245) and Air Medals (163), including Oak Leaf Clusters. This was more than twice the number of decorations any of the other nineteen Squadrons received during the entire WWII from 7 December 1941, to 2 September 1945.

During all of World War II the 374th Troop Carrier Group, which included Group Headquarters, the 6th, 21st, 22nd and 33rd Troop Carrier Squadrons, were awarded 528 Distinguished Flying Crosses and 519 Air Medals. For the period of 13 October 1942, to 2 October 1943, the 6th Troop Carrier Squadron was awarded 245 Distinguished Flying Crosses and 163 Air Medals. The 6th Troop Carrier Squadron was awarded three Presidential Citations and two Battle Stars.

While in New Guinea, I air-evacuated at least 1,500 sick and wounded patients out of jungle air strips to Moresby. Several died enroute. Never during any of my flights did I have a male or female doctor, nurse or medical corpsman on board when we were evacuating wounded. To my knowledge none of the other aircraft in the 6th at that time had any medical personnel aboard while evacuating wounded personnel. Later on in the war, after we left

New Guinea, the Army was able to assign male medical nurses or technicians on all flights evacuating wounded. In the Pacific the wounded chances of survival were much higher than ever before primarily due to air evacuation. Our C-47s were fitted with a maximum of 24 litters. On occasion four additional stretchers were laid in the aisle.

I was awarded six (6) Distinguished Flying Crosses as a result of my combat missions in New Guinea. According to military criteria, the Distinguished Flying Cross (DFC) is awarded to a person who distinguishes himself by heroism or extraordinary achievement while participating in flight. The performance of the act must be evidenced by voluntary action above the call of duty. The extraordinary achievement must result in an accomplishment so exceptional and outstanding as to clearly set the individual apart from his comrades or from other persons in similar circumstances.

While the 6th was in New Guinea there were more than 100 air raids in the Port Moresby area. It is remarkable that only two fatalities were sustained by members of the Squadron as a result of these raids. In the early days of the struggle in New Guinea, when the enemy had air superiority, the raids were methodical. From January 1943, on the raids were mainly nuisance raids of one or two planes mostly at night in an attempt to destroy the morale of the troops and interrupt their sleep. On a moonlit night you could usually plan on spending one or two hours a night in a slit trench.

Prior to March 1943, there were no organized religious services for the Group. Protestant personnel had to journey to the Main Army Hospital at Port Moresby.

During the first months in New Guinea no attention was given by the Squadron to organized recreation. Most of the daylight hours were devoted to flying and feeding the troops. Aircraft maintenance worked around the clock. The only thing that stopped their work was air raids. At night lack of lighting facilities and enemy bombings discouraged such activities, but the maintenance work had to carry on. During this period, occasionally at night the Squadron would load a truck with men and venture through dust, rain and or mud until they could locate a camp where a movie was being shown. For the year I spent in New Guinea I only went to one movie. Fighting the mosquitoes to see a movie was not worth it.

The Troop Carrier's claim to the important part it played in the New

Guinea War is based upon a declaration by General George C. Kenney, Allied Air Forces chief in the Southwest Pacific, who in October 1943, said, "The 'forty-and-eight' railway car of the last war has been replaced by the C-47 airplane. Men, food, munitions, all their equipment, medical, jeeps, gasoline, bulldozers, PSP, artillery, and mail now go by air and are maintained by air. Beginning with the Papuan campaign last October (1942), war as waged in New Guinea would be impossible without air transportation."

Port Moresby did not fall, thanks to the splendid fighting spirit of the Australian "diggers", the American "dough boy," and the brave men who flew the Troop Carriers that did not let them down.

How those brave men were supported by Troop Carriers is summed up magnificently by George Johnston, official Australian war correspondent. In an article in *Collier's*, 4 December 1942, he wrote:

> ". . . In August 1942, a pitifully small Australian force of 650 men were still trying desperately to defend the pass leading through the Owen Stanley Mountains to Port Moresby against 3,000 Japanese. Douglas transports twisted and turned through the high pass, parachuting stores to the hard-pressed Australians.
>
> "In the middle of the month this flying organization, just getting into shape, was almost wiped out in one blow. The transports were loading stores on a Port Moresby airfield when twenty-four Japanese bombers came over. Something had gone wrong with the warning system, and our interceptors were still on the ground. The control tower and operations hut were blown to pieces. Plane after plane, caught in parking areas, was riddled by bomb fragments.
>
> "Nine days later the Japanese launched an all-out attack on the weary Australians still holding Kokoda. The battered 39th Battalion, which alone had held Kokoda for more than a month, retreated with 252 of the original 650 marching out alive. The retreat through the Owen Stanley's had begun. The position was serious. On September 1, I wrote in my diary: 'If the Japs attempt to follow up this breakthrough we are in a very tough spot in these mountains. There are terrible problems associated with supply and evacuation of wounded. There is something approaching chaos up on the Kokoda

Trail, with some A.I.F. units cut off and lost, and burdened by sick and wounded, others decimated. Reinforcements are attempting to struggle up the slippery mountain track. It's very doubtful that we can send food and ammunition for any greater than the miserably small band we have up there which is exhausted by weeks of battle and outnumbered by fresh Japs, four or five times our strength, who can be maintained over a relatively simple supply road. Everything will probably depend on what air support we can get—and what air support the Japs get!' Everything did depend on air support and, eventually, on the magnificent courage of the personnel of the Army Air Forces Troop Carrier Command—the boys flying the 'bully-beef bombers.'"

I flew up to Cooktown, Australia. This is where Captain Cook first landed in Australia on 17 June 1770. There is a nice good-sized monument, plaque and large ship gun, in memory of the event. I have pictures of me standing in front of the statue.

On 19 October 1943, the 6th lost another C-47 in weather at Cloncurry, Queensland, Australia. The crew was Captain John C. Fredrickson, pilot, co-pilot First Lieutenant Fred R. Mentzer, crew chief Master Sergeant Michael Kullich, Assistant crew chief Sergeant Robert L. Kerr, and radio operator Corporal Marvin D. Middleton.

Now that we were in Australia back in civilization, we were told that we would once again act like soldiers. Authority (Army) and Discipline (ours) were expected. No "spit and polish," inspections or parades. We were to wear uniforms, no ties, be an example to the younger troops, to be good soldiers and to reflect respect to our host the Australians.

All flights to and from New Guinea had been on hold for the better part of two days due to two typhoons out over the Coral Sea between Australia and the southeast tip of New Guinea. Our base received an urgent request from GHQ in Brisbane! "Could a volunteer crew be found that would fly blood plasma to the dying troops at Milne Bay as soon as possible?" I volunteered. Operations were not able to locate my regular crew, so I took those who would make the flight. Irene was out for maintenance so we were assigned one of the old C-47s. There were only four crew members on this mission and no passengers. This was one ROUGH, ROUGH HAIRY FLIGHT!! The only two maneuvers on this flight that we did not do were to fly upside down and backwards. All other flight maneuvers were repeated hundreds of times. Most of the 6:55 hours enroute was spent below 500 feet. We made many drift corrections up to 30°, first to the right, then to the left. We had no navigator and the co-pilot did not know how to read a drift meter so I ricocheted off the cabin walls many times going back and forth from the cockpit to the tail of the aircraft. At the altitude we were flying and the heights of the waves, getting any kind of a drift correction was strictly a wild guess. It seemed that the waves were washing the underside of the aircraft. The "eye" of the storm was very calm and eerie. The squall line stretched from horizon to horizon. Then we fly back into "Hell with all its fury." Most of the time in the violent weather the co-pilot and I were both on the rudders trying to hold a heading. I was trying to hold the wings level with the ailerons and the altitude with the elevators. We were both drenched and exhausted.

If we missed the tip of the island to the right we would run out of gas somewhere out over the Solomon Sea. With the near zero forward visibility and if we made a left landfall we would be heading straight into the side of a 3-4,000-foot chain of mountains with not enough warning to avoid the mountains. At this time, we were trying to hold a right course correction of 30° straight out to the open sea. That 29 October 1943, flight was one to remember. We entered the mouth of the harbor at Fall River, dropped the gear and turned on the landing lights. We were scraping the bottom of the clouds and flying below the decks of most of the larger Navy War ships that were in the harbor. We did not have to worry about the Navy trying to shoot at us. In most cases we were to low for their guns to shoot or they would hit one of their own war ships. Most likely we were past and behind another of their ships before they realized we had been there. We were below all radar and if anyone had been on deck they could not have heard us over the roar of the raging typhoon. The blowing sheets of rain and wind would have been good for any movie. We buzzed the tower twice. On the third time we received a green light from the front entrance of Base Operations. The Tower had been abandoned for the last two days. I made a quarter flap, power on wheel landing at 100 mph and taxied up in front of Operations. I had the crew chief put the pins in, chocks, all control locks, and wing-tip and tail-wheel tie downs before cutting the engines. This had been one punishing long 6-hour and 55-minute flight.

Everyone had given us up as lost at sea and the Hospital's "Meat Can" had returned to the Hospital. Within thirty-five minutes a Lieutenant Colonel and two Army Medical Corpsman from the Army Field Hospital arrived. The Colonel wanted to thank us and to see what kind of pilots would fly in this kind of weather. We told him that as soon as we could get gassed up we would be leaving for Moresby. He had already sent the blood back to the Hospital in the "Meat Can." He asked if we had any room. He had some people who had been trying for a week to get to Australia. I told him we could take twenty-eight. If they would be aboard within an hour, we'd get them to Townsville by tomorrow evening. I told him that I did not think any litter or real sick patients should go because the first hour of flight would be very rough. He thanked me and said there would be none. He then got on the phone and passed the word.

After the call he wanted to know about our flying background. He was surprised that I had already completed a combat tour. The passengers arrived. There were three Army Nurses and two male officers. The rest were GIs from the US Army, Navy, and Aussies. The Doctor shook hands with each of us, thanked us again, and wished us a safe flight. It was still raining like "Cats and Dogs" with very strong steady winds straight down the PSP runway just as when we came in. Milne Bay is protected on three sides. The airdrome is located in a boxed in-canyon. The wind is funneled in off the ocean from the east between two rows of mountains with one on the north and the other on the south side of the field. There are also mountains just beyond the west end of the runway. The wind came in from the east over the field and up the mountains to the west. Once you got lined up on the runway you were in pretty good shape. Otherwise you would never make it. I'd been there several times before and knew that if we could locate the runway we should be able to land and take-off. The Operations Officer asked if we really wanted to go in this kind of weather. I told him that anything would be better than what we flew up in. He said, "Since you have your own clearing authority have a good and safe flight." Between the sheets of blowing rain we got off the steel mat strip and were in wild weather before the wheels were up. We climbed straight out as fast as the bird could. At 8,000 feet I made a right bank and headed for Wards. One hour out over the Coral Sea I started letting down breaking out at 1,000 feet. I made a right land fall till we reached the coast somewhere east of Hood Point.

Barf Bags were the order of the day. Only we did not have any, so the passengers had to pass the two 14-qt mechanic's buckets. We RONed at Wards. The mosquitoes were waiting for us. With the high humidity it was just like being in a Turkish bath. How could I ever forget Port Moresby??!!

Next morning in our old Operations Hut at Wards, I was filling out the Form 23 Flight Clearance for Garbutt when an Army full Colonel came up and asked if it was possible to fly him and his boss, a Brigadier General, to Fall River. He understood that we'd flown up the night before and everything was grounded on the eastern end of the island. I told him that we had a full load with no vacant seats and of course, no parachutes, Mae Wests, or life boats for anyone. I told the Colonel to "wait a minute," I'd see what I could do. I went out to where the co-pilot was talking to the three nurses. I told the four of them about the request and asked the nurses if they would mind standing up front in the companionway with the crew all the way back to Milne Bay. This should be about a two-hour flight and the weather should be somewhat better than yesterday. Then from there we would be going on to Townsville. On that leg of the flight they could either stay up front or go back to their old seats. They would love to come up front. I told the co-pilot to start loading everyone aboard taking the nurses up front now. Leave three seats up front clear for the General and the Colonel. I returned to Operations and filled in our two new passenger's names. The Colonel said that he understood that we already had a full load. I told him that was correct, that we just shifted them around and three are now standing in the cockpit with the crew. He said that they could stand in that case. My reply was, "No General or Colonel will be standing on any plane I'm flying while other able bodied troops are seated."

The weather to Fall River was considerably improved over that of the evening before, although at times the nurses standing in the aisle were hanging on for dear life. I do not believe any of them ever volunteered to become Flight Nurses because that one flight was enough. The Operations Officer was surprised to see us. I told him that we were running a taxi service for the General and his Aide, but we're glad to be able to do it. My two flights were the only flights they had in three days. The flight to Garbutt was 1000% better than coming up. We just had strong head winds and it took 1:45 hours longer to make the same flight back to Australia. This was another flight where not even the birds were walking. It would have blown off their wings.

I've had several encounters with typhoons and hurricanes since this flight in 1943. I still believe that my first experience was the worst even though there was no injury to the crew or damage to the aircraft. In 1950, I was resting on a cot in a secured, cabled-down Quonset hut at Naha, Okinawa. At this time I was stationed in Japan flying C-54 aircraft. We were waiting for the typhoon to blow over so we could continue on to Dahahran, Saudi Arabia. The huts were built so that only one of the end doors should be opened at one time. In that way the tin roof would stay on. However, if both doors were opened at the same time the incoming wind would rip and tear the roof off between the steel tie-down cables. That is just what happened. In high winds only the door at one end of the Quonset was to be used. The other was blocked off and locked shut. One "jerk" unblocked and unlocked the "closed door," as he later said in case of a fire. Another transient went out that door as someone else came in the other end of the building. A howling 155 mph wind did the rest. It seemed to be quiet for a second or so then the rain and wind both hit us at the same time and everything that did not blow away got drenched.

Once again I was in Okinawa on 29 September 1957. This time I was at Kadena on my way from Korea to Taiwan. Our aircraft was parked on the ramp, tied down with steel cables at both wing tips, and the three landing gear with control locks were in place. Operations had five 6X6 heavy loaded trucks parked all around our bird. This was to deflect the wind up and over the aircraft. The wind was so forceful that the C-47 was completely ripped free from all moorings and flipped over on its back and was Classed 26'd. All five of the trucks were turned over on their sides with major damage. The crew and all twenty-eight passengers were in storm proof buildings and no one was injured. The wind was clocked at 216 mph. Twenty-six aircraft were completely destroyed and many were damaged. The Air Force Commanding General and the Base Weather Officer were both relieved for letting flyable aircraft get caught on the ground. I had flown in with thirty-two aboard with all their gear and with one fan feathered so this bird could not be flown out.

But many could have been saved if only they had been ordered to fly out.

In 1947, while stationed at Lawson Field, Columbus, Georgia, the US Army assigned two flight crews: Louis A. Moran and me as pilots, in two different aircraft to the Weather Bureau. We had two primary missions, seeding clouds with silver iodide particles and flying through hurricanes in the Gulf of Mexico. This project was run by the University of Georgia School of Technology.

I took part in two other civilian flying projects. Right after World War II the railroad unions went on strike for higher pay. At that time almost all U.S. mail was sent by rail. The Army was called in to fly the mail. We were flying C-46s. My route was from Kansas City to Memphis, New Orleans, and return. I made this night flight for one week. Then President Harry S. Truman told the Union to call off the strike and go back to work or they would all be drafted 4-F, over age or not, and do the same jobs as Privates in the US Army on a Private's pay. The strike was over.

During the winter of 1948-49 there were terrible blizzards in Nevada that lasted for over a month. It was so cold and the snow and wind were so high that the cattle, horses, and sheep could not get to the feed troughs, and the ranchers could not take hay to them. Without our help thousands of livestock would have died. Even with the Air Force's help many did die. At that time we were flying C-82s which was an ideal aircraft for this type of aerial delivery. I flew to Ely, Nevada loaded with hay. A Rancher would climb aboard. He would direct us to his herd of cattle, horses, and/or sheep. We would bail out a few bales of hay and then fly to the next herd and bail out some more. When the plane was empty we'd fly back to the airport for another load of hay and repeat the same procedure for another rancher flying to three different ranches each day. Our C-82s stayed for eleven days and we were replaced by another squadron of Fairchilds. We were billeted in a nearby motel with all ground transportation furnished by the Nevada National Guards. The American Red Cross ran a free soup line with all the sandwiches, coffee, and hot soup you wanted. The hot soup was the best.

At no time while stationed at Garbutt Field did I run into any of the personnel that I had run-ins with during my early flights from New Guinea to Australia. It could be that my letters not only corrected the problems but moved the violators on their way.

Homeward Bound

IN MID-OCTOBER 1943, I WAS WALKING down the street in Darwin, Australia when a tall, skinny American Army Air Force First Lieutenant from across the street yelled: "Ford, you stole a foot locker from me." The last time I had seen him we were both PFCs. He was the acting Supply Sergeant, 91st Observation Squadron at Gray Field, Fort Lewis, Washington. Here was Lucky Leach! Now we were both First Lieutenants. When I left for flying school, I was on Detached Service, before WWII. Once the war started, if you washed out you were sent to an infantry outfit overseas. If I graduated, I would be assigned to a flying organization. If I had washed out in peace time, I would have gone back to the 91st Observation Squadron at Gray Field. So when I graduated and received my Pilot Wings, the foot locker went with me, and Leach had a lot of paper work to do in order to balance the books.

After much talk he offered to drive our four crew members "out back in the bush" into the country to shoot kangaroos and see some termite mounds. We were glad to accept. He drove us by his Supply Squadron and each of us picked up a M-1 rifle and several clips of ammo. He filled the old command car up with gas and strapped two 5-gallon Jerri cans of gas on the back, drinking water, and sandwiches. And off we went. I would judge about twenty miles southeast of Darwin we came upon some 18-22-foot tall termite mounds. They were about 4 X 6 feet at the base and tapered to a very dull top like a two-edged digger. The two edges faced south and north. Notice, I said south and north. The reason is we're in the southern hemisphere and the compass points to the south. No one seems to know why all the mounds always seem aligned with the south and north poles.

After looking over the tall mud-dirt mounds, taking a few shots at their adobe home and some pictures, we left to look for kangaroos. When we first saw a heard of kangaroos they all seemed to look up at us at the same time. They just stood on their hind legs, chewed their cud and looked at us. We found out that if we shot and made a kill we'd be able to bag one. Otherwise, forget it. They would scatter, bounding off by jumping high in one direction, then change directions, just skimming over the grass land, next jump in a different height, speed, and direction. Having hunted as a kid, I had no problem in making a kill each time I took a shot. I have a picture of my kill. We took some more pictures, had

In October 1943, after I completed my term of duty in New Guinea, I was reassigned to northern Australia. On one of my flights to Darwin I had the opportunity to travel into the outback. Here I am standing next to a large termite mound. Before I left Australia in December 1942, I had flown completely around Australia and much of the interior.

something to eat, walked around and then headed back. It was a lot of fun.

On the way back from Darwin we flew out over the Northern Desert and at one point we saw a large flock of wild Emus. They looked and acted like a large flock of dumb turkeys. We let down and chased them until they ran off a small bluff into a dry gulch. On the same flight we saw many Dingos (wild dogs) and the famous rabbit fence that had been strung across Australia from the far north to the far south. We then flew on back to Townsville.

One of the new Medics assigned to the Squadron handed me a report that the Medics had just completed with their version of the history of the Squadron's health since arriving in the Theater. He asked several of the troops that flew over with the original flight crews to read and make comments. It

I am holding a kangaroo I "bagged." A large termite mound can be seen in the background.

was not the exact way I remembered it, but the new guys were trying to turn in a report that should have been made out monthly starting with our arrival in New Guinea fourteen months before. One item not listed below should have been in their report. During the months of April-December 1943 the Squadron had 308 cases of Malaria and Dengue Fever. At this time the "New Guys" were trying to make a written record for each of the Squadron's Section so it could be forwarded to 5th AF. While in New Guinea we did not have the man power or time for nonessential paper work and besides that we had a war to fight. Later we found out that some units spent more time with the "paper war," than the "fighting war" and their record proves it.

HEALTH

During the months of October, November, December, 1942, and January 1943, while the crews of the squadron were billeted and rationed at Arcadia, medical facilities were highly inadequate. Medical supplies were non-existent in that area, and the nearest facilities were at the 10th Evacuation Hospital, a distance of six miles. The latrines did not comply with Army Regulations. Water supply was inadequate, both as to quantity and quality. It was frequently impossible to shower, either because the water tanks were empty or because the water was too hot for comfort, having run through pipes exposed to the sun. Food consisted mainly of bully beef and hash.

During the 18 days the squadron stayed at Arcadia in October, 1942, it is reported that meals were served but twice a day, and that within three days of arrival epidemic diarrhea was evident, affecting at one time or another fifty percent of the personnel. Patients hitch-hiked to the 10th Evacuation Hospital where they were given sulfaguanidine powder. Due to lack of transportation, flying personnel had to hitch-hike from Arcadia to the strip three miles distant.

On October 19, 1942, the flying personnel of the squadron moved its organizational equipment to a newly selected camp site at Wards' Drome. Sleep was interrupted during this period at least one out of every two nights by enemy bombing raids. After planes and crews had completed their last mission for the day, personnel, including pilot officers, pitched their tents and dug slit trenches. Medical attention in the squadron in those early days in New Guinea consisted of a detachment of four enlisted men with meager first aid equipment. Epidemic diarrhea continued. Sanitary measures were deplorable and the first latrine was not in use until 20 November 1942. Water supply was still a problem because of lack of transportation and the necessity for hauling all the water. Between 13 November 1942, and 1 December 1942, an open mess tent was pitched and showers were constructed. Water transportation was improved so that water was available 74% of the time.

On 1 December, 1942, the ground echelon of the squadron arrived in New Guinea and began to function as a unit once more. At this time sanitary conditions were unsatisfactory, there being but one latrine, poor garbage disposal, an unworkable soaking pit, and a mess tent too small to accommodate the troops. Water was also being improperly chlorinated. By requisition, medical supplies were made available and with proper recommendations from the Medical Department improvements began at once. During the month of December, the water problem was gradually solved by obtaining transportation facilities. The food supply improved in quality but there was still a lack of fresh meat, fresh and canned fruits, fresh vegetables and milk. Preventative medicine was limited to vaccination of personnel, supervision of sanitation projects, mess inspection, test chlorination of water, and mosquito elimination measures.

By March, 1943, all the squadron had the advantage of piped water for bathing purposes. Drinking water was delivered by truck to conveniently located lister bags and was then chlorinated.

By April, 1943, supplementary rations from the mainland having become available, the food situation was satisfactory, both as to quality and quantity of food.

Mosquito control continued to be an outstanding problem during the period January, 1943, to April, 1943. Respiratory diseases were infrequent; even the common cold was seldom encountered.

A Group dentist was assigned 16 March 1943, and excellent dental care became available to all squadron personnel.

During April, 1943, the squadron constructed a new dispensary. It was raised five feet above the ground, completely screened, and was provided with running water. Two pyramidal tents joined together constituted the roof.

In May and June, 1943, there was a marked increase in nasopharyngitis cases. This was attributed mainly to colds and infections resulting from leaves and furloughs to the mainland.

During the first week of October, 1943, the squadron moved to APO 922, taking over the area formerly occupied by the 317th Troop Carrier Group. Here each squadron maintains its own dispensary in a wooden building in or near squadron headquarters. Water supply and sewage is furnished by the City of Townsville.

Medical supplies were easily obtained from Base Section 2 Medical Supply Depot, and from the 12th and 13th Station Hospital pharmacies. Hospital cases were sent to the 12th Station Hospital located in the City of Townsville, or to the 13th Station Hospital located approximately 3 miles southeast of the city.

During the last of November and the first part of December, 1943, RAAF Sergeant Pilot Cox, Grassi, Gregg and I were sent on an extended eleven-day tour of the outer perimeter of Australia, plus one night in the middle of the country at Alice Springs. Cox was the unofficial tour guide. The official reason for the flight was to ferry troops from one airdrome to the next station enroute. In other words, I was told to see the country, go all the way around the perimeter of the continent in eleven days, have a good time and make up the itinerary as you go.

In a nut shell, here was our trip. When we departed from Townsville the

Coral Sea was on our left. Three hundred miles later it was the South Pacific
Ocean. We stopped off at Brisbane, refueled and went on to Sydney and
RONed. Next morning we flew inland and made a four-hour stop in Can-
berra, Capital of Australia. By now the ocean on our left was called the Tas-
man Sea. Then we flew an hour and a half on to Melbourne where we spent
our second night. The next night we spent in Adelaide. Between these two
cities the water to the south of us was called Bass Strait. That is the water
between the southeast tip of Australia and Tasmania. From there we made an
860 mile inland flight over the desert up north to Alice Springs. During the
night there was a dust storm. It was not nearly as bad as we had in Western
Kansas in the early and mid-thirties. From there 200 miles to the southwest
there is a very large, high, flat red toped mound called Ayers Rock. We flew
over and around it on the way to Perth with a refueling stop at Kalgoorlie. We
got to see both ends of the famous 800 mile railroad that ran straight from
Adelaide to Perth without a single curve, so they claim. After two days in the
desert it was nice to see the Indian Ocean and feel a cool breeze. During the
last two days we had missed seeing the Great Australian Bight of water far
south of our route. Perth is half way around the continent and the farthest
from Townsville. It is diagonally across the continent to the southwest. It is
about as far south of the equator as San Diego is north.

The sixth day flight was the shortest leg of the eleven day tour. The water
on our left was the Indian Ocean. We spent that afternoon on the beach north
of Geraldton, Western Australia. While walking on the beach and looking
for shells and rocks which I always do, I picked up five small, thumb size,
milky white sparkly rocks. Sergeant Cox looked at them and said that they
were Opals. Of Course, I did not know what an Opal was. A few years later
when my family and I were stationed with the Occupation Forces in Japan,
we had one of the stones made into a nice large Dinner Ring for Etta. She
still has it and wears it often. The next morning we flew on up the coast to
Port Hedland and another walk on the beach. It was just a little warmer. The
next leg took us up the coast for a refueling stop at Derby and then on to
Darwin. By this time the water on our left was the Timor Sea. Only six weeks
before, I'd spent two nights in Darwin and had heard many stories of the
many air raids and bombings by the Japs Darwin suffered. Later I learned
that the Japs had bombed Darwin sixty-four times during WW II.

Cox had one place in particular that he wanted to stop and spend the night. He had never been there. That was Borroloola in the Northern Territory off the Gulf of Carpentaria. There we spent several hours visiting in a native aborigine village. This is truly out-back bush country as far out-back as you can get and still be in Australia. The weather was similar to Port Moresby, hot, sticky, and humid. The natives all were thin, had black leathery skin, fuzzy black hair, and they wore little or no body covering. These aborigines hunted with boomerangs and they did kill game with them. They also used a long bamboo pole sharpened on one end like a fish hook to fish and to catch crocodiles. In the morning, we flew on to Cooktown on the northeast coast. The Coral Sea and the Great Barrier Reef were again on our left. And then we flew back to Captains Cook's statue and onto Cairns where we RONed. Between Cooktown and Cairns the weather was good so we flew a few miles out to sea over the Great Barrier Reef. It was beautiful. Most of the islands had a ribbon of white sand stretching most of the way around them. By noon on our eleventh day after sixteen landings, 7,137 miles and 43:35 hours of flying time we landed back at Garbutt Airdrome at Townsville. Later we found out that the 5th AF had approved this R&R ("Fat Cat" trip) cross-country for the entire crew. I'm sure at the most we flew fifty passengers, no freight, and very little mail on this entire flight. At that time it was my opinion that if you were going to live in Australia it had to be Sydney. Sydney was different from all the rest of Australia. Sydney is the largest city in Australia. At that time the entire continent had a population less than that of New York City and was almost geographically as large as the "48 States."

A few years later while on my first tour in occupied Japan, I had a very similar type of flight. As the Wing Flying Safety Officer I was assigned for a ten-day period to fly the US Navy, Pacific Fleet Commander, Admiral Tomilson, anywhere and everywhere in Japan he wished to go. He flew as co-pilot and we had a crew chief. It was another "Fat Cat" deal. We flew to many of the cities in Japan and to most of the air fields where American Troops were stationed. A few months later one of my friends and I were invited to Yokohama aboard his flag ship, the USS Baxter, for a tour of the ship and to have dinner in the Admiral's Mess with the Admiral and his staff. It is a long story, but most interesting. I still cannot figure out why the Air Force flew the Admiral, instead of the Navy, but there were no complaints on my part. These were two real "boondoggles."

On my twenty-second birthday while on the way to Darwin, we were scheduled to stop at Cloncurry to let off some supplies and troops. Cloncurry is noted for two things. It is the hottest place in Australia and it has a mountain of iron. The iron deposit in the mountain is of such high quality that at a distance of two hundred miles when flying at 10,000 feet or higher, if there are no thunderstorms in the immediate area, the Radio Compass needle would point straight to the mountain. About thirty minutes out No. 1 engine began to run rough, backfire and have surges of power. I feathered the left prop and continued on. I made a normal single engine landing and was towed in. It was only 09:10 in the morning with a thirty mile an hour wind and blistering hot. As the day progressed the heat intensified into shimmering, searing, beastly hot heat. The only shade was in a building and the temperature there was even hotter. It was worse than Death Valley when the wind was factored in. Grassi said we would need an engine change and it would have to come from Garbutt. A built-up engine was ordered. It was flown in early the next evening. That night after 2100 hours the newly arrived engine was installed. No outside maintenance could be done from about 0900 to 2100 hours due to the intense heat. All tools were too hot to touch and could not be picked up.

Fifty years later, in 1992, Etta and I were in Australia. I contacted the Brisbane Weather Bureau and found that the official Cloncurry temperature on 12 December 1943, was the second to the hottest day in recorded history for all of Australia. Without the wind factor being computed in, the official reading was 127° Fahrenheit. But there was a steady wind of 35 mph. With the wind factored in, it was like being inside a heated oven. That was one long, lousy, three-day period waiting for an engine change. The crew that flew the engine in took our load on to Darwin. When the repairs on Irene were completed we returned to Garbutt. We were a very happy crew to get away from that blast furnace.

During this tour of duty, I flew over and near many islands with miles of gleaming sugar-white, sandy beaches in the blue South Pacific. I do not have the words to describe their beauty. From the unrestricted view of the cockpit of an aircraft it is breathtaking. One such flight was the 125-mile stretch of water across the Torres Strait between Daru, Western Papua, New Guinea and Thursday Island, Queensland, Australia. This is close to where we had been instructed to "Walk from New Guinea to Australia." From 2,000 feet up you could see several islands, many coral reefs and rocks sticking out of the calm sea. Most of the water appeared to be very shallow. It was easy to see why the passage of ships between the Coral Sea and the Gulf of Carpentaria was so treacherous. You would have to go far and search a lot to find something more interesting, exciting, and stimulating than flying. Flying could become my home in the sky!!

If I should forget, here are a few things to remember about New Guinea:

THE ISLAND: The most beautiful landscapes, the beauty of the scenery cannot be explained or imagined until seen. It has long wide sandy sugar-white beaches with a 1,500 mile long chain of high mountains running down the middle of the island parallel to the coast. The birds are beyond description. But the snakes, lizards, crocodiles, sharks, flies, gnats, ants and mosquitoes—these they can keep.

AIR STRIPS: Short, grassy, rocky, bumpy, muddy, dusty, uphill, downhill, curved air strips with bomb and mortar craters, along with enemy snipers shooting at our aircraft.

WEATHER: Clouds so high the fighters could not get over the tops, or climb as fast as they were building up. Radar tracked thunder heads over 79,000 feet, with severe turbulence, hail, and rain like you could not believe—places on the island received over 400 inches a year. There was wind, heat, humidity, mud, and dust.

MOSQUITOES: Swarms of mosquitoes, large, small and vicious!! Malaria, Atabrine, which gave you a yellow bronze complexion. Mosquito headgear, mosquito bar, and "T" bars for your cot.
FOOD: Bananas, coconuts, mutton, hash, bully beef, C-rations, K-rations, canned peaches, peas, beans, powdered potatoes, eggs and milk, many dehydrated foods, fresh fish, and later, the Army's regular mess.

THE NATIVES: The nudity of the natives, headhunters, canni-
bals, hand shake, and the strange penis attachment at Bena Bena.
At this time the natives of New Guinea were frozen in a "TIME
WARP," 5,000 years behind us.

Our fanatical enemy was a worthy opponent. They did not play by the
same rules and for the most part they had inferior equipment. The ZERO
was the one big exception. The aircraft had capabilities about which books
will continue to be published. In the hands of a skillful, aggressive pilot it
was a lethal weapon. Until mid-1943, Japanese pilots were excellent. After
that they had lost most of their professional pilots. The new rookies were not
as good marksman and not as aggressive. But the enemy had determination
that was to be reckoned with. His devotion to duty was to accomplish the
assigned mission or die trying. Hundreds of thousands did die. The Japanese
were fanatical fighters. They fought like wild men who seldom retreated and
seldom surrendered with very, very few exceptions during my tour in New
Guinea. I must not forget Tokyo Rose and her music and propaganda.
WORLD WAR II has been referred to as The SAMURAI-SWASTIKA WAR.

The fanatic and barbaric treatment of American POWs by the Japanese
can best be illustrated in a news article compiled by the National Parks Service, published by the Veteran's Press, California Edition, dated 6 April 2001:

For the following number of American POWs in captivity one died.
Number of POWs who died per number of POWs captured

Civil War: 1 died per 178 Union territory prisoners captured
1 died per 7 Confederate territory prisoners captured

WWI: 1 died per 280 US prisoners captured
WWII: 1 died per 850 European Theatre US prisoners captured
1 died per 2.7 Pacific Theatre US prisoners captured

Korea: 1 died per 2.6 US prisoners captured
Vietnam: 1 died per 6.7 US prisoners captured
Gulf War: 0 died per the 23 US prisoners captured

As you can see from the above, for every three Americans that became Japanese POW's in WWII better than one out three died. While in Germany it was one out of eight hundred and fifty. Another way of looking at it is that you had a 315 TIMES better chance of living if captured by the Germans, to say nothing about the inhuman treatment!! That is why we ALWAYS carried an extra round of live ammunition in the chamber, a full clip in our 45, and at least four loaded clips on our gun-belt. One 45-clip against an enemy patrol, or the "Headhunters or cannibals" in New Guinea is almost a guaranteed suicide.

As of this writing I have now been in ninety foreign countries and all fifty States. In all my travels, reading, and conversations since leaving New Guinea, I have never found any evidence to lead me to believe any other place on earth has as many vicious blood sucking mosquitoes. One way to compare the summer mosquitoes of Minnesota with those in New Guinea is to compare a Pre-Flight Flying School Pilot to a seasoned Combat Pilot. They are just not in the same league. They came in all sizes and speeds. The thickness of the swarms reminded me of the clouds of grasshoppers in Western Kansas during the dust bowl days of the early to the 30s. The mosquitoes were one of our worst and most deadly enemies every single day while in New Guinea.

As I was packing to leave the Squadron to return to the United States, I received a wonderful gift of appreciation from the enlisted men of the 6th Troop Carrier Squadron. Where the idea came from and who paid for it I do not know. The carpenter shop made a beautiful chest a little smaller than a GI footlocker. It was made from some kind of extinct exotic Australian wood with brass hinges and hasp. It is most beautiful and practical, and I've used it ever since. I feel this was a gift from their hearts.

On the next to the last night I spent at Garbutt Airdrome my three crew members and I had the evening meal at the NCO Club. Most of the Base Enlisted Men knew that in a couple of days I would be returning to the States. Up to that time I had never shaken so many hands at one time. I was glad to be going home, but it was sad to say goodbye. This was in December 1943. Until one has shared the fears and hardships of combat you cannot understand the faith and trust one has in GOD and your comrades in arms. Most would lay down their life for you even though you were not a friend or a close buddy. Some sixty plus years later my only true military friends that are still alive and the ones I still keep in contact with turned out to be active Church members.

Years later I learned that T/Sgt AMERIGO GRASSI and S/Sgt JOHN C. GREGG both were rotated back to the States for "Combat Replacement" in January 1945. Since then they have both passed away. God bless both of them for the outstanding service they performed for their country in such a time of great wartime need. Not only were they outstanding and devoted crew members they were good friends and my life depended on them on every mission.

Most Troop Carrier Combat Pilots in New Guinea during the period of 1942 and the first few months of 1943 had no psychological problems about flying combat in C-47s. However, it was a real problem when fighter or bomber pilots had to fly combat in C-47s. After being protected by all their flak suits, armor plating, the many machine guns, cannons, self-sealing fuel tanks, and good fighter escort the bomber pilots found flying C-47s was so scary and life-threatening. When flying the unarmed, unprotected transports in combat, in all kinds of weather and landing in very small dirty, wet, rocky, muddy short strips and landing on both sides of the front lines, few could make the transition. With few exceptions our missions were flown behind enemy lines. A few months later when the Allies had gained air superiority and we had good fighter cover it was different. The "Gooney Bird" was one of the most vulnerable of all wartime aircraft. I guess it is mostly what you start out in. Like I told the Navy submariners at Pearl Harbor, "I would not want to be in one of your little tin sardine cans, but thank God we do have you and your submarines."

Before we left New Guinea our Wing eventually was assigned two or three Army Air Corps Reserve Officers and commercial airline pilots from the States with thousands of hours of flying time mostly in DC-3s. They were ten to twenty years older than any of our line pilots. They had always flown with high built-in safety margins, with very low gross take-off and landing weights, in weather with high ceiling and good visibility for take-off and landing, and with very limited cross wind for take-offs and landings. They were use to long hard-surfaced runways, maps, navigational aids, radio towers and airways always ready to assist, always a full functioning instrument panel, and never any thought about enemy air or ground fire to say nothing about the kind of weather we experienced in New Guinea. With all of these hazards they simply could not "cut the mustard." Combat flying is for the "kids" who have not had all those safety factors drilled into them. Otherwise they will never make it.

A pilot must know his and his crew's abilities, the limits of the aircraft, and he must not be afraid to use them on every flight to the fullest. This is one time where each First Pilot MUST KNOW HIS ABILITIES AND LIMITATIONS AND THE CAPABILITIES OF THE AIRCRAFT FOR THIS SPECIFIC CONFIGURATION AND NOT IGNORE THEM or many lives and an aircraft will be lost. After each of the Airline pilots' first combat missions they came back and reported to Operations that none of us young pilots would ever live to be old pilots as this flying is crazy. Few of them ever flew a second combat mission. It is true that the C-47, when flying combat, was considered the most vulnerable of all wartime aircraft. At that time when we thought about coming home, it was "the Golden Gate in '48, maybe if we are still alive." What it took was courage, skill, and total attention to flying. The written word cannot express the horrors and terror when flying in this environment. The true facts cannot be appreciated until one is on the scene and lived through the experience. That is why combat is for the kids, for old men's heart would not stand the strain.

In July 1979 when our youngest daughter Nancy graduated from high school, Etta, Nancy, and I drove to the east coast. We were gone for seven weeks and drove over 7,900 miles. Prior to leaving Sacramento I made arrangements to spend one evening with Grassi and his family. It was most enjoyable. He had reserved a dining room for sixteen of us in a very nice restaurant in downtown Erie, Pennsylvania. Attending were his wife, their three grown children, their spouses, and children. After the meal and lots of talk, Grassi, his wife, Etta, Nancy, and I went over to his brother-in-law's for dessert. What a surprise! He was the Mayor of Erie, Pennsylvania, Louie J. Tullis was Mrs. Grassi's brother. We had cake and ice cream. Then the Mayor presented me with the keys to the city in recognition of my war record. This was thirty-six years after my last combat flight in New Guinea!! How often we have thought or said, "Why didn't I say that." For when I first met Mrs Grassi I should have said, "So you are the IRENE that we flew half way around the world and at last after thirty-six years we finally meet!!"

On this tour of combat (13 October 1942-2 October 1943), the 6th TROOP CARRIER SQUADRON spent three hundred and fifty-four days (354) in the combat zone before being rotated out of the war zone and back to Australia. The Squadron's flight crews had been awarded The Distinguished Unit Citation Device with two Oak Leaf clusters, two Battle Stars, two hundred forty-five Distinguished Flying Crosses (245) and one hundred sixty-three Air Medals (163) including Oak Leaf Clusters. From this it could be said that the 6th flew more hazardous and dangerous missions than any Troop Carrier Squadron. Extracted from the "History of the 374th TROOP CARRIER GROUP in WORLD WAR II," "The 374th TCG cited by General PAUL PRENTICE as the "most highly decorated" group in the military forces of the United States of America of comparable size." On this tour of combat, the pilots of the 6th flew and routinely performed maneuvers in a C-47 aircraft that no civilian pilot would believe, understand, or think possible.

By the end of World War II, there were nineteen Troop Carrier Squadrons in the Pacific Theater of Operations. No Troop Carrier Squadron in the Pacific Theater during ALL of WWII came close to being awarded as many decorations as this one Squadron received during its' first year of combat. This was the 6th's first tour of combat during the war, and it was accomplished in only 26% of the days of fighting in the Pacific. During this period the 6th was awarded 15% of the combined total of all DFCs awarded to the nineteen (19) Troop Carrier Squadrons. Not a bad record for a Squadron that had more Enlisted Pilots than Officers. It is said, "there is honor in fighting for your country."

Weather was also one of the biggest enemies to flying in New Guinea. The weather proved to be as formidable an enemy as the Japanese. When flying was called off for the day for being below minimums, Group Operations of the 374th Troop Carrier Group would call some of the eager, capable First Pilots and ask if they would like to "volunteer" to round up a crew and fly. FORD and VAUGHTER were always eager, ready, and waiting to fly!! That was why we flew the most combat missions of any pilots in the United States Army Air Corps. We always were ready to deliver the urgently needed troops, supplies, equipment, and return the wounded. And we did so without one single accident. When ERNEST C. FORD flew his last combat mission in New Guinea, his record was three hundred sixty-four (364) as a C-47 Troop

Carrier Pilot. I was decorated for valor, heroism, and extraordinary achievement, and received six Distinguished Flying Crosses. The coveted, prestigious DFC is the highest Armed Forces decoration awarded for airmanship. In addition, I received two Air Medals, the Army Good Conduct Medal, and several Service Medals, with stars and clusters. Returning to the United States I went on Bond Tours for six months, where I was billed as having the most combat Missions of any pilot in the UNITED STATES ARMY AIR FORCES. Lieutenant Vaughter, a great pilot, was only a few combat missions behind my record.

After I had departed Australia, the 6th forwarded a letter. The subject of "Flying Time," stated that I had "Total Combat Missions: 360" (plus 4 missions not recognized by the Fifth Air Force.) On 6 March 1944, when I arrived at Stout Field, Indianapolis, Indiana, they had received this letter and notification that the four contested missions had been approved. All Military news releases thereafter stated that I had flown 364 Combat Missions.

Thank God, in World War II, the military ran and fought the war—not the politicians—and we won!! But this was not true in either Korea or Vietnam. In Desert Storm the military was once again in command and the war was over in less than one month!! By 2000 the U.S. Air Force once again has been reduced in strength, equipment, parts and supplies to nothing more than a good Boy Scout Troop. Their PILOTS have been placed on the "National Resource List." Their morale appeared to be below rock bottom.

If politicians had to fight the wars, there would be no wars!! Too many politicians vote to "USE, ABUSE, and LOSE" the military once the war is over. Two good examples are: not authorizing, financing, or approving for the VA to treat battle exposed sick vets after the Vietnam War for Agent Orange and Nerve Gas after Desert Storm.

A "Goldbrick" would have been hard to find in the 6th. I'm sure in our Squadron there might have been someone that considered his duties very mundane, humdrum, day-to-day work, but not me. It has been said that in the "combat zone it is a time of boredom or sheer terror!" Flying combat keeps you on your toes and vigilant with your peripheral vision going in every direction, every second you're in the air. I considered that time in my life very exciting for I got to fly mostly when and where I wished. Sure it was long, fatiguing, dangerou,s and life threatening, but as a whole it was most

A number of years later, a peace-time photo of the author in the pilot seat of a B-17, still looking like a young boy, looking out of his airplane.

interesting and challenging. To paraphrase JIMMY DOOLITTLE: "I would not want to live my flying life over, for I doubt if my flying would turn out as good as it did." For a few of us it was a time of high adventure, unbelievable danger, and great achievement. It was said that the US Army Staff Sergeant Pilots were made of "The Right Stuff." As the Australians said, "We served the Flag well." From the President of the United States on down the Chain of Command, the 6th Squadron received special recognition for an outstanding job well done for their first year spent flying combat in New Guinea. After I left the 6th the Squadron returned to fly combat in New Guinea, Philippines, Okinawa and on to Japan. The 6th Troop Carrier Squadron was stationed in Tokyo all through the occupation of Japan and after the Korean War.

Epilogue

The photo on the left was taken in May 1944, in front of Pratt and Whitney Aircraft in Hartford, Connecticut, the manufacturer of the C-47 aircraft engines for military and civilian use. The aircraft engine manufacturer selected me to speak to more than 2,000 of its employees to acknowledge the importance of their contribution to the war effort. When Pratt and Whitney learned that I planned to marry the end of that month, they offered to give me and my bride a three-day, all-expenses paid, honeymoon at the New York Waldorf Astoria as part of my speaking tour. Unfortunately, Etta, my bride-to-be, chose not to speed up the wedding plans to mid-May since her sister, her bridesmaid who was a teacher in a rural one-room school in North Dakota, could not be available until the end of May. We were married in Indianapolis on May 30, 1944, and instead of honeymooning at the Waldorf Astoria, Etta and I honeymooned at McCormick's Creek State Park in Indiana. As I recall, it was beautiful! I figure it all worked out since we were still married after 65 years.

The next two pages are from the October 1945, issue of *Mechanix Illustrated* featuring an article highlighting war experiences recorded during a bull session of Troop Carrier Pilots that I was asked to participate in. It recognized my 364 C-47 missions as "one of the greatest number of combat missions amassed by any pilot in WW II."

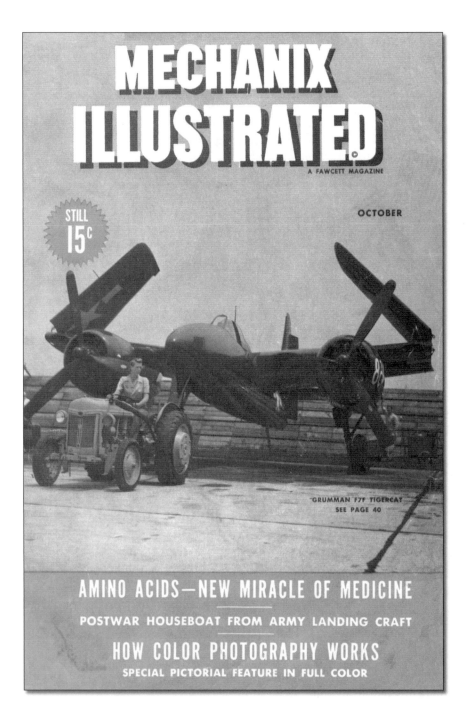

Everything Happens to a Pilot!

When veteran pilots get together for a bull session, their "true" stories are astonishing, to say the least.

Adapted from Douglas Airview

AT A certain Troop Carrier Command Base there were gathered a number of pilots who had flown their transports in virtually every country in the world. A "bull session" was in progress, as is wont to occur when oldtimers get together, and the tall stories were flying thick and fast.

One of these men was Lt. Ernest C. Ford of Manzanola, Colorado, with 364 missions in a C-47, one of the greatest number of combat missions amassed by any pilot in the war. Ford, then a sergeant pilot, left the United States in October, 1942, with the first squadron of C-47s to be flown over the Pacific. They flew to Australia and were the first TCC outfit under General MacArthur.

"I was only a sergeant but I was first pilot on my ship—and outranked by everyone else on board," Ford said. "My co-pilot, radio operator, navigator, four passengers and even the crew chief outranked me."

Mechanix Illustrated October, 1945

80

351

From January through May 1946, I was assigned to the American Embassy in Bogotá, Columbia. My duty—and I'm not kidding—was to fly to the major capitals of Central and South America to "show the U.S. Flag." In less than five months, I gladly accomplished this objective. The photo above shows 2nd Lieutenant Tomlinson (my co-pilot) and me posed in front of a Catholic Church high in the Andes mountains above the city of Bogotá, Columbia. While flying at an altitude of nearly 22,000 feet in a State Department plane (that, by regulations, could not be modified to provide oxygen) my hands froze to the wheel and I nearly passed out. Fortunately, a passenger in the plane, pilot Dick Overfield, a flying school classmate of mine, came to the cockpit and took over the controls. The crew pried my frozen hands from the wheel, carried me to the back of the plane, and wrapped me in blankets while Dick dove down to a lower altitude. He landed the plane in Cali, Columbia without further incident.

In August 1950, Lieutenant General George E. Stratemeyer, Far East Air Forces Commander during the first year of the Korean War, congratulated me by pinning on the very first Air Medal awarded to a pilot during the Korean War. I flew 21 combat missions during the first month of the Korean War. When additional pilots arrived to augment U. S. forces in July 1950, I was able to return to my duty station in Haneda, Japan as Director of Safety for the 5th Air Force Command.

Separation from the family for long periods of time is a price military personnel pay in the service of their country. In June 1957, my 5-year-old daughter, Kathy, looked through the fence at Travis Air Force Base, California as my plane awaited departure for Korea. This trip was difficult for her, for my family, and for me, too, as I embarked on a 13-month assignment in Korea away from my family. Seven years before on June 25, 1950, the night the Korean War broke out, I was flying from Japan to Korea and was immediately caught up in the conflict. Now, I was going back, posted to a base known as K-55 outside of Seoul, Korea assigned to the UN Peace-Keeping effort. (Refer to the Foreword, "My Daddy...My Hero," that appears in the front of this Diary and our picture on the back cover.) Today, I am proud to have four grown children, including Kathy, and seven grandchildren.

Prior to my retirement in 1963, I was awarded the Air Force Commendation Medal by General Joe W. Kelly. The top left photograph on the next page shows that memorable moment.

On October 31, 1963, at age 42, I retired from the U.S. Air Force after 23 years of service. At the time of my retirement I had the good fortune to be one of the most decorated officers in the military. My last duty assignment prior to retirement was at Scott Air Force Base, Illinois where I served as Chief of the Air National Guard and Reserve Force Maintenance Affairs for the Maintenance Engineering Division, and Deputy Chief of Staff, Material, Headquarters Military Air Transport Service.

On the left, at age 80, I stood beside my wife in front of the United States Capitol Building in Washington, D.C., always proud to be an American.

Mr. Ernest C. Ford & Family
25 Oct 2002

Attendees: Mr. Ernest C. Ford, Mrs. Etta Ford, Mr. Steven Ford
Mrs. Linda Ford, Mr. Jeff Lacy-Ford, Ms. Elizabeth Hanson

10:00A.M. **Guests arrive at Main Gate** (Thunderbird) and are directed to Bldg 1150. Directed by Barbara Johnson, 56th Fighter Wing Public Affairs

10:05A.M. **Arrive Bldg 1150 for visit with Mr. Gustave Vinas** (Wing Historian)

11:50A.M. Van picks up Family and drives to Officer's Club

12:00P.M. **Lunch at Officer's Club** (Escorted by Major Fox)

1:00P.M. Depart for Wing Headquarters

1:05P.M. **Guests arrive at Wing Headquarters for Interview with SSgt. Drury**, Greeted by Maj Laurent "Swamp" Fox, Chief 56th Fighter Wing Public Affairs

1:30P.M. **Wing Mission Brief**. Greeted by Lt. Col David McMickell, 56th Fighter Wing Director of Staff

2:00P.M. **Walk to 62nd Fighter Squadron**

2:15P.M. **Arrive 62nd Fighter Squadron for Tour**, Greeted by Major John Parker, 62nd Fighter Squadron

3::00P.M. **Board Van for Windshield Tour.** Escorted by Major Fox

3:30P.M. **Air Park Tour** (if time permits) Escorted by Major Fox

4:00P.M. **Officer's Club for O'call**
COLONEL PHILIP M. BREEDLOVE Commander 56th Fighter Wing. Escorted by Major Fox

5:00P.M. **Depart Base**

Ernie and Lt. Col David McMickell,
56th Fighter Wing Director of Staff

Luke Air Force Base Tribute

Left photograph includes members of my family in front of the
world's largest fighter base.

The page on the left shows the
printed program for the cremony.

On October 25, 2002, I was invited to return to Luke Air Force on the occasion of the 60th Anniversary of my receiving my pilot's wings at Luke. My family and I were honored by a day-long tribute that included an Officer's Call presided over by Colonel Philip M. Breedlove, Commander 56th Fighter Wing, with hundreds of officers in attendance. It was a great personal honor. The day's events also included a tour of the world's largest fighter base and a hands-on opportunity to sit in an advanced fighter simulator. It was truly amazing to experience how far aviation technology has progressed over the past 60 years.

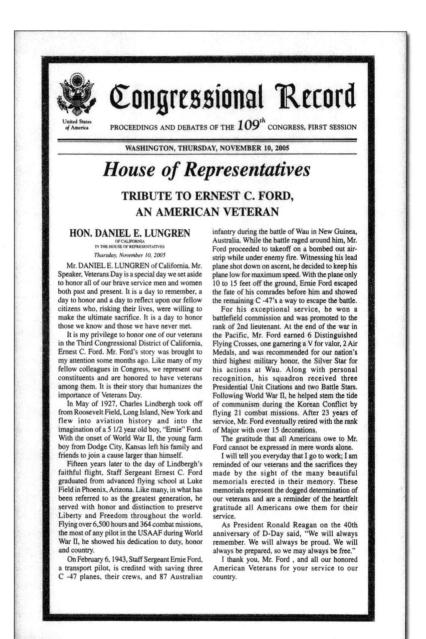

Congressional Record

United States
of America

PROCEEDINGS AND DEBATES OF THE 109th CONGRESS, FIRST SESSION

WASHINGTON, THURSDAY, NOVEMBER 10, 2005

House of Representatives

TRIBUTE TO ERNEST C. FORD, AN AMERICAN VETERAN

HON. DANIEL E. LUNGREN
OF CALIFORNIA
IN THE HOUSE OF REPRESENTATIVES
Thursday, November 10, 2005

Mr. DANIEL E. LUNGREN of California. Mr. Speaker, Veterans Day is a special day we set aside to honor all of our brave service men and women both past and present. It is a day to remember, a day to honor and a day to reflect upon our fellow citizens who, risking their lives, were willing to make the ultimate sacrifice. It is a day to honor those we know and those we have never met.

It is my privilege to honor one of our veterans in the Third Congressional District of California, Ernest C. Ford. Mr. Ford's story was brought to my attention some months ago. Like many of my fellow colleagues in Congress, we represent our constituents and are honored to have veterans among them. It is their story that humanizes the importance of Veterans Day.

In May of 1927, Charles Lindbergh took off from Roosevelt Field, Long Island, New York and flew into aviation history and into the imagination of a 5 1/2 year old boy, "Ernie" Ford. With the onset of World War II, the young farm boy from Dodge City, Kansas left his family and friends to join a cause larger than himself.

Fifteen years later to the day of Lindbergh's faithful flight, Staff Sergeant Ernest C. Ford graduated from advanced flying school at Luke Field in Phoenix, Arizona. Like many, in what has been referred to as the greatest generation, he served with honor and distinction to preserve Liberty and Freedom throughout the world. Flying over 6,500 hours and 364 combat missions, the most of any pilot in the USAAF during World War II, he showed his dedication to duty, honor and country.

On February 6, 1943, Staff Sergeant Ernie Ford, a transport pilot, is credited with saving three C -47 planes, their crews, and 87 Australian infantry during the battle of Wau in New Guinea, Australia. While the battle raged around him, Mr. Ford proceeded to takeoff on a bombed out airstrip while under enemy fire. Witnessing his lead plane shot down on ascent, he decided to keep his plane low for maximum speed. With the plane only 10 to 15 feet off the ground, Ernie Ford escaped the fate of his comrades before him and showed the remaining C -47's a way to escape the battle.

For his exceptional service, he won a battlefield commission and was promoted to the rank of 2nd lieutenant. At the end of the war in the Pacific, Mr. Ford earned 6 Distinguished Flying Crosses, one garnering a V for valor, 2 Air Medals, and was recommended for our nation's third highest military honor, the Silver Star for his actions at Wau. Along with personal recognition, his squadron received three Presidential Unit Citations and two Battle Stars. Following World War II, he helped stem the tide of communism during the Korean Conflict by flying 21 combat missions. After 23 years of service, Mr. Ford eventually retired with the rank of Major with over 15 decorations.

The gratitude that all Americans owe to Mr. Ford cannot be expressed in mere words alone.

I will tell you everyday that I go to work; I am reminded of our veterans and the sacrifices they made by the sight of the many beautiful memorials erected in their memory. These memorials represent the dogged determination of our veterans and are a reminder of the heartfelt gratitude all Americans owe them for their service.

As President Ronald Reagan on the 40th anniversary of D-Day said, "We will always remember. We will always be proud. We will always be prepared, so we may always be free."

I thank you, Mr. Ford , and all our honored American Veterans for your service to our country.

In November 2005, I was honored by the U.S. House of Representatives for my distinguished military service. The tribute that appears in the Congressional Record is displayed at left. California Congressman Daniel E. Lungren presented me a plaque commemorating the event.

In 2008, at age 87, I was honored by the del Campo Junior ROTC cadets in Carmichael California as I stood at Salute in a V "for Valor" Formation, while ROTC instructor Col. Earl Farney and my wife, Etta, reminisce to the side about my service experiences (photo by Susan Maxwell Skinner). Forty-four years after retirement, I could still fit into my Air Force uniform!

THE SACRAMENTO BEE

Wednesday, March 10, 2010 ••   sacbee.com   75¢

OBITUARY

Ernest Ford flew 364 WWII combat missions

By ROBERT D. DÁVILA
bdavila@sacbee.com

Ernest C. Ford
Born: Dec. 12, 1921
Died: March 4, 2010
Survived by: Wife, Esther of Sacramento; sons, Steven of Phoenix, and Terry of Sacramento; daughters, Kathy Shea of Calgary, Alberta, and Nancy Weaver of Houston; brother, Marvin of Flint, Texas; and seven grandchildren
Services: Viewing, 3-7 p.m. today at Sierra View Funeral chapel, 6201 Fair Oaks Blvd., Carmichael; memorial service, 11 a.m. Thursday at Fair Oaks Presbyterian Church, 11427 Fair Oaks Blvd., Fair Oaks

Ernest C. Ford, a decorated Air Force veteran who was believed to have flown the most combat missions by a U.S. pilot during World War II, died Thursday of cancer at age 88.

Mr. Ford joined the Army in 1940, graduated from flying school and piloted C-47 transport planes in the Pacific as a staff sergeant. He had flown 91 missions by age 21 and was assigned to New Guinea, where he distinguished himself at the battle of Wau.

Under a heavy Japanese attack that shot down his lead plane on takeoff, Mr. Ford flew his aircraft 10 to 15 feet off the ground at maximum speed to escape. His actions led the way for other C-47s on take off. Credited with saving three planes, their crews and 87 Australian infantrymen, he received a battlefield commission as a second lieutenant. He was hailed as an American

hero and was sent on a national war bond tour.

Mr. Ford returned to duty in the Pacific and was credited with a total of 364 combat missions during the war, as cited in the Congressional Record in 2005 by Rep. Dan Lungren, R-Gold River, the most by any Army Air Forces pilot. He earned six Distinguished Flying Crosses – including one with a V for valor – and two Air Medals.

Mr. Ford, who flew another 21 missions during the Korean War, retired from the Air Force with the rank of major in 1963 and settled in Sacramento. Several years ago, he wrote an account of his war experiences that his family is planning to publish.

"My dad was someone who was exceedingly loyal and a hard worker," said his son, Terry. "He understood that this was war, and you had to get the mission done. He'd fly a mission, come back and be ready for the next one."

Ernest Clayton Ford was born in 1921 in Inez, N.M., and reared during the Dust Bowl in Kansas by a service station operator and a housewife. He worked his way to San Francisco after high school and signed up for the Army after his plans to sail to South America to become an oil field worker fell apart.

He spent 27 years as a New York Life Insurance agent in Sacramento and retired during the early 1990s. He had four children with his wife of 65 years, the former Esther "Etta" Trautner.

A religious man, Mr. Ford was an usher and deacon at First Baptist Church in Sacramento, Southside Community Church and Fair Oaks Presbyterian Church. He enjoyed spending time in his home workshop and making repairs for family members.

Mr. Ford was a man of quiet dignity who enjoyed working and helping others. He was proud of his service during

war but never considered himself a hero, his son said.

"He always said it took everyone to win the war, from Rosie the riveter to the guys in battle," Terry Ford said. "He said it just happened to be his duty to fly the plane."

Call The Bee's Robert D. Dávila, (916) 321-1077.

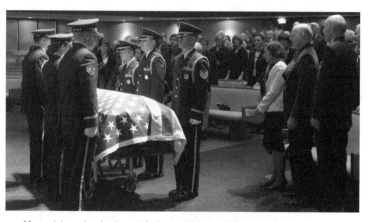

Memorial service for Ernest C. Ford with full military honors took place at Fair Oaks Presbyterian Church in Fair Oaks, California, March 11, 2010.

Ernest C. Ford Loses His Final Battle to Cancer

The author died at age 88, on March 4, 2010, after a long bout with cancer. His funeral, with full military honors, was a celebration of his life of goodwill and service to others. Following the War, when the author was asked about his accomplishments, he would respond, "It took everyone to win the war, from Rosie the Riveter to the guys in the battle." He would then add, "It just happened to be my duty to fly the plane."

UNKNOWN SOLDIER

I would feel honored if I were chosen to lay the wreath on the Tomb of the Unknown Soldier. This tomb represents those soldiers who died protecting our freedom while representing our country in war time.

I come from two proud military families. Both of my grandfathers had long-term careers in the service. My father's dad served 30 years in the Army and my mother's dad served 23 years in the Air Force.

Command Sergeant Major Andrew C. Weaver retired from the Army in 1973, after proudly serving our country for 30 years. My grandfather was at Normandy Beach on D-Day. His unit did not deploy until day two. However, he and his unit watched the battle from their ship while they awaited their orders. Thankfully, he made it out alive on that fateful day. He continued to serve in World War II, in the Korean War, and in the Vietnam War.

Major Ernest C. Ford retired from the Air Force in 1963. He flew 364 combat missions, the most of any pilot in the US Armed Services during World War II. He earned six Distinguished Flying Crosses and was recommended for the Silver Star. As a result of my grandfather's dedication to our country during World War II and the Korean Conflict, he was voted Veteran of the year in 2005 by the US Congress.

I would like to honor both my grandfathers for the sacrifices they made to protect our freedom. How lucky I am to go to this wonderful Christian School and worship in the church of my choice. By laying this wreath, my grandfathers would be very proud of me.

Written by Morgan Weaver, age eleven, my granddaughter, who was selected in 2008 to lay a wreath on the tomb of the Unknown Soldier in Arlington, Virginia.

Praise for *My New Guinea Diary*

"I highly recommend *My New Guinea Diary* to any reader interested in the greatest generation and all they did in their dedication to duty, honor, and country. All Americans owe a debt of gratitude to these great patriots."

—Daniel E. Lungren, U.S. Congressman

"A remarkable story. Fascinating reading of great historical significance."

—George Beverly Shea

"It's a heroic tale of a faithful pilot, whose skill and daring saved hundreds of lives. Ernie flew the C-47, with God's hands on his shoulders, through foggy mountain passes, in and out of tiny jungle airstrips, delivering vital supplies and ammo to the troops; then, carrying the wounded to safety, while dodging circling enemy fighters. He brings you into the busy cockpit and soaking tent, detailing the life of an air corps enlisted pilot."

—Gary S. Fritts, MSgt, Chief Aircrew, USAF (Retired),
Board of Directors, Aerospace Museum of California

"You are holding the diary of Ernie Ford's harrowing combat experiences that he lovingly recreated a few years before his death in 2010, at age 88. He did what he had to do in New Guinea—fly the assigned missions with no maps or charts, few, if any, radio navigation aids in a hostile land with Japanese soldiers just a few miles away, all while being awarded six Distinguished Flying Crosses. You will learn that the aircrews in New Guinea had nothing to rely upon but their own wits, their devotion to their country, and trust in God. You will be awe struck and uplifted after reading Ernie's combat diary. He was a true hero."

—Richard Shultz, Captain, US Naval Reserve (Retired)

"Moments after I met Major Ernest C. Ford, he politely turned down our commanding officer's offer and said he would rather bunk with us at the enlisted mens' barracks and eat at our mess hall. The idea that Major Ford, an officer, would sleep and eat with the enlisted men greatly impressed me.

Continued on next page

He honored his country with his military service in the Pacific and in Korea. He was a very religious man with high morals and integrity. The words *Duty, Honor,* and *Country* describe one of America's best citizens, Ernie Ford."

—James D. Doering, Entrade Inc., (V.P., Treasurer and C.F.O.)

"This book is written by a man who knows what it means to be faithful under fire. Ernie Ford's life was one of devotion and dedication: devotion to God and dedication to his country. This story is a first hand account of a period in his life of constant danger from enemy fire and nature's fury. His life was a blessing. You will be blessed by reading his own words."

—Dr. William H. Goddard, Pastor

"In one of WWII's Pacific conflicts credited with turning back Japan's invasion of Australia, a desperate Ernie Ford piloted a plane load of military evacuees ten feet above rocky terrain. Against the odds (and 70 enemy planes bombing from above) he heroically manuvered his C-47, helping two following aircraft and 90 passengers escape destruction. Ernie, just 21 years old, became an overnight national hero. His life story is interwoven with danger, innocence, humor, and the belief that no victory is achieved alone."

—Susan Maxwell Skinner; royal columnist, author of *Diana: Memory of a Rose,* and *Carmichael: Americana on the Move*

"It is with great pleasure that I endorse this book about my big brother, Ernie Ford—his life and military service. Ernie was an exceptional father, a devoted husband and a loving brother. He was a devoted Christian, an asset to his community, a kind and gentle man, and an inspiration to all who knew and loved him."

—Marvin Ford

"When I read Ernie Ford's New Guinea notes many years ago, I said, 'This would make a great book!' And, it truly is that! Kudos honorable brother-in-law! You are a truly great American hero, serving God, country, family, and duty. Great legacy, you earned it!"

—Jane Hanson